OXFORD REVISION GUIDES

A Level

Advanced

PSYCHOLOGY
through diagrams

Grahame Hill

Oxford University Press

Oxford University Press, Great Clarendon Street, Oxford OX2 6DP

Oxford New York
Athens Auckland Bangkok Bogota Buenos Aires
Calcutta Cape Town Chennai Dar es Salaam
Delhi Florence Hong Kong Istanbul Karachi
Kuala Lumpur Madrid Melbourne Mexico City
Mumbai Nairobi Paris São Paulo Singapore
Taipei Tokyo Toronto Warsaw

and associated companies in
Berlin Ibadan

Oxford is a trade mark of Oxford University Press

First published 1998

ISBN 0 19 917168 8

For Valérie Férec – it would not have been possible without you!
I would also like to thank all the following for their support:
my family, my friends at the Sixth Form College Colchester
(especially David, Morag, Rosemary, and Sue), and my students

150/

Illustrated by Oxford illustrators
Typeset and designed by Hardlines, Charlbury, Oxford
Printed in Great Britain

CONTENTS

Perspectives in Psychology

Approaches to psychology

Controversies in psychology

Ethical issues in psychology

What is psychology?

THE HISTORY OF PSYCHOLOGY

WHERE DID PSYCHOLOGY COME FROM?
Psychology developed from three main areas of study:

PHILOSOPHY
- Many of the problems which psychology has investigated were first most clearly outlined by Greek philosophers such as Socrates, Plato, and Aristotle in the 5th century BC. Two more recent philosophical influences on the development of psychology as a science were:
1 **Empiricism** - which argued that humans should only measure data that is *objectively observable*, such as behaviour.
2 **Positivism** - which argued that the *methods* and principles of *science* should be applied to human behaviour.

BIOLOGY
Biology has had two important influences:
1 Evolution - Darwin's suggestion that humans have *evolved* from other animals. The discoveries in *genetics* that followed from his evolutionary theory have had many important implications for the study and understanding of behaviour.
2 Physiology - the discoveries, mostly by the medical profession, of the structure and function of the brain, nervous, and endocrine systems have significantly contributed to the understanding of behaviour.

PHYSICS
- A subject that because of its great success has been adopted as the ideal model by scientists in psychology, who have borrowed its *scientific methods* and *principles*.
- Physicists, such as Fechner, started applying their subject to human behaviour and experience (psychophysics) in the nineteenth century, with some success.

WHEN DID PSYCHOLOGY START?
The date **1879** is usually said to be the start of psychology as a **separate scientific discipline**, since it was when Wilhelm Wundt created the first psychology laboratory in Leipzig. Wundt is, therefore, regarded as the 'founding father' of psychology, although Americans tend to suggest that William James should have this honour since his 1890 book (which took 12 years to write) entitled *Principles of Psychology* was a major landmark in psychology's literature and he began teaching a course on the relationship between physiology and psychology at Harvard University in 1875.

HOW DID PSYCHOLOGY DEVELOP?
- **Structuralism** - was the first approach to investigating psychology, pioneered by Wundt himself, who thought that the object of psychological investigation should be the *conscious mind,* and that it should be studied by *introspection* (looking inwards at one's own mental experience) in order to *break it down* into its component parts (such as images, sensations and feelings) like the science of chemistry had done with chemicals. One structuralist, Titchener, claimed there were a total of 46,708 basic sensations that combined to form the structure of the human mind, but the approach was very limited in its ability to explain and was replaced by functionalism.
- **Functionalism** - the approach William James advocated. James was influenced by Darwin's views and argued that the workings of the mind are functional, to survive and adapt, so we should investigate *what behaviour and thoughts are for.* Many of James's insights remain valid today, but functionalism was superseded by the next two very powerful approaches that both started around the turn of the century.
- **Psychoanalysis** - was in fact a method of *therapy* developed by Sigmund Freud in Austria, but in many major books, such as *The interpretation of dreams* (1900), Freud began describing in detail an underlying theory of the human mind and behaviour that has had an enormous (and controversial) impact on psychology. Freud argued that the proper object of psychological investigation should be the *unconscious mind*, and that our behaviour is determined by processes of which we are not aware.
- **Behaviourism** - Behaviourists, such as John Watson, were extremely critical of all the approaches that concerned themselves with 'minds', and proposed that psychology should only investigate *observable behaviour* if it wanted to be an objective science. This approach dominated experimental psychology until the 1950s, when a strong resurgence of interest in the 'mind' developed in the form of the cognitive and the humanistic approaches, which suggested that behaviourism ignored all the most important and interesting things that go on in our heads.
- **Cognitive psychology** - aims to investigate the mind by using *computer information processing* ideas to arrive at testable *models* of how the brain works, and then applying *scientific methods* to confirm these models. The cognitive approach has enjoyed much success and is a very dominant one in psychology today.
- The **Humanistic approach**, however, has had less of an impact on psychology, since it has deliberately adopted a *less scientific* view of the human mind by arguing that psychology should focus on each *individual's conscious experience* and *aims* in life.
- The **Biological approach** has advanced *evolutionary, physiological,* and *genetic* explanations for human behaviour throughout the history of psychology.

The psychoanalytic approach to psychology

ORIGINS AND HISTORY

- The psychoanalytic approach was started and developed mainly by **Sigmund Freud,** a Viennese doctor who specialised in neurology. Freud became interested in hysteria - the manifestation of physical symptoms without physical causes - and became convinced that **unconscious mental causes** were responsible not just for this disorder but for all disorders and even 'normal' personality. Freud developed techniques for **treating** the unconscious causes of mental disorders and built up an underlying explanatory **theory** of how human personality and abnormality develop from childhood.

- Freud's theory and approach were influenced by the technology of the time (such as the steam engine), and his early work with Charcot, the Parisian hypnotist, and Breuer the pioneer of the cathartic method. Freud's psychoanalytic approach had a great impact on psychology and psychiatry, and was developed in different ways by other psychoanalysts such as Jung, Adler, Klein, Anna Freud (his daughter), and Erickson.

Sigmund Freud (1856-1939)
'...I set myself the task of bringing to light what human beings keep hidden within them... the task of making conscious the most hidden recesses of the mind is one which it is quite possible to accomplish.'

ASSUMPTIONS
Psychoanalysis proposes:
- **Unconscious processes** - the major causes of behaviour come from that part of the mind which we have no direct awareness of.
- **Psychic determinism** - all we say and do has a cause (usually unconscious), even slips of the tongue or 'Freudian slip'.
- **Hydraulic drives** - behaviour is motivated by the two basic instinctual drives, the sex drive from Eros the life instinct, and the aggression drive from Thanatos the death instinct. The drives create psychic energy which will build up (like steam in a steam engine) and create tension and anxiety if it cannot be released in some form.
- **Psychodynamic conflict** - different parts of the unconscious mind are in constant struggle as the rational ego and moralistic superego seek to control the id expressing its sexual and aggressive urges.
- **Stages of development** - personality is shaped as the drives are modified by different conflicts at different times in childhood.

METHODS OF INVESTIGATION
Freud used the **case study** method when treating his clients (seeing them individually several times a week for many months), and **deeply** analysed and **interpreted** all they said and did. Two techniques Freud used for investigating the unconscious were:
- **Free association** - involving the uninhibited expression of thought associations, no matter how bizarre or embarrassing, from the client to the analyst.
- **Dream analysis** - the 'royal road to the unconscious'. The analyst attempts to decode the symbols and unravel the hidden meaning (the latent content) of a dream from the dreamer's report (the manifest content).

AREAS OF EXPLANATION
Freud used his theory to explain a vast number of topics, such as:
- **Personality development** - due to fixation/defence mechanisms.
- **Moral/gender development** - the result of the Oedipus complex.
- **Aggression** - caused by hydraulic drives and displacement.
- **Abnormality** - the consequence of early trauma and repression.
- **Memory** - Forgetting caused by repression.
+ Slips of the tongue, the shaping of civilisation and customs, etc.

PRACTICAL APPLICATIONS
The purpose of psychoanalysis was as a therapy to treat mental disorder. Once the unconscious cause of disorder was identified through dream interpretation, etc., then a cure could be effected through catharsis - discharging the repressed emotions associated with problems by getting them 'out in the open' to be discussed/resolved.

STRENGTHS
- Freud's ideas made a large impact on psychology and psychiatry and are still discussed and used today, around a 100 years after he started developing them.
- Freud regarded case studies like 'Little Hans' and 'Anna O' as firm empirical support for his theory, and thought his belief in determinism and detailed collection of data were scientific.
- Freud's theory has had some experimental support in certain areas, such as repression and fixation.
- Psychoanalysis has enormous explanatory power and has something to say on a huge variety of topics.

WEAKNESSES
Many psychologists today reject psychoanalysis because:
- It has been accused of being **unrefutable** (incapable of being proved wrong) and so **theoretically unscientific** - it seems to explain everything but predicts very little.
- Freud's methods have been regarded as unscientific because he based his theory on studying an 'abnormal' sample of people, using the case study method and techniques that were not fully objective and, therefore, open to bias.
- Much experimental research carried out on Freudian hypotheses has failed to support his theory and ideas.
- The success of psychoanalytic therapy has been criticised.

The behaviourist approach to psychology

ORIGINS AND HISTORY

- The behaviourist approach was influenced by the philosophy of **empiricism** (which argues that knowledge comes from the environment via the senses, since humans are like a 'tabula rasa', or blank slate, at birth) and the physical sciences (which emphasise scientific and objective methods of investigation).
- **Watson** started the behaviourist movement in 1913 when he wrote an article entitled 'Psychology as the behaviourist views it', which set out its main principles and assumptions. Drawing on earlier work by Pavlov, behaviourists such as Watson, Thorndike and Skinner proceeded to develop theories of **learning** (such as classical and operant conditioning) that they attempted to use to explain virtually **all** behaviour.
- The behaviourist approach dominated experimental psychology until the late 1950s, when its assumptions and methods became increasingly criticised by ethologists and cognitive psychologists. The behaviourist theories have been modified to provide more realistic explanations of how learning can occur, for example by psychologists such as Bandura with his social learning theory.

John Watson

'Give me a dozen healthy infants... and my own specified world to bring them up in and I'll guarantee to take any one at random and train him to become any type of specialist I might select - doctor, lawyer... and yes, even beggarman and thief.'

ASSUMPTIONS

The behaviourists believed:
- the majority of all behaviour is **learned** from the **environment** after birth (behaviourism takes the nurture side of the nature-nurture debate), and so a psychology should investigate the **laws** and **products** of learning
  - **a** psychology should investigate the **laws** and **products** of learning
  - **b** behaviour is **determined** by the environment, since we are merely the total of all our past learning experiences, freewill is an illusion.
- only **observable** behaviour not minds should be studied if psychology is to be an objective science, since we cannot see into other people's minds, and if we ask them about their thoughts they may lie, not know, or just be mistaken.

METHODS OF INVESTIGATION

The behaviourists adopted a very nomothetic approach, using strict laboratory experimentation, usually conducted on animals such as rats or pigeons. Animals were tested because the behaviourists believed:
- the laws of learning were universal
- there was only a quantitative difference between animals and humans
- animals are practically and ethically more convenient to test

AREAS OF EXPLANATION

The behaviourists' discoveries concerning the laws of learning were vigorously applied to explain many aspects of behaviour, such as:
- **Language acquisition,** e.g. Skinner's theory.
- **Moral development,** e.g. conditioned emotional responses of guilt and conscience.
- **Attraction,** e.g. Byrne & Clore's reinforcement affect model.
- **Abnormality,** e.g. the classical conditioning of phobias and their treatment.
- aggression, prejudice, gender role identity, etc.

PRACTICAL APPLICATIONS

- The behaviourist learning theory approach has produced may practical applications for education (such as programmed learning) and the treatment of those suffering behavioural disturbances (such as systematic desensitisation for phobias, behaviour shaping for autism, and token economies for institutionalised patients).
- Operant conditioning principles have been used in training animals to perform tasks, from circus animals to guide dogs.
- Watson applied behaviourist theory to both child rearing and advertising, while Skinner offered many suggestions regarding the large scale manipulation of behaviour in society in his books such as *Beyond Freedom and Dignity* and *Walden Two*.

STRENGTHS

Behaviourism contributed to psychology in many ways:
- Behaviourism was very scientific and its experimental methodology left a lasting impression on the subject.
- It provided strong counter-arguments to the nature side of the nature-nurture debate.
- The approach is very parsimonious, explaining a great variety of phenomena using only a few simple (classical and operant) principles.
- Behaviourism has produced many practical applications, some of which have been very effective.

WEAKNESSES

Behaviourist views have been criticised by other approaches for a number of reasons.
- Ethologists argued that the behaviourists ignored innate, built-in biases in learning due to evolution, but also disagreed with the behaviourists' use of animals and laboratory experimentation, saying that there is a biologically qualitative difference between humans and other animals and that experiments only demonstrate artificial, not natural learning.
- Cognitive psychologists think that behaviourism ignores important mental processes involved in learning; while the humanistic approach disliked their rejection of conscious mental experience.

The humanistic approach to psychology

ORIGINS AND HISTORY

- The humanistic movement developed in America in the early 1960s, and was termed the third force in psychology since it aimed to replace the two main approaches in the subject at that time, behaviourism and psychoanalysis. Influenced by gestalt psychology's idea of studying **whole units,** and existential philosophy with its belief in **conscious free will,** humanists argued that behaviourism's artificial and dehumanising approach and psychoanalysis's gloomy determinism were insufficient to provide a complete psychology.
- The humanistic approach aimed to investigate all the uniquely **human** aspects of **experience** such as love, hope, creativity, etc. and emphasised the importance of the individual's interaction with the environment. Humanists, such as **Maslow,** believed that every individual has the need to **self-actualise** or reach their potential, and **Rogers** developed client-centred therapy to help individuals in this process of self-actualisation.

Carl Rogers
'Humanistic psychology has as its ultimate goal the preparation of a complete description of what it means to be alive as a human being.' Bugental (1967)

ASSUMPTIONS

Bugental (1967), the first president of the American Association for Humanistic Psychology, described some of its fundamental assumptions:

- A proper understanding of human nature can only be gained from **studying humans,** not other animals.
- Psychology should research areas that are **meaningful** and important to human existence, not neglect them because they are too difficult. Psychology should be **applied** to enrich human life.
- Psychology should study **internal experience** as well as external behaviour and consider that individuals can show some degree of **free will.**
- Psychology should study the **individual** case (an idiographic method) rather than the average performance of groups (a nomothetic approach).
- In general, humanistic psychologists assume that the **whole person** should be studied in their environmental **context.**

METHODS OF INVESTIGATION

Humanists take a phenomenological approach, investigating the individual's conscious experience of the world. For this reason they employ the idiographic case study method, and use a variety of individualistic techniques such as

- flexible open ended interviews.
- the Q-sort technique, where the participant is given one hundred different statements on cards, such as 'I don't trust my emotions' or 'I have an attractive personality' which they have to sort into piles for personal relevance

AREAS OF EXPLANATION

The humanistic approach has been applied to relatively few areas of psychology compared to other approaches. The main areas of explanation have been in

- **personality/self identity,** e.g. Rogers's self theory
- **motivation,** e.g. Maslow's hierarchy of needs and self-actualisation
- **abnormality,** e.g. due to imposed conditions of worth by others or the inability to accept the true self. Humanists are against the nomothetic classification of abnormality

PRACTICAL APPLICATIONS

The humanistic approach's primary application has been to therapeutic treatment for anybody suffering 'problems with living'. Some humanistic therapies include

- client-centred therapy - whereby the client is encouraged to develop positive self-regard and overcome mismatch between their perceived self, true self, and ideal self
- gestalt therapy - developed by Fritz Perls, the aim is to help the client become a 'whole' (gestalt) person by getting them to accept every aspect of themselves

STRENGTHS

The humanistic approach has contributed to psychology by

- re-emphasising the need to study consciousness and human experience for a complete study of the subject
- serving as a valuable agent of criticism against the extremes of the earlier major approaches
- highlighting the value of more individualistic and idiographic methods of study, particularly in the areas of personality and abnormality
- emphasising the importance of self-actualisation, responsibility, freedom of choice, and social context in therapy

WEAKNESSES

Humanistic psychology has not, however, had the significant impact on mainstream academic psychology that the other approaches have. This is probably because humanists deliberately take a less scientific approach to studying humans since

- their belief in free will is in opposition to the deterministic laws of science
- they adopt a more idiographic approach, seeking the more unique aspects of individuals, rather than producing generalised laws of behaviour that apply to everyone
- the issues they investigate, such as consciousness and emotion, are amongst the most difficult to objectively study

The cognitive approach to psychology

ORIGINS AND HISTORY

- The cognitive approach began to revolutionise psychology in the late 1950s and early 1960s, to become the dominant paradigm in the subject by the 1970s. Interest in mental processes had been gradually resurrected through the work of people like Tolman and Piaget, but it was the arrival of the **computer** that gave cognitive psychology the terminology and metaphor it needed to investigate human minds.
- Cognitive psychology compares the human mind to a computer, suggesting that we too are **information processors** and that it is possible and desirable to study the **internal mental processes** that lie between the stimuli we receive and the responses we make. Cognition means 'knowing' and cognitive processes refer to the ways in which knowledge is gained, used and retained. Therefore, cognitive psychologists have studied perception, attention, memory, thinking, language, and problem solving.
- Cognitive psychology has influenced and integrated with many other approaches and areas of study to produce, for example, social learning theory, cognitive neuropsychology, and artificial intelligence.

Jerome Bruner

'...cognition refers to all those processes by which sensory input is transformed, reduced, elaborated, stored, recovered and used... cognition is involved in everything a human being might possibly do.'
Neisser (1966)

ASSUMPTIONS

Cognitive psychologists assume that
- mental processes **can** and **should** be investigated scientifically
- **models** of psychological functions can be proposed
- **research** on these models can be carried out to confirm, refute or modify them by testing observable behaviour and conscious report
- cognitive processes **actively** organise and manipulate information that we receive - humans are not merely passive responders to their environment

METHODS OF INVESTIGATION

Cognitive psychologists mostly employ a nomothetic approach to discover human cognitive processes, but have also adopted idiographic techniques at times:
- Laboratory experimentation - for example, many subjects have been exposed to memory tests under strictly controlled conditions.
- Case study - Piaget studied the cognitive development of his children using the clinical interview method.

AREAS OF EXPLANATION

Cognitive psychologists have sought to explain:
- **memory,** e.g. Atkinson and Shiffrin's multi-store model of the input, storage and loss of information, etc.
- **perception,** e.g. Gregory's theory on the role of mental processes in influencing/organising visual stimuli
- **attention,** e.g. Broadbent's filter model
- **artificial intelligence,** e.g. Rumelhart and McClelland's parallel distributed network models
- **social cognition,** e.g. the effects of stereotypes on interpersonal perception
- **cognitive development,** e.g. Piaget's stage theory of cognitive development

PRACTICAL APPLICATIONS

Cognitive psychology has had a broad range of applications, for example to
- **memory** - to help improve memory through mnemonic devices or to aid the police in eyewitness testimony
- **education** - Piaget' theory has been applied to improve educational techniques
- **therapy** - such as the use of Ellis's rational emotive therapy to restructure faulty thinking and perceptions in depression, for example. When combined to form cognitive-behavioural techniques, effectiveness is improved
- **personality assessment** - e.g. Kelley's personal construct measurement

STRENGTHS

Cognitive psychology is probably the most dominant approach today:
- It investigates many areas of interest in psychology that had been neglected by behaviourism; yet, unlike psychoanalysis and humanism, it investigates them using more rigorous scientific methods.
- In contrast to the biological approach, it bases its explanations firmly at a functional, psychological level, rather than resorting to reductionism to explain human behaviour.
- The approach has provided explanations of many aspects of human behaviour and has had useful practical applications.
- The cognitive approach has combined with other approaches to strengthen its explanations and usefulness, e.g. cognitive neuropsychology.

WEAKNESSES

Cognitive models have been accused of being
- over simplistic - ignoring the huge complexity of human functioning compared to computer functioning
- unrealistic and over hypothetical - ignoring the biological influences and grounding of mental processes
- too cold - ignoring the emotional life of humans, their conscious experience and possible use of freewill

The biological approach to psychology

ORIGINS AND HISTORY

- Sometimes known as the physiological, biopsychological, neurophysiological, nativist (considering nature rather than nurture) or innate approach.
- The biological approach to psychological matters has integrated with and run parallel to the rest of psychological thought since early Greek times - the Greek physician Galen suggested that personality and temperament may be linked to the levels of body fluids such as blood and bile in the body.
- As knowledge of human anatomy, physiology, biochemistry, and medicine developed, important insights for human behaviour and experience were gained. Penfield for example mapped the role of various areas of the cerebral cortex through microelectrode stimulation with conscious patients. Sperry investigated the effects of splitting the cerebral hemispheres on consciousness and psychological function.
- The field will progress still further as the technology to isolate the effects of genes and scan the living brain develops.

Roger Sperry
'All that is psychological is first physiological' Anon.

ASSUMPTIONS

Biologically orientated psychologists assume that
- all that is psychological is first physiological - that is since the mind appears to reside in the brain, all thoughts, feelings and behaviours ultimately have a physical/biological cause
- human genes have evolved over millions of years to adapt behaviour to the environment. Therefore, much behaviour will have a genetic basis
- psychology should, therefore, investigate the brain, nervous system, endocrine system, neurochemistry, and genes
- it is also useful to study why human behaviour has evolved in the way it has, the subject of evolutionary/sociobiological theory

METHODS OF INVESTIGATION

The biological approach mainly adopts a nomothetic approach to generalise biological influences on behaviour to all humans with similar physiology, but finds the use of particular 'special case studies' very useful.
Most common techniques include
- laboratory experimentation - stimulating, giving drugs to, or removing parts of the body to see what effect it has on behaviour
- laboratory observations - controlled observations of physical processes, e.g. sleep

AREAS OF EXPLANATION

Biopsychological researchers have contributed to an understanding of
- **gender development** - e.g. the influence of genetic and hormonal predispositions on gender behaviour and identity
- **aggression** - e.g. investigating the role of the limbic system
- **abnormality** - e.g. the dopamine hypothesis and enlarged ventricle theory of schizophrenia
- **memory** - e.g. brain scans of areas involved during memory tests or the effect of brain damage on memory
- **motivation** - e.g. the role of the hypothalamus in homeostasis
- **awareness** - e.g. biological theories of sleep, dreams and body rhythms

PRACTICAL APPLICATIONS

Biopsychology's main applications have been to
- **localisation of function** - e.g. the effect on behaviour of brain damage to certain areas such as language control centres on the left side of the brain
- **therapy** - such drug treatment, psychosurgery, or electroconvulsive therapy for mental disorders such as schizophrenia or depression

STRENGTHS

Biopsychology has contributed to psychology in many ways:
- The approach is very scientific, grounded in the hard science of biology with its objective, materialistic subject matter and experimental methodology.
- It provides strong counter-arguments to the nurture side of the nature-nurture debate.
- Biopsychology's practical applications are usually extremely effective, e.g. the treatment of mental disorder.

WEAKNESSES

- Reductionism - the biopsychological approach explains thoughts and behaviour in terms of the action of neurones or biochemicals. This may ignore other more suitable levels of explanation and the interaction of causal factors.
- The approach has not adequately explained how mind and body interact - consciousness and emotion are difficult to study objectively.
- Over simplistic - biopsychological theories often over-simplify the huge complexity of physical systems and their interaction with environmental factors.

The reductionism debate in psychology

REDUCTIONISM	HOLISM & INTERACTIONISM

ASSUMPTIONS

Reductionism involves explaining a phenomenon by **breaking** it **down** into its **constituent parts - analysing it.** Reductionism works on the scientific assumption of **parsimony** - that complex phenomena should be explained by the **simplest underlying principles** possible.

Holism looks at same/higher level explanations. Interactionism shows how **many aspects** of a phenomenon or **levels** of explanation can **interact together** to provide a **complete** picture. Both approaches involve taking a gestalt approach, assuming that *'the whole is greater than the sum of its parts'.*

EXAMPLES IN PSYCHOLOGY

There have been many reductionist attempts to explain behaviour in psychology, for example:
- Structuralism - one of the first approaches to psychology pioneered by Wundt and Titchener involved trying to break conscious experience down into its constituent images, sensations, and feelings.
- Behaviourism - assumed that complex behaviour was the sum of all past stimulus-response learning units.
- Biopsychology - aims to explain all at the psychological or mental level in terms of that at the physiological, neurochemical or genetic level. Ultimately, psychology would be replaced by biology and the other natural sciences lower down on the reductionist ladder.

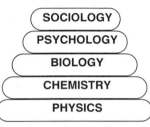

A simple reductionist hierarchy of explanation.

Other approaches have proposed higher level holistic and/or interactionist explanations of human behaviour, for example:
- **Humanistic psychology** - investigates all aspects of the individual as well as the effect of interactions between people. Gestalt therapy developed by Fritz Perls aims to enable people to accept and cope with all aspects of their life and personality.
- **Social psychology** - looks at the behaviour of individuals in a social context. Group behaviour may show characteristics that are greater than the sum of the individuals which comprise it (or *less* in the case of social loafing!).
- **Psychoanalysis** - Freud adopted an interactionist approach, in that he considered that behaviour was the result of dynamic interaction between id, ego, and superego.
- **Abnormal psychology** - mental disorders are often explained by an interaction of biological, psychological, and environmental factors. Schizophrenia may be due to a genetic predisposition triggered by environmental stress. An eclectic approach to therapy is often taken using drugs and psychotherapy.
- **Perception** – illusions show that humans perceive more than the sum of the sensations of the retina.

FOR

- Reductionist explanations in psychology adopt a very **scientific** and **analytical** approach, which has worked very well with the natural sciences.
- By breaking phenomena down into smaller simple components (as behaviourism did with stimulus-response units) these constituent parts are often more **easily tested.**
- By explaining behavioural phenomena in terms of their underlying physical basis, psychology gains the scientific **support** and **credibility** of these well established and robust sciences, and **unifies** with them to provide a **consistent** picture of the universe.

- The interactionist approach can **integrate** many **different levels** of explanation to provide a more **complete** and **realistic** understanding of behaviour.
- Holism does **not ignore** the **complexity** and the **'emergent properties'** of higher level phenomenon. For example, there may be aspects of crowd behaviour that could not be explained in terms of the individuals in that crowd.
- **Functional** explanations are only possible at higher levels - examining the social reasons **why** we show a certain aggressive behaviour is often more useful than providing a detailed neuronal, hormonal and physiological explanation of the act.

AGAINST

- **Oversimplification** - reductionist explanations often ignore many important interactions and the emergent properties of phenomena at higher levels. The whole may be greater than the sum of its parts.
- **Value of explanation** - higher level explanations may be less detailed and more useful than lower level ones. The **meaning** of an action, such as a hand wave, is only gained from its situation (e.g. greeting or drowning) not its underlying physiological description.
- **Validity of reductionism** - Rose (1976) argues that different levels of discourse cannot be substituted for each other. This raises the problem of the relationship between the **mind** and the **brain** - is a feeling of pain the same as the activation of nerve cells in a particular part of your brain? A neurologist may follow the 'neuronal path' of a pin prick up the arm and into a reception area of the brain, but the neurologist would have to rely on your conscious (psychological level) verbal report to know whether you *felt* pain or not.

- There is a great **practical difficulty** in investigating the integration of explanations from different levels. Research into mental disorders is beginning to understand the interaction of environmental, psychological, and biological explanations of disorders like depression.
- Holistic explanations of psychological phenomena that assume the mind is not the same as the body, tend to **ignore** the huge **influence** of biology on behaviour.
- Holistic explanations tend to get more **hypothetical** and divorced from physical reality the higher they go up the reductionist ladder. Higher level theories appear to **lack** the **predictive** power of the physical sciences (although there is a corresponding increase in the complexity of the systems investigated).

The nature-nurture debate in psychology

NATURE   **NURTURE**

APPROACH

Roots of the approach - nativist philosophy, biology (physiology and genetics), evolutionary theory.
Causes of behaviour - genetic determinism, inherited influence, maturational blueprint, neurochemical and hormonal influences, brain activity.
Methods employed - gene/chromosome mapping, twin and adoption studies, brain scanning, brain stimulation or damage studies, drug testing.
Implications - due to biological determinism, behaviour can only be changed through physical means, such as selective breeding (eugenics), gene therapy, brain surgery, or drugs.
Criticisms - reductionist, may neglect environmental influences.

Roots of the approach - empiricism philosophy, behaviourism, social psychology.
Causes of behaviour - the mind is regarded as a 'tabula rasa' (blank slate) at birth; therefore, knowledge and behaviour are the result of experience and learning from the environment.
Methods employed - use of classical and operant conditioning techniques to affect behaviour, manipulation of social environment to change behaviour.
Implications - due to environmental determinism, behaviour can only be easily changed through manipulating reinforcement and environmental conditions. Anybody could be trained to do anything.
Criticisms - reductionist, may neglect innate influences.

AREAS OF EXPLANATION

Perception - Research conducted by Fantz, Bower, and Gibson and Walk on new-born babies indicated pattern detection, size constancy and depth perception are innate abilities.
Aggression - The ethologist Lorenz and psychoanalyst Freud believed aggression is an innate drive. Bio-psychologists have examined the role of hormones and brain areas in aggression.
Sex-role behaviour - Bio-psychologists propose gender identity is a direct result of genetic and hormonal influences.
Abnormality - The biomedical approach has isolated genetic and neurochemical causes of mental disorders.
Language acquisition - Chomsky proposed language is gained through the use of an innate language acquisition device.

Perception - Research into perception by Hebb on cataract removal and Turnbull on cross-cultural differences indicated that perceptual identification is a learnt ability.
Aggression - Social learning theory argues that aggression is learnt from the environment through observation and imitation. Social psychologists study conformity to aggressive norms.
Sex-role behaviour - Cultural relativism and learning theory argue that gender is socially constructed and reinforced.
Abnormality - The environment plays a role in the development of phobias, post-traumatic stress disorder, and anorexia.
Language acquisition - Skinner argued that language is learnt from other people via natural behaviour shaping techniques.

INTERACTIONISM

While some researchers have aimed to investigate the relative contributions of innate and environmental factors in psychology, it is now accepted that the two influences form a **continuum** and interact so thoroughly with each other that they are virtually inseparable. Even seemingly direct genetic influences, such as those on the physical development of the brain, are affected by environmental factors from the inside of the womb to the pollution of the atmosphere. Many genes could impose a **susceptibility** to develop in certain ways or provide a 'norm of reaction' - a genetic potential that may or may not be realised by environmental circumstances. In a similar way, environmental experiences are **mediated** by not only innate abilities but even by the physical structure of the body, e.g. what gender or skin colour it has.

EXAMPLES OF NATURE-NURTURE INTERACTION IN PSYCHOLOGY

Perception - Blakemore and Cooper showed restricted environmental experience could physically affect the visual cortex of the brain.
Cognitive development - Piaget suggested that innate schemata develop and expand through interaction with the environment to adapt the child to its surroundings, although development was always limited by biological maturation.

Abnormality - Many mental disorders, such as schizophrenia, may have a genetic predisposition - those with an inherited susceptibility may be more likely to develop the disorder if they experience certain stressful environmental conditions. Animal studies have looked at the effect of aversive environmental stimuli upon the brain's neurotransmitters to explain depression.

Sex-role behaviour - The Biosocial approach proposes that factors such as the physical sex and innate temperament of a new born baby elicits sex typing behaviour from the people around it, leading to a self-fulfilling prophecy in terms of its gender identity.

THE STANDING OF THE DIFFERENT APPROACHES IN PSYCHOLOGY

NATURE 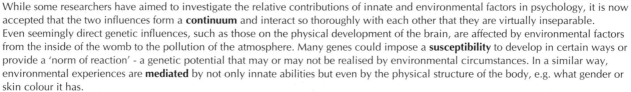 **NURTURE**

| **BIOPSYCHOLOGY** | **PSYCHOANALYSIS** | **COGNITIVE PSYCHOLOGY** | **HUMANISM** | **BEHAVIOURISM** |
| Focuses on genetic, physiological, hormonal and neurochemical explanations of behaviour. | Focuses on instinctual drives of sex and aggression, expressed within the restrictions imposed by society via the ego and superego. | Focuses on innate information processing abilities or schemata that are constantly refined by experience. | While accepting basic physiological needs, the focus is upon the person's experience of their social and physical environment. | Focuses on the acquisition of virtually all behaviour from the environment via conditioning. |

The freewill vs. determinism debate in psychology

FREEWILL

DETERMINISM

ASSUMPTIONS

The freewill approach assumes that humans **are free to choose their behaviour,** that they are essentially **self-determining.** Freewill does not mean that behaviour is uncaused in the sense of being completely random, but assumes that influences (biological or environmental) can be rejected at will.
Soft determinism (William James, 1890) suggests that freewill is not freedom from causation, but freedom from coercion and constraint - if our actions are voluntary and in line with our conscious desired goals then they are free.

The determinism approach assumes that **every physical event is caused,** and, since human behaviour is a physical event, it follows that it too is caused by preceding factors.
If all events are caused and perfect knowledge is gained of the current state of the universe, it follows that future events are entirely **predictable.**
Determinism, with its emphasis on **causal laws** is, therefore, the basis of science, which aims to reveal those laws to provide prediction and **control** of the future.

EXAMPLES IN PSYCHOLOGY

Humanistic psychology, proposed by the likes of Rogers and Maslow, is the strongest advocate of human freewill, arguing that we are able to direct our lives towards self-chosen goals. The emphasis on freewill is most apparent in humanistic based therapies, where the terms client and facilitator are used to indicate the voluntary nature of the situation, and the idea that the individual has the power to solve their own problems through insight. Humanistic therapies are usually non directive.
Cognitive psychology appears to adopt a soft determinism view considering problem solving and attentional mechanisms as the 'choosers' of thought and behaviour. While it seems that we select what we pay attention to, these mechanisms operate with the parameters of their innate capabilities and our past experience (just as a computer cannot choose to do something it was not built or programmed for) e.g. 'perceptual set' suggests that we are not free to choose what we see. However, language and metacognitive abilities may allow humans to choose from among many possible influences (Johnson-Laird,1988).

The majority of approaches in psychology adopt a fairly strict deterministic view of human behaviour.
Behaviourism took an extreme environmental determinism approach, arguing that learning from the environment 'writes upon the blank slate of our mind at birth' to cause behaviour. Watson's belief that the deterministic laws of learning could predict and control the future were reflected in his claim that he could take any infant at random and turn them into any type of specialist he might select. Skinner argued that freewill is completely an illusion created by our complexity of learning.
Psychoanalysis took the view of unconscious determinism - that our behaviour is controlled by forces of which we are unaware - the reasons for our actions are merely rationalised by our conscious minds. Later psychoanalysts, such as Erikson, looked at more conscious ego processes than Freud, however.
Biological approaches to psychology look at the deterministic influence of genetics, brain structure and biochemistry. Sociobiologists investigate evolutionary determinism.

FOR

- **Introspection** upon our decisions when many possible and equally desirable options are available often seems to indicate free choice. Subjective impressions should be considered.
- Even if humans do not have freewill, the fact that **they think they do** has many implications for behaviour. Rotter (1966), for example, has proposed that individuals with an external locus of control who feel that outside factors (e.g. chance) control their life, suffer more from the effects of stress than those who feel they can influence situations (an internal locus of control). Brehm (1966) argued people react if their freedom is threatened.

- The illusion of freewill is shattered very easily by **mental disorders** (obsessive compulsives lose control of their thoughts and actions, depressives their emotions) and psychoactive drugs (which can produce involuntary hallucinations and behaviour).
- Determinism is one of the key assumptions of **science** - whose cause and effect laws have explained, predicted and controlled behaviour (in some areas) above the levels achieved by unaided commonsense.
- The **majority** of all psychologists, even those sympathetic to the idea of freewill, accept determinism to some degree.

AGAINST

- It is **difficult to define** what freewill is and what the 'self' that 'does the choosing' consists of. Philosophers such as Descartes regarded it as the non-physical soul or spirit, while the existentialist philosopher Sartre preferred to think that freewill was a product of consciousness.
- The **evidence** for the existence of freewill is mostly **subjective** - where 'objective' studies have been conducted the results are a little disturbing - Libet (1985a) claims that the brain processes that initiate the movement of a hand occur almost half a second *before* the moment a subject reports choosing to move it!
- A pure freewill approach is **incompatible** with the deterministic assumptions of **science.**

- Determinism is **inconsistent** with society's ideas of self-control and responsibility that underlie all our moral and legal assumptions. Only extreme examples of determinism are taken into account (e.g. insanity).
- Determinism can never lead to complete prediction, due to
a The vast complexity of influences upon any behaviour
b The nature of induction - never being able to prove 100%
c The notions of unpredictability (e.g. Heisenberg's 'uncertainty principle') and non-causality that physics has produced
- Determinism is **unfalsifiable** since it always assumes a cause exists, even if one has not been found yet.

Idiographic vs. nomothetic approaches to psychology

NOMOTHETIC APPROACH	IDIOGRAPHIC APPROACH

DEFINITIONS

The approach of investigating **large groups** of people to try to find **general laws** of behaviour that apply to everyone.	The approach of investigating **individuals** in personal, **in-depth,** detail to achieve a **unique understanding** of them.

ASSUMPTIONS & METHODS

The nomothetic approach (from the Greek word 'nomos' meaning 'law') assumes that since individuals are merely complex combinations of many universal laws, people are best studied by **large scale,** preferably **experimental,** methods to identify those laws. The individual will be **classified** with others, measured as a score upon a **dimension,** or be a **statistic** supporting a **general principle.**	The idiographic approach (from the Greek 'idios' meaning 'private or personal') assumes that since each human is unique, they are best investigated by the **case study method** to provide a more complete and global understanding of the individual. Individuals are studied using more **flexible, long term** and **detailed procedures** and may be put 'in a class of their own'.

EXAMPLES FROM PSYCHOLOGY

Nomothetic research is the main approach taken in scientifically orientated psychology: **The behaviourists' experiments** on the principles of learning were conducted on many subjects, and replicated until the general principles of learning were well established. Most of the experiments were conducted on rats and pigeons, but the behaviourists' belief in the universal nature of the laws they discovered allowed them to generalise their findings to humans. **The social psychology experiments** of Asch and Milgram also used the nomothetic approach, aiming to reach general conclusions. **All psychological theories** that propose generalised principles of behaviour have nomothetic assumptions - Eysenck's personality theory places individuals along a universal **dimension** of **extro-version**, intelligence tests measure people along the **scale of IQ** scores, the medical model **classification manuals**, e.g. the DSMIV, classify people as suffering from particular **types** of disorder.	There are many examples of idiographic studies in psychology: **Freud (1909)** used the clinical case study method, seeing patients frequently, over long periods of time, and keeping detailed notes of his interpretations. Freud's techniques were deliberately unstructured (as in free association) and he wrote up his notes at the end of the day to allow a more free and natural expression of the patients thoughts. **Piaget (1953)** carried out longitudinal studies of the cognitive development of his children, keeping frequent notes and using the flexible clinical interview method and informal experiments to gain detailed and ecologically valid understanding. **Gardner and Gardner (1969)** spent long periods of time interacting with and observing the chimpanzee Washoe as they attempted to teach it sign language. **Gregory and Wallace (1963)** studied the perceptual progress of a man who recovered his sight after 50 years of blindness.

ADVANTAGES

The nomothetic approach is in tune with the deterministic, law-abiding nature of **science**, and has been applied very successfully in other sciences as well as psychology. The ability to generalise laws from limited instances is very useful in **predicting & controlling** behaviour. Personality questionnaires and mental disorder classification manuals have proven useful in the selection of personnel and the diagnosis and treatment of disorders. Nomothetic findings from psychological studies may prove useful in reducing global problems such as prejudice and aggression.	The idiographic approach provides a **more complete** and global **understanding** of the individual. This approach may be the most efficient in the area concerned (as Freud and Piaget claimed) or it may be the only viable one available (as in the case of Washoe - long and detailed study was necessary to teach language and measure the progress). Idiographic studies are often financially necessary and may spark off interest and lead to experimental research in an area (eg Piaget).

DISADVANTAGES

The drawback, however, is that this approach leaves us with a more **superficial understanding** of any one person - you and I may have the same IQ, but I may have answered different questions from you. Also a piece of nomothetic research may tell me I have a 1% chance of becoming schizophrenic, but it will not tell me if I am in that 1%. Nomothetic generalisations may be too inaccurate for the individual. This is a criticism of the medical model classification systems whose diagnosis may not accurately describe or help the subject.	However, the disadvantage of using this approach is that we **cannot legitimately generalise** (or apply) any findings carried out on just one person to other people. Freud and Piaget have been accused of creating global theories from limited and unrepresentative samples and methods. Idiographic techniques also tend to be more **unreliable** and **unscientific** due to their more subjective, long term, flexible and unstandardised nature.

COMPROMISE

Clearly both approaches seem necessary for a complete study of Psychology - if the aims of science are to describe, understand, predict and control, then idiographic methods may be more suitable for the first two aims and nomothetic methods for the latter two.
As Kluckholm and Murray (1953) have pointed out, every person is in some respects **1** like no other person, **2** like some other people, and **3** like all other people. If there were no common points between individuals then nobody would be able to understand each other! In the case of abnormality, classification allows research to be carried out on groups of people suffering similar symptoms in the hope that a similar cause and cure can be identified. However, an idiographic approach may be useful to deal with the particular and perhaps unique set of problems encountered by each patient.
A healthy balance between nomothetic and idiographic approaches is needed if psychology is to succeed in all of its aims.

Psychology and science 1

- Mainstream psychology, since its emergence as a separate scientific discipline (Wundt, 1879), has always claimed to be a science.
- The early structuralists tried to bring the scientific methods of **pure observation** and **analysis** to the study of human experience, aiming to break consciousness down into its constituent parts, as chemistry had done with the elements.
- The behaviourists prided themselves on the strictness of their application of the scientific method, being influenced perhaps by Pavlov who, being a physiologist, took extreme care in the **control** and **standardisation** of his methods (going so far as to construct a 'Tower of Silence' with airtight doors and a moat filled with straw to prevent outside distractions to his experiments on conditioning reflexes).
- Freud himself always maintained that he was a scientist, despite criticism of his methods; and, although the humanists deliberately took a step away from the scientific method in the 1960s, the vast majority of current psychology (mostly cognitive) is funded on the basis of its scientific nature.

- However, psychology has come **under attack as** being a **pseudo science**, pretending to be a science but achieving nothing like the results and success of the natural sciences.
- Worse still, it has been **dismissed** by some as nothing more than **common sense**. Why might this be? There are several possible reasons:

1. Everybody is a natural psychologist themselves, and the subject matter of psychology (thoughts and behaviour) is freely available to everyday speculation.
   - However, one thing psychology has demonstrated is that there are many instances when we **do not or cannot know the reasons** for our behaviour (Nisbet and Wilson, 1977), but when psychology comes up with its findings, the tendency is for the individual to say (in a very 'ad hoc' manner), 'Oh, I knew that all along'.
   - This is because common sense psychology is full of contradictory proverbs ('birds of a feather, flock together' or 'opposites attract') but it is the role of psychology as a science to put these to the **objective** test, to provide *evidence* to support these views or to decide between them. As a science, psychology has to aim for 'understanding prediction and control above the levels achieved by unaided commonsense' (Allport, 1946).
   - Psychology has come up with many **counter-intuitive findings** - in his obedience experiment, Milgram took the precaution of asking qualified people to estimate the percentage of subjects who would give a potentially lethal 450 volt shock to another person, just because a psychologist told them to, and found that the actual percentage (65%) was far greater than the highest estimate (3%).

2. Psychology is a relatively young science but aims to investigate one of, if not the, **most complex subjects** in the universe - the human brain's physical complexity is stunning, and just think of the huge amount of learnt information it contains.
   - The human subject is the victim of **so many variables** and influences (genetic, neurochemical, environmental) that the idea of controlling out all the possible extraneous variables and isolating just one variable to manipulate, is impossible in practice.

3. Psychology is beset, more so than most other subjects, with many philosophical, practical, and ethical problems.
   - **Philosophically** - the notion of **consciousness** in humans raises difficulties in explaining how apparently non-physical thoughts, feelings and experiences can be explained by physical processes (how can my feeling of 'happiness' be the same as neurones firing in a particular part of my brain?) and also raises the possibility of **freewill** (we alone, as humans, have claimed the ability to be able to reject or choose amongst all of the influences that affect us). There is also the problem of choosing which level of explanation on the **reductionist** ladder to use to describe human behaviour (the social, psychological, physiological?).
   - **Practically** - apart from the above mentioned difficulties in investigating a complex system, there is also the problem that **we are our own subject matter**. Investigating ourselves proves problematic since we **react** to being studied, unlike chemicals, and may be unwilling to participate in research for reasons of self-esteem, for example, or may react differently in the artificial and controlled conditions of an experiment. Worse still, our results may be hopelessly distorted by our own psychological and theoretical biases.
   - **Ethically** - again since we are our own subject matter, there are **moral** problems with studying human behaviour. We do not have unrestricted access to and control of our subject matter, we cannot deliberately damage or kill human subjects in the name of science, or deprive them of all interaction with an environment to discover what is nature and what is nurture! We have to consider their informed consent, their right to withdraw and their right not to suffer any harmful consequences (although psychologists have not always obeyed these principles).

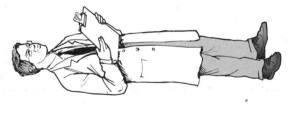

Psychology and science 2

To fully investigate whether psychology, despite its problems, is justified in calling itself a science, we must first outline what a science consists of, and then see how well psychology matches these criteria.

A science consists of various components:
- A **subject matter**
- Good **theories** and **hypotheses**
- Scientific **methodology**

THE SCIENTIFIC METHOD

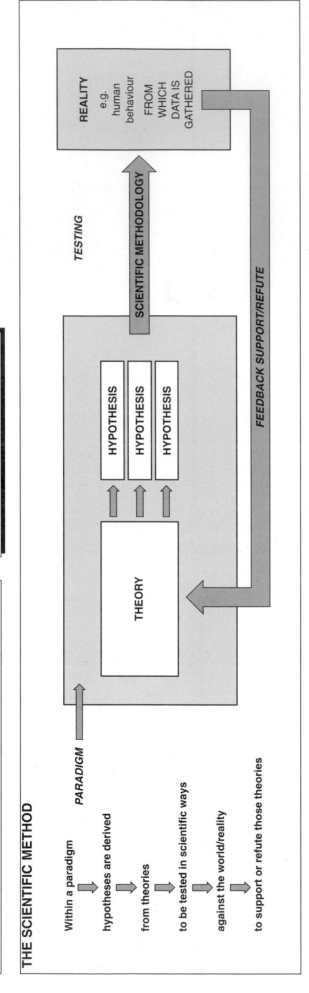

Within a paradigm

hypotheses are derived

from theories

to be tested in scientific ways

against the world/reality

to support or refute those theories

A SUBJECT MATTER

- The subject matter of a science is what the science is about. There should be agreement amongst researchers about *what* should be studied and *how*. **Kuhn** (1962) used the term '**paradigm**' to describe this **shared set of assumptions, methods and terminology**.

- According to Kuhn's theory of the progression of science, paradigms go through changes over time, through three historical stages:

  a **Pre-science**, where there is no universally accepted paradigm.
  b **Normal science**, where researchers work sharing the same paradigm.
  c **Revolution**, where conflicting evidence becomes so overwhelming that a paradigm-shift occurs to a new perspective.

- Thus, the majority view at one time was that the earth was flat and was the centre of the universe, but this view became more and more criticised until it was superseded. Similarly, the Newtonian paradigm of physics was replaced by Einstein's which better fitted the facts of, for example, planetary motion.

PSYCHOLOGY'S SUBJECT MATTER

Does psychology have a unified subject matter and paradigm? **Kuhn** argues that psychology is in a state of **pre-science**, because there are so many conflicting approaches to the subject that there is **no overall paradigm**. However, it could be argued that psychology has already gone through **several paradigm shifts**, from structuralism, to behaviourism, to cognitive psychology. Perhaps psychology is in the process of selecting the best set of approaches to form an integrated paradigm. Certainly most psychologists accept the definition of Psychology as the study of mind **and** behaviour.

Valentine (1982) proposes that **behaviourism** is the closest psychology has come to having a unified **paradigm**, since it had a clear subject matter (observable behaviour), assumptions (environmental determinism, learning, etc.), methods (strict laboratory experimentation), and terminology (conditioning, reinforcement, etc.). This paradigm dominated psychology for many years.

Other philosophers of science, such as **Feyerabend** (1975), argue that **science** does **not** progress in an **orderly** way through paradigms, but does and should progress **anarchistically** - as each researcher sticks tenaciously to their own theories, often in the face of opposition from others. Feyerabend argues that conforming to paradigms may limit creativity and progress, 'The only principle that does not inhibit progress is anything goes'. This view seems much more realistic of how psychology has developed, with many psychologists working as individuals or in small teams to defend their own particular area of research in the subject.

Psychology and science 3

THEORIES AND HYPOTHESES

A science should involve theories which should provide hypotheses to be tested in order to support or refute the theories. The theories themselves should provide *general laws* or principles to fulfil the aims of science - **understanding, prediction,** and **control.**

1 **Understanding** - Theories should provide understanding by being
   * **orderly** (theories should organise facts and find regularities and patterns to generate laws).
   * **internally consistent** (different parts of the theory should not contradict each other).
   * **parsimonious** (provide the greatest possible explanation in the most economic way).
   * **true!** (theories should correctly explain reality).

2 **Prediction** - A good theory should generate lots of **bold, precise hypotheses** to stimulate research to support or refute the theory.
   * According to **Karl Popper** (1959) scientific theories should be **refutable** (able to be shown wrong) and research should aim to falsify rather than support theories - since it is all too easy to find support to fit your theory, especially if you expect to find it. **Falsification** is best achieved by advancing bold and precise hypotheses, and if a theory is falsified then it should be rejected. Thus Popper is suggesting that science advances through refutation rather than support. This is why we ensure that we include a null hypothesis.
   * Another philosopher of science, **Imre Lakatos**, suggests that theories should be given a chance to prove themselves first, so they can develop. Lakatos proposes that theories or paradigms should have a **hard core** of crucial assumptions and a **protective belt** of auxiliary hypotheses - this belt can support being falsified to a certain extent (perhaps the first experiments made type 2 errors) but the hard core should remain unfalsified for the theory to remain credible. Good theories, he added, should also provide a **positive heuristic** - a future research program to generate new hypotheses and to produce unexpected findings.
   * Theories provide laws and principles to predict the future, but this can only occur if
     a a **deterministic**/nomothetic view is taken, rather than a freewill or idiographic approach.
     b **induction** is accepted, i.e. that we can generalise from a limited number of observations to general laws. Induction can **never prove** anything 100%, however, because it is impossible to observe all possible data at any one time and we can never prove that our next observation will not refute our law. Induction is the basis for inferential statistics which talk about the **probability** of chance factors causing the results.

3 **Control** - Theories should be **useful** and have **practical implications,** such as solving problems and improving the human condition. However, complete control may be impossible in practice, due to the complexity of situations and the probabilistic nature of scientific laws. Knowing the high probability that something will occur 99/100 will not guarantee that it will occur on a certain occasion. Ethical issues are also raised concerning control - who should have it and whose purposes should it serve?

SCIENTIFIC METHODOLOGY

* A science should test its hypotheses in fair and objective ways, meaning its terms should be operationalised and its methods should be standardised, controlled and replicable.

PSYCHOLOGICAL THEORIES AND HYPOTHESES

The different approaches to psychology fulfil these principles to varying degrees:

1 **Psychoanalysis** has **great explanatory power** and understanding of behaviour, but has been accused of only explaining behaviour after the event, **not predicting** what will happen in advance and of being **unfalsifiable**/unrefutable. Some have argued that psychoanalysis has approached the status more of a religion than a science, but it is not alone in being accused of being unfalsifiable (evolutionary theory has too - why is anything the way it is? Because it has evolved that way!) and like all theories that are difficult to refute - the possibility exists that it is actually right. Kline (1984) argues that psychoanalytic theory **can** be broken down into testable hypotheses and tested scientifically. For example, Scodel (1957) postulated that orally dependent men would prefer larger breasts (a positive correlation), but in fact found significantly the opposite (a negative correlation). Although Freudian theory could also be used to explain this finding (through reaction formation - the subjects were showing exactly the opposite of their unconscious impulses!), Kline has nevertheless pointed out that theory would have been refuted by *no significant correlation.*

2 The **humanistic approach** in psychology deliberately steps away from a scientific viewpoint, **rejecting determinism** in favour of freewill, aiming to study the **individual** to arrive at a unique and in depth understanding. The humanistic approach does not have an orderly set of theories (although it does have some core assumptions) and is not interested in prediction and controlling people's behaviour - the individuals themselves are the only ones who can and should do that. **Miller** (1969) in 'Psychology as a Means of Promoting Human Welfare' criticises the controlling view of psychology, suggesting that understanding should be the main goal of the subject as a science, since he asks who will do the controlling and whose interests will be served by it?

3 **Behaviourism** had **parsimonious** theories of learning, using a few simple principles (reinforcement, behaviour shaping, generalisation, etc.) to explain a vast variety of behaviour from language acquisition to moral development. It advanced **bold, precise and refutable hypotheses** (such as Hull's drive theory equations) and possessed a **hard core of central assumptions,** such as determinism from the environment (it was only when this assumption faced overwhelming criticism by the cognitive and ethological theorists that the behaviourist paradigm was overthrown). Behaviourists firmly believed in the scientific principles of **determinism** and orderliness, and thus came up with fairly consistent **predictions** about when an animal was likely to respond (although they admitted that perfect prediction for any individual was impossible). The behaviourists used their predictions to **control** the behaviour of both animals (pigeons trained to detect life jackets) and humans (behavioural therapies) and indeed Skinner, in his book *Walden Two* (1948), described a whole society controlled according to behaviourist principles.

4 Cognitive Psychology - adopts a scientific approach to unobservable mental processes by advancing precise models and conducting experiments upon behaviour to confirm or refute them.

* Full understanding, prediction and control in psychology is probably unobtainable due to the huge complexity of environmental, mental and biological influences upon even the simplest behaviour.

PSYCHOLOGICAL METHODS

* Behaviourist, cognitive and biopsychological approaches have used the most objective method, the laboratory experiment. Humanists point out many problems of using this method for human study.

Gender bias in psychological theory and research

EXAMPLES OF GENDER BIAS IN PSYCHOLOGY

Moral development - Kohlberg applied his stages of moral development derived from male subjects, to female subjects, and concluded that the latter reached lower levels. Gilligan (1982) has suggested that female morality is based on different priorities.

Interpersonal relationships - the research focus on brief acquaintances rather than long term kin relationships may reflect a male bias.

Childcare - Bowlby's research on maternal deprivation implied that women needed to stay at home and care for the children.

Socialisation - many psychoanalytically orientated psychologists proposed gender biased views on women. Freud argued that women fall 'victim to "envy for a penis", which will leave ineradicable traces on their development and the formation of their character' such as the 'physical vanity of women, since they are bound to value their charms more highly as a late compensation for their original sexual inferiority' (Freud, 1933a). Erickson proposed women were destined to bear and take care of the offspring of men.

THEORETICAL BIAS

Hare-Mustin and Maracek (1990) distinguish between alpha and beta bias in theories:

- **Alpha bias** exaggerates differences between men and women, serving to reinforce gender stereotypes.
- **Beta bias** minimises real differences between men and women, causing important parts of women's life experiences to be ignored.

These biases exist because **androcentric** (male biased) views are used as the standard or norm to explain the psychological experiences of both sexes. If women show different behaviour from the male norm, it is seen as inferior, and what does not concern the androcentric world view is not investigated.

REPORTING BIAS

- **Interpretation of results**
  Results that show gender differences may be reported in a way that emphasises female stereotypes or inferiority, e.g. concluding that women are more 'field dependent' rather than 'context aware' in visual perception, or have less self-confidence, rather than saying men are over-confident (Tavris, 1993). Gender differences in results are only average differences - variation in male and female scores means that, for example, some women will be superior to some men.
- **Selection of material to be published**
  Male biased editors and reviewers of psychology journals and books may filter out research on women, and studies that report no differences or findings contrary to male opinion (e.g. those that report very little pre-menstrual syndrome in women).
- **Use of results**
  Those studies that report genuine difference between men and women should not be used to discriminate against whichever sex seems weaker, but should be used to support the argument for increased training opportunities.

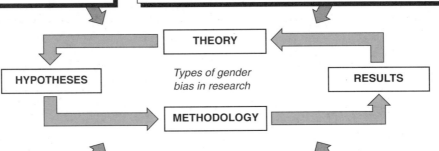

Types of gender bias in research

THEORY · HYPOTHESES · RESULTS · METHODOLOGY

RESEARCHER BIAS

Gender bias in research is likely to be caused by

- **lack of researchers**
  Researcher bias may occur because women are not appointed to, or promoted in, academic positions in male dominated universities. Alternatively, female academics may find themselves marginalised into areas outside mainstream psychology.
- **nature of researchers**
  Androcentric researchers are likely to propose hypotheses that
  a investigate stereotypical differences rather than real ones or similarities.
  b do not investigate important issues to women, such as pregnancy or female harassment and discrimination.
  c perpetuate biased ideas by, for example, searching for causes within women for different or abnormal behaviour (e.g. pre-menstrual syndrome) but in the environment for men (e.g. violent upbringing).

METHODOLOGICAL BIAS

Gender bias in the methodology of studies is found in

- the biased sampling of subjects - many famous studies in psychology (e.g. by Asch, Sherif, Kohlberg, Erikson) only used male subjects and generalised the results to women.
- the use of 'male preferred' techniques, such as the laboratory experiment with its 'manipulation' and 'control' of 'subjects'. Many feminists prefer less distant and hierarchical techniques, such as interviews where the emphasis is on personal experience and joint participation.
- the lack of controls to distinguish differences that are innate from those that are the product of gender socialisation or biased stereotypes (Weisstein 1993).

CONSEQUENCES OF GENDER BIAS

Feminists suggest that although gender differences may be minimal or non-existent, they are used against women to maintain male power. Judgements about an individual woman's ability are made on the basis of average differences between the sexes or biased sex role stereotypes, and this also has the effect of lowering women's self-esteem; making them, rather than men, think they have to improve themselves (Tavris, 1993).

VALIDITY OF GENDER BIAS

Maccoby and Jacklin (1974), in a thorough review of the research into sex differences, concluded that in the majority of areas no significant differences were found, and where they were found they were very small. The gender biased views of famous figures in psychology, such as Freud and Bowlby, have been disproved.

REDUCING GENDER BIAS

Equal opportunity legislation and feminist psychology have performed the valuable functions of reducing institutionalised gender bias and drawing attention to sources of bias and under-researched areas in psychology. More and more women are becoming psychologists and gender bias should be redressed as they become the majority in academic psychology.

Cultural bias in psychological theory and research

EXAMPLES OF CULTURAL BIAS IN PSYCHOLOGY

Social influence - Cross-cultural replications of obedience and conformity studies have revealed wide differences in resistance to influence.

Interpersonal relationships - Cultural bias in Western research on this topic, is revealed by its focus on
- brief, new acquaintances, rather than long term, kin relationships.
- the idea that marriage on the basis of romantic love is more desirable than on the basis of companionate love.

Helping behaviour - Western economic theories on the costs and rewards of helping behaviour may not be suitable for other cultures.

Abnormality - The increased diagnosis of mental disorder in immigrants may reflect prejudice or misunderstanding by a native diagnoser.

Psychometric testing - IQ and personality tests have been culturally biased in terms of content, phrasing, application, and assessment.

THEORETICAL BIAS

Cultures differ in many important ways from each other, for example in terms of their values, norms of behaviour and social structure - such as whether they emphasise individualism or collectivism, masculine or feminine values, etc. (Triandis, 1990).

Since cultural values strongly shape the construction of theories, a major problem is **ethnocentrism**, which involves
- inappropriately generalising the values and research findings of one culture to another without bothering to test other cultures. This limits the validity of theories and neglects important cross-cultural differences.
- imposing those values upon other cultures when conducting cross-cultural research. This distorts the validity of research, over-emphasises differences and can lead to unfavourable comparisons being made.

Nobles (1976) points out that the 'Eurocentric' approach (based on concepts such as 'survival of the fittest', 'competition' and 'independence') to the study of African people (who believe in 'the survival of the tribe', 'co-operation' and 'interdependence') amounts to an act of scientific colonialism.

REPORTING BIAS

- **Interpretation of results**
  Results that show cultural differences may be reported in a way that make non-American/European cultures appear deviant from the 'norm' or inferior.
- **Selection of material to be published**
  The predominantly white establishment in American and European psychology has filtered out research on black psychology, leading to the need to publish journals and books specifically for black psychology. Around two thirds of psychology in the world is North American.
- **Use of results**
  Results may be interpreted to fit political ideology and thus 'scientifically sanction' racist policies such as the eugenics driven policy of restricting immigration into the USA during the 1920s and 1930s based on the results of (biased) IQ tests.

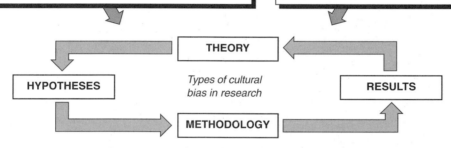

Types of cultural bias in research

THEORY

HYPOTHESES

METHODOLOGY

RESULTS

RESEARCHER BIAS

Cultural bias in research is likely to be caused by
- **lack of researchers**
  Researcher bias may occur because researchers from other cultures are not appointed to, or promoted in, academic positions in universities. 'Token' black psychologists in a predominantly white department, for example, may find themselves marginalised into areas outside mainstream psychology.
- **nature of researchers**
  Culturally biased or racist researchers are likely to propose hypotheses that
  a investigate stereotypical differences between 'races' (arbitrary and over-simplified categories based on skin colour) which may ignore cultural influences and perpetuate the stereotypes.
  b do not investigate important cross-cultural differences or similarities.

METHODOLOGICAL BIAS

Cultural bias in the methodology of studies is found in
- the biased sampling of subjects - the vast majority of the most famous studies in American and European psychology only used white subjects. Reviews of research in these countries frequently reveal less than 5% of subjects tested are not white.
- the use of Eurocentric scientific methods (based on 'control over nature', objective 'separateness' from the subject, and the investigation of individual 'differences' and 'uniqueness'), such as the laboratory experiment, is alien to the African concepts of 'oneness with nature', 'groupness' and 'similarity' (Nobles, 1976). These methods represent an imposed 'etic' (the study of a culture from the outside) when ecologically valid data can only be gained from an 'emic' study (from within the culture). Imposed 'etics' can lead to very culturally biased tests such as those on IQ described by Gould (1982).

CONSEQUENCES OF CULTURAL BIAS

Nobles (1976) argues that western psychology has been a tool of oppression and dominance. Cultural bias has also made it difficult for psychologists to separate the behaviour they have observed from the context in which they observed it.

VALIDITY OF CULTURAL BIAS

Culturally biased views have been exposed in many areas of psychology.

REDUCING CULTURAL BIAS

Equal opportunity legislation aims to rid psychology of cultural bias and racism, but we must be aware of merely swapping old, overt racism for new, more subtle forms of racism (Howitt and Owusu-Bempah, 1994).

Controversial applications of psychology - psychometric testing

Kline (1992) suggests that psychological tests fall into one of five categories:
- Ability tests - those measuring intelligence, general reasoning, verbal, numerical or spatial ability.
- Aptitude tests - those measuring specialised skills, such as hand-eye co-ordination or attention in pilot selection.
- Personality tests - those measuring traits or characteristics such as Eysenck's personality inventory (which assesses extroversion, etc.).
- Motivational tests - those measuring drive and interest for the purpose of vocational guidance.
- Other tests - those measuring mental disorders or learning deficits.

A psychometric test is one that measures some aspect of a person's psychological functioning to provide a score which can
- enable comparisons to be made with the scores of other people (some tests are standardised around a population average or norm, enabling scores to be more accurately compared).
- enable predictions to be made concerning future behaviour and performance.

Psychometric tests are, thus, obviously of use in selection purposes, to distinguish between individuals and to decide which are the most suitable for certain tasks, careers or special treatment. Given their significant potential importance, the key controversial issues become:

IS THE TEST FAIRLY CONDUCTED?
The psychologist must take into account
- conditions of testing - which must be the same for all those being tested or differences may be due, for example, to distractions
- experience of testing - experience of testing may lead to better performance due to practice, or just familiarity leading to less anxiety
- motivation and intentions of those tested - unmotivated subjects will perform under their capability, highly motivated subjects may give socially desirable answers or lie

IS THE TEST FAIRLY CONSTRUCTED?
Tests constructed to measure a universal ability should not be biased in favour of one type of population. This is especially important if tests are applied in cross-cultural contexts

CONTROVERSIAL ASPECTS OF PSYCHOMETRIC TESTING

IS THE TEST TECHNICALLY SOUND?
Tests need to show
validity - measure what they are supposed to measure
reliability - measure consistently and fairly
standardisation and **discriminatory power** - to be able to properly differentiate between subjects taking the test

ARE THE TEST RESULTS PROPERLY USED AND APPLIED?
Psychologists should take care that they
- do not assume the results are perfectly stable - abilities may change over time, so a single assessment may be unfair
- do not assume results are perfectly predictive - there may not be a correspondence between test responses and real life behaviour
- do not use the results to label people - negative as well as positive effects can follow testing, e.g. a self-fulfilling prophecy
- do not use the results to compare people if the test was not devised for the purpose - tests not standardised on a common scale should not be used to compare different people, e.g. ipsative tests
- do not fail to take into account other important factors, or use the test results as the only source of data

Given their potentially controversial aspects and applications, why are psychometric tests still employed?
Psychometric testing has several advantages

- It is easy, quick and cheap to conduct
- If the tests are well constructed they can be more objective and fairer than the subjective views of an interviewer for selection purposes.
- They have been shown to be very useful for
  a employers
  b employees
  c people suffering problems

'A nation of morons' Gould (1982)

AIM

To describe one part of the early history of intelligence testing as a way of discussing the following issues in psychology:

- The problematic nature of psychometric testing in general and the measurement of intelligence in particular.
- The problem of theoretical bias influencing research in psychology, in particular how psychological theories on the inherited nature of intelligence and the prejudice of a society can dramatically distort the objectivity of intelligence testing.
- The problem of the political and ethical implications of research, in this case the use of biased data to discriminate between people in suitability for occupation and even admission to a country.

THE HISTORY OF YERKES' TESTING OF INTELLIGENCE

What did Yerkes aim to do?

Yerkes aimed to

- show that psychology could prove itself as a respectable science by using intelligence testing to aid recruitment, and
- find support for the hereditarian view of intelligence (that intellectual ability was inherited through the genes).

How did Yerkes test intelligence?

Yerkes tested 1.75 million army recruits during the First World War, using three intelligence tests:

- Army alpha - a written exam for literate recruits
- Army beta - A pictorial exam for illiterate recruits and those who failed the alpha
- Individual exam - for those who failed the beta

Every individual was given a grade from A to E (with plus and minus signs), for example:

C- indicated a low average intelligence, suitable for the position of ordinary private in the army

D indicated a person rarely suited for tasks requiring special skill, forethought, resourcefulness or sustained alertness

What did Yerkes find?

- White American adults had an average mental age of 13, just above the level of moronity.
- Nations could be graded in their intelligence based on immigrants' intelligence test scores - people from Nordic countries scored higher than those from Latin or Slavic countries, with American 'Negroes' at the bottom of the scale.

What was wrong with Yerkes' findings?

Lots - they were a methodological, ethical, and practical disaster!

Methodological problems:	- Validity errors - the tests did not measure innate intelligence, since questions were often based on American general knowledge that recent immigrants would be unlikely to know e.g. 'The number of Kaffir's legs is - 2, 4, 6 or 8 ?' (Army alpha test) The Army beta asked often poor and illiterate immigrants to spot errors in pictures of things they had probably never seen before (e.g. a tennis match without a net) and then write their answer. - Reliability errors - unstandardised procedures were followed, with individuals being given the wrong test, being rushed, and not given the appropriate re-tests - especially during the testing of black subjects.
Interpretation of findings errors:	- Ignored experience issue - the finding that immigrants scored higher the longer they stayed in America - Ignored education issue - the finding that there was a positive correlation between number of years in education and the IQ test scores - Yerkes interpreted causation from this by arguing that intelligent people chose to stay longer in education.
Negative implications of faulty conclusions:	- Intelligence can be objectively measured - therefore, people were assigned military positions and tasks according to their scores. - Intelligence is inherited - therefore, providing illegitimate evidence for those who advocated eugenics (selective breeding in humans), racist politics, and immigration restriction (the tests were influential in denying the immigration into America of up to 6 million people from Southern, Central, and Eastern Europe, many seeking political refuge, from 1924 to 1939). - IQ tests can predict future performance - thus providing biased support for the argument that special educational measures were a waste of time and money.

EVALUATION

Methodological:	Gould's criticism is based primarily on a methodological and theoretical critique of Yerkes' testing without presenting any empirical support for his own views.
Theoretical:	Contributes to an evaluation of an area of psychology which has many important implications. IQ tests have improved in sophistication, although there is still debate over their validity.
Links:	The ethics of socially sensitive research, the nature-nurture debate in intelligence, the validity and reliability of psychometric testing, bias in cross-cultural testing (see Deregowski).

Controversial applications of psychology - advertising

WHY IS ADVERTISING A CONTROVERSIAL ISSUE?

Advertising involves a communication of the existence and nature of a product (goods or services) from the advertiser to the consumer. This at first sight does not seem a very controversial area for psychological research - indeed one might argue that advertising performs a valuable service to consumers by informing them of the range of goods available to enable them to make the best choice.

Advertisers, however, are not in business to perform altruistic services for consumers but to make profit, and have conducted or funded extensive psychological research to determine the most effective ways in which to persuade consumers to buy their products. This notion of advertising relates to sociobiological ideas of communication as manipulation (Dawkins and Krebs, 1978, Dawkins, 1982) - ultimately the advertiser wants to control people's behaviour by getting them to change or maintain their consumption of a product.

The key controversial issues, therefore, become:
- Are consumers really buying what is in their interests or the advertiser's? The advertiser obviously wants to sell as much as possible of their own product, while the consumer wishes to purchase only enough of the most suitable product for them to satisfy their needs. The answer to this question perhaps depends upon two inter-related issues:
  a The extent to which the consumer is regarded as having free choice (this ties in with the freewill vs. determinism debate) - do we always have the ability and insight to objectively assess our motivations and purchasing behaviours?
  b The extent to which advertising methods can manipulate behaviour - some methods are more effective than others.
- Are fair methods used to advertise? In other words, although trading standards organisations aim to prevent overt deception over the nature of goods and services, do advertisers employ techniques that are more subtly deceptive and exploit aspects of our psychological functioning (this ties in with the issue of conscious vs. non-conscious behaviour)?

The answers to these questions are probably best provided by looking at examples of advertising methods to examine whether they work in a manipulative way or not. A useful distinction in advertising methods is made by Petty and Cacioppo (1981) who argue that there are two main routes to persuasion:
- **The central route**, where a reasoned argument is made to a motivated buyer who can consciously consider the benefits of the product.
- **The peripheral route**, where attempts are made to influence the buyer in ways that are not directly concerned with the product itself. Such peripheral or indirect routes of influence aim to take advantage of the various behavioural, cognitive, motivational or perceptual tendencies that psychological research has revealed in humans, and thus represent a controversial application of psychology.

EXPLOITING BEHAVIOURAL TENDENCIES OF CONSUMERS

Market research on the buying behaviour of sub-groups of the population is used to match products to consumers. The collection and storage of data (especially without the knowledge of the consumer) and the subsequent targeting of advertising to the home may be perceived as an invasion of privacy.

Milliman (1982) claimed that shoppers matched their pace of shopping to the tempo of the music played at supermarkets, buying almost 40% more when the music was at a slower tempo, because they spent longer in the building.

EXPLOITING THE COGNITIVE ABILITIES OF CONSUMERS

Many sales techniques aim to create cognitive dissonance (mental unease) that can be reduced by buying a product, e.g.
- Providing free gifts to make people feel obliged to buy due to the norm of reciprocation.
- using the 'foot in the door' technique where the seller gets the buyer to begin the buying process to encourage a momentum of compliance - having already attended a long product presentation it becomes more difficult to justify backing out of buying.

Advertisers encourage deeper processing of an advert by deliberately making it bizarre or puzzling.

EXPLOITING THE PERCEPTUAL ABILITIES OF CONSUMERS

Perceptual habits are exploited in supermarkets by positioning certain goods in prime viewing locations, for example placing tempting sweets near the checkouts where resistance is weakened by longer exposure while waiting.

Advertisers exploit the human tendency to shift attention to stimuli that are vivid or novel by focusing on the presentation of the message, not just the message itself. Adverts are thus made entertaining - humorous, vivid, unique or bizarre.

Subliminal advertising, where messages are presented so quickly that they are only received unconsciously, probably does not have a significant effect on buying behaviour (Pratkanis and Aronson, 1992).

EXPLOITING MOTIVATIONAL TENDENCIES OF CONSUMERS

Adverts create pleasant associations of success, happiness, sex, etc. with a product that are not directly related to it. This is usually achieved by linking the product (probably via classical conditioning) to famous and attractive promoters, humour, or appealing fantasy situations. Positive emotions bypass the more analytical parts of the mind and appeal directly to the desires and needs a person finds important.

Advertising leaflets aim to create the impression of group belonging and acceptance (another important need) by using terms such as 'Dear friend' or 'exclusive member'.

Evaluation
- Although the central route to persuasion is meant to be more successful, the fact that so many peripheral techniques are still employed in advertising implies that they must be effective.
- Deliberate attempts to influence in advertising may backfire - they are often recognised and cynically ignored.
- Peripheral techniques of persuasion can have other negative effects - they often reinforce stereotypes and distort reality.
- Studying psychological techniques of persuasion in advertising can lead to methods of resisting it (Pratkanis and Aronson, 1991).

Controversial applications of psychology - the psychology of warfare

PROPAGANDA

Propaganda involves the dissemination of messages intended to change or consolidate attitudes and behaviour for political purposes.

Propaganda is similar to advertising in its
- use of biased, one-sided communication
- objective of changing behaviour and attitudes
- use of emotion and occasional disregard for logical analysis

Propaganda is different to advertising in that
- political ideas and information are what is 'bought'
- a more complete and general behaviour and attitude change is sought.
- being more socially sanctioned, the use of bias and deception is more likely to extend beyond any 'Consumer Protection Act'

Propaganda achieves its aims through a variety of techniques:
- Proliferation of information and dominance of communication channels - in order to establish their 'unquestionable truths' the propagandists have to limit the airing of alternative views in any media, e.g. television, radio, the press, etc.
- Establishment of narrow and rigidly defined norms of acceptable thinking and behaviour - encouragement is given to reject and sanction alternative ideologies, reinforcement through social acceptance is given for conforming to the correct ideology.
- Dehumanisation of the enemy - to justify persecutory propaganda and reduce inhibitions about biased behaviour in the receiver.
- Strengthening of central fears and stereotypes - to promote and motivate intergroup discrimination.

BRAINWASHING
- Brainwashing is a more coercive form of persuasion, where powerful techniques are used to remove the ability of voluntary thought in a more complete way, thereby leading to behaviour that is not in the individual's own interest.
- Brainwashing is applied in varying degrees of severity, for a variety of purposes, but there are similar principles involved. Tavris and Wade (1995) have outlined some of these principles and applied them to the brainwashing of cult members, but we can also see how easily these ideas can be used in warfare - to brainwash troops and prisoners of war into obedience.

	CULTS	ARMIES	PRISONERS OF WAR
THE AIM OF BRAINWASHING	To establish dependence upon, and fanatical attachment to, the cult - thus giving up time, wealth and belongings to it.	To establish unquestioning obedience to authority - thus following orders that may result in damage or death.	To change loyalties and establish obedience to the captors - encouraging the rejection of previous attitudes and defection.
TECHNIQUES **The use of physical and emotional distress**	Cults may recruit those suffering from emotional problems and use initiation rituals (e.g. deprivation of food, repetitive chanting, or constant activity) to keep them disoriented, weak and vulnerable.	Army routines involve vigorous and constant activity schedules with little sleep and constant commands to carry out in order to encourage uncritical, automatic acceptance of command and obedience to orders.	Physical torture (pain infliction, starvation, etc.) and psychological torture (sensory or social deprivation) may be applied to produce disorientation and lack of critical thought.
The offering of simple solutions	Encouraging recruits to think that all the problems of life can be easily solved by following the cult's beliefs.	Encouraging potential recruits to think that the problems of life are removed, e.g. no need to search for employment, housing, excitement.	Encouraging P.O.W.s to think that torture can stop and a new life begin if they comply with demands and reject former values.
The creation and enforcement of a new social identity, through: • **attire and name changing** • **conditional in-group acceptance** • **physical and informational entrapment** • **out-group denigration**	Cults often provide new names and clothing to encourage the change of identity and the appearance of unconditional acceptance to make the new member feel part of the group. In reality group acceptance is conditional upon complying with the demands of the cult. Cults use communal residences to cut off communication with the outside world, the faults of which are emphasised to promote withdrawal.	Service numbers, ranks and uniform remove individual identity and promote the change to an army identity. Disobedience is punished. Location of residence is controlled and operational information is given on a need to know basis. Distinctions from civilians are emphasised and dislike/dehumanisation of the enemy encouraged to promote in-group identity consolidation.	Captors often dehumanise and remove all tokens of individuality (such as clothing and personal possessions) from their prisoners. The withholding of punishment is conditional upon compliance with expected behaviours. Physical confinement isolates the prisoner from all contact with their previous life - any information allowed from it is only permitted to be negative.

EVALUATION
- There are many differences as well as similarities in the various situations that brainwashing or coercive persuasion is employed in.
- There are individual differences in the ability to resist brainwashing. Psychological techniques often produce greater brainwashing.
- The issue of 'voluntary' thinking and decision making in brainwashing is a difficult issue. If subtly carried out, the influenced individual will strongly feel that the change in their attitudes and behaviour was completely their own decision.

OTHER APPLICATIONS OF PSYCHOLOGY TO WARFARE
- Interrogation techniques - using psychological techniques in the delivery and context of questioning and the reinforcement of answers.
- Psychological warfare - disrupting wartime communication, demoralising troops, analysing psychological causes and responses to war.

Ethics of animal experimentation - the arguments for testing animals

THE REASONS FOR CONDUCTING ANIMAL RESEARCH IN PSYCHOLOGY

Ethical reasons - Many experiments that psychologists want to conduct are deemed unethical for human testing, but important enough to be justified for animal testing. Such experiments might involve controlled interbreeding, deprivation studies, brain surgery, or the trial testing of drugs.

Evolutionary continuum - Some psychologists, such as the behaviourists, claimed that animal research was justified because humans have evolved from other animals and so the difference between them is only quantitative. Since humans are just more complex animals, it makes sense to study more simple organisms first, and then generalise to humans by 'scaling up' the results.

Convenience - Animals are 'good subjects', they do not try to understand the purpose of the experiment, are more controllable, and their faster breeding cycles allow tests to be conducted on the influence of heredity and environment on behaviour.

Skinner box

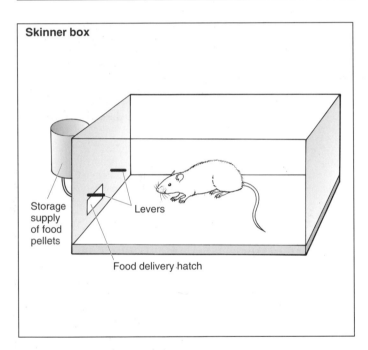

Storage supply of food pellets

Levers

Food delivery hatch

THE ETHICAL DEFENCE OF ANIMAL RESEARCH

- Humans have a moral obligation to help humans first (a rather 'speciesist' assumption!) and the alternatives to animal research are either ethically undesirable (i.e. testing humans) or practically undesirable (using less reliable methods such as non experimental observations or computer simulations).
- Anti-vivisectionists have been accused of only drawing attention to a minority of the most vivid cases of animal suffering in psychology (although many would argue that such a minority of cases is still ethically unjustifiable).
- There are now many safeguards in place to prevent the unnecessary use of animal research in psychology.

THE CONTRIBUTION OF ANIMAL RESEARCH TO PSYCHOLOGY

Theoretical knowledge - Animal studies have contributed to our understanding of many topics in psychology, for example

- learning theory, e.g. from Skinner's rats and pigeons
- parental deprivation, e.g. from Harlow's rhesus monkeys
- perception, e.g. from Held and Hein's 'kitten carousel'
- language acquisition, e.g. from chimpanzee and gorilla studies
- aggression, e.g. from ethological and physiological studies of other species
- abnormality, e.g. from Seligman's work on the preparedness of phobias and the role of learned helplessness in depression

Practical applications of animal findings, for example

- behavioural treatments and therapies based on the principles of operant and classical conditioning, such as the systematic desensitisation of phobias derived from Wolpe's work on cats.
- education - again based on the behaviourists' discoveries of learning using animals.

Practical uses of animals, for example as

- animal helpers, e.g. guide dogs, monkey home helps, air-sea rescue pigeons, police drug-detecting dogs - all trained using learning theory principles.
- Military tools, e.g. the use of trained dolphins to deliver mines to the hulls of enemy ships or pigeons to deliver messages.

ETHICAL GUIDELINES FOR THE USE OF ANIMALS IN PSYCHOLOGICAL RESEARCH

The Experimental Psychology Society (1986) has issued guidelines to control animal experimentation based on the legislation of the 'Animals (Scientific Procedures) Act' (1986), by stressing that all researchers should:

- Avoid or minimise stress and suffering for all living animals, and always consider the possibility of other options to animal research.
- Acquire a Home Office Licence to conduct animal research (which can only be obtained if the research aims are approved and certain conditions are met, such as suitable knowledge of the species and its living conditions, limits on the maximum level of electric shock allowed, etc.).
- Be as economical as possible in the numbers of animals tested.

Bateson (1986) has specified some of the factors involved in deciding on the viability of animal research. Often the decision will involve a trade off between
a the certainty of benefit from the research.
b the quality of the research.
c the amount of suffering involved for the animals.

Home offices licences are most likely to be awarded if factors '**a**' and '**b**' are high, and factor '**c**' is low.

Ethics of animal experimentation - the arguments against testing animals

ETHICAL CRITICISMS OF ANIMAL RESEARCH IN PSYCHOLOGY

The two key ethical arguments against animal testing in psychology are:

- The animals tested often **suffer** greatly. There is little doubt that a number of objective and behavioural measures indicate that animals can be said to suffer stress, pain and anxiety. Inflicting suffering upon another creature is morally objectionable. In many cases, the suffering of animals (the means) has not been justified by the knowledge gained from the studies (the ends).
- The suffering inflicted upon animals is often **unnecessary** for a number of practical and methodological reasons.
  - a Humans are **physically qualitatively different** to other animals, for example in terms of brain structure, complexity and specialisation (e.g. the human areas for language) and may react differently to drugs. Although there is only a 1.6% difference in the DNA of humans and chimpanzees, this 1.6% may be the most crucial for understanding human uniqueness.
  - b Humans are **mentally qualitatively different** to other animals, for example the humanists would regard human consciousness as a key difference. Superficial similarities in behaviour between rats and humans may lead to faulty over-generalisations of rat findings to humans ('ratomorphism') while the projection of human-like traits onto animals (anthropomorphism) may also lead to an exaggeration of similarity.
  - c Laboratory studies on animals are often even more likely to **lack ecological validity** than those conducted on humans, and so these invalid findings are even less useful for generalisation to human behaviour.

Biologically orientated research
Lashley, (1929) removed parts of rats brains in order to monitor later behaviour.
Delgado (1969) implanted electrodes into animals brains to stimulate behaviour.
Hubel & Wiesel (1959) inserted measuring electrodes into the visual cortex of cats.

Obedience
Sheridan and King's (1972) later variation of Milgram's obedience study involved subjects being instructed to give real electric shocks to puppies. As usual, high levels of obedience were shown.

Deprivation studies
Harlow raised rhesus monkeys in complete social deprivation. Their later behaviour was extremely maladaptive, being unable to properly interact with other monkeys or look after their young.

Perception studies
Riesen (1950) raised chimpanzees in complete darkness and then tried to condition them to fear a visually presented object by pairing it with an electric shock. It took many pairings to get the chimpanzee to whimper when presented with the visual stimuli.
Sperry (1943) surgically rotated the eyes of salamanders through 180 degrees in perceptual re-adaptation studies.

EXAMPLES OF ANIMAL SUFFERING IN PSYCHOLOGICAL RESEARCH.

Learning studies
Pavlov classically conditioned 'experimental neurosis' into his dogs.
Seligman and Maier (1967) demonstrated a 'failure to escape traumatic shock' in animals by repeatedly administering unavoidable electric shocks.
Garcia and Koelling (1966) used radiation to induce sickness in their rat taste aversion studies.

FIGURES

A British Psychological Society survey of animal testing in British university psychological research in 1977 found:
- 43,196 animals were tested
- 3929 were given electric shocks
- 6851 were exposed to drugs
- 4761 underwent surgery
- 8980 were deprived of water and/or food
- The majority of animals tested (around 95%) were rats, mice and birds

Thomas and Blackman (1991) compared the research use of animals in 62 out of 67 British psychology departments in 1989 with the use in 1977 and found:
- 13,286 animals were tested
- Almost 90% fewer electric shocks were used on animals
- A third fewer animals were tested with drugs
- Two thirds fewer animals underwent surgery
- Around 50% fewer animals were deprived of water and/or food
- More observational research was conducted
- Even fewer species were studied, only 1.5% were not rodents or birds

It appears that less psychological research on animals is being conducted today, and animal studies only account for a very small percentage of psychological research.

Ethical issues in human experimentation in psychology 1

WHY CONSIDER ETHICAL ISSUES IN HUMAN RESEARCH?

The aim of psychology is to provide us with a greater understanding of ourselves and, if required, to enable us to use that understanding to predict and control our behaviour for **human betterment**.

To achieve this understanding psychologists often have no other choice but to investigate human subjects for valid results to be obtained. Humans, however, not only experience physical **pain** and **anxiety** but can be affected mentally - in terms of **embarrassment** or **loss of self-esteem**, for example. Humans also have **rights** of **protection** and **privacy** above the levels granted to animals, and so this leads us to ethical dilemmas:

- How far should psychologists be allowed to go in pursuing their knowledge?
- Should humankind aim to improve itself by allowing people to be dehumanised in the process?
- Do the **ends** of psychological research **justify** the **means**?
- Can we ever know whether a piece of research will justify abusing the rights of individuals before we conduct it?

The existence of ethical constraints is clearly a serious but necessary limitation on the advancement of psychology as a science, and the major professional psychological bodies of many countries have published ethical guidelines for conducting research. In Britain, the British Psychological Society (1993) has published guidelines such as the **'Ethical Principles for Conducting Research with Human Participants',** which deal with ethical issues such as consent, deception, debriefing, withdrawal from the investigation, confidentiality, protection of participants, observational research, and giving advice.

CONSENT

Researchers are obliged, whenever possible, to obtain the informed consent of participants in a psychological study.
Consent is especially an issue when testing involves children or those unable to give their own consent, e.g. those with serious brain damage.

Examples in psychology

Milgram (1963) - The subjects in Milgram's study had volunteered to participate in a study of learning, not obedience. Having not been told of the researcher's objectives, their informed consent was not given.

Bystander intervention studies - Such as those conducted by Darley and Batson (the 'Good Samaritan' study) or Piliavin (subway studies) where subjects were not asked for their consent at all. However, one could argue that people see the plight of others every day without consent.

Zimbardo et al (1973) - The subjects in the prison simulation experiment signed a formal 'informed consent' statement specifying there would be a loss of some civil rights, invasion of privacy and harassment.

Children studies - Such as Rosenthal amd Jacobson's 'Pygmalian in the classroom' experiment, or Sherif's 'Robbers Cave' study. In each case, consent was not given but the consequences of the former study (improved I.Q.) were more favourable that the latter (discrimination). Should consequences make a difference?

DECEPTION

The BPS Ethical Principles (1993) states that 'Participants should never be deliberately misled without extremely strong scientific or medical justification. Even then there should be strict controls and the disinterested approval of independent advisors'. Many psychology studies would not achieve valid results due to demand characteristics if deception was not employed, and so a cost-benefit analysis of the gains vs. the discomfort of the participant must be considered.

Examples in psychology

Milgram (1963) - The subjects were led to believe that they were giving real electric shocks to another in an experiment on learning rather than obedience. Orne and Holland (1968) have suggested that the subjects were involved in a 'pact of ignorance' with the experimenter (they did not really believe they were harming anyone).

Computer dance studies - Conducted by Walster et al (1966), for example, in the area of interpersonal attraction. Subjects filled out questionnaires believing that they were going to be matched with an ideal partner, but in fact were rated for physical attractiveness without their knowledge and assigned a partner at random.

Rosenhan (1973) - In the study 'On Being Sane in Insane Places' eight 'normal' people gained admission to psychiatric hospitals merely by pretending to hear voices and faking their name and occupation. One might argue that this case of deception was one that the victims were able to avoid.

Drug testing - Often involves the use of placebo control groups. Patients may be given either the real drug or pills that have no effect, but are not told which they have been given. Perhaps a necessary case of deception but what about the patients' rights to receive the best care?

Craik and Tulving (1975) - Tested Levels of processing ideas by using incidental learning (subjects were not told they would be tested on their memory). A case of minor deception.

MILGRAM'S EXPERIMENT

Ethical issues in human experimentation in psychology 2

DEBRIEFING

Involves informing those tested of the reasons for the research and ensuring that they leave the testing in as similar a state as possible as they entered it. This is especially important if deception has been employed and the procedures could cause long term upset.

Examples in psychology

Milgram (1963) - All subjects were fully debriefed and reassured after the experiment. They were shown that the learner was unharmed and had not received any shocks.

CONFIDENTIALITY

Under the Data Protection Act (1984) participants and the data they provide should be kept anonymous unless they have given their full consent. If clients are dissatisfied after debriefing they can demand their data is destroyed.

Examples in psychology

Confidentiality is of particular importance in case studies, especially involving data gained as part of a client-patient relationship. There are many examples in psychology of pseudonyms used to maintain anonymity, e.g. Genie, H.M., Anna O, etc.

WITHDRAWAL

Any participants in psychological studies should be informed of their right to withdraw from testing whenever they wish.

Examples in psychology

Milgram (1963) - The study abused the right of subjects to withdraw from a psychology study - those wishing to leave were told 'you have no other choice, you *must* go on'. However, subjects had the right to leave, they were not physically restrained, in fact the subsequent variations of the experiment were designed to discourage obedience.

Zimbardo et al (1973) - Stopped their prison simulation study after just 6 days instead of the two weeks it was meant to run because of extreme reactions shown by the participants.

OBSERVATIONAL RESEARCH

Hidden observational studies produce the most ecologically valid data but inevitably raise the ethical issue of privacy. The importance of this issue will obviously be greater in certain areas of psychology (e.g. intimate behaviour in interpersonal relationships) than others (e.g. crowd behaviour).

PROTECTION OF PARTICIPANTS

Participants should leave psychological studies in roughly the same condition in which they arrived, without suffering physical or psychological trauma.

Examples in psychology

Milgram (1963) - Baumrind (1964) criticised Milgram's study as being unethical because it caused distress and anguish to the subjects. One had a seizure and all subjects could have suffered psychological damage. Milgram himself commented that 'In a large number of cases the degree of tension reached extremes that are rarely seen in sociopsychological laboratory studies'. However, the results obtained were completely unexpected (Milgram asked for estimates beforehand), and although the subjects appeared uncomfortable with their obedience, Milgram concluded that 'momentary excitement is not the same as harm'. Milgram argued that it was the shocking nature of his findings that provoked a moral outrage.

A follow up opinion survey conducted a year later found that nearly 84% were 'glad to have been in the experiment', 15% were neutral, and only 1.3% were 'sorry or very sorry to have been in the experiment'. Around 80% of the respondents said there should be more experiments like Milgram's conducted, and around 75% said they had learnt something of personal value from their experience. The subjects were examined one year after the experiment by a psychiatrist who found no signs of harm.

Zimbardo et al (1973) - Zimbardo's prison simulation procedures were more stressful than the volunteer students playing the prisoner role expected. A surprise city police arrest and processing was followed by brutal treatment from the students playing the role of the guards, which caused psychological stress in the form of crying, rage and depression, and even the development of a psychosomatic rash.

Sherif et al (1961) - Experimentally produced discrimination and hostility between two groups of boys in their 'Robber's Cave' study through tournaments and staged situations, leading to verbal abuse and even fighting. Conflict was reduced by the end of the experiment.

Watson and Raynor (1920) - Conditioned a phobia of rats into an emotionally stable 11 month old infant, 'Little Albert', by repeatedly startling the child with a loud noise every time a white rat was presented. The fear response generalised to other objects including rabbits, white fur coats and even facial hair (including that on a Santa Claus mask!) but was never removed from the subject.

Bandura et al (1961) - Showed how aggression could be learnt in children through observational learning in their Bobo Doll experiment. However is it right to produce aggression in children experimentally, even if they may acquire it from their own environment anyway?

Ethical issues in human behaviour change in psychology

If the aim of psychological understanding is to provide prediction and control for human betterment, then several issues need to be raised:

1 Should behaviour be controlled?

2 Who should do the controlling?

3 What behaviour should be controlled?

4 How should behaviour be controlled?

SHOULD BEHAVIOUR BE CONTROLLED?

The answer to this question often depends on the approach taken to psychology.

- Miller (1969) in 'Psychology as a means of promoting human welfare' argued that the primary goal of psychology should be to provide understanding and prediction only and, by making psychological knowledge available to the public, allow individuals to apply it to their own lives. This disagreement with the controlling aspects of psychology is in accord with humanist principles and assumptions of **self-actualisation**, but was opposed by behaviourist orientated psychologists such as

Skinner who argued that, since freewill is an illusion and all behaviour is controlled by the environment anyway, it makes sense to have experts (psychologists!) doing the controlling.

- Clearly the issue of whether behaviour should be controlled is dependent on which side of the freewill vs. determinism debate one takes - the degree to which self-responsibility is bestowed on humans. If a degree of determinism is accepted, however, then the issue of whether behaviour should be controlled then revolves around the issues of **who** is doing the controlling and **how far** behaviour should be controlled.

WHO SHOULD DO THE CONTROLLING?

This concerns the issue of who is doing the controlling and for what purpose.

- **What should the ratio of power be between the individual and their society?**
  If we consider the area of abnormality then clearly there is a range of possible power arrangements depending upon the approach taken to treating disorders and the seriousness of the disorder itself. Humanist therapists would aim to clarify the client's problems with living in order to provide insight and encourage **self** improvement, whereas cognitive psychologists and psychoanalysts would take a more **directive** approach, aiming to persuade the subject to change their thinking/accept unconscious truths. At the other end of the continuum, the medical model approach would hold the majority of power with serious psychoses, and may insist on administering physiological treatments, which they could **enforce** if the patient was sectioned under the Mental Health Act (1983) - thereby assuming complete responsibility, even over the rights

of the nearest relative if necessary. Thus the control of society can range from giving advice, to persuasion, to enforced treatment. The main ethical problem with social control of behaviour is deciding who controls the controllers.

- **Whose goals is behaviour being changed for - the benefit of the individual or society?**
  The goals of the therapy and the extent to which the individual can decide when therapy has been completed again depend upon the approach taken - psychology is not 'value-free'. Humanists such as Laing and Szasz are rather pessimistic about the seemingly caring approach of the medical model to abnormality, suggesting that society uses medical labels as a form of social control based on motives of fear and prejudice, and that institutionalisation and treatment merely perform the function of reducing atypical individuals into passive and 'model citizens'. The behaviourist Skinner firmly believed behaviour should be engineered and controlled by expert state psychologists.

WHAT BEHAVIOUR SHOULD BE CONTROLLED?

The issue of control crops up many times in psychology, and again represents a continuum in the desirability of behaviour change.

- Abnormality is generally accepted as an area in which behaviour change is accepted and often desired, even if mistakes have been and still are occasionally made (e.g. the former use of aversion therapy on homosexuals).

- Other areas of psychology such as education, advertising, social influence, attitude change and the reduction of prejudice and aggression all have ethical problems with the behavioural changes they wish to bring about. Most would agree, for example, that discrimination should be controlled, but what about prejudiced attitudes/opinions?

HOW SHOULD BEHAVIOUR BE CONTROLLED?

- Biological approaches - such as drugs, ECT, psychosurgery, or even gene therapy. Often these techniques are used before we have attained a proper understanding of how they work and what their effects might be. The techniques and the changes produced may often benefit society more than the patient in the long run, e.g. drugs controlling rather than curing, but we should not underestimate how anti-schizophrenic and anti-depressant drugs have changed many people's lives for the better.

- Behavioural techniques - such as flooding and aversion therapy. These can produce effective changes, usually on a voluntary basis, but can involve some trauma in the process. As with all types of therapy, a cost-benefit analysis on the benefits vs. side-effects should be considered. The use of electric shocks has controlled childhood eating disorders that might otherwise have killed their victims.

The ethics of socially sensitive research

Many of the studies conducted and topics researched in psychology have wider implications for those who are investigated and society as a whole. The ethics of socially sensitive research involves the psychologist being aware of:
- The implications of investigating certain controversial topics.
- The possible uses to which their research findings will be put.
- The amount of influence the psychologist has on public policy.
- The basis or validity of their research findings in controversial areas.
- The availability, understanding and interpretation of the data they provide.

DECIDING WHAT TO RESEARCH

Even the very act of phrasing hypotheses - deciding who and what is to be investigated - has ethical implications.
- Investigating potentially socially sensitive areas, such as race and its effects on IQ or the genetic basis of homosexuality, may serve to legitimise or perpetuate socially constructed differences and prejudices. Alternatively, one might argue that the only way to dispel such prejudices or tackle genuine difference is to investigate them objectively and scientifically to reach the truth. Avoiding controversial topics just because they are controversial (and may involve stress to the researchers) could be regarded as an avoidance of social responsibility.
- Whether objectivity in the phrasing and investigation of research hypotheses is possible is debatable. As the humanist psychologist Rogers (1956), in his debate with the behaviourist Skinner, commented 'In any scientific endeavour - whether "pure" or "applied" science - there is a prior subjective choice of the purpose or value which that scientific work is perceived as serving'.
- We must remember that what is investigated, even in seemingly pure academic research, is subject to social values. Much psychology, especially in the USA, has been (and still is) funded by the military and large businesses, for example Zimbardo's research into the psychological effects of imprisonment was funded by the US navy.

THE USE OF KNOWLEDGE

Psychologists should consider how their findings will be used and who will be affected by them.
- Knowledge is rarely neutral in practice, it can be used to improve the human condition or worsen it. The application of psychological knowledge to warfare is a good example. Watson (1978) has commented 'Psychology can be a worrying science in the hands of the military' - research on deindividuation and attitude change can be used to train soldiers to kill or brainwash prisoners of war, yet psychological research on intergroup conflict and post-traumatic stress disorder can also help prevent war or treat the victims of it.
- Even the same research findings, such as those on the operant conditioning of animals, can be applied to train animals to help the disabled, e.g. guide-dogs, or to deliver explosive weapons, e.g. 'Project Pigeon' (Skinner, 1960).

THE INFLUENCE OF THE PSYCHOLOGIST IN SOCIETY

The impact of socially sensitive research depends upon the influence the psychologists have in a society. Segall (1976) in 'Human Behaviour and Public Policy' identifies three main ways in which psychologists could affect political and social policies, by acting as:
- expert witnesses, e.g. giving evidence in court cases. The problem with this role for psychologists is that they lose control of their knowledge - policy makers can use or reject psychological expertise and knowledge at will. On the plus side, opposing psychological views can be presented for judgement, reducing the possibility of biased views influencing outcomes, e.g. alternative views on the value of testimony retrieved under hypnosis.
- Policy evaluators, e.g. helping research the impact of proposed political and social measures, such as new laws. Psychological research on the harmful effects of American school segregation for blacks and whites was influential in causing desegregation laws. The problems of this role for psychologists are that it is dependent upon the quality of research and prevailing social conditions of the time.
- Social-psychological engineers - to devise ways of ensuring desirable behaviour. Skinner (1971) advocated this view for psychologists in his book *Beyond Freedom and Dignity*. The problems with this role for psychologists are those of behavioural control in general (Who decides what behaviour is desirable? Who controls the controllers? etc.) and the possible unreliability of psychological research.

It follows that the potentially harmful effects of socially sensitive research become magnified with the power of psychologists in society.

THE BASIS OF PSYCHOLOGICAL KNOWLEDGE

With socially sensitive research, the psychologist must be particularly careful to avoid bias and error, and thus must make clear their **theoretical background**, the **limitations of their research** and the **generalisability of their findings.** Howitt (1991) argues that, since it is impossible to be objective and value free, psychologists should always be cautious when applying their findings. There are many examples of biased or faulty psychological research influencing social views and policies.
- Bowlby's (1951) maternal deprivation research drew attention to the adverse effects of early disrupted child-care but wrongly added support to the social view that it was the role of the woman to care for children.
- Gould (1981) in 'The Mismeasure of Man' describes how biased IQ tests carried out by Yerkes on immigrants to the USA led to eugenicists limiting immigration from Europe for people wanting to escape Nazi persecution.
- Cyril Burt's questionable view that 80% of IQ was genetically determined, influenced ideas on selective education at age 11.
- Gerard (1983) argued that the Social Science Statement supporting the 1954 Brown vs. Board of Education U.S. Supreme Court Decision which led to school desegregation was based on 'well meaning rhetoric rather than solid research'.

Although the premature application of psychology to political issues diminishes public confidence in the social sciences, all knowledge is relative to the time and decisions have to be made on currently available knowledge.

THE AVAILABILITY OF RESEARCH

In the case of socially sensitive research, psychologists have a responsibility to clarify the communication of findings to the media, public and policy makers to minimise any distortion or abuse of findings (they may only want to hear findings that confirm their own prejudices or policies). Miller (1969) argues that psychological knowledge should be freely given away to the public to prevent its exploitation.

Research methods

Variables

WHAT DO PSYCHOLOGISTS INVESTIGATE?

VARIABLES

A variable is any object, quality or event that changes or varies in some way. Examples include: aggression, intelligence, time, height, amount of alcohol, driving ability, attraction.

OPERATIONALISATION

Many of the variables that psychologists are interested in are **abstract concepts,** such as aggression or intelligence. Operationalisation refers to the process of making variables physically measurable or testable. This is done in psychology by recording some aspect of **observable behaviour** that is assumed to be indicative of the variable under consideration. For example:
Aggression - a psychologist may record the number of punches thrown.
Intelligence - a psychologist may record the number of puzzles solved in an hour, or calculate the score on an IQ test.

Reification (regarding hypothetical variables like intelligence as having a real physical existence) is a danger, however.

INVESTIGATING VARIABLES

OBSERVATIONS, CASE STUDIES, SURVEYS, ETC.

In these methods variables are precisely measured in varying amounts of detail.

CORRELATIONS

Variables are measured and compared to see how they co-vary with each other (what relationship they have together).

EXPERIMENTS

One variable (the **independent variable**) is **altered** to see what **effect** it has on another variable (the **dependent variable**).
The independent variable is the variable that is manipulated in two or more conditions to see what effect it has on the dependent variable.
The dependent variable is the main measured outcome of the experiment, hopefully due to the manipulation of the independent variable.
For example, the independent variable (IV) of alcohol could be manipulated to see what effect it had on the dependent variable (DV) of driving ability by testing in two conditions, one with no alcohol and the other with four pints of lager.
However, many **extraneous variables** (other variables that could potentially influence the dependent variable apart from the independent variable), could spoil the experiment and so **controls** are employed to prevent extraneous variables from becoming confounding variables (those that actually affect the dependent variable strongly enough to distort the effect of the independent variable). Extraneous variables can be either **random** (unsystematic variables that can affect the dependent variable but should not affect one condition more than another) or **constant** (those that have a systematic effect on one condition more than another). While random errors will reduce the accuracy of the results, only constant errors usually truly confound the experimental results.

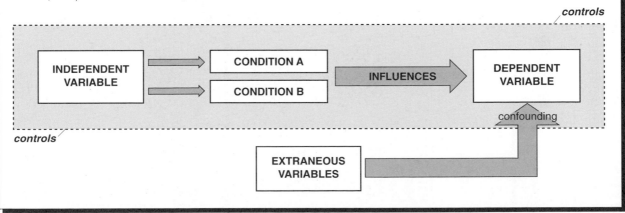

controls

| INDEPENDENT VARIABLE | → | CONDITION A |
| | → | CONDITION B | INFLUENCES → | DEPENDENT VARIABLE |

controls

confounding

| EXTRANEOUS VARIABLES |

Hypotheses

HOW DO PSYCHOLOGISTS MAKE THEIR PREDICTIONS?

HYPOTHESES are *precise, testable statements*

THEY SHOULD BE → **BOLD**

THEY CAN BE →

BOLD

2-tailed hypotheses simply predict an effect, such as a difference or correlation.

1-tailed hypotheses predict a particular direction in the effect, e.g. that one condition will do better than another, or that a positive correlation will occur.

PRECISE

Precise hypotheses should contain fully **operationalised variables** and the words 'statistically significant' if inferential statistics are to be conducted on the results.

REFUTABLE

To be scientific every hypothesis should be capable of being **shown to be wrong**. For this reason a **null hypothesis** is proposed that states that there will be **no significant effect** (either difference or correlation). Sometimes, however, it is the null hypothesis which researchers wish to study.

EXPERIMENTAL HYPOTHESES

Predict significant differences in the dependent variable [DV] between the various conditions of the independent variable [IV].

BOLD

2 - tailed
There will be a significant **difference in** [the DV] **between** [condition A of the IV] **and** [condition B of the IV].

1 - tailed
There will be a significant **increase in** [the DV] **in** [condition A of the IV] **compared to** [condition B of the IV].
or
There will be a significant **decrease in** [the DV] **in** [condition A of the IV] **compared to** [condition B of the IV].

PRECISE

2 - tailed example
There will be a **statistically significant** difference in **I.Q. scores** between **male subjects** and **female subjects**.

1 - tailed examples
There will be a **statistically significant** increase in **I.Q. scores in male subjects** compared to **female subjects**.
or
There will be a **statistically significant** decrease in **I.Q. scores in male subjects** compared to **female subjects**.

REFUTABLE

2 - tailed example
There will be **no** statistically significant difference in I.Q. scores between male subjects and female subjects.

1 - tailed examples
There will be **no** statistically significant increase in I.Q. scores in male subjects compared to female subjects.
or
There will be **no** statistically significant increase in I.Q. scores in female subjects compared to male subjects.

CORRELATIONAL HYPOTHESES

Predict significant patterns of relationship between two or more variables.

BOLD

2 - tailed
There will be a significant **correlation between** [variable 1] and [variable 2].

1 - tailed
There will be a significant **positive correlation between** [variable 1] and [variable 2].
or
There will be a significant **negative correlation between** [variable 1] and [variable 2].

PRECISE

2 - tailed example
There will be a **statistically significant** correlation between **hours of psychology revision conducted** and **A level grade gained in psychology**.

1 - tailed example
There will be a **statistically significant** positive correlation between **hours of psychology revision conducted** and **A level grade gained in psychology**.

REFUTABLE

2 - tailed example
There will be **no** statistically significant correlation between hours of psychology revision conducted and A level grade gained in psychology.

1 - tailed example
There will be **no** statistically significant positive correlation between hours of psychology revision conducted and A level grade gained in psychology.

Experimental methods

HOW DO PSYCHOLOGISTS INVESTIGATE THEIR HYPOTHESES?

EXPERIMENTS

An experiment involves the **manipulation of the independent variable** to see what effect it has on the dependent variable, while attempting to **control** the influence of all other **extraneous variables**.

TYPES

LABORATORY
In the laboratory the researcher **deliberately manipulates** the independent variable while maintaining **strict control** over extraneous variables through standardised procedures.

FIELD
The researcher **deliberately manipulates** the independent variable, but does so in the subject's own **natural environment.**

NATURAL/QUASI
The independent variable is **changed by natural occurrence**; the researcher just records the effect on the dependent variable. Quasi experiments are any where control is lacking over the IV.

EXAMPLES

BANDURA ET AL (1961)
Bandura manipulated the independent variable of 'exposure to aggression' to see what effect it had on the dependent variable of 'imitation of aggression in children' under controlled laboratory conditions by randomly allocating children to either a condition where they saw
- an adult being violent towards a Bobo doll, or
- an adult showing no violence.

The number of aggressive acts shown by each child was later also measured in the laboratory.

FESHBACH AND SINGER (1971)
Feshbach and Singer manipulated the independent variable of 'exposure to aggression' to see what effect it had on the dependent variable of 'imitation of aggression in children' by showing boys in a residential school either
- aggressive television or
- non-aggressive television.

This field study was conducted over 6 weeks, during which the boys' aggression was rated.

JOY ET AL (1977)
Joy et al investigated the independent variable of 'exposure to aggression' to see what effect it had on the dependent variable of 'imitation of aggression in children' by measuring levels of aggression in children of a small Canadian town
- before television was introduced to the town, and
- after television was introduced to the town.

STRENGTHS

LABORATORY
The most scientific method because the
- manipulation of the independent variable indicates **cause** and **effect.**
- laboratory **increases control** and accurate measurement of variables thus more **objectivity.**
- laboratory standardisation means greater ability to replicate (repeat again) the study.

FIELD
- Has **greater ecological validity** than laboratory experiments, since behaviour occurs in its own natural environment.
- **Less bias** from sampling (subjects do not have to be brought into the laboratory) and demand characteristics (if subjects are unaware of being tested).

NATURAL/QUASI
- Has **great ecological validity**, since a 'natural' change (not induced directly by the experimenter) occurs in a natural environment.
- **Very little bias** from sampling or demand characteristics (if subjects are unaware of being observed by experimenters).

WEAKNESSES

LABORATORY
- **Total control** over all variables is **not possible.**
- **Artificial** laboratory conditions may produce unnatural behaviour that **lacks ecological validity** (results do not generalise to real life).
- Results more likely to be **biased** by sampling, demand characteristics, experimenter expectancy.
- May raise ethical problems of deception, etc.

FIELD
- **More bias** likely from extraneous variables, due to **greater difficulty of controlling** all aspects of experiment outside the laboratory.
- More **difficult to replicate** exactly.
- Possibly more time consuming.
- **Ethical problems** of consent, deception, invasion of privacy, etc.

NATURAL/QUASI
- **Hard to infer cause and effect** due to **little control** over extraneous variables and no direct manipulation of the independent variable.
- **Virtually impossible to replicate** exactly.
- Bias if subjects are aware of being studied.
- **Ethical problems** of consent, deception, invasion of privacy, etc.

Non-experimental methods 1

HOW DO PSYCHOLOGISTS INVESTIGATE THEIR HYPOTHESES?

OBSERVATIONS
Observations involve the precise measurement of naturally occurring behaviour in an objective way.

TYPES

NATURALISTIC
Naturalistic observations involve the recording of spontaneously occurring behaviour in the subject's own natural environment.

CONTROLLED
Controlled observation involves the recording of spontaneously occurring behaviour, but under conditions contrived by the researcher.

PARTICIPANT
Participant observations involve the researcher becoming involved in the everyday life of the subjects, either with or without their knowledge.

EXAMPLES

NATURALISTIC
- Fagot's (1973) naturalistic observation of parent-child interaction in gender socialisation in the home.
- Sylva et al's (1980) naturalistic observation of types of play in children's playgroups.
- Ethological observations of animal behaviour in the animal's natural habitat.

CONTROLLED
- Sleep studies - laboratory equipment is needed to record eye movements and changes in brain activity as subjects naturally fall to sleep.
- Parent-child interaction - observed through one way mirrors.
- Human sexual response, e.g. Masters and Johnson's work.

PARTICIPANT
- Rosenhan (1973) used eight 'normal' undisclosed participant observers to gain admittance to psychiatric hospitals through faking symptoms and then record their experiences of being a psychiatric inpatient.
- Whyte's (1955) participant observation of Italian gang behaviour in the USA.

STRENGTHS

NATURALISTIC
- **High ecological validity** (realism) of observed behaviour if observer is hidden.
- Can be used to **generate ideas** for or **validate findings** from experimental studies.
- Sometimes the only ethical or practical method.

CONTROLLED
- **More control** over environment which leads to **more accurate** observations.
- Greater control leads to **easier replication**.
- Usually avoids ethical problems of consent, unless research purpose and observer are hidden.

PARTICIPANT
- Very **high ecological validity** if participant undisclosed, less if disclosed depending upon level of integration with subjects.
- Extremely **detailed** and **in depth knowledge** available, not gained from any other method.

WEAKNESSES

NATURALISTIC
- **Cannot legitimately infer cause and effect** relationships between variables that are only observed but not manipulated.
- **Lack of control** over conditions makes **replication more difficult**.
- **Ethical problems** of invasion of privacy.

CONTROLLED
- **Participant reactivity** may distort the data if subject is aware of being observed, e.g. abnormal sleep patterns in unnatural laboratory conditions.
- **Lower ecological validity** than naturalistic observations, can cause demand characteristics.
- Cause and effect can not be inferred.

PARTICIPANT
- **Difficult to record data promptly** and **objectively**, and impossible to **replicate** exactly.
- Participant's behaviour may **influence subjects**.
- **Ethical problems** of deception with undisclosed participants.
- Cause and effect can not be inferred.

Data recording techniques

TECHNIQUE	ADVANTAGES	DISADVANTAGES
BEHAVIOUR SAMPLING METHODS		
• **Event sampling.** Key behavioural events are recorded every time they occur.	Limits the behaviours observed, thus reducing the chance that the behaviour of interest will be missed.	It is difficult to observe all incidents of key behaviour over large areas. Other important behaviour may be ignored.
• **Time sampling.** Behaviour is observed for discrete periods of time.	Reduces the amount of time spent in observation and thus may increase accuracy.	Behaviour may be missed if random time samples are not taken across the day.
• **Point sampling.** The behaviour of just one individual in a group at a time is recorded.	Increases the accuracy of observation and number of behaviours that can be recorded.	May miss behaviour in others that is important for an understanding of the individual.
DATA RECORDING TECHNIQUES		
• **Frequency grids.** Nominal data is scored as a tally chart for a variety of behaviours.	Quick and easy to use and can record a larger number of behaviours at a time.	Nominal data provides little information, e.g. it cannot say how long or intensely a behaviour was shown.
• **Rating scales.** Scores ordinal level data for a behaviour, indicating the degree to which it is shown.	Provides more information on the behaviour.	Rating using opinion rather than fixed scales, such as timing, introduces subjectivity.
• **Timing behaviour.**	High accuracy of data.	Loss of descriptive detail of behaviour.
DATA RECORDING EQUIPMENT		
• **Hand-written** notes or coding systems.	Less intimidating than more mechanical methods of recording.	Data may be missed or subjectively recorded.
• **Audio-tape** recording.	Accurately records all spoken data for later leisurely and accurate analysis.	Omits important gestures and non-verbal communication accompanying speech.
• **Video.**	Accurately records all data in view for later analysis - increases objectivity.	May produce participant reactivity and unnatural behaviour due to intimidation.
• **One way mirrors** in laboratories.	Reduces participant reactivity.	Unethical if subjects are not informed.
CONTENT ANALYSIS A **quantitative** method for analysing the **communication** of people and organisations, e.g. in their conversations, or media records. The researcher first decides what media they are going to sample and then devises the **coding units** they are interested in measuring, e.g. the frequency of, or amount of time and space devoted to, certain words or themes.	Content analysis is a useful tool for gathering data on a variety of topics, from rhetorical devices used in political speeches to the stereotyping or aggressive content of books and films. It can be used to assess what is omitted from speech, not just what is included. The data gained is usually of high ecological validity.	It is sometimes difficult to arrive at objectively operationalised coding units and the technique can be time consuming. Content analysis can be used to examine the function that a person's or organisation's communication serves, e.g. justifying or criticising, but the analyst's interpretations are also open to interpretation!
QUALITATIVE DATA ANALYSIS The analysis of qualitative data in its own right, without reducing it to quantitative numbers, can be very useful. Qualitative data can be gained from a variety of methods, such as observations, interviews, case studies and even experiments - for example in terms of **how** the subject **behaved** during testing and what they **said**.	Qualitative data is useful to describe information lost in the quantified and narrowed analysis of figures. Interviews with subjects after experiments can often reveal the causes of their behaviour and provide ideas for future research. However, qualitative analysis can be a useful research tool in its own right - arriving at an in-depth analysis and discussion of behaviour.	Qualitative analysis is often attacked for its lack of objectivity. However, • techniques exist to check its reliability and validity, e.g. triangulation (using more than one method of investigation) and repetition of the research cycle (to check previous data). • subjective opinion and participant consultation is regarded as a strength by many researchers, e.g. feminists.

Non-experimental methods 2

HOW DO PSYCHOLOGISTS INVESTIGATE THEIR HYPOTHESES?

QUESTIONING PEOPLE

There are many techniques for gathering **self report** data, which can be employed in varying detail – from the superficial survey of many people to the in-depth assessment of individuals.

TECHNIQUES	EXAMPLES	STRENGTHS	WEAKNESSES
INTERVIEWS All interviews involve direct verbal questioning of the subject by the researcher, but differ in how structured the questions are:		Generally, interviews generate a large amount of detailed data, especially about internal mental states/beliefs.	Generally interviews rely on self report data which may be untrue. Cause and effect can not be inferred.
• **Structured interviews** - contain fixed predetermined questions and ways of replying (e.g. yes/no).	Usually used in large scale interview-based surveys, e.g. market research.	Easy to quantify and analyse. Reliable, replicable and generalisable.	Less validity - distorts/ignores data due to restricted answers or insensitivity.
• **Semi-structured interviews** - contain guidelines for questions to be asked, but phrasing and timing are left up to the interviewer and answers may be open-ended.	Schedule for affective disorders and schizophrenia – a diagnostic interview. Most employment interviews.	Fairly flexible and sensitive. Fairly reliable and easy to analyse.	Flexibility of phrasing and timing could lead to lower reliability. Open-ended answers are more tricky to analyse.
• **Clinical interview** - semi-structured guidelines but further questioning to elaborate upon answers.	Piaget's interviewing of his children. Freud's interviewing of his patients.	Very flexible, sensitive and valid. Fairly reliable and easy to analyse.	Flexibility leads to more difficulty in replication and bias from interviewer.
• **Unstructured interview** - may contain a topic area for discussion but no fixed questions or ways of answering. Interviewer helps and clarifies interview.	Often used in humanistic based therapy interviews.	Highly detailed and valid data. Extremely flexible, natural and un-constrained.	Very unstandardised, therefore, not very replicable, reliable or generalisable. Difficult to quantify and analyse.
QUESTIONNAIRES Questionnaires are written methods of gaining data from subjects that do not necessarily require the presence of a researcher. They include:		Generally questionnaires collect large amounts of standardised data relatively quickly and conveniently.	Generally questionnaires lack flexibility, are based on self report data and are biased by motivation levels.
• **Opinion surveys**, e.g. attitude scales and opinion polls. Questions can be closed or open-ended and should be precise, understandable and easy to answer.	Likert attitude scales.	Highly replicable and easy to score (unless open-ended answers).	Biased by socially desirable answers, acquiescence (agreeing with items) and response set (replying in the same way).
• **Psychological tests**, e.g. personality and I.Q. tests. Items need to be standardised for a population and tested to show reliability, validity and discriminatory power.	Eysenck's personality inventory (to measure extroversion for example) or Bem's sex role inventory (to assess gender role identity).	Highly replicable and standardised between individuals. Easy to score.	Difficult to construct highly reliable and valid tests.

Non-experimental methods 3

HOW DO PSYCHOLOGISTS INVESTIGATE THEIR HYPOTHESES?

TECHNIQUES AND EXAMPLES

STRENGTHS

WEAKNESSES

CASE STUDY

An idiographic method involving the **long term** and **detailed** study of an **individual** or particular group. The case study method is often applied to unusual or valuable examples of behaviour which may provide important insights into psychological function or refutation of psychological theory. Examples of case studies include: Freud's studies of his patients and Piaget's studies of his children.

Highly detailed and in depth data is provided which superficial methods might miss or ignore.

High ecological validity of data obtained.

Often the only method suitable for studying some forms of behaviour, e.g. investigating the acquisition of human language in primates.

Often the only method possible due to rarity of behaviour, e.g. natural cases of human environmental deprivation, such as the case of Genie.

No cause and effect can legitimately be inferred.

Lack of generalisability to the population due to single cases being too small and unrepresentative a sample.

Low reliability due to
- many case studies involving recall of past events, which may be open to memory distortion.
- subject reactivity
- lack of observer objectivity

Difficult or impossible to replicate.

Time consuming and expensive.

CORRELATIONS

A method of data analysis which measures the relationship between two or more variables to see if a trend or systematic pattern exists between them. Inferential statistics can be used to arrive at a correlation coefficient which indicates the strength and type of correlation, ranging from:

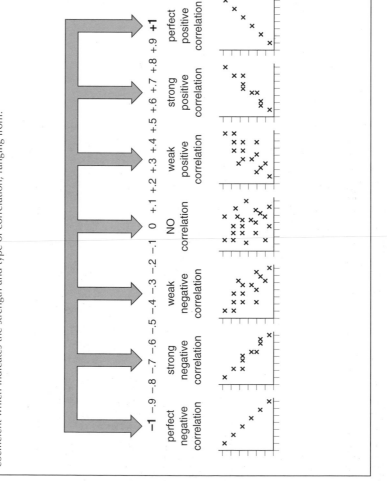

Precise information on the degree of relationship between variables is available in the form of the correlation coefficient. It can readily quantify observational data.

No manipulation of behaviour is required.

Strong significant correlations can suggest ideas for experimental studies to determine cause and effect relationships.

No cause and effect can be inferred.

Correlations should be plotted out on scattergrams to properly illustrate the relationship between variables - a zero correlation coefficient may not form a random pattern.

For example, both of these patterns would not yield a significant correlational result.

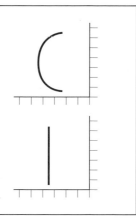

Sampling

HOW DO PSYCHOLOGISTS SELECT THEIR SUBJECTS?

SAMPLING

- Sampling is the process of selecting subjects to study from the **target population** (a specified section of humankind).
- Since the results of the study on the sample will be generalised back to the target population (through inference), samples should be as **representative** (typical) of the target population as possible.
- Samples should be of a sufficient size (e.g. 30) to represent the variety of individuals in a target population, but not so large as to make the study uneconomical in terms of time and resources.

TARGET POPULATION

REPRESENTATIVE SAMPLING

SAMPLE

TYPES OF SAMPLING

RANDOM

Truly random sampling only occurs when **every member** of a target population has an **equal chance** of being selected.
For example:
Putting the names of every member of the target population into a hat and pulling a sample out (without looking!).

STRATIFIED

Involves **dividing** the target population into important **subcategories** (or strata) and then selecting members of these subcategories in the **proportion** that they occur in the target population.
For example:
If a target population consisted of 75% women and 25% men, a sample of 20 should include 15 women and 5 men.

OPPORTUNITY

Opportunity sampling simply involves selecting those subjects that are around and **available at the time.** An effort may be made to not be biased in selecting particular types of subject.
For example:
University psychologists may sample from their students.

SELF-SELECTING

Self-selecting samples consist of those individuals who have consciously or unconsciously **determined their own involvement** in a study.
For example:
Volunteers for studies or passers by who become involved in field studies, i.e. in bystander intervention studies.

STRENGTHS

Random sampling (in large numbers) provides the **best chance of an unbiased representative sample** of a target population.

A **deliberate effort** is made to identify the characteristics of a sample most important for it **to be representative** of the target population.

It is **quick, convenient** and often the most economical method of sampling.
It has, therefore, been the most common type of sampling.

Self-selecting samples are relatively convenient and, if volunteering is made on the basis of informed consent, ethical.

WEAKNESSES

The larger the target population, the more difficult it is to sample randomly, since compiling a selection list of everyone becomes more impractical. True random sampling is, therefore, very rare.

Stratified sampling can be very **time consuming,** since the subcategories have to be identified and their proportions in the target population calculated.

Opportunity sampling gives very unrepresentative samples and is often **biased** on the part of the **researcher** who may choose subjects who will be 'helpful'.

Self-selecting samples are often unrepresentative - being **biased** on the part of the **subject.** Volunteers are unlike non-volunteers in many ways.

Experimental design

REPEATED MEASURES

DESIGN

A repeated measures design involves using the **same subjects** in each condition of an experiment, e.g. giving a group of subjects a driving test with no alcohol, followed at a later time by the same test after a pint of lager

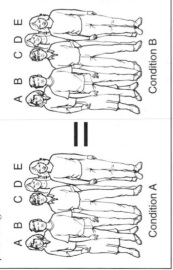

Condition A = Condition B

STRENGTHS

- **Subject variables** (individual differences shown by every subject, e.g. intelligence, motivation, past experience, etc.) which could become extraneous variables are **kept constant** between conditions.
- **Better statistical tests** can be used because of less variation between conditions.
- **Fewer subjects** are required (because each is used more than once) therefore more economical.

WEAKNESSES

- **Order effects** such as learning, fatigue or boredom may become constant errors when one condition is done after another, e.g. a subject given the same test may do better due to practice.
- **Demand characteristics** may become a problem - as the subject does both conditions of the experiment, they may guess the aim of the study and act differently.
- **Different tests** may be needed.

INDEPENDENT MEASURES

An independent measures design involves using **different subjects** in each condition of the experiment, e.g. giving one group of subjects a driving test with no alcohol, and a different group of subjects the same test after a pint of lager.

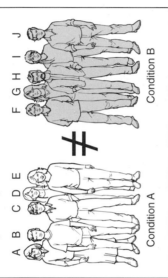

Condition A ≠ Condition B

- **Order effects** such as learning, fatigue or boredom do not influence a second condition, since the subject only participates in one condition.
- **Demand characteristics** are less of a problem as the subject only participates in one condition so is naive to the test, and is less likely to guess the aim of the study and act differently.
- The **same test** can be used.

- **Subject variables differ,** which could become confounding variables unless controlled for.
- **Worse statistical tests** can be used because of more variation between conditions.
- **More subjects** are required (because each is used only once) and is, therefore, less economical.

MATCHED PAIRS

A matched pairs design involves using **different but similar subjects** in each condition of an experiment. An effort is made to match the subjects in each condition in any important characteristics that might affect performance,
e.g. in driving ability, alcohol tolerance, etc.

A B C D E   1 2 3 4 5

Condition A ≠ Condition B

- **Subject variables** are kept **more constant** between conditions.
- **Better statistical tests** can be used because of less variation between conditions.
- **Order effects** do not occur since the subject only participates in one condition.
- **Demand characteristics** are less of a problem as the subject only participates in one condition.
- The **same test** can be used.

- **Subject variables** can never be perfectly matched in every respect.
- Matching subjects is very **time consuming** and **difficult.**
- **More subjects** are required (because each is used only once) and is, therefore, less economical.

Controlling extraneous variables and bias

HOW DO PSYCHOLOGISTS CONTROL EXTRANEOUS VARIABLES AND BIAS IN THEIR STUDIES?

TYPE OF PROBLEM	PROBLEM	METHOD OF CONTROL
SUBJECTS	**INDIVIDUAL DIFFERENCES** Subject variables can become a problem especially in an independent measures design, creating random or even constant confounding effects.	**Sample large** and **randomly** to gain a representative sample. **Allocate** subjects **randomly** to each condition of an independent measures experiment to balance out subject variables.
METHOD	**ARTIFICIALITY** Laboratory environments and operationalised variables may lack ecological validity.	Use a **non**-laboratory environment instead, e.g. field study. Broaden or increase the number of definitions for the operationalised variable.
DESIGN	**ORDER EFFECTS** Where learning, boredom or fatigue can influence the second condition of an experiment using a repeated measures design.	Use independent measures design instead. **Counterbalance** the conditions, by getting half the subjects to perform condition A before condition B, and the other half to perform condition B before condition A, thereby balancing the order effects equally between conditions.
	DEMAND CHARACTERISTICS Working out the aim of the study and behaving differently (e.g. trying to please the researcher or spoil the study).	Use independent measures design to stop exposure to both conditions of the experiment, therefore reducing chances of guessing the aim of the study. Use **deception** to hide research aim. However, there are ethical problems with this. Use **single blind method** - the subject does not know which condition of the experiment they are in, e.g. whether they have been given placebo or real pills.
	EXPERIMENTER EXPECTANCY Where the expectations of the researcher influence the results either by consciously or unconsciously revealing the desired outcome or through unconscious procedural or recording bias.	Use **double blind method** - neither the subject nor the researcher carrying out the procedure and recording the results knows the hypothesis or which condition the subjects are in. Use **inter-observer reliability** measures to overcome biased observation. An observer with no vested interest in the result, simultaneously, but separately, rates the same piece of behaviour with the researcher. When results are compared, a high positive correlation should be expected.
PROCEDURE	**DISTRACTION AND CONFUSION** Both sources of extraneous variables which could confound studies unless controlled for.	Standardised instructions should be given in a clear and simple form and the subject should be asked if they have questions, so each participant receives equal information. Standardised procedures should be employed so each subject is tested under equal conditions with no distractions.

Assessing the quality of studies

HOW DO PSYCHOLOGISTS TEST THE QUALITY OF STUDIES?

RELIABILITY
The reliability of a method of measurement (whether it be an experimental test, questionnaire or observational procedure) refers to how **consistently** it measures.

INTERNAL RELIABILITY
Internal reliability refers to **how consistent a method measures within itself**. If methods of measurement were not **standardised** they would give distorted final scores.
For example, internal reliability would be lacking if
- a ruler consisted of variable centimetres,
- an I.Q. test was made up of half ridiculously easy questions and half ridiculously difficult questions (virtually everyone would score half marks and be equally intelligent!) or
- different observers using the same observational definitions simultaneously scored the same individual differently.

Internal reliability could be checked for test items by the **split half method** - correlating the results of half the items with the other half (e.g. the odd numbers with the even numbers of the test) and gaining a high positive correlation coefficient.

EXTERNAL RELIABILITY
External reliability refers to **how consistent a method measures over time when repeated**. Methods of measurement should give similar scores when repeated on the same people under similar conditions.
For example external reliability would be lacking if
- a ruler measured an unchanging object different lengths each time it was used,
- an I.Q. test scored the same person a genius one day but just average a week later.

External reliability could be checked for test items by the **test-, re-test method** - correlating the results of the test conducted on one occasion with the results of the test conducted on a later occasion (with the same subjects) and gaining a high positive correlation coefficient.

VALIDITY
The validity of a method of measurement (whether it be an experimental test, questionnaire or observational procedure) refers to whether it **measures what it is supposed to measure** - how realistically or truly variables have been operationalised.

FACE/CONTENT VALIDITY
Face or content validity involves **examining** the content of the test to see if it **looks** like it measures what it is supposed to measure.
For example, examining the test items of an intelligence test to see if they seem to measure general intelligence, not just general knowledge or linguistic comprehension.

CONCURRENT VALIDITY
Concurrent validity involves **comparing** a **new** method or test **with** an already well **established** one that claims to measure the same variable(s). A high positive correlation should be gained between the results of the two tests.
For example, correlating the results from the same people tested by a new intelligence test and an older established one.

CONSTRUCT VALIDITY
Construct validity refers to whether the test or method can be used to **support** the **underlying theoretical constructs** concerning the variable that it is supposed to be measuring.
For example, if theory suggests the offspring of two highly intelligent parents raised in a stimulating environment should be intelligent, an IQ test should confirm this.

PREDICTIVE VALIDITY
Predictive validity refers to whether the test will **predict future performance** indicated by its results.
For example, high scorers on an I.Q. test at a young age should be predicted to later perform better in studies or jobs requiring intelligence.

ECOLOGICAL VALIDITY
Ecological validity refers to whether a test or method measures behaviour that is representative of naturally occurring behaviour. Too specifically operationalised tests may ignore many aspects of spontaneously occurring behaviour.
For example, do the items on an intelligence test represent all the types of behaviour we would describe as intelligent in everyday behaviour.

Data analysis - numerical summaries

HOW DO PSYCHOLOGISTS SUMMARIZE THEIR DATA NUMERICALLY?

LEVELS OF DATA

NOMINAL
Nominal data is a simple **frequency headcount** (the number of times something occurred) found in **discrete categories** (something can only belong to one category).

For example, the number of people who helped or did not help in an emergency.

Nominal data is the simplest data.

ORDINAL
Ordinal data is measurements that can be put in an **order**, **rank** or **position.**

For example, scores on unstandardised psychological scales (such as attractiveness out of 10) or who came 1st, 2nd, 3rd, etc. in a race.

The **intervals** between each rank, however, are **unknown,** i.e. how far ahead 1st was from 2nd.

INTERVAL AND RATIO
Both are measurements on a **scale**, the **intervals** of which are **known and equal**. **Ratio** data has a **true zero** point, whereas **interval** data can go into **negative** values.

For example, **temperature** for interval data (degrees centigrade can be minus) **length** or **time** for ratio data (no seconds is no time at all).

The most **precise** types of data.

MEASURES OF CENTRAL TENDENCY

MODE
The value or event that occurs the most frequently.
The most suitable measure of central tendency for nominal data.
Not influenced by extreme scores; useful to show most popular value.
Crude measure of central tendency; not useful if many equal modes.

MEDIAN
The middle value when all scores are placed in rank order.
The most suitable measure of central tendency for ordinal data.
Not distorted by extreme freak values, e.g. 2, 3, 3, 4, 4, 4, 4, 4, 5, 5, 6, 42.
However, it can be distorted by small samples and is less sensitive.

MEAN
The average value of all scores.
The most suitable measure of central tendency for interval or ratio data.
The most sensitive measure of central tendency for all data.
However, can be distorted by extreme freak values.

MEASURES OF DISPERSION

RANGE	ADVANTAGE	DISADVANTAGE
the difference between the smallest and largest value, plus 1. For example, 3, 4, 7, 7, 8, 9, 12, 4, 17, 17, 18 **(18 - 3) +1 = Range of 16**	• Quick and easy to calculate.	• Distorted by extreme 'freak' values, an extra value of 43 would give a range of 41.
SEMI-INTERQUARTILE RANGE When data is put in order, find the first quartile (Q1) and third quartile (Q3) of the sample, subtract the Q1 value from the Q3 value and divide the result by two. For example, 3, 4, 7, 7 8, 9, 12, 14, 17, 17, 18 (Q1 ↑ 7, Q2 ↑, Q3 ↑ 17) 17 - 7 = 10 10 ÷ 2 = **Semi-interquartile range of 5**	• Less distorted by any extreme 'freak' values.	• Ignores extreme values.
STANDARD DEVIATION The average amount all scores deviate from the mean. The difference (deviation) between each score and the mean of those scores is calculated and then squared (to remove minus values). These squared deviations are then added up and their mean calculated to give a value known as the variance. The square root of the variance gives the standard deviation of the scores.	• The most sensitive measure of dispersion, using all the data available. • Can be used to relate the sample to the population's parameters.	• A little more time consuming to calculate but no important disadvantages.

Standard deviation calculation table:

score		mean		d	d squared
6	–	10	=	–4	16
8	–	10	=	–2	4
10	–	10	=	0	0
12	–	10	=	+2	4
14	–	10	=	+4	16
					40

mean of 40 = 8 = variance
square root of variance
= standard deviation = 2.8

Data analysis - pictorial summaries

HOW DO PSYCHOLOGISTS SUMMARIZE THEIR DATA PICTORIALLY?

FREQUENCY POLYGON

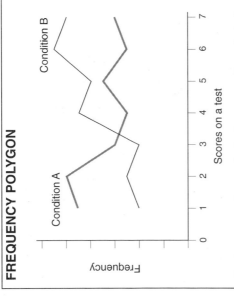

Also known as a line graph, the frequency polygon is similar to the histogram, except that it allows two or more sets of data to be shown on the same graph.

NORMAL DISTRIBUTION

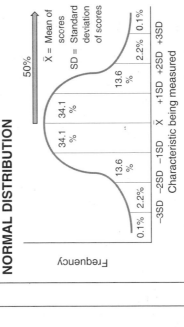

Normal distribution curves occur in the populations of many continuous psychological variables and are involved in parametric statistics. They are bell shaped and symmetrical at the midpoint where the mode, median and mean all fall. The percentage of scores covered by the areas between the standard deviations of the curve are known.

HISTOGRAMS

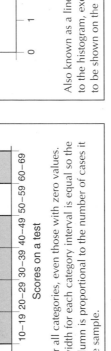

Shows data for all categories, even those with zero values. The column width for each category interval is equal so the area of the column is proportional to the number of cases it contains of the sample.

SCATTERGRAMS

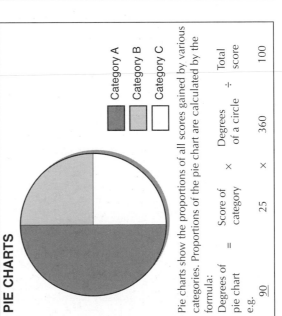

Scattergrams plot pairs of scores against each other to show their correlational relationship.
Emergent patterns or trends in the data can be calculated to show a line of best fit.

BAR CHARTS

Shows data only for those categories that the researcher is interested in comparing, e.g. two or more conditions in an experiment.

PIE CHARTS

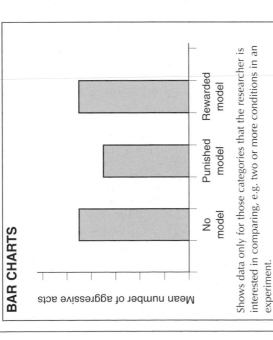

Pie charts show the proportions of all scores gained by various categories. Proportions of the pie chart are calculated by the formula:

Degrees of pie chart	=	Score of category	×	Degrees of a circle	÷	Total score
e.g.						
90		25	×	360		100

Data analysis - inferential statistics

HOW DO PSYCHOLOGISTS KNOW HOW SIGNIFICANT THEIR RESULTS ARE?

WHAT IS MEANT BY SIGNIFICANCE?

DEFINITION: A significant result is one where there is a **low probability that chance factors** were responsible for any observed difference, correlation or association in the variables tested.

FOR EXAMPLE

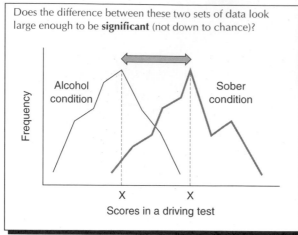

Does the difference between these two sets of data look large enough to be **significant** (not down to chance)?

Alcohol condition   Sober condition

Frequency

X   X

Scores in a driving test

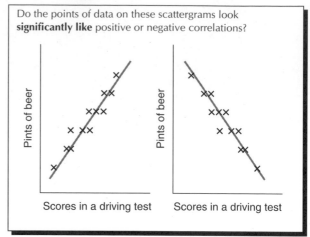

Do the points of data on these scattergrams look **significantly like** positive or negative correlations?

Pints of beer

Scores in a driving test

Pints of beer

Scores in a driving test

HOW SIGNIFICANT DO RESULTS HAVE TO BE?

LEVELS OF SIGNIFICANCE

How large an effect (difference or relationship) is required for psychologists to conclude that a result is significant (not probably due to chance factors)?

Significance levels are expressed as a decimal in the form **P < 0.00** where '**P**' stands for probability that chance factors are responsible for results

Psychologists have concluded that for most purposes in psychology, the 5% level of significance (**P < 0.05**) is appropriate; a result that is significant at this level can be said to be less than 5% likely to be due to chance factors (a 1 in 20 chance it was a 'fluke' result).

There are many other possible levels of probability but the P < 0.05 seems reasonable since:

- Significance levels of: **P < 0.5** (a 50% or 50:50 probability that chance factors were responsible) or **P < 0.3** (a 30% or roughly 1 in 3 probability that chance factors were responsible)

  are regarded as **too lenient** - the effect (difference or correlation) is too likely to have happened by chance and a **type one error** is more likely to be made (the **null hypothesis may be falsely rejected** - the researcher may falsely claim an effect exists).

- Significance levels of: **P < 0.01** (a 1% or 1 in a 100 probability that chance factors were responsible) or **P < 0.001** (a 0.1% or 1 in 1000 probability that chance factors were responsible)

  are regarded as **too strict or stringent** - a strong effect (difference or correlation) is too likely to be ignored because the level is overly demanding and a **type two error** is more likely to be made (the **null hypothesis may be falsely accepted** - the researcher may falsely claim an effect does not exist).

N.B. - Stringent levels are required when greater certainty of significance is needed, e.g. during safety tests.

WHAT DO INFERENTIAL STATISTICAL TESTS TELL PSYCHOLOGISTS?

INFERENTIAL STATISTICAL TESTS

Inferential statistical tests provide a calculated value based on the results of the investigation.

This value can then be compared to a critical value (a value that statisticians have estimated to represent a significant effect) to determine whether the results are significant.

The critical value depends upon the level of significance required (P < 0.05, P < 0.01, etc.) and other factors such as the number of subjects used in the test and whether the hypothesis is one or two tailed.

In the Chi squared, Sign test, Spearman's Rho, Pearson's product and Related or Unrelated T-tests, the **calculated** value has to **exceed** the **critical** value for a significant result.

Inferential statistics allow us to **infer** that the **effect gained from** the results on a **sample** of subjects is **probably typical of** the **target population** the sample was derived from.

Data analysis - choosing inferential statistical tests

HOW DO PSYCHOLOGISTS CHOOSE AN APPROPRIATE STATISTICAL TEST?

1 TEST OF DIFFERENCE OR RELATIONSHIP REQUIRED?
2 WHAT EXPERIMENTAL DESIGN HAS BEEN USED?
3 WHAT LEVEL OF DATA IS BEING USED?
4 ARE ALL THREE PARAMETRIC CONDITIONS MET?
  a Interval or ratio data
  b Both sets of data normally
    distributed or from normally
    distributed populations
  c Both sets of data have
    similar variance.

	TESTS OF DIFFERENCE		TESTS OF RELATIONSHIP
	INDEPENDENT MEASURES DESIGN	REPEATED MEASURES OR MATCHED PAIRS DESIGN	CORRELATION OR ASSOCIATION
NOMINAL DATA	CHI SQUARED TEST	SIGN TEST	CHI SQUARED TEST
ORDINAL DATA	MANN WHITNEY U TEST*	WILCOXON SIGNED RANKS TESTS*	SPEARMAN'S RHO CORRELATION
INTERVAL OR RATIO DATA	UNRELATED T-TEST	RELATED T-TEST	PEARSON'S PRODUCT MOMENT CORRELATION COEFFICIENT

PARAMETRIC TESTS
The most powerful and sensitive tests.

* NB The two ordinal level tests of difference are the only ones where the calculated value of the test has to be LESS THAN the critical value.

Research methods 45

Timing and location of investigations

WHEN SHOULD PSYCHOLOGISTS INVESTIGATE?

CROSS-SECTIONAL STUDIES
In cross-sectional studies subjects of **different** ages are investigated **at one particular point in time.** It is a form of independent measures design.

LONGITUDINAL STUDIES
In longitudinal studies the **same** subjects are investigated **over a long period of time.** It is a form of repeated measures design.

WHERE SHOULD PSYCHOLOGISTS INVESTIGATE?

CROSS-CULTURAL STUDIES
In cross-cultural studies subjects from **different cultures** are given the same test and their results are compared.

EXAMPLES

ASCH (1951)
Kohlberg (1981) compared the moral development of three groups of boys aged 10, 13 and 16. Asch's findings on conformity were not replicated, indicating that his findings may have been influenced by factors present in his society *at that particular time.*

KOHLBERG (1971)
Kohlberg conducted a twenty year longitudinal study of moral reasoning.
Developmental psychologists concentrate on how abilities and behaviour may vary over time, from infancy to adulthood, and so may find that studying the same subjects over a long period of time is the most accurate way of discovering the principles and processes of development.

MEAD (1935)
Mead studied three different tribes in New Guinea and compared their gender role behaviours.

STRENGTHS

- Immediate results can be gained, therefore, they are convenient.
- Cheaper and less time consuming than longitudinal studies.
- Less likelihood of losing subjects between conditions.

- Less bias from subject variables.
- In some areas of psychology, such as mental illness, a longitudinal study may be the only way of determining how a disorder progresses.

- Combats an ethnocentric culturally biased view of human psychology.
- Widens the generalisability of results.
- Provides data on cultural differences or similarities which may increase understanding of psychological development.

WEAKNESSES

- Cross-sectional studies may be overly influenced by the social environment of the time, and therefore need to be regularly replicated.
- All disadvantages of independent measures design, e.g. subject confounding variables, greater number of subjects needed, etc.
- Cohort effect may bias data.

- Time consuming, expensive and high likelihood of losing subjects between conditions.
- Extremely difficult or impossible to replicate.
- Longitudinal studies can be carried out retrospectively by examining the history of subjects, but this has many disadvantages, such as memory distortion and lack of objectivity.

- More time consuming, difficult (due to language barriers etc.) and expensive.
- Open to ethnocentric misinterpretation by cross-cultural research.
- Subject reactivity may increase with cross-cultural observer.

Cognitive psychology

Perception

Attention

Memory

Visual perceptual organisation 1

Perception is the process of interpreting and organising the environmental information received by the senses.

For visual perception, this involves taking the constantly fluctuating patterns of light which arrive from all over the environment, upside-down, onto our two-dimensional retinas and

- **detecting the shape** of objects in the environment,
  e.g. distinguishing features from each other and their background.

- **establishing location** in three-dimensional space,
  e.g. interpreting a two-dimensional retinal image as a three-dimensional object at a specific distance in three-dimensional space.

- **recognising an object** in terms of its shape, size, brightness and colour,
  e.g. identifying an object on the retina despite its
  a **viewpoint** - an object seen from different angles will cast images of different shapes upon the retina, yet will be recognised as being the same object (a phenomenon known as **shape constancy**).
  b **distance** - the same object at longer distances will cast smaller images on the retina but will be identified as the same size (a phenomenon known as **size constancy**).
  c **Luminescence** - an object will be perceived as the same brightness despite changes in the overall level of luminosity (a phenomenon known as **brightness constancy**).

The difference between sensation and perception can be illustrated by visual illusions, such as the Necker cube.
The **perception** of this ambiguous figure alternates between 2 three-dimensional cubes seen from different angles, despite an **unchanging retinal image** of a two-dimensional line drawing.

Any theory of visual perception, therefore, has to explain the key phenomena of perceptual organisation:
- Feature or object detection
- Depth perception
- Object recognition
- Perceptual constancy

Theories have also been proposed to investigate the development of perception - to find out which perceptual organisational abilities are innate and which are learned.

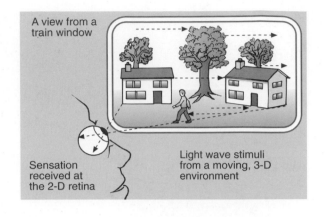

A view from a train window

Sensation received at the 2-D retina

Light wave stimuli from a moving, 3-D environment

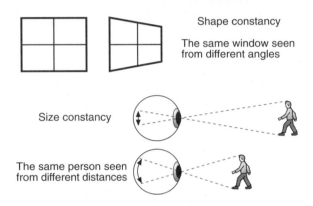

Shape constancy

The same window seen from different angles

Size constancy

The same person seen from different distances

The Necker cube

or

THEORIES OF PERCEPTION

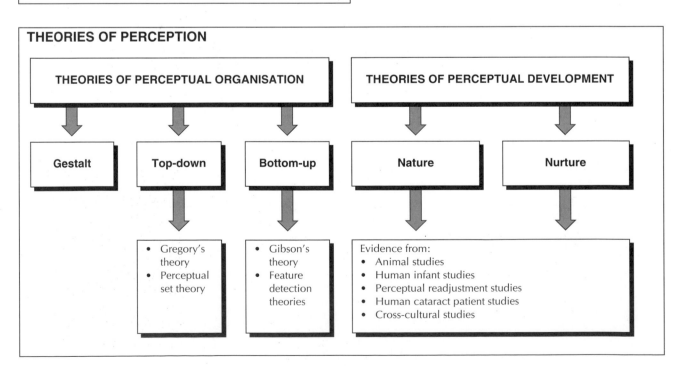

THEORIES OF PERCEPTUAL ORGANISATION	THEORIES OF PERCEPTUAL DEVELOPMENT

Gestalt	Top-down	Bottom-up	Nature	Nurture

Top-down:
- Gregory's theory
- Perceptual set theory

Bottom-up:
- Gibson's theory
- Feature detection theories

Evidence from:
- Animal studies
- Human infant studies
- Perceptual readjustment studies
- Human cataract patient studies
- Cross-cultural studies

Visual perceptual organisation 2

GESTALT THEORY OF PERCEPTUAL ORGANISATION

Gestalt psychologists, such as Wertheimer and Koffka, believed that the brain possesses innate organisational properties with which it structures, orders and makes coherent sense of sensations from the environment.

1   The organisation of environmental stimuli into groups produces **'emergent properties'** in them - that is to say, groups of stimuli have **'gestalt'** or 'whole' properties that produce perceptions that are more than the sum of the sensory stimuli that make them up (the whole is greater than the sum of its parts).

EVIDENCE:

*   Wertheimer's phi phenomenon - a series of separate lights turned off and on, one by one, in sequence will give the perception of continuous movement.
*   Navon (1977) found, using figures like those opposite, that subjects were able to identify the large (whole) letter without being influenced by the smaller letters (parts) that made it up, but took longer to identify the smaller letters if the larger one did not correspond. This is evidence for the gestalt notion that the whole image is perceived before the parts that make it up.

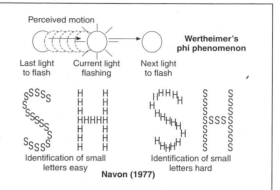

2   Gestalten (organised wholes) are derived from combinations of sensations via the **'Law of Pragnanz'** - the organisation of sensory stimuli will always follow the most simple or stable shape. The organisation will always be as 'good' as possible, so for example:
*   The patterns or figures perceived will always be the ones requiring the least descriptive information.
*   The unseen or missing parts of figures will be predicted from the seen parts in the most economical way.

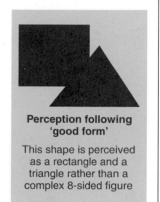

Perception following 'good form'

This shape is perceived as a rectangle and a triangle rather than a complex 8-sided figure

EVIDENCE:

Pomerantz (1981) found that subjects would join dots in the same way to produce 'good', simple figures. For example, when shown the dots arranged in configuration 'a', subjects tended to join them as pattern 'b' rather than 'c' or 'd'.

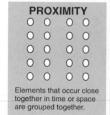 joined as 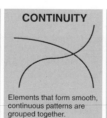 rather than 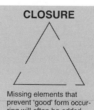 or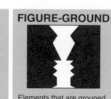

a   b   c   d

Pragnanz, and thus perceptual grouping and feature detection, is achieved through organising principles such as proximity, similarity, continuity, closure, figure-ground, and common fate.

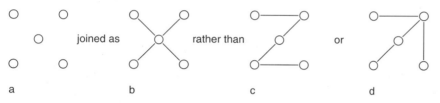

PROXIMITY	SIMILARITY	CONTINUITY	CLOSURE	FIGURE-GROUND	COMMON FATE
Elements that occur close together in time or space are grouped together.	Similar elements are grouped together.	Elements that form smooth, continuous patterns are grouped together.	Missing elements that prevent 'good' form occurring will often be added.	Elements that are grouped together are then separated from their background.	Elements that move or change together are grouped together.

EVALUATION:

*   Gestalt principles tended only to be applied to two-dimensional drawings rather than three dimensional objects.
*   However, Johansson (1975) found that subjects watching films of actors made completely invisible (by wearing black on a black background) except for dots of lights attached to their joints, could identify the actors' movements, posture and even gender. Cutting and Kozlowski (1977) even found subjects could identify their friends filmed under these conditions (requiring quite a degree of joining the dots!).
*   The objects gestalt psychologists investigated were usually viewed in isolation, not as part of real scenes.
*   Some gestalt concepts are rather vague - what is a 'good' figure and why?
*   Gestalt psychology describes how features are grouped rather than explains.

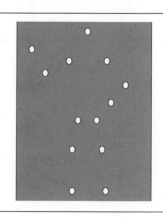

Johansson (1975)

Top-down theories of perception

TOP-DOWN THEORIES

- Sometimes referred to as constructivist theories, these theories stress the factors in the construction of reality that go beyond the information received from the senses.
- Gregory's theory and perceptual set theory regard perception as a very active process, whereby the individual's past knowledge, expectations and stereotypes seek out sensory data to 'complete the picture'.

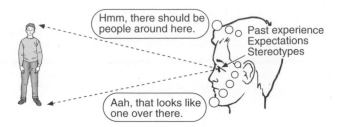

Hmm, there should be people around here.

Past experience
Expectations
Stereotypes

Aah, that looks like one over there.

GREGORY'S PERCEPTUAL INFERENCE THEORY

Gregory suggests that we go beyond the available sensory information in perception, 'a perceived object is a hypothesis, suggested and tested by sensory data'. Gregory points out that sensory information alone cannot account for perception - often all the information required is not present or we need to select information to prevent sensory overload - and he uses illusions and perceptual constancy to support his suggestion.

1 ILLUSIONS

Distortions
e.g. The Ponzo illusion. The retinal images of the horizontal lines are equal, yet the top one is usually perceived as longer due to the diagonal lines acting as depth cues from our memory.

Ambiguous Figures
e.g. The Necker cube. Perception of the cube's angle differs according to our focus of attention.

Fictions
e.g. The Kanizsa triangle. The subjective contours of the triangle go beyond the available information.

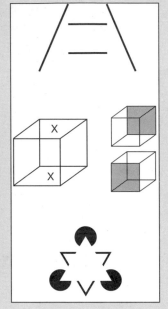

2 PERCEPTUAL CONSTANCY

e.g. Size constancy. The same sized object seen from different distances will cast different sized images upon the retina, yet will be perceived as the same size due to the brain scaling the image.

e.g. Shape constancy. An object seen from different angles will cast different images upon the retina, yet will still be recognised by the brain.

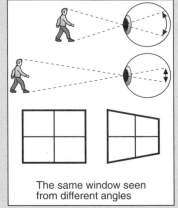

The same window seen from different angles

e.g. Location constancy. Despite head movements changing stimulation across the retina, we see the world as stationary, since information from the eye muscles and brain's motion detectors allows the brain to compensate.

For: Illusions and constancy show how the brain uses memory, expectation and unconscious processing to interpret environmental stimuli.
Against: Illusions are artificial stimuli and do not contain the rich amount of detail and information naturally received by the retina.

PERCEPTUAL SET THEORY

Perceptual set theory stresses the idea of perception as an active process involving selection, inference and interpretation. Perceptual set is a bias or readiness to perceive certain aspects of available sensory data and to ignore others. Set can be influenced by many factors such as:

1 Expectation and context

Minturn and Bruner (1951) showed the middle figure would be more likely to be perceived as a letter if presented amongst other letters and a number if presented amongst other numbers.

$$
\begin{array}{c}
12 \\
A \; 13 \; C \\
14
\end{array}
$$

Similarly, expectation and context lead to the mis-reading of phrase triangles.

Paris in the the spring

2 Expectation and past experience

Bruner and Postman (1949) showed playing cards with black hearts and red spades at very fast speeds on a tachistoscope and found that these unusual cards would be seen as normal cards at first but at slower speeds 'compromise' perceptions emerged, e.g. brown or purple hearts were seen.

3 Motivation

Gilchrist and Nesberg (1952) found that pictures of food and drink were perceived as brighter than other pictures by subjects who had been deprived of food and liquid.

4 Emotion

McGinnies (1949) found perceptual defence of taboo words using a tachistoscope - they would be recognised less quickly than non-emotionally arousing words. Worthington (1969) showed this was not just due to the reluctance to report them or their frequency.

For: Set theory links with many other areas in psychology, such as schemata and stereotypes, and has been supported by many studies.
Against: The experimental findings concerning perceptual defence and the validity of tachistoscope presentation have been much debated.

Bottom-up theories of perception

BOTTOM-UP THEORIES

- These theories emphasise the richness of the information entering the eye and the way that perception can occur from using all the information available.
- Gibson believes perception occurs directly from sensation, feature detection theories examine the processes involved in assembling perception from sensations.

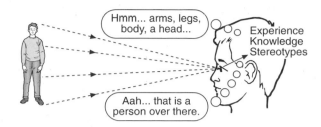

Hmm... arms, legs, body, a head...

Experience Knowledge Stereotypes

Aah... that is a person over there.

GIBSON'S THEORY OF DIRECT PERCEPTION

Gibson proposed that the optical array contains all the information needed to directly perceive a three dimensional world with little or no information processing needed. Light reaching the eye contains invariant information about the depth, location and even function of objects. 'Sensation is perception'.

1 DEPTH
Monocular depth cues
(capable of perception by one eye)

- **Texture gradients** - closer objects can be seen in greater detail than distant ones.
- **Overlap and motion parallax** - closer objects obscure more distant ones.
- **Linear perspective** - lines known to be parallel converge in the distance.

Binocular depth cues

- **Retinal disparity** - each eye sees a slightly different view, which gives us a three dimensional impression.
- **Ocular convergence** - our eyes converge the closer an object is to us.

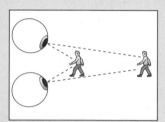

2 LOCATION
Optic flow patterns
The point to which we are moving remains stationary while the rest of the view rushes away from it, giving information on speed and direction of movement.

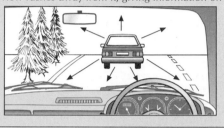

3 FUNCTION
Affordances
Gibson even argued that the perceptual system has evolved to inform us directly of the function of a perceived object, i.e. chairs are for sitting on.

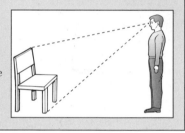

For: Gibson put perception back into the real world, stressed the importance of movement for perception and richness of information available at the retina.

Against: Affordances are debatable and the theory neglects much of the processing that must take place in perception. Direct perception may apply more to innate reflexes where environmental stimuli directly affect behaviour, but much of human behaviour is governed by higher-order intervening processes between stimulus and response.

FEATURE DETECTION THEORIES, E.G. SELFRIDGES PANDEMONIUM MODEL

Selfridge's pandemonium model is a feature detection approach that can be used to explain how the perception of objects can be built up from the detection of their elementary features. Lindsay and Norman (1972) applied the model to letter recognition, showing how letters can be analysed in terms of line, angle, pattern and decision 'demons' to be correctly identified. The processing occurs in parallel as each specialist line demon 'shrieks' with a loudness that reflects how similar its feature speciality is to those features found in the target letter.

This shriek 'weighting' determines which angle demons will be activated and shriek themselves to activate the pattern demons, and so on.

For: the model received experimental support from Neisser's target letter recognition tests and has gained credibility from:

a its use of parallel processing,

b its conceptual links to Hubel and Wiesel's neurological findings of feature detection cells in the visual cortex.

Against: it has been less successful detecting three dimensional objects under real life conditions. The model does not deal with how expectation (perceptual set) can influence feature analysis - perhaps if a more dynamic, 'two-way' flow was provided in the model (as in connectionist networks) expected pattern demons could 'shout back' down the system to bias the weighting of analysed features.

Image demon

Line demons

Angle demons

Pattern demons

Decision demon

Interactionist theories of perception

INTERACTIONIST THEORIES
- These theories provide a synthesis of bottom-up and top-down aspects to explain perception.
- As Eysenck and Keane (1995) point out, bottom-up processes probably account better for viewing under optimal conditions where clear and detailed information is available from the environment, whereas top-down theories become more important under sub-optimal viewing conditions where extra interpretation is required.

NEISSER'S PERCEPTUAL CYCLE

Neisser (1976) proposed an 'activation-by-synthesis' approach, whereby top-down and bottom-up processes are **constantly cycled** through during perception.

The individual starts the perceptual process with a **set of schemata** that
- provide **expectations** about what **features** will be seen in certain environmental **contexts,** and
- act to **direct** perceptual **exploration** of the **environment** towards those expected relevant features.

This is the **top-down** aspect of the model.

The schemata themselves are **derived from past experience** in certain environments and the **available sensory information** arriving from a perceptual exploration of an environment has either
- an **elaborative effect** on the anticipatory schema which initiated the search if that schema was correct, causing more appropriate information to be added to it.
- a **corrective effect** on the anticipatory schema which initiated the search if that schema was wrong, causing a more appropriate schema to be activated.

This is the **bottom-up** aspect of the model.

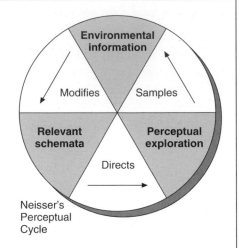

Neisser's Perceptual Cycle

For: The theory makes the process of perception a more flexible, dynamic and continuous process. Expectations are taken into account but are less fixed than Gregory's perceptual hypotheses and are constantly changing with environmental conditions and the person's developing understanding of those conditions. It explains how different perceivers are aware of different aspects of their environment.
Against: The theory lacks detail on the precise processes involved in directing, sampling and modifying, and is difficult to test.

MARR'S COMPUTATIONAL THEORY

Marr (1982) aimed to show how perception and recognition could occur by building (from the **bottom up**) an image from:

A) a grey level description...	B) to a primal sketch...	C) to a 2.5-dimensional sketch...	D) to a 3-dimensional object.

Consists of the intensity of light at each point in a picture or retinal image.	The analysis of light contrast leads to detection of edges and lines.	Consists of a picture of the object from the viewpoint of the observer, including the orientation and depth of **visible** features of a scene. It is difficult to identify 2.5-D sketches as objects because of unseen parts.	Consists of recognising the three-dimensional identity of the object by matching it to cylinder prototypes in memory. Cylinders were proposed since they add volume to an axis and the axes of an object are easy to detect regardless of viewpoint. Prototype matching to establish identity is a **top-down** process.

Marr (1982) proposed that visual perception should be explained at three levels:
- The computational level - i.e. what is the function or goal of perception?
- The algorithmic level - i.e. what rules and processes are used to achieve that goal?
- The hardware level - i.e. how are these functions and rules physically incorporated in the brain?

For: Warrington and Taylor (1978) found that certain brain damaged patients who have problems with object recognition, cannot turn viewpoint dependent 2.5-D sketches into 3-D objects. These patients could not recognise pictures of objects taken from unusual angles, but could recognise the same objects presented from typical angles (where the 2.5-D sketch would have provided enough information).
Against: Biederman (1987) took the 3-D prototype matching ideas of object recognition further than Marr, suggesting all shapes could be recognised using combinations of around 36 'geons', such as:

The development of perception 1

THE NATURE-NURTURE DEBATE IN THE DEVELOPMENT OF PERCEPTION

The research in this area aims to determine what particular aspects of perception are present at birth and what aspects are developed through experience with the environment. The physiology of the eye and brain can only tell us so much about this debate, so many different approaches have been taken to investigate it. All the approaches have their own strengths and weaknesses, however, and there is evidence for both nativist and empiricist views - suggesting an interaction of innate and environmental factors in the development of perception.

HUMAN INFANT STUDIES

Neonates (new born babies) are born with most of the features, such as rods and cones, of the adult eye and quickly demonstrate many perceptual abilities as their eyes and brain systems mature.

EVIDENCE SUPPORTING THE ROLE OF NATURE IN PERCEPTUAL DEVELOPMENT

Pattern and shape perception
- Fantz (1961) argued that very young babies are able to distinguish between patterns, and by 2-3 months prefer looking at complex stimuli if given a choice.
- Bower (1966) conditioned 2 month olds to respond to a triangle with a bar across it and found the response was generalised to a complete triangle (more than other possibilities), indicating the presence of the gestalt law of continuity and closure.

Depth perception
- Gibson and Walk (1960) argued that depth perception was innate using the visual cliff apparatus. Six month old babies would not crawl over the cliff edge onto the deep side, neither would newly born chicks or lambs.
- Campos et al (1970) placed two month old babies (who cannot crawl) onto the deep side of the visual cliff and found a decrease in heart rate compared to the shallow side, reflecting interest and a recognition of the difference.
- Bower et al (1970) found 20 day old babies would show an avoidance response to a large approaching box, but not if it was filmed and projected on a screen.

Constancy perception
- Bower (1966) found evidence that 2 month old babies possess size constancy. Having conditioned them to turn their head whenever they saw a 30 cm cube at a distance of 1 metre (using an adult playing 'peek-a-boo' as a reinforcer), Bower found they would respond more to the same 30 cm cube at a distance of 3 metres than they would to a 90 cm cube at 3 metres (which would cast the same size retinal image as the original 30 cm cube).
- Bower (1966) also showed shape constancy develops in the first few months by conditioning babies to respond to a shape and then rotating it.

Evaluation:
- Obviously it is impossible to rule out any environmental experience since birth.
- If neonates lack a perceptual ability, it may be due to a lack of biological maturation rather than lack of experience.
- The certainty of perception in babies is less reliable because of their lack of verbal report. Therefore, non-verbal methods of perceptual response have to be used, such as preferential looking, conditioned body movement or sucking, heart and brain activity changes.

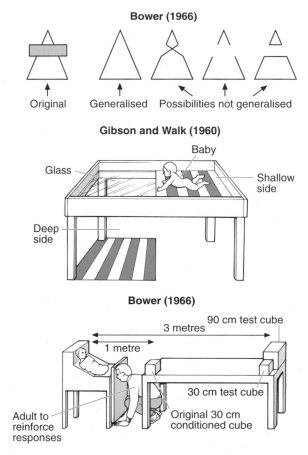

Bower (1966)

Original Generalised Possibilities not generalised

Gibson and Walk (1960)

Baby
Glass
Shallow side
Deep side

Bower (1966)

3 metres
90 cm test cube
1 metre
30 cm test cube
Adult to reinforce responses
Original 30 cm conditioned cube

PERCEPTUAL ADAPTATION & READJUSTMENT STUDIES

These studies assume that if perception can be adjusted to cope with artificial perceptual distortions, then perceptual abilities are more flexible and open to environmental influences - lending support to the nurture side of the nature-nurture debate in this area.

Evidence supporting the role of nature in perceptual development
- Studies on animals, e.g. Sperry's (1943) rotation of salamander eyes through 180 degrees, found they could not adjust their perception.

Evidence supporting the role of nurture in perceptual development
Using devices which invert or distort visual stimuli many researchers have found that human perception can readjust itself, e.g.
- Stratton (1896) wore an inverting telescope and had adjusted completely after 8 days, with only a location constancy after image afterwards.
- Ewart (1930) found inverting binoculars only produced motor

adaptation (vision-body co-ordination) not true perceptual adaptation.
- Snyder and Pronko (1952) used inverting and reversing goggles and found that the adaptation gained after 30 days lasted for years.

Evaluation:
- What is learnt is not necessarily a new way of perceiving but a new set of body movements.
- Showing that adults can learn to perceive does not mean that babies learn to perceive.

The development of perception 2

ANIMAL EXPERIMENTS

Animal studies into the development of perception usually involve the deprivation or distortion of the animal's normal visual experience from birth and noting the consequences for later perceptual abilities. Much of the evidence appears to emphasise the need for environmental stimulation for normal perception to develop. However, whether this involves learning to perceive, is less certain.

Evidence supporting the role of nurture in perceptual development

These studies imply that there are no innate abilities in perception and show that **active environmental stimulation** of **normal patterned light** is necessary for normal perceptual development in animals, e.g.

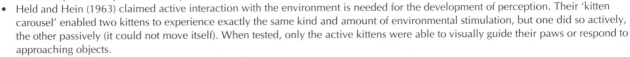

Blakemore and Cooper (1970)

- Riesen deprived animals such as chimpanzees and kittens of either:
  - **a** All light - for the first 16 months of life and found no visual perception because retinal cells failed to develop properly. When then allowed light, normal object recognition was shown at 21 months, although if light was denied until 33 months, the subsequent development of perceptual abilities was poorer.
  - **b** Just patterned light - the animals wore translucent goggles, which only allowed unpatterned light to be seen, and found that only general aspects of brightness, colour and size could be responded to. No object or pattern recognition was immediately evident.
- Blakemore and Cooper (1970) exposed kittens to an environment consisting of either only vertical or only horizontal lines and found that they would only respond to a pointer presented in the same orientation. Furthermore, the cells of each cat's primary visual cortex would only fire in response to lines presented in the orientation they had been raised in and not to lines of the opposite orientation.
- Held and Hein (1963) claimed active interaction with the environment is needed for the development of perception. Their 'kitten carousel' enabled two kittens to experience exactly the same kind and amount of environmental stimulation, but one did so actively, the other passively (it could not move itself). When tested, only the active kittens were able to visually guide their paws or respond to approaching objects.

Evaluation:

- There are major ethical problems with these studies. In one study Riesen tested the blindness of a light deprived chimpanzee by seeing if it would avoid a visually presented object that was associated with a painful electric shock.
- These studies aim to prevent or distort environmental experience or learning to **stop perceptual abilities being acquired** from the environment and thus may imply that there are no innate abilities in perception. However,
  - **a** deprivation may physically **damage** or **prevent** the **maturation of innate abilities** rather than prevent learning - chicks kept in the dark from birth to 10 weeks cannot recognise and peck at grain, whereas normal chicks can do this immediately on hatching without learning (Govier and Govier, cited in Radford and Govier, 1991).
  - **b** distortion of normal visual experience may merely **distort** the **development of innate abilities** - in Blakemore and Cooper's study, the stimulated visual cortex cells may have grown to dominate cells of other orientations that would otherwise have naturally responded.
- Animals cannot report their subjective experience and their perception can only be inferred from behaviour - Held and Hein's passive kitten probably lacked the ability to co-ordinate motor actions with perception rather than perception itself.
- Animal perception and development may be qualitatively different to human perceptual development.

HUMAN CATARACT PATIENTS

- Patients who have undergone cataract operations are provided with sight for the first time as adults and may shed light upon whether perceptual abilities are innate, i.e. shown immediately after the cataracts are removed, or are dependent upon experience and learning.
- Hebb (1949) studied the reports of 65 cases of cataract removal by von Senden and concluded that some aspects of vision were innate (figural unity) while others were learned (figural identity).
- Gregory and Wallace (1963) studied a 52 year old patient, S.B., who had undergone a corneal graft to restore his sight after being blind since he was 6 months old. Some aspects of vision were very quickly shown, others were not - implying a mixture of nature and nurture.

Evidence supporting the role of nature in perceptual development

- Hebb found that figural unity - the ability to fixate upon, scan, follow and detect shapes from their background (figure-ground perception), was shown by those patients whose sight had been restored, indicating these abilities were innate.
- Gregory and Wallace found that S.B. could quickly detect objects, walk around the hospital guided by sight alone and identify objects by sight that he had experienced through touch (showing good cross-modal matching). These abilities may have been aided by his experience of vision in his first 6 months of life.

Evidence supporting the role of nurture in perceptual development

- Hebb found that the cataract patients had great problems with figural identity - recognising objects. The patients could detect and scan a shape such as a triangle but would not be able to identify it by sight unless they counted the angles. They also lacked perceptual constancy.
- Gregory and Wallace found that S.B. had problems with identifying objects by sight that he had not experienced through touch before, detecting mood by visual facial expressions and depth perception (thinking a 40 foot drop from a window was manageable).

Evaluation:

- The adult patients' sensory systems would not be the same as those of babies due to adaptation to the loss of vision. Visual systems present at birth may have deteriorated through disuse or other sensory systems have over-developed to compensate, so interfering with vision.
- Methodologically these studies can be regarded as natural experiments, and so there is a lack of control over variables such as the degree of visual experience before the cataract developed, the age when the cataract was removed, and the emotional trauma of cataract removal.

Individual, social and cultural differences in perception

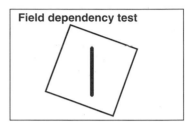

INDIVIDUAL DIFFERENCES

- **Experience** - Many studies have shown individual experience can affect perceptual set and thus perception.
  Bugeleski and Alampay (1961) discovered that subjects presented with pictures of animals and then the ambiguous 'rat-man' figure were more likely to see the rat than a control group who were more likely to see the man.
- **Personality** - Postman et al (1948) found subjects recognised words at faster presentation speeds on a tachistoscope which were related to their previously judged personal values. Words like 'helpful' and 'friendly' were recognised faster than words like 'logical' and 'analysis' in subjects who possessed social rather than theoretical values. Introverts are usually more visually sensitive, e.g. in tasks requiring sustained visual attention, than extroverts.
- **Cognitive style** - Witkin suggested that 'field-independent' subjects (who can position a rod vertically inside a frame regardless of the orientation of that frame) are more analytical and self-confident than 'field-dependent' subjects (who are more influenced by the frame and are thought to be more conforming and sensitive to context).

Evaluation:
The studies typically use stimuli that are ambiguous or lacking in ecological validity, presented at very fast speeds.

Rat-man illusion

Field dependency test

SOCIAL DIFFERENCES

- **Social class** - Bruner and Goodman (1947) found that poor children perceived more valuable coins as larger than they really were compared to children from richer families or a control group. The children had to adjust a beam of light to match the size of the coin they could see. However, other studies have only found overestimation of valuable coin size in poor children if they attempt to judge the size from memory.
- **Gender** - Females appear to be more field-dependent than males, less able at spatial rotation tasks and detecting embedded figures, and show poorer vision just before and during menstruation. Males are more likely to show colour blindness and adapt less quickly to dim light levels.
- **Ethnic group** - The attitudes of groups within a culture have been shown to affect perception. Pettigrew et al (1958) stereoscopically presented members of different ethnic groups in South Africa (e.g. white Afrikaners, Indians and Native South Africans) with pairs of facial pictures, one to each to eye, for a couple of seconds. When, for instance, the picture presented to one eye was of a white face and the other a black face, the White Afrikaners were more likely to report only one of the faces, compared to the members of the other ethnic groups who were more likely to report both or a perceptual fusion of the two. This was taken to imply strong social group attitudes affect perception.

Evaluation:
It is difficult to determine whether social differences are innate or learnt. Gender differences in spatial ability have been linked to the action of the hormone androgen, poor visual acuity during menstruation with progesterone, and colour blindness to sex-linked chromosomes.

CROSS-CULTURAL DIFFERENCES

Illusion studies

- Rivers (1901) in a very early study discovered that Murray Islanders, both adults and children, were more susceptible to the vertical-horizontal illusion, but less susceptible to the Muller-Lyer illusion, than English subjects.
- Allport and Pettigrew (1957) found that a rotating trapezoid was more likely to be seen as a swaying rectangle by western cultures and urban Zulus who are used to seeing rectangular windows, but more likely to be seen for what it was by non-urban Zulus.
- Segall et al (1963) conducted a very large scale study, testing around 1,900 subjects over a six year period, and argued that Africans and Filipinos were less susceptible than European subjects to the Muller-Lyer illusion, because they did not live in such a 'carpentered world' where right angles are so frequently encountered that they are readily learnt as depth cues. However, the 'carpentered world hypothesis' cannot account for findings that some groups of subjects living in rectangular constructed environments also fail to show susceptibility to the Muller-Lyer illusion (Mundy-Castle and Nelson, 1962), or that no difference has been found in its perception between urbanised and non-urbanised aborigines (Gregor and McPherson, 1965).

Vertical-horizontal illusion
the vertical line is perceived as longer than the horizontal line but is not

Muller-Lyer illusion
the right hand side vertical line is perceived as longer but is not

Carpentered world

Non-carpentered world

Size constancy

- Turnbull (1961) suggested that size constancy may be lacking in pygmies living in dense rain forests without the open space required to develop the ability. When taken to an open plain to see a herd of buffalo in the distance, they reported being unable to identify such 'strange insects' and were amazed at what happened as they were driven closer to the herd.

Depth perception

- Hudson (1960) discovered that African cultures have difficulty perceiving two-dimensional pictures as three-dimensional objects.
  However, the unnatural materials, the lack of natural depth cues such as texture gradient and the different artistic styles used in the pictures may have influenced the African subjects' perception.

Evaluation:
Cross-cultural differences in perception are often regarded as evidence for the idea that perception is flexible and so influenced by learning. However, the evidence is not conclusive, may only reflect the artificial methodologies used, and may even be due to biological factors since, for example, there is evidence that people with blue irises are more susceptible to the Muller-Lyer illusion than those with brown irises.

'Pictorial perception and culture' Deregowski (1972)

AIM
To present studies to show that different cultures perceive pictures in different ways. Cross-cultural studies of picture perception:
1 provide an insight into how perception works (indicating the role played by learning in perception) and
2 investigate the possibility of a universal cross-cultural means of communication (a 'lingua franca').

EVIDENCE
Pictorial object recognition studies

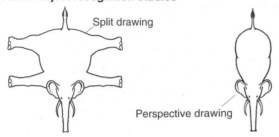

Split drawing

Perspective drawing

Pictorial depth recognition studies

What is the man doing?

2-dimensional picture

3-dimensional model

2-dimensional model

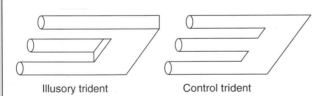

Illusory trident   Control trident

- Anecdotal reports from missionaries and anthropologists living among remote cultures have shown these cultures to have difficulties recognising objects from pictures, especially from accurate perspective drawings which do not represent all aspects of an object. Some studies have shown that African subjects from remote villages can pick out the correct toy from pictures of familiar animals (e.g. lions) though not unfamiliar ones (e.g. kangaroos).
- Hudson showed that African children and adults prefer split drawings to correct perspective drawings.

Hudson tested South African Bantu workers to see whether they could interpret a combination of three pictorial depth cues as a three dimensional representation:
- Familiar size - where the larger of two objects is drawn further away,
- Overlap - where nearer parts of a picture obscure farther away parts, and
- Perspective - where lines known to be parallel converge at the horizon.

The subjects were asked questions about the relationship between objects in the picture to see whether they had two- or three-dimensional vision. For example in the picture opposite, a three-dimensional viewer would say that the man is about to throw his spear at the antelope, a two-dimensional perceiver would say that the man is about to throw his spear at the elephant.

Hudson found two-dimensional perception in African tribal subjects across all ages, educational and social levels, and this finding was confirmed by pictorial depth measuring apparatus developed by Gregory.

Hudson showed Zambian subjects a drawing of two squares (arranged so that western subjects perceive them as a three-dimensional cube) and asked them to build a model of it out of modelling clay and sticks. Most of the Zambians built two-dimensional models, whereas the few who showed three-dimensional perception built a three-dimensional cube.

A group of Zambian school children, having been divided into two- and three-dimensional perceivers, were shown a picture illusion which three dimensional western perceivers become confused by (since they attempt to see it as a three-dimensional picture of a trident). Three-dimensional perceivers spent longer looking at the illusory trident than a normal control trident, compared to the two-dimensional perceivers who showed no significant difference in viewing the two, when asked to copy the tridents.

EVALUATION
Methodological:

Design - A wide range of methods used in the subject's own environment. However, most involve natural experiments, with a consequent lack of experimenter control over the independent variable (culture) and extraneous variables during testing.

Apparatus - Pictures lacked important depth cues, such as texture gradient, and were presented on paper rather than on ecologically natural materials.

Theoretical: Three explanatory theories are given, but little evidence is used to support or decide between them. There is an ethnocentric assumption that western methods of pictorially representing objects especially involving depth cues are more correct than others and should be universally recognised.

Links: Nature-nurture debate in perception. Cross-cultural psychology.

Attention

- Definition - The focusing and concentration of mental effort that usually results in conscious awareness of certain aspects of external sensory stimuli or mental experiences (although most study has focused on the former).
- The vast amount of sensory information from all our senses has to be cut down to manageable proportions - while reading this you are probably not aware of the smells around you or the pressure on whatever part of your body you are resting on.

- Some studies have looked at **focused** or **selective** attention - how certain stimuli are selected over others through allocating attention.
- Other studies have looked at **divided** attention - how, within a limited capacity, attention can be allocated to more than one task at a time.
- The two senses most investigated by psychologists researching attention are vision and hearing.

FOCUSED VISUAL ATTENTION

- Even with just one sense, such as vision, there is too much information to precisely process at any one time - we cannot read all the words on this page at the same time. Since the two eyes work in unison, providing one input channel of visual information, attention serves to focus on different areas of the visual field, and thus physically limits the flow of information.
- There are many theories that aim to explain how attention focuses on and selects particular information from its background visual field.

THEORY		EVIDENCE FOR & AGAINST

Zoom lens
• Visual attention is like the beam of a spotlight, which can be adjusted to cover a large area in little detail or a small focused area in greater detail.
	+	• LaBerge (1983) presented 5 letter words with the task of either
		  1 identifying the middle letter - requiring a narrow attentional beam, or
		  2 identifying the whole word - requiring a broad attentional beam.
		
		A stimulus probe was randomly presented in the position of one of the five letters and it was located more quickly in the word than the letter identification task (unless it occurred in the position of the middle letter).

	−	• Juola et al (1991) found attention could be just as quickly and accurately focused at the periphery of the 'beam' as at the centre. • Neisser & Becklen (1975) displayed two films at once in the same area and found that attention could be paid to either one of the superimposed images at the expense of the other.
Feature detection • Neisser suggested basic features of a scene are automatically processed in a pre-attentive (not requiring conscious attention) and parallel (all at the same time) way, allowing several basic but separate features to be analysed at once. • Subjects aiming to locate a particular item do not have to be aware of the identification of all non-relevant items.	+	• Neisser showed that subjects could spot any one of up to ten possible target items equally quickly, indicating that the search had to be conducted in a parallel simultaneous way for all possible target items. In further visual search studies, Neisser found that subjects could locate a target letter from amongst many other letters if they were non-similar rather than similar.
	−	• Neisser's subjects did, however, make more mistakes searching for one of ten possible target items, than one of two or three possible items.

Feature integration
• Treisman proposed that all basic features of a scene are processed rapidly in a parallel, automatic and pre-attentive way.
• Integrated features (involving more than one basic feature at a time) are processed more slowly in a serial (one at a time), automatic way requiring concious attention.
	+	• Treisman & Gelade (1980) asked subjects to visually search from an increasing number of surrounding distracter items for either
		  1 a single feature target item, e.g. a particular colour or letter, or
		  2 a conjunction target item - composed of two features integrated, e.g. an item consisting of a particular colour and shape.
		Single feature items were spotted equally well regardless of the number of distracter items indicating parallel processing. Conjunction items were more difficult to detect with increasing distracter items, indicating serial processing.

	−	The experiments were artificial using meaningless conjunctions of features, whereas most 'real-life' objects have meaningful combinations of features that may be pre-attentively recognised, e.g. the shape of a lemon and its colour.

Attentional engagement
• Duncan & Humphreys proposed that all integrated items are analysed in terms of their features and segregated from each other. Any item searched for is then matched to its likeness in visual short term memory, the speed of this being determined by the amount of desegregation required and the similarity present in the non-target items.
	+	• Studies have shown that searching for a target item takes longer when:
		  1 More segregation is required, e.g. when there is greater dissimilarity between non-target items.
		  2 More matching problems are encountered due to greater similarity between the target and non-target items.

	−	• There is much disagreement between researchers over the concepts of desegregation and conjunction of features.

Focused auditory attention 1

- Unlike visual attention, auditory attention involves many possible '**channels**' of information from the environment, since the ears can not be directed to provide one channel like the eyes can.
- Auditory attention serves to direct perception towards one of these channels, for example to pick out one conversation from amongst many surrounding us, as Cherry noticed with the 'cocktail party effect'.
- Psychologists have proposed that for auditory attention to work, the many channels must be **filtered** and one selected for further action. They differ, however, in whether they think this filtering (or '**bottleneck**' in the system) occurs early or late in the processing of information.

BROADBENT'S FILTER THEORY

Channels of information   Single selected channel

| **INPUT STIMULUS** from many sources via ears | → | **SENSORY REGISTER** briefly holds up information | → | **SELECTIVE FILTER** selects one channel based on physical characteristic of its information | → | **LIMITED CAPACITY PROCESSOR** | → | **OUTPUT RESPONSE PROCESSES** |

- Broadbent's filter model assumes that attended information is selected **early** in the system according to its **physical characteristics**.

EVIDENCE FOR

Cherry - binaural tests
Cherry presented **two** different messages simultaneously to **both** ears.
Result - Differences in the **physical aspects** of the messages, such as voice intensity and gender of the speaker, affected how easily they were attended to. If there were no physical differences (e.g. same voice and intensity) it was very difficult to distinguish between the two messages in terms of meaning.

CHERRY (1953)

"The cat sat on the mat"
"The dog hid the bone"

I can't tell what the two messages say

Different messages presented in the **same voice** at the **same time** to **both ears**

Cherry - dichotic tests
Cherry presented **one** different message simultaneously to **each** ear with instructions to shadow (repeat out loud) one of the messages.
Result - Subjects could only notice the physical aspects of the **non-attended** (non-shadowed) message such as the gender of the speaker but could **not** discern any aspects of its **meaning** (even after numerous repetitions or if it was played backwards or changed to another language).

"The cat sat on the mat"   **Different** gender **voices** presented **simultaneously** to **different ears**   "The dog hid the bone"

The cat sat on the mat ... I can't tell what the other message said but it had a male voice

CHERRY & TAYLOR (1954)

Broadbent - Split-span tests
Broadbent used a dichotic test where, for example, three different items of information are simultaneously presented to each ear in pairs.
Result - Subjects preferred, and were better at, recalling the information **by the ear of presentation** rather than by the order of presentation (one pair at a time). This implied to Broadbent that the ears functioned as separate channels and that it is difficult to change between channels.

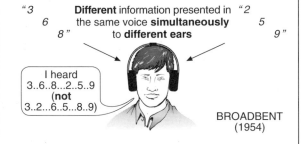

"3 6 8"   **Different** information presented in the same voice **simultaneously** to **different ears**   "2 5 9"

I heard 3..6..8...2..5..9 (**not** 3..2...6..5...8..9)

BROADBENT (1954)

EVIDENCE AGAINST

- Broadbent's theory assumes that non-attended information is not processed for meaning. However, at 'cocktail' parties, for example, people are capable of detecting their name being mentioned in other conversations that they thought they were not paying attention to.
- **Many studies** have shown that non-attended information can be processed for **meaning,** e.g. Moray (1959) found that a subject would detect their own name in the non-attended message of a dichotic shadowing test on around a third of occasions. See the evidence for Treisman's theory for more studies against Broadbent's idea that only physical features are selected early.
- Studies have shown that **attention can be switched** between channels far more easily and quickly than Broadbent thought possible, e.g. Gray and Wedderburn (1960). See evidence for Treisman's theory for more details.
- The early dichotic listening experiments used subjects unpractised in shadowing, who had to concentrate more on the task. Underwood (1974) found subjects highly experienced in shadowing could detect 67% of non-shadowed digits, compared to non-experienced subjects who only detected 8%.

Focused auditory attention 2

TREISMAN'S ATTENUATION THEORY

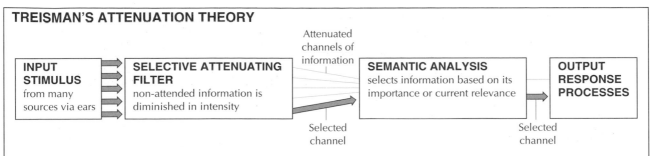

- Treisman proposed that non-attended (or non-shadowed) information is not rejected based upon physical characteristics (as Broadbent suggested), but is diminished or '**attenuated**' compared to attended information. All attenuated channels then proceed to a **semantic analysis** where information is noticed with an ease determined by its threshold of importance or relevance. Information that has some **personal importance** (e.g. your name or your baby crying next door) or current **temporary relevance** (e.g. things that you expect to hear in your present context, such as certain words in a sentence) will probably be recognised even in non-attended, poorly attenuated channels.

EVIDENCE FOR

Gray and Wedderburn (1960)
Gray and Wedderburn used a split-span dichotic listening test similar to Broadbent's where, for example, 'what..6..hell' was played to one ear at the same time as '2..the..9' was played to the other.
Result - Subjects found that they could easily report 'what..the..hell' or '2..6..9', showing Broadbent was wrong and that:
1 analysis of meaning must have occurred in the filter before selection
2 it is not difficult to change between channels

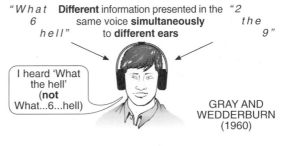

Treisman (1960)
Treisman found in a dichotic shadowing test that certain words from a non-attended sentence would intrude into an attended sentence if it made the latter more meaningful.

Mackay (1973)
Mackay found that the meanings of ambiguous word such as 'bank' in the attended channel could be influenced by words in the non-attended channel, e.g. 'river' or 'money'.

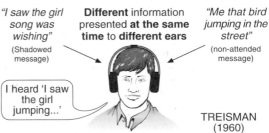

EVIDENCE AGAINST
- Treisman's theory seems overly complex - is the attenuator actually needed? The Deutsch-Norman theory criticises early processing ideas.

DEUTSCH-NORMAN LATE SELECTION THEORY

All channels of information proceed to semantic analysis · Selected channel

| INPUT STIMULUS from many sources via ears | → | SEMANTIC ANALYSIS selects information based on its importance or current relevance | → | OUTPUT RESPONSE PROCESSES |

- The Deutsch-Norman Theory argues that **all** channels of information are analysed for **meaning** equally and the filter is a **late selection** one.

EVIDENCE FOR
- Norman (1969) found the last few words of non-attended messages could be remembered if the subject stopped halfway through shadowing.
- Their theory also accounts for the studies supporting Treisman's theory, but is more parsimonious (explains the same in a more simple way).

EVIDENCE AGAINST
- Treisman & Riley (1969) found target words were better detected in shadowed than non-shadowed messages. Why would this occur if all channels are processed semantically to the same degree as the Deutsch-Norman theory predicts?
- Filter theories generally lack flexibility. Johnston and Wilson (1980) found that selection can be made early or late depending upon the demands of the situation.

Divided auditory attention 1

- Divided attention concerns the ability to perform two tasks simultaneously.
- Eysenck and Keane (1995) identify three factors which affect the performance of dual tasks:

1 TASK DIFFICULTY
Task difficulty is not easy to define, but tasks become harder to perform at the same time, the more difficult they are (Sullivan, 1976).

2 TASK PRACTICE
Tasks can be performed more easily together if one or both are well practised. Allport et al (1972) found skilled pianists were able to sight read music and shadow speech at the same time. Practice may have its effects by
a using attentional resources more economically, thus freeing them up for other tasks
b developing new strategies to minimise interference between tasks (see 3).

3 TASK SIMILARITY
Non-similar tasks interfere with each other less and can be more readily performed at the same time. Allport et al (1972) found subjects could shadow speech and learn pictorial information at the same time, since the tasks used different modalities. Shaffer (1975) found skilled typists could type from sight and shadow speech, but could not type from speech and shadow speech, at the same time. Tasks disrupt each other if they require the use of
a the same modality, e.g. sight or hearing
b the same processing stage, e.g. word analysis or problem solving
c the same response mechanism, e.g. speech or manual response.

- Many types of theory have been proposed, including limited capacity, modular and synthesis theories.

KAHNEMAN'S LIMITED CENTRAL CAPACITY THEORY

- Kahneman (1973) views attention as a **skill**, rather than a process, and argues that there is just **one central processor** which **allocates** a central pool of attentional **resources** in a **flexible** manner across a variety of different tasks.
- Despite its flexibility, the central processor has a **limited capacity** or pool of attentional resources that it can allocate at any one time.
  1 Tasks requiring little capacity need **little mental effort** or attentional resources and so leave more **room** for performing **additional** tasks. Attention can be divided as long as the capacity is there - a task requiring a large amount of mental effort will leave no room for other tasks.
  2 The amount of capacity or mental effort tasks need, depends upon their **difficulty** and the individual's **past experience** (practice) of them.

3 The amount of total **capacity available** depends on **arousal levels** - the more alert someone is, the more attentional capacity they have.
4 The limited **capacity** available is **allocated** amongst tasks depending on
  a an evaluation of attentional demands - if the degree of mental **effort** required **exceeds capacity**, the central processor has to decide upon an **allocation policy**
  b momentary intentions - attentional resources are likely to be directed towards tasks related to **current goals**
  c enduring dispositions - some stimuli will **override** the **attention** paid to current goals because of their **importance,** e.g. new, startling or personally relevant (like the calling of your name) stimuli. This usually occurs naturally and without voluntary control.

Evidence for
- The model is far more flexible in processing than the filter theories.
- It can explain many of the findings of previous models, plus studies they found difficult to account for, e.g. the problems novice, compared to experienced, subjects had in attending to non-shadowed messages (Underwood, 1974) or the flexibility of processing (Johnston and Wilson, 1980).
- The theory has practical implications. It could explain Gopher and Kahneman's (1971) evidence that the efficiency of a pilot's attention-switching ability (presumably a reflection of the skill of the central processor) is positively correlated (r = .36 for 100 flight cadets) to their success in flight training.

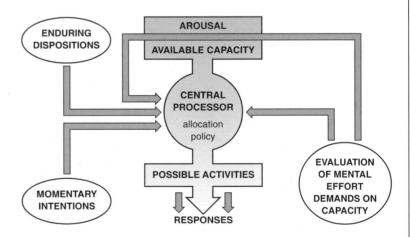

Evidence against
- The theory is not specific enough about how much capacity there is. Spelke et al (1976) trained two students to simultaneously perform two fairly complex tasks requiring the same processes (reading short stories while writing down auditory dictation), perhaps implying a much larger overall capacity than previously assumed, since they could eventually process both sources of information for meaning.
- The theory assumes that processing resources are general and undifferentiated rather than specialised. Module theories disagree with this.

- Norman and Bobrow's (1975) central capacity interference theory suggests that Kahneman neglected the importance of interference. They point out that **resource limitations** can be solved by allocating more attentional resources, but **data limitations** (where two tasks require the same type of resource, e.g. word usage) cannot be solved this way. Task similarity interference tests, e.g. Shaffer (1975) support this idea, and although the theory is descriptive rather than explanatory, it did lead to the idea of specialised resource modules.

Divided auditory attention 2

ALLPORT'S MODULE RESOURCE THEORY

- Allport proposes that attention consists of several **specialised** information processing **modules** for information, each with its **own resources** and **capacity**, rather than one central capacity processor.
- Tasks that are similar use the **same module's resources** and **interfere** with one another if they are attempted at the same time, preventing dual task performance.

- Tasks that are **not similar** use different modules and can be processed in **parallel,** without interfering with each other in any way.
- Wickens (1984) further suggests that resources are specialised to different aspects of a task, e.g. the input mode, processing mechanism, and output modality.

Evidence for

- Module theories can account for the way that dual tasks can be performed and attention divided if the tasks are non-similar. They, therefore, explain studies such as Allport et al's (1972) where the experienced piano players could sight read music and shadow spoken messages.
- Module theories have practical applications to everyday issues, such as whether the use of car phones interferes with driving. Despite the fact that car phones have been devised to make them 'hands free', so that manual responses are not interfered with, there is some evidence that calls demanding decision making can interfere with the perceptual and decision making skills made under difficult driving conditions. Brown et al (1969) got drivers to negotiate a set of obstacles while simultaneously verbally solving problems presented through headphones. Although the drivers usually drove more slowly, and the automatic, basic aspects of driving were unaffected by the auditory task, the demanding logical reasoning did interfere with the more difficult driving decisions - the drivers attempted to get through gaps between obstacles that were far too small. The quality of problem solving also decreased.
- Brain modularity has received support from brain damage studies which have found very specific skill deficits from specific damage.

DUAL TASKS	POSSIBLE MODULES INVOLVED		
	Input mode	Processing mechanism	Output mode
Sight reading music	Vision	Music recognition	Manual
Shadowing speech	Auditory	Speech recognition	Vocal
	No interference-good performance		
Demanding driving conditions	Vision	Decision making	Manual
Hands free demanding car phone call	Auditory	Problem solving	Vocal
	Interference-poor performance		

Evidence against

- Module theories do not specify
  1 how many modules there are - making the theory irrefutable, since another module can always be proposed to account for new findings.
  2 what types of module exist - Spelke et al's (1976) students were trained to accomplish two tasks that should have

demanded similar modules. Shallice et al (1985), however, have provided some evidence that speech perception and production systems are functionally separate, perhaps accounting for the ability of some translators to listen, translate and speak their languages simultaneously.
  3 how the modules interact so smoothly with each other.

BADDELEY'S SYNTHESIS THEORY

- Baddeley proposed the working memory model, which combines a modality free, central, limited capacity processor (the central executive) plus specific modality processing systems (the phonological loop and visuospatial sketchpad).
- There is much experimental support for the model through the use of concurrent tasks and brain imaging techniques that verify different areas of the brain are active when different modules are active.
- Aspects of the model, such as the role of the central executive, need more investigation.
- See material on memory for more detail on working memory.

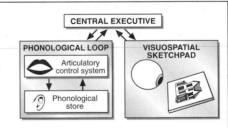

EVALUATION OF DIVIDED ATTENTION THEORIES

- Filter processing theorists still point out that central, modular and synthesis theories **cannot explain** the 'bottleneck' in information processing that is reflected by the **psychological refractory period effect**. This occurs when two stimuli requiring responses are presented rapidly one after the other and the response to the second stimulus is slower than the response to the first, even when the two tasks are not competing for modules (and, therefore, should be processed in parallel) and the subject is highly practised (so resources should not have to be allocated). This refractory period, estimated at around **one tenth of a second**, is possibly due to the time it takes to **switch attention** from one serial channel to another. Although small, as Barber (1988) points out, the consequences for a record breaking 100 metre sprinter of not attending to the starter's gun would be a lost metre on an attending rival.
- Studies and theories of divided attention have practical importance. Trainee pilots often fail, and bus drivers partly have accidents, 'because of a failure to divide attention among concurrent activities or among concurrent signals, or else because they are slow to recognise the significance of crucial signals which arrive on unattended channels' Gopher and Kahneman (1971), quoted in Barber (1988).

Automatic processing

Research has shown that if tasks are practised enough, they become automatic, need less attention, and can be successfully performed with other tasks, e.g. Allport et al's (1972) skilled pianists who were able to sight read music and shadow speech at the same time.

SCHNEIDER AND SHIFFRIN (1977)

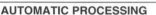 Schneider and Shiffrin distinguish between controlled and automatic processing.

CONTROLLED PROCESSING
- requires direction of attention
- occurs in a serial manner
- is slow
- makes heavy demands on attentional resources
- is capacity limited - therefore affects the performance of other tasks attempted at the same time
- allows very flexible processing

AUTOMATIC PROCESSING
- always occurs - is unavoidable
- occurs in a parallel manner
- is fast
- makes no demands on attentional resources
- is unaffected by capacity limitations - does not affect the performance of other tasks attempted at the same time
- is inflexible in processing and difficult to modify

Evidence for

- Treisman's studies of the feature integration approach to focused visual attention support the above distinction - some aspects of a task (e.g. the detection of basic features) can be processed automatically in parallel, whereas others (e.g. those involving the detection of feature combinations) need a more complex analysis using conscious attention and have to be processed serially.
- Schneider and Shiffrin (1977) demonstrated using visual detection tests that
  1 automatic processing occurs rapidly and in parallel when a subject is searching for numbers among letters
  2 controlled attention processing occurs slowly and in a serial manner when a subject is searching for letters among other letters.
- Shiffrin and Schneider (1977), however, found that the search for letters among other letters could become automatic with extensive practice. After over 2000 trials, the letter detection times decreased until they were as fast as the automatic detection shown in the first study.
- Shiffrin and Schneider (1977) also demonstrated that once acquired, automatic processes become unavoidable and difficult to modify. When the target letters or their location in the detection area were changed, subjects found it difficult not to automatically search for the letters they had practised before, in areas they were used to looking. It took subjects around a 1000 trials of the new letters to even start showing automatic detection with them.
- The distinction between controlled and automatic processing has been useful in explaining other psychological phenomenon, such as social facilitation or inhibition. For example, subjects attempting a new or difficult task will show worse performance in front of an audience than on their own. The individual's lack of automatic processes means the distraction of conscious attention by other people will have dire consequences on performance.

Evidence against

- The idea that automatic tasks do not use up attentional resources, are unaffected by capacity limitations, and so do not affect the performance of other tasks attempted at the same time, is not strictly correct. Automatic tasks can interfere with simultaneously performed consciously controlled processing, as in the Stroop effect, where subjects asked to identify **the colour that words are written in** cannot ignore the content of the word if it describes a different colour, e.g. subjects will often report the colour of the word 'green' written in red ink as green rather than red. This occurs as reading skills are automatically triggered and intrude upon the attentional resources of the consciously processed colour detection task.
- How automatic processing occurs is not specified - does the speed of processing increase with practice or is there a change in the type of processing involving more efficient, economical techniques? Logan (1990) argues that automaticity develops through practice because the **retrieval of appropriate responses** becomes more rapid and does not require any intervening conscious thoughts or effort - just the accessing of 'past solutions'. Children, for example, will first have to continuously and laboriously work out addition sums such as '9 + 7 =' but each time they do that sum they leave a memory trace of the answer until eventually they can access that answer directly, without having to 'work it out'. Logan's ideas indicate that there are probably different degrees of task automaticity depending on the amount of past experience with them, a notion that Norman and Shallice (1986) have taken a little further.

NORMAN AND SHALLICE (1986)

Norman and Shallice propose different levels of automaticity:

- Fully automatic processing - which involves no conscious awareness and is controlled by schemata.

- Partially automatic processing - involves slightly more conscious awareness and is not deliberately controlled but governed by a contention scheduling control system, which resolves conflicts amongst schema so they do not interfere with each other.

- Deliberate control - involves conscious awareness governed by a supervisory attentional system, which allows decision making and flexibility of response in new situations.

Action slips

REASON'S (1992) THEORY

- Reason (1992) regards action slips - actions performed but not intended - as important contributions to our understanding of attention and automatic processing.
- Reason asked 35 subjects to keep a diary record of action slips over a 2 week period and found that, out of the 433 slips recorded between the subjects, the majority could be categorised into one of the following five types:

1 Storage failures
40% of slips involved forgetting or recalling inaccurately intentions and actions which lead to the same action being repeated,
e.g. sugaring a cup of tea twice without remembering the first time.

2 Test failures
20% of slips involved forgetting or switching a goal because of a failure to monitor a planned sequence sufficiently,
e.g. going to make a cup of coffee but making tea instead.

3 Sub-routine failures
18% of slips involved omitting or re-ordering stages in an action sequence, e.g. pouring cold water into a teapot or hot water into a teapot without tea in.

4 Discrimination failures
11% of slips involved failing to discriminate between two objects involved in different actions, e.g. mistaking drinking yoghurt for milk, or shaving cream for toothpaste.

5 Programme assembly failures
5% of slips involved incorrectly combining the action sequences of different goals,
e.g. putting the tea bags in the refrigerator and the milk in the cupboard.

- Reason (1992) suggests that actions are under two types of control, either:
  1 'open loop' (automatic and non-conscious) control - which is fast but error prone, or
  2 'closed loop' (deliberate and conscious) control - which is slower but less prone to error.

Evidence for
Reason found that action slips happen with tasks that are highly practised and are, therefore, under open loop, automatic control. Since such tasks are performed without monitoring by conscious attention, automatic routines can occur inappropriately. For example,
a actions carried out by non-attended automatic channels are likely to be forgotten - leading to storage failures.
b automatic actions common to many situations may get confused if not monitored at crucial points in a sequence - leading to test failures.

Evidence against
- The data gained using the diary method may be unreliable since it is not known how many slips went unnoticed or on how many occasions slips could have occurred.
- Laboratory attempts to set up action slips (which could control for the faults of the diary method) lack ecological validity. They do not provide the same conditions under which natural 'absent-mindedness' occurs, and so may not produce slips caused by the same factors.
- The precise mechanisms underlying action slips are not specified - Sellen and Norman (1992) aimed to provided more detail on these.

SELLEN AND NORMAN'S (1992) THEORY

- Sellen and Norman suggest that action slips are the result of schemata - cognitive structures that enable us to deal with the world. They propose that there are two main types of schema:
1 parent schemata - which are concerned with overall intentions such as making a cup of tea, and
2 child schemata - which consist of the actions required to accomplish the parent schema's intention, such as filling the kettle with water, plugging it in, putting a tea bag in the cup, pouring the water in, etc.

- Each schema has a particular activation level for producing its behaviour which depends upon current intentions or triggering environmental conditions.
- An action slip will, therefore, occur if, for example, an error was made in forming a parent schema intention (so a whole set of inappropriate child schemata are activated) or incorrect child schemata are triggered (while making tea you walk past the coffee jar and unconsciously trigger the child schema for putting coffee in the cup rather than tea).

EVALUATION OF ACTION SLIP THEORIES

- The type of action slips investigated above usually occur when conscious attention is not being paid to a task, usually it is already 'pre-occupied' with a heavy workload of information. However, the theories do not take into account automatic errors made in tasks that subjects are paying close attention to. Healy (1976) found that subjects asked to circle all the letter 't's in a passage, missed out the 't' in 'the', one of the most common words in the English language. Although the task required conscious effort, since the word 'the' tends to be processed automatically as a whole unit, performance was disrupted. The stroop effect also involves automatic action slips despite conscious effort.
- Action slips are of practical importance. Langan-Fox and Empson (1985) found that air-traffic controllers made more action slips as workload (measured in terms of the number of aircraft in radio contact at any one time) increased.

Types of memory

ENCODING TYPES OF MEMORY

The human sensory systems, such as our eyes and ears, receive many different forms of stimulation, ranging from sound waves to photons of light. Obviously the information reaching our senses is transformed in nature when it is represented in our brains, and encoding refers to the process of representing knowledge in different forms.

IMAGERY MEMORY

- Some memory representations appear to closely resemble the raw, unabstracted data containing original material from our senses, such as the extremely brief iconic (visual) and echoic (auditory) after images that rapidly fade from our eyes and ears. Yet even after these have gone, we retain the ability to recall fairly vivid visual images of what we have seen and to hear again tunes we have experienced.
- Baddeley and Hitch (1974) have investigated this sort of short term imagery ability by suggesting that we have a 'visuospatial scratchpad' for summoning up and examining our visual imagery.
- Although extremely rare in adults, photographic (eidetic) memory is an ultra enhanced form of imagery memory, shown by perhaps 5% of young children (Haber, 1979).

PROCEDURAL MEMORY

- Also known as implicit memory, this is the memory for **knowing how** to do things such as talk, walk, juggle, etc. Although we retain these skills and abilities, we are often completely **unable to consciously introspect upon or describe** how we do them. Procedural memory is similar to Bruner's enactive mode.
- Procedural knowledge is very resistant to forgetting (we never forget how to ride a bicycle) and is also resistant to brain damage that eradicates other forms of memory - anterograde amnesiac patients, who forget simple events or verbal instructions after a few moments, are often able to learn new procedural skills such as playing table-tennis.

DECLARATIVE MEMORY

- Sometimes termed explicit memory, this type concerns all the information that we can **describe or report**, and as such has been the focus of the *majority* of research on memory. Declarative memory includes:
- **a** **semantic memory** - this concerns memory for meaning, the storage of abstract, general facts regardless of when those facts were acquired e.g. *knowing what* a word means.
- **b** **episodic** - this is 'knowing when' memory based upon personal experience and linked to a particular time and place in our lives. Episodic memory can be quite precise - Lindsay and Norman (1977) asked students "what were you doing on a Monday afternoon in the 3rd week of September, 2 years ago?", and found many actually knew. Very vivid episodic memories have been termed 'flashbulb' memories (Brown and Kulik, 1977) which involve recalling exactly what you were doing and where you were when a particularly important, exciting or emotional event happened.

DURATION TYPES OF MEMORY

Ever since William James (1890) distinguished between *primary* memory which feels like our present conscious experience, and *secondary* memory which seems like we are 'fishing out' information from the past, cognitive psychologists have been very interested in the possibility of different types of memory store based on the duration of time memories last for. Cognitive psychologists have proposed **three types** of time based store, each with differences in duration, capacity, coding and function.

SENSORY MEMORY

(sometimes called the short term sensory store or sensory register)

- The sense organs have a limited ability to store information about the world in a fairly unprocessed way for less than a second, rather like an afterimage. The visual system possesses **iconic** memory for visual stimuli such as shape, size, colour and location (but not meaning), whereas the hearing system has **echoic** memory for auditory stimuli.
- Coltheart et al (1974) have argued that the momentary freezing of visual input allows us to select which aspects of the input should go on for further memory processing. The existence of sensory memory has been experimentally demonstrated by Sperling (1960) using a tachistoscope.

SHORT TERM MEMORY

- Information selected by attention from sensory memory, may pass into short term memory (STM).
- STM allows us to retain information long enough to **use** it, e.g. looking up a telephone number and remembering it long enough to dial it. Peterson and Peterson (1959) have demonstrated that STM lasts approximately **between 15 and 30 seconds,** unless people rehearse the material, while Miller (1956) has found that STM has a **limited capacity** of around **7 'chunks'** of information.
- STM also appears to mostly **encode** memory **acoustically** (in terms of sound) as Conrad (1964) has demonstrated, but can also retain visuospatial images.

LONG TERM MEMORY

- Long term memory provides the lasting retention of information and skills, from **minutes** to a **lifetime**.
- Long term memory appears to have an almost **limitless capacity** to retain information, but of course its capacity could never be measured - it would take too long!
- Long term information seems to be encoded mainly in terms of **meaning** (semantic memory), as Baddeley has shown, but also retains procedural skills and imagery.

Research on the sensory register, short term and long term memory

SENSORY MEMORY

- Since sensory memory lasts less than a second, most of the material in it will have been forgotten before it can be reported! **Sperling** studied the sensory memory for vision (the iconic store) by using a **tachistoscope** - a device that can flash pictoral stimuli onto a blank screen for very brief instances. Using this device, Sperling was able to ask subjects to remember as many letters as they could from a **grid of 12 symbols** that he was going to display for just **one twentieth of a second**, and found that while they could only recall around **four** of the symbols before the grid faded from their sensory memory, they typically reported seeing a lot more than they had time to report.

- **Capacity** Sperling presented the 12 symbol grid for 1/20th of a second, followed immediately by a **high, medium** or **low tone,** which indicated which of the three rows of four symbols the subject had to attend to from their iconic memory of the grid. In this partial report condition, recall was on average just over 3 out of the 4 symbols from any row they attended to, suggesting that the iconic store can retain **approximately 76%** of all the data received.

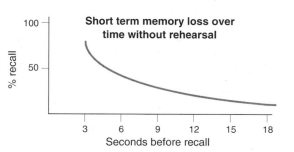

Step 1 Show grid	Step 1 Ring tone	Step 1 Recall letters
7 1 V F		? ? ? ?
X L 5 3	Medium tone	X L 5 3
B 4 W 7		? ? ? ?

- **Duration** If there was a delay between the presentation of the grid and the sounding of the tone, Sperling found that more and more information was lost (only 50% was available after a 0.3 second delay and only 33% was available after a 1 second delay).

SHORT TERM MEMORY

- **Duration** - Peterson and Peterson (1959) investigated the duration of short term memory with their **trigram experiment**. They achieved this by
  1. asking subjects to remember a single nonsense syllable of three consonants (a trigram of letters such as FJT or KPD).
  2. giving them an *interpolated* task to stop them rehearsing the trigram (such as counting backwards in threes from one hundred).
  3. testing their *recall after* 3, 6, 9, 12, 15 or 18 seconds (recall had to be perfect and in the correct order to count). While average recall was very good (80%) after 3 seconds, this average dropped dramatically to just 10% after 18 seconds.

Short term memory loss over time without rehearsal

y-axis: % recall (0, 50, 100)
x-axis: Seconds before recall (3, 6, 9, 12, 15, 18)

- **Capacity** - Many early researchers in the area of memory, including Ebbinghaus, noted that short term memory appears to have a limited storage capacity. *Miller* (1956) investigated this limited capacity experimentally, refering to it as '**The magical number seven, plus or minus two**'. Miller found that the amount of information retained could be increased by **chunking** the information - packaging it into larger items or units, although the STM can still only retain 7 + or - 2 of these chunks. Chunking is greatly improved if the chunks already have **meaning** from LTM.

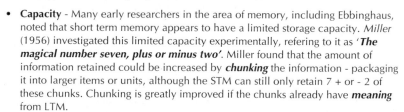

Unchunked items
0 1 0 3 3 8 9 8 2 1 8 6 5 7
M P I B M I T V A A F B I R A F
Chunked items
010 33 898 21 8657
MP IBM ITV AA FBI RAF

- **Encoding** - It has been argued that the main way information is encoded or retained in STM is through sound - an **acoustic code**. Regardless of whether we see or hear material, we tend to find ourselves repeating the information verbally to ourselves to keep it in mind (STM), and hopefully pass it on to long term storage. Conrad (1964) demonstrated acoustic STM encoding, finding that rhyming letters were significantly harder to recall properly than non rhyming letters, mostly due to acoustic confusion errors. Conrad found similar effects for rhyming vs. non rhyming words.
Den Heyer and Barrett (1971) showed that STM stores visual information too.

1) **B T C P G E D**
2) **F T Z Q W R N**
3) **MAT, CAT, SAT, BAT, HAT, RAT, FAT**
4) **PIE, SIX, TRY, BIG, GUN, HEN, MAN**

Acoustic confusion errors are made when recalling lists 1 & 3, even though the letters are visually presented. This shows the material is retained acoustically in STM.

LONG TERM MEMORY

- **Duration** - While it is impossible to predict the duration of any one piece of information, researchers have investigated general trends in the durability of memory. Ebbinghaus found that a large proportion of information in LTM was lost comparatively quickly (within the first hour) and thereafter stabilised to a much slower rate of loss.
Linton used a diary to record 3 'every day' events from her life each day, and randomly tested her later recall of them. She found a much more even and gradual loss of data over time (approx. 6 % per year).
- **Capacity** - Enormous but impossible to measure.
- **Encoding** - Baddeley (1966) showed that LTM stores information in terms of meaning (semantic memory), by giving subjects four lists to remember.
If recall was given immediately, list A was recalled worse than list B, but there was little difference between the recall of lists C and D.
After 20 minutes, however, it was list C that was recalled worse than D, with little difference between lists A and B.

Baddeley's (1966) lists:

List A - Similar sounding words
e.g. man, map, can, cap.

List B - Non similar sounding words
e.g. try, pig, hut, pen.

List C - Similar meaning words
e.g. great, big, huge, wide.

List D - Non similar meaning words
e.g. run, easy, bright.

Multi-store model of memory

- Much research was devoted to identifying the properties of sensory, short term, and long term memory, and cognitive psychologists such as Atkinson and Shiffrin (1968) began to regard them as **stores** - hypothetical holding structures.
- Atkinson and Shiffrin proposed the two-process model of memory, which showed how information flowed through the two stores of short term and long term memory, but like many of the models, they assumed the existence of a sensory memory that precedes the short term memory, and so it is sometimes termed the multi-store model.

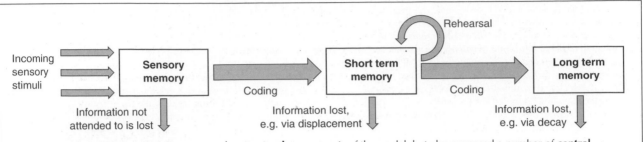

- Atkinson and Shiffrin regarded the stores as the **structural components** of the model, but also proposed a number of **control processes,** such as attention, coding and rehearsal, which operate in conjunction with the stores.

There are two main lines of evidence that support the model's assumptions about the way information flows through the system and the distinct existence of short term and long term memory stores - free recall experiments and studies of brain damaged patients.

FREE RECALL EXPERIMENTS

- In free recall experiments, subjects are given a number of words (for example 20) in succession to remember and are then asked to recall them in any order ('free recall'). The results reliably fall into a pattern known as the **serial position curve**. This curve consists of

  a a **primacy effect** - Subjects tend to recall the first words of the list well, which indicates that the first words entered short term memory and had time to be rehearsed and passed on to long term memory before the STM capacity was reached. The primacy effect, therefore, involves recall from long term memory.

  b an **asymptote** - The middle portion items of the list are remembered far less well than those at the beginning and the end. This is probably because the increasing number of items fills the limited capacity of the STM and these later items are unable to be properly rehearsed and transferred to LTM before they are displaced.

  c a **recency effect** - Subjects usually recall those items from the end of the list first, and tend to get more of these correct on average than all the earlier items. This effect persists even if the list is lengthened (Murdock, 1962), and is thought to be due to recall from the short term memory store - since the items at the end of the list were the last to enter STM and were not displaced by further items.

- Further evidence for the primacy/recency effects comes from two other findings:

  a Slower rates of presentation can improve the primacy effect, but have little or no influence on the recency effect.

  b The recency effect disappears if the last words are not recalled straight away. Glanzer and Cunitz (1966) gave subjects an interference task immediately after the last word of the list and found a primacy but no recency effect.

STUDIES OF BRAIN DAMAGED PATIENTS

Cases of **anterograde amnesia** such as H.M. (Milner et al, 1978) or Clive Wearing (reported in Blakemore, 1988) provide strong evidence for the distinction between STM and LTM. Anterograde amnesia is often caused by brain damage to the hippocampus and those suffering from it seem incapable of transferring information from STM to LTM. With this inability, they are essentially trapped in a world of experience that only lasts as long as their short term memory does.

Patients afflicted by anterograde amnesia often retain most of their long term memory for events up until the moment of brain damage and maintain their procedural memories. While they seem incapable of gaining new long term declarative memory for semantic or episodic information most are able to learn new procedural skills like mirror writing)

If these people are given free recall experiments, they show good recency effects but extremely poor primacy effects (Baddeley and Warrington, 1970).

CRITICISMS OF THE ATKINSON AND SHIFFRIN MODEL

- It is too rigid and simplistic - Information must flow in both directions for the model to be realistic, since here is a good deal of interaction between the stores. For example, long term memory must influence not only STM (think of how effective chunking is achieved by imposing meaning on material - M P, I B M, B B C, I T V, C I A, etc.) but even sensory memory (we tend to pay attention to relevant information from the sensory registers, but this 'relevance' must be stored in a long term way).

The model does not take into account the *type* of information taken into memory (some items seem to flow into LTM far more readily than others), and the model ignores factors such as the effort and strategy subjects may show when remembering.

- The model does not explain why information changes in coding from one memory store to another.
- Other approaches have proposed alternative explanations of memory processing that do not draw such as clear line between short and long term memory - allowing more of a continuum, e.g. Craik and Lockhart's levels of processing theory (1972).

Alternative models of memory processing

LEVELS OF PROCESSING APPROACH TO MEMORY - CRAIK AND LOCKHART (1972)

THE APPROACH

- Craik and Lockhart's important article countered the predominant view of fixed memory **stores**, arguing that it is what the person **does** with information when it is received, i.e. how much attention is paid to it or how deeply it is considered, that determines how long the memory lasts.
- They suggested that information is more readily transferred to LTM if it is *considered, understood* and related to past memories to gain *meaning* than if it is merely *repeated* (maintenance rehearsal). This degree of consideration was termed the **'depth of processing'** - the deeper information was processed, the longer the **memory trace** would last.
- Craik and Lockhart gave three examples of **levels** at which verbal information could be processed:
  1 **Structural** level - e.g. merely paying attention to what the words *look* like (very shallow processing).
  2 **Phonetic** level - processing the *sound* of the words.
  3 **Semantic** level - considering the **meaning** of words (deep processing).

EVIDENCE

- Craik and Tulving (1975) tested the effect of depth of processing on memory by giving subjects words with questions that required different levels of processing, e.g.
  'table'
  Structural - 'Is the word in capital letters?'
  Phonetic - 'Does it rhyme with "able"?'
  Semantic - 'Does it fit in the sentence "the man sat at the _____"?'
- Subjects thought that they were just being tested on reaction speed to answer yes or no to each question, but when they were given an unexpected test of recognition, it was found that those words processed at the semantic level were recognised more often than those processed structurally.

MODIFICATIONS

Many researchers became interested in exactly what produced **deep** processing:

- **Elaboration** - Craik and Tulving (1975) found complex semantic processing (e.g. 'The great bird swooped down and carried off the struggling __') produced better cued recall than simple semantic processing (e.g. 'She cooked the ___').
- **Distinctiveness** - Eysenck and Eysenck (1980) found even words processed phonetically were better recalled if they were distinctive or unusual.
- **Effort** - Tyler et al (1979) found better recall for words presented as difficult anagrams (e.g. 'OCDTRO') than simple anagrams (e.g. 'DOCTRO').
- **Personal relevance** - Rogers et al (1977) found better recall for personal relevance questions (e.g. 'Describes you?') than general semantic ones (e.g. 'Means?').

EVALUATION

- **Strengths** - good contribution to understanding the processes that take place at the time of learning.
- **Weaknesses** - There are many problems with defining 'deep' processing and why it is effective.
- Semantic processing does not always lead to better retrieval (Morris et al, 1977).
- It describes rather than explains.

THE WORKING MEMORY MODEL - BADDELEY AND HITCH (1974)

THE MODEL (AS OF 1990)

The working memory model challenged the unitary and passive view of the multi-store model's short term memory store.

Working memory is an **active** store to hold and manipulate information that is currently being consciously thought about. It consists of 3 separate **components:**

- **The central executive** - a modality-free controlling attentional mechanism with a limited capacity, which monitors and co-ordinates the operation of the other two components or slave systems.
- **The phonological loop** - which itself consists of two subsystems,
  a The **articulatory control system** or 'inner voice' which is a verbal rehearsal system with a time-based capacity. It holds information by articulating sub-vocally material we want to maintain or are preparing to speak.
  b The **phonological store** or 'inner ear' which holds speech in a phonological memory trace that lasts 1.5 to 2 seconds if it does not refresh itself via the articulatory control system. It can also receive information directly from the sensory register (echoic) from long term memory.
- **The visuospatial sketchpad** - or 'inner eye' which holds visual and spatial information from either the sensory register (iconic) or from long term memory.

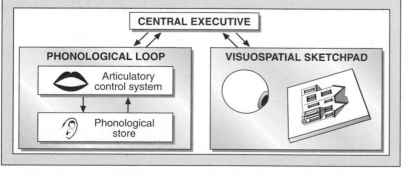

EVIDENCE

- The existence of separate systems in working memory has been shown experimentally by using concurrent tasks (performing two tasks at the same time) - if one task interferes with the other, then they are probably using the same component.
- Thus, if articulatory suppression (continually repeating a word) uses up the phonological loop, another task involving reading and checking a difficult text would be interfered with, but not a spatial task.

EVALUATION

- Working memory provides a more thorough explanation of storage and processing than the multi-store model's STM.
- It can be applied to reading, mental arithmetic and verbal reasoning.
- It explains many STM deficits shown by brain-damaged patients.
- However, the nature and role of the central executive is still unclear.

Organisation in memory

THE IMPORTANCE OF ORGANISATION

- Memory must be organised, considering the speed of access we have to a lifetime of stored data.
- Bousfield (1953) showed LTM spontaneously categorises information in his free recall studies. Subjects given 60 words **randomly** presented from 4 categories (e.g. names, vegetables, etc.), tended to recall those words in **clusters** of similar meaning.
- Bower et al (1969) found that material learnt in organised hierarchies was more easily recalled.
- Most research has focused on the organisation of semantic memory (e.g. factual knowledge).

HIERARCHICAL NETWORK MODEL

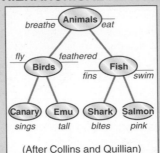

(After Collins and Quillian)

- Collins and Quillian suggested that knowledge was organised hierarchically - from general concepts to more specific ones.
- The model was tested by measuring reaction times to verify statements such as 'A canary can fly' and 'A canary can breath'. It took longer to verify the latter statement (a 2 level search) than the former (a 1 level search). This model cannot explain the typicality effect.

THE SPREADING ACTIVIATION MODEL

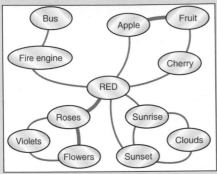

- Collins and Loftus (1975) overcame the typicality effect by abandoning the hierarchical structure.
- Speed of access depends on the distance between nodes and the strength of connection between them (often used links become stronger).
- The model seems to mimic the way neurones in the brain spread excitation to each other, but appears to explain rather than predict.

CONNECTIONIST NETWORKS

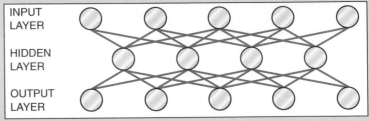

INPUT LAYER
HIDDEN LAYER
OUTPUT LAYER

- Parallel distributed processing or connectionist networks suggest that information is not stored in a single place but is organised in a **distributed** way over a **network** as a **pattern of activation** across many nodes (McClelland, 1981).
- Connectionist networks consist of layers of nodes that are intricately linked together. From an input layer, the nodes excite or inhibit each other in the hidden layers until the desired output pattern is reached - the network 'teaches' itself. The same network can store many different patterns using different combinations of the same nodes.
- As information about objects is distributed across many nodes, the system can function with imperfect knowledge or with a loss of some nodes to produce a 'best guess' (known as 'graceful degradation'). PDP networks can produce spontaneous generalisations and can infer information not provided through default assignments.
- Connectionist networks seem a more biologically realistic and productive way of explaining organisation in memory

SCHEMAS

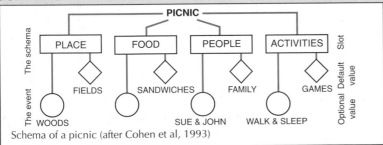

Schema of a picnic (after Cohen et al, 1993)

- Schemas are knowledge holding structures much **larger** and more **complex** than the nodes of the network models.
- Schemas are **active recognition devices** - they attempt to make sense of the world in terms of what is already known (Bartlett called this 'effort after meaning') and may therefore distort unfamiliar information to make it more understandable (e.g. Bartlett's War of the Ghosts story was recalled in a westernised way) or 'fill in' expected information (in the picnic schema above, if the food eaten at a particular picnic was forgotten, then it may be assumed that sandwiches were eaten by default).
- Brewer and Treyens (1981) tested memory for objects in an office that subjects had waited in for 35 seconds. **Expected** objects (e.g. a desk) that were in the room were recalled well but **unexpected** objects (e.g. a pair of pliers) were usually not. Some subjects **falsely** recalled **expected** objects that were not actually in the room (e.g. books and pens).

BIOLOGICAL THEORIES OF MEMORY ORGANISATION

- Biologically orientated researchers have argued that cognitive models of memory organisation overly ignore how these systems may be realised physically in the brain.
- Penfield (1955) activated vivid memories by electrical stimulation to the surface of the brain.
- Lashley (1950) tried and failed to localise the 'engram' (neural representation) of memory in the brain.
- Modern cognitive neuropsychology has discovered parts of the brain responsible for particular memory deficits, e.g. the hippocampus in anterograde amnesia, and PET scans have shown brain activity in specific locations when tasks are given to different components of working memory.
- McConnell (1962) has controversially proposed that memory could be stored in protein molecules and even transferred from one animal to another.

Retrieval

TYPES OF RETRIEVAL

There are many ways that information may be either retrieved from long term storage or demonstrate its existence in storage in a less direct manner. Some types are more powerful and accurate than others:

Recall - This involves the active searching of our memory with very few external memory cues, e.g. recalling a list of previously memorised digits or the timed essay situation (we have the question but have to search for the answer).

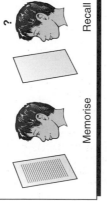

Memorise   Recall

Recognition - This involves a sense of familiarity with external material whether we can name/identify it or not, for example recognising a face or the correct answer in a multiple choice. In recognition, the material to be retrieved is matched to its external likeness. Recognition is an extremely powerful form of retrieval compared to recall - Standing (1973) showed that subjects in a memory test could correctly identify 10,000 previously presented photographs in recognition tests with very low error rates and little sign of an upper boundary for its capacity.

Subject shown picture   Later has to correctly identify original

Re-learning - This involves not necessarily being able to recall or even recognise previously presented material, but being better able to re-learn it on later occasions. Ebbinghaus investigated this type of retrieval and found that there were re-learning savings (it took less time to re-learn material perfectly the more times the list was re-learnt). An everyday example could be re-learning a language that you have not studied for years - you may be unable to recall or even recognise some of the words you had previously learnt, but it would take you less time to re-learn them compared to other, unexperienced words.

Reconstruction - This involves retrieval that has **distorted** the original information due to our interpretation of it - based upon our past experiences, beliefs, schemas and stereotypes. Bartlett's subjects not only remembered less of the 'War of the Ghosts' story he presented them, but distorted the story when retelling it by making it more coherent and westernised.

Confabulation - This involves the usually unintentional **manufacture** or invention of material to fill in missing details during retrieval. The material added often serves the purpose of making the story more coherent and is likely to occur under conditions of high motivation or emotion.

Redintegration - This is where patchy details of an experience will pop into consciousness regardless of what is currently thought about and gradually become more coherent.

PROBLEMS WITH RETRIEVAL (FORGETTING)

When considering theories of forgetting it is useful to distinguish between the concepts of availability and accessibility.

Availability of memory refers to whether the material is actually there to be retrieved - it is not possible to retrieve what has not reached/lasted in long term storage.

Accessibility of memory refers to the problems involved in retrieving available information - the tip of the tongue phenomena illustrates this type of difficulty.

There is however a **'grey area'** of ambiguity between these two concepts since we can never be 100% sure that what we have forgotten is unavailable - we may not have found the correct memory cue to 'jog our memory', and what cannot be directly recalled or recognised may still exist as a memory trace to aid re-learning.

FORGETTING

AVAILABILITY   GREY AREA   **ACCESSIBILITY**

Information not stored
Due to the **limited information processing** ability of human memory, material may not reach long term storage due to
- limited attentional **capacity** in sensory memory.
- limited capacity and, therefore, **displacement** in short term memory.

Information stored then permanently lost
Material may reach long term storage only to be lost there either rapidly due to
- **prevention of consolidation** where memory fixation is disrupted.
- Or over a longer time due to
- **trace decay** where memory traces gradually fade.

Information 'hidden'
Some experiences may be so traumatic and emotionally disturbing that according to Freud they may be **repressed** - deliberately hidden in the unconscious as a defence mechanism. Such memories are available but need psychoanalysis to access them.

Information awaiting a suitable prompt
Humans frequently experience problems accessing material through unaided recall but may benefit from external cues, as in
- **tip of the tongue phenomena** where a single letter may cue the word that is on the verge of recall
- **state/context dependent recall**

Interference

Permanent distortion/replacement

Amnesia

Permanent destruction of memory

Temporary confusion/bias

Temporary concussion

Forgetting - availability problems

MULTI-STORE MODEL INFORMATION PROCESSING LIMITATIONS

- The multi-store model can be thought of as a set of filtering mechanisms that reduce the vast amount of information received by the senses down to manageable and useful proportions. Thus, information not paid attention to in sensory memory will decay, while, due to the limited capacity of 7 plus or minus 2 items in the short term memory, any information not rehearsed or passed into long term memory will be displaced by new incoming material and will, therefore, be lost.

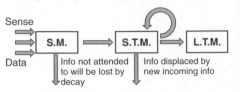

Sense

Data

S.M. → S.T.M. → L.T.M.

Info not attended to will be lost by decay

Info displaced by new incoming info

INSUFFICIENT INFORMATION PROCESSING

- According to the levels of processing model, if information is only processed at a shallow level (e.g. structural level) then the resulting memory is unlikely to persist for very long and will be forgotten.

INFORMATION STORED BUT THEN PERMANENTLY LOST

Material may reach long term storage but may then become unavailable either rapidly, because it has failed to be consolidated (i.e. permanently fixed in L.T.M.), or slowly, because that consolidated memory trace fades in strength over time.

PREVENTION OF CONSOLIDATION

- A number of researchers have demonstrated that a period of time is required for information to become permanently consolidated in the nervous system. It has been suggested that biochemical/structural changes in the nervous system occur, and that if these are disrupted during the consolidation time period then the information is lost.
- Disruption can be caused by concussion, brain surgery, electro-convulsive therapy (ECT) or some drugs, and leads to the loss of long term memory for the duration of the disruption.
- Yarnell and Lynch (1973) questioned American football players suffering from concussion about the events leading up to their injury:
  1 immediately after injury
  2 after 20 minutes.
  The players remembered if asked immediately, but could not after 20 minutes, since consolidation was disrupted.

What happened?

The big guy No 7. got me!

20 minutes later

I don't know!

What happened?

- Hudspeth et al (1964) identified the approximate amount of time that ECT disrupts consolidation for, by training subjects at different times before their shocks. Training was completely undisturbed if it took place one hour before treatment, but became increasingly disrupted the nearer it took place to the electric shocks.
- Dingman and Sporn (1963) prevented the consolidation in rats learning a water maze by injecting them with protein synthesis inhibitors and found no long term learning occurred while the drug was active.

TRACE DECAY

- A very popular but debatable concept in memory research has been the memory trace or engram - the neural representation of a memory. Decay or weakening of the memory trace has been applied to forgetting in both short and long term memory.
- Donald Hebb (1949) argued that trace decay only applied to short term memory, which he suggested might be the result of brief neural excitation between nerve cells, whereas long term memory would involve lasting structural changes.
- However, while research has indicated some role for decay in short term memory (Shallice, 1967), displacement seems to play a much larger role. Waugh and Norman (1965) used a serial probe technique to find out if presenting digits at faster speeds increased the ability to accurately recall information from short term memory. If trace decay was responsible for STM forgetting then faster presentation should lead to better recall since the information has less time to decay before being tested. Waugh and Norman found no relationship between speed and recall.
- Trace decay has been applied to long term memory too - decay through disuse - but anecdotal evidence of elderly people being able to ride bicycles after decades, or to remember previously forgotten incidents from their childhood seems to counter this idea.

Jenkins and Dallenbach (1924) found that more than decay was involved when they gave 2 groups nonsense syllables to learn. One group learnt them in the morning, the other at night before sleeping. When tested after 1, 2, 4 and 8 hours both groups recalled less but the day group had forgotten significantly more.

Group 1	Group 2
Learns	Learns
Active	Sleeps
Recalls less	Recalls more

Forgetting - accessibility problems

INFORMATION 'HIDDEN'

Many theorists have suggested that emotions can have a marked effect on our memories, in particular that negative or stressful experiences may actually be less well recalled.

FREUD AND MOTIVATED FORGETTING

- Freud proposed that forgetting is motivated by the desire to avoid displeasure. Unpleasant or anxiety producing experiences would, therefore, be repressed by the ego - pushed down into the unconscious.
- Repression of memory involves active blocking by the ego - direct recall attempts will either fail, lead to distorted recall or digression from the topic. Psychoanalytic techniques, such as dream interpretation, free association, etc., are necessary to access repressed memories.
- Experimental evidence is difficult to gather due to the ethical problems of probing for traumatic memories or creating them by exposing subjects to unpleasant experiences. The results of those studies that have been done show mixed findings, and where repression effects have been found, there has been debate over the cause - emotion can affect memory without the need for an ego.

EMOTION AND FORGETTING

- Lóftus and Burns (1982) showed two groups a film of a bank robbery, but exposed one of the groups to a far more violent version where a young boy was shot in the face. The group that saw this version later showed far poorer recall of detail than the control group.
- Freud would have suggested repression, but there are other ways in which negative emotions may cause forgetting. Loftus (1987) has demonstrated the weapons focus effect, whereby the fear provoking/stressful aspects of a scene channel attention towards the source of distress and away from other details.
- Alternatively, Holmes (1974) argues that anxiety produces a whole host of negative thoughts that interfere with recall, while Bower (1981) proposes a context explanation - people need to be in the same context (i.e. anxious) to recall properly.

INFORMATION AWAITING A PROMPT

Information may be available but temporarily inaccessible to recall, as the tip of the tongue phenomenon shows. Memory prompts may, therefore, be necessary to access information, such as being in the same context as the learning took place in.

THE TIP OF THE TONGUE PHENOMENA

- Brown and McNeill (1966) investigated the 'tip of the tongue' phenomena which they described as 'a state in which one cannot quite recall a familiar word but can recall words of similar form and meaning'. They induced this state several hundred times in undergraduate students by reading them definitions of infrequently encountered words, such as:

  'A navigational instrument used in measuring angular distances, especially the sun, moon and stars at sea'
  The answer word, 'sextant', occurs approximately once per million words.

- They found that the students could frequently identify some of the letters (usually the first or last), the number of syllables and even where the stress was in the word before they could completely recall it.
- Often similar sounding words were recalled such as 'secant' or 'sextet', or words with similar meanings such as 'protractor' or 'compass'.
- Brown and McNeill suggested this experiment has important implications for how verbal information is organised in long term memory.

CONTEXT DEPENDENT MEMORY

- Many researchers have investigated the idea that information apparently inaccessible under some circumstances can be retrieved if tested under the conditions in which it was learnt. Baddeley (1982) distinguishes between extrinsic and intrinsic contexts.

1 **Extrinsic context** refers to indirect cues, such as the physical state or environment present when material is learnt (***state-dependent memory***). Godden and Baddeley (1975) found, for example, that divers who had learned a list of words on land recalled them almost twice as well when tested on land than underwater, and vice versa for divers who learnt underwater. However, no effect was seen if a recognition test was used. Bower (1981) found that his subjects recalled more memories learnt when sad if he tested them when hypnotised to be in a sad mood than a happy one, and vice versa for happy memories. However, Bower's study has not been replicated, although state-dependent effects have been found for alcohol.

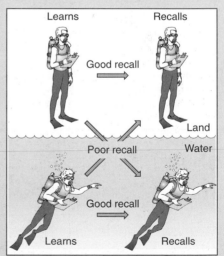

2 **Intrinsic context** refers to direct cues which are meaningfully related to the material to be remembered. This intrinsic context has been investigated by Tulving and Pearlstone (1966) who asked subjects to memorise lists of words from different categories. Those subjects who were given the category headings as retrieval cues recalled more of the words than those who were not. Tulving's ***encoding specificity principle*** proposes that any item committed to memory is encoded with the precise semantic context present at the time of learning. Thomson and Tulving (1970) confirmed this.

Forgetting - other problems

INTERFERENCE

- Another explanation of long term memory forgetting with age is that more and more material will be stored and confused over time. Research is divided, however, over the exact form that interference takes - whether information permanently distorts or replaces other information (an availability reason for forgetting) or whether the interference only confuses the recall rather than the original stored memories (an accessibility problem).

OLD MATERIAL	→ PROACTIVE INTERFERENCE →	NEW MATERIAL
	← RETROACTIVE INTERFERENCE ←	

TYPES OF INTERFERENCE

- **Proactive interference** is where material learnt first interferes with material learnt later (this is often the effect that stereotypes have on new information).
- **Retroactive interference** is where material learnt at a later time interferes with material learnt earlier.

RESEARCH ON INTERFERENCE EFFECTS

The major influences on the degree on interference are:

- **Similarity of information** - McGeoch and Macdonald (1931) presented subjects who had learnt a list of words with various types of interference list to learn for ten minutes afterwards. Recall of the original words was then tested and those students given an interference list of *similar meaning* words recalled on average far less (12.5%) than those given unrelated words (21.7%) or nonsense syllables (25.8%). Best recall (45%) was gained for subjects who were given no interference test at all.
- **Timing of information** - Underwood (1957) claimed information suffers most from retroactive interference if learning takes place soon after the original material. Proactive interference seems to have a stronger effect after a longer delay.

EVALUATION

- **Artificiality** - interference theory has declined in popularity as an explanation of forgetting because it has been mostly demonstrated with only meaningless word pairings under laboratory conditions. However, Anderson and Myrow (1971) have shown interference with meaningful material by reading students' descriptive passages.
- **Reason for interference** - Some believe interference occurs when information is unlearned (Underwood, 1957), or over-written (Loftus, 1979) by other information. Tulving, however, would argue that interference of retrieval cues rather than stored material is responsible. If recall of a list is tested on three separate occasions, different items may be recalled each time, probably because of the different cues in each test.

AMNESIA

- Trauma, either physical or psychological can profoundly affect memory. However, the type of retrieval failure shown (availability or accessibility) depends upon the reason for the amnesia. Even with severe physical damage, unavailability is not guaranteed.

TYPES OF AMNESIA

- **Retrograde amnesia** - where memory is lost for events *before* the trauma.
- **Anterograde amnesia** - where new long term memory is disrupted for events *after* the trauma.
- **Psychogenic amnesia** - amnesia caused by *psychological* trauma.

RESEARCH ON AMNESIA

- There are many possible causes of amnesia, including damage from head blows, strokes, disease, alcohol and ageing.
- Post mortem studies and now brain scanning technology have been used to locate the precise areas responsible for deficits in both working memory and long term memory.
- For example, cases of viral infection and surgical accidents have indicated that the temporal lobe and hippocampus are involved in anterograde amnesia.
- Alzheimer's disease and Korsakoff's syndrome (found in chronic alcoholics) both show more widespread damage to areas of the frontal and parietal cortex as well as the temporal, and lead to retrograde amnesia. Alzheimer patients also show short term memory deficits.

EVALUATION

- Cases of amnesia are still far from understood. For example, it was originally thought that damage to the hippocampus and temporal lobe produced anterograde amnesia because these structures were involved in laying down new long term semantic and episodic memory (what things mean and when things happened), but not procedural memory (how to do things).
- More recent research, however, has indicated that long term semantic memory *can* be acquired, but can only be retrieved implicitly rather than explicitly (it is not able to be *consciously* remembered). Graf et al (1984) found that amnesic patients shown a word list performed significantly worse than a control group when later given recall, recognition and cued recall tests. If the test involved completing word fragments (e.g. 'STR___') and writing down the first word they thought of (e.g. 'STRIP' or 'STRAP'), then amnesics were just as likely to use the words in the list as the control group.

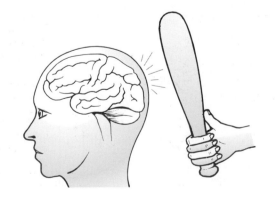

Practical applications of memory research – improving memory

RECOMMENDATION	RESEARCH BASED ON	EVALUATION
REPETITION • **Practice** makes perfect. The more times information is memorised, the more accurate the recall and the less time it takes to **re-learn** the material. Revise more than once!	• Ebbinghaus (1895) found re-learning savings - the greater the number of repetitions the less time it took to re-learn the lists. Since the majority of material was lost within the first day, perhaps the best time to test memory is after that time delay. Linton found that everyday memories last longer if they are occasionally remembered.	• Ebbinghaus only tested himself and used nonsense syllables. • Advertisers and psychologists have found that simple verbal repetition is not very effective. • Bekerian and Baddeley found that frequently repeated radio information did not produce strong memory.
ELABORATION • Information to be remembered should be made as **meaningful** as possible. New material will be remembered better if it is **integrated** with **existing** knowledge and if it is richly **associated** with other information.	• Craik and Tulving found deep semantic level processing increased recall. • Morris et al (1981) found that football fans recalled a list of football results far better than non football fans. The fans' interest and knowledge made the scores more meaningful and deeply processed. • Ley (1978) found patients remembered medical information better if they had existing background medical knowledge.	• Many mnemonic techniques work by creating associations with existing memories (the method of loci links items on a list to well known locations) or enriching associations (Bower (1972) found linking material with vivid visual imagery is especially effective). These methods involve extra learning.
MEMORY CUES • Often memorising cues or **memory jogs** will **help access** larger amounts of information. **Recreating** the **conditions** under which material was learnt can act as a trigger for memory.	• Tulving and Pearlstone (1966) found that cues such as category headings could improve recall of lists of words under those headings. • Godden and Baddeley (1975) showed how state or context could act as a powerful memory jog when testing diver's recall of material under water and on land.	• Mnemonic techniques such as acronyms (like ROY.G.BIV to stand for the colours in the spectrum) or the peg word system and method of loci work by providing memory cues. • Freudian free association may also jog repressed memories.
ORGANISATION • Information is better remembered if it is **presented** in a **structured** way. The structure may aid recall by **linking** infomation in a **meaningful** way, **grouping** or **ordering** material more **manageably** or by taking advantage of the mind's existing ways of **representing** knowledge (for example in semantic categories).	• Bousfield found in free recall studies that information is automatically organised in LTM in semantic clusters. Bower et al found higher recall for words organised in meaningful hierarchies. • Miller showed how the capacity of STM could be improved by organising/chunking information into larger meaningful units, while many studies have supported the primacy/recency effect where word order affects memory.	• Ley et al (1973) found presenting medical information in a structured way improved patient's recall by 25%. • In a later study Ley (1978) found that many patients remembered the first information received better (the primacy effect). This finding and others were included in an advice booklet for doctors, which improved patient's recall of medical information by 15%.
IMPROVING CONSOLIDATION • Memory can be improved by limiting disruption to it (e.g. through preventing interference or trauma) or by strengthening it (e.g. through the use of memory enhancing drugs).	• Jenkins and Dallenbach (1924) found memory was less disturbed if material was learnt before going to sleep, while McGeoch and MacDonald (1931) found interference effects were greatest if two sets of information were learnt close together in time and were similar. • Cameron et al (1963) has claimed that heavy doses of RNA can improve the memory of elderly people with memory difficulties, while a precursor of RNA, orotic acid, is commonly included in 'smart drugs'.	• Cameron's results were tainted by a lack of proper control data (perhaps memory improvement was due to a Hawthorne effect from the attention the elderly received) and replication failure. • While memory retention can be affected by drugs in laboratory animals, there is little evidence for smart drug effectiveness. • Caffeine may improve memory indirectly by increasing attention, or via a state dependent effect.

Practical applications of memory research - eyewitness testimony

NATURE OF EVENT

- **Stress** - Loftus and Burns (1982) showed subjects a film of a hold up. The experimental group saw a young boy shot in the face at the end and later showed significantly worse memory for 16 details they were asked to recall than the control group who saw a non violent end.
- **Content** - Certain aspects of an event will be more memorable than others, although this 'detail salience' often depends on the type of witness. Loftus et al (1987) found evidence for 'weapon focus' - memory for details is reduced if a weapon is present during an event, presumably because of its attention focusing properties.
- **Timing** - Events that take place very rapidly reduce the amount of detail recalled. The duration of events is usually overestimated.

NATURE OF WITNESS

- **Expectations** - the stereotypes and schemas of witnesses can profoundly affect their memory. Allport and Postman (1947) found that prejudice influenced the recall of whether a black or white person was holding a cut throat razor in a picture. Harris (1978) found that over 60% of subjects would infer information not present in testimony based on their expectations, even when trained not to. For example if given the testimony 'I ran up to the burglar alarm in the hall' many would later assert that the burglar alarm had been rung.
- **Type** - There are many individual differences that can influence testimony, including culture, age, gender, anxiety levels, and profession.
- **Confidence** - The confidence of a witness is not a good predictor of their accuracy.

FACTORS AFFECTING INPUT AND STORAGE OF MEMORY FOR EVENTS

EYEWITNESS TESTIMONY

FACTORS AFFECTING THE RETRIEVAL OF EYEWITNESS TESTIMONY

IDENTIFICATION TECHNIQUES

- **Identification parades** - false identification is most likely with small line ups and a failure to warn that the culprit may not be present (Wells, 1993).
- **Type of interview** - Open ended interviews give more accurate recall than structured questions.

HYPNOSIS

- Geiselman et al (1985) found interviews conducted under hypnosis produced a greater average number of correct responses (38) than a standard police interview (29.4).
- However, some argue that the use of hypnosis may lead to confabulation and false memory syndrome.

POST EVENT INFORMATION

Loftus has demonstrated how information received after the witnessed event (especially in the form of leading questions) can have a retroactive interference effect on the memory of that event. Information can be

- **added to an account** - Loftus and Zanni (1975) showed subjects a film of a car accident, and got more subjects to incorrectly recall seeing a broken headlight by asking 'did you see *the* broken headlight?' than asking 'did you see *a* broken headlight?'. Loftus (1975) even got subjects to recall seeing a non-existent barn in a picture by using a similar technique of adding post event information.
- **distorted** - Loftus and Palmer (1974) received higher estimates of speed when asking 'how fast were the cars going when they *smashed* into each other?' than when the verb '*hit*' was used.
- **substituted** - Loftus et al (1978) changed the recognition of a 'stop' sign to a 'yield' sign with misleading questions.

However, there are many debatable issues involved in this area:
- **Artificiality of results** - Yuille and Cutshall (1986) have demonstrated that real life eyewitness testimony can be very accurate.

- **Demand characteristics** - McCloskey and Zaragoza (1985) suggest that subjects may just be following the expectations to recall the (misleading) information that was last given to them. However, warnings that incorrect post event information has been given does not appear to stop incorrect information being recalled (Lindsay, 1990).
- **Degree of interference possible** - Loftus (1979) has shown that *obviously* incorrect post event information has little or no effect on accurate recall, interference is most likely to occur with minor details and if post event information is given after a long time delay.
- **Nature of interference** - Loftus (1979) is convinced that post event information replaces the original information - which cannot be recalled even if money is offered for accurate information. McCloskey and Zaragoza (1985) disagree - they showed that if subjects are given misleading information and are later offered a choice of the original or a neutral alternative, they tend to choose the original, indicating that the original material is not 'overwritten' or permanently distorted.

IMPLICATIONS OF EYEWITNESS TESTIMONY RESEARCH

- Advice should be given to jurors to warn them against convicting on the basis of a single eyewitness testimony alone, unless it is made under ideal circumstances or corroborated with other evidence.
- Interviewing techniques need to be improved. The Home Office now recommends that police interviews progress from free recall, to open ended questions to more specific questions to facilitate recall. Fisher et al (1987) have developed the 'enhanced cognitive interview' using techniques such as mental recreation of context, unstructured and perspective based recall, sensitivity to pace of the interview and the state of the interviewee, etc. These techniques have produced larger amounts of accurate information than standard police interviews under both laboratory and field conditions.

'Reconstruction of automobile destruction'
Loftus and Palmer (1974)

BACKGROUND

There is much support for the idea that most people, when they are witnesses to a complex event, such as a traffic accident, are very inaccurate when reporting numerical details like time, distance, and especially speed, even when they know that they will be questioned on them (e.g. Marshall, 1969). As a consequence, there can sometimes be large variations in estimates between witnesses and so it seems likely that such inaccurate testimony could easily be influenced by variables such as the phrasing of questions or 'leading' questions.

AIM

Loftus and Palmer, therefore, aimed to investigate the effect of leading questions on the accuracy of speed estimates in, and perceived consequences of, a car crash.

EXPERIMENT ONE

Subjects: 45 students, tested in groups of different sizes.
Design: Laboratory experiment.

Procedure:

7 films of traffic accidents, ranging in duration from 5 to 30 seconds, were presented in a random order to each group. After each film, the subjects had to give a general account of what they had just seen and then answer more specific questions about the accident. The critical question, 'About how fast were the cars going when they hit each other?' acted as the independent variable, since it was manipulated in five conditions. Nine subjects heard the sentence with the verb 'hit' in it, and then an equal number of the remaining subjects were asked the same question but with either the verb 'smashed', 'collided', 'bumped' and 'contacted' instead of 'hit'. The estimated speed was the dependent variable.

Results

Speed estimates for the verbs of experiment one		Significance of result	Accuracy of subjects' speed estimates		
Verb	Mean speed estimate	Results were significant at the P < .005 level, according to analysis of variance of the data.	In 4 of the 7 films the speed of the cars was known.		
				Actual speed of collision	Mean speed estimate
Smashed	40.8		Film 1	20 mph	37.7 mph
Collided	39.3		Film 2	30 mph	36.2 mph
Bumped	38.1		Film 3	40 mph	39.7 mph
Hit	34.0		Film 4	40 mph	36.1 mph
Contacted	31.8				

Discussion

The results indicate that not only are people poor judges of speed, but they are systematically and significantly affected by the wording of a question. However, this finding could be attributed to either response-bias (the subject remembers accurately but is pressured by the word to increase or decrease the estimate) or a genuine change in the subject's memory of the event (the word makes the subject recall the event as worse than it was). If the latter explanation is true, then the subject might be lead into recalling details that did not occur. This second experiment was designed to determine which explanation of different speed estimates was correct.

EXPERIMENT TWO

Subjects: 150 students, tested in groups of different sizes.
Design: Laboratory experiment.

Procedure:

A film lasting just less than a minute was presented to each group which featured four seconds of a multiple traffic accident. After the film, the subjects had to give a general account of what they had just seen and then answer more specific questions about the accident. The critical question concerning the speed of the cars was the independent variable, and it was manipulated by asking 50 subjects 'About how fast were the cars going when they hit each other?' another 50 'About how fast were the cars going when they smashed into each other?' and another 50 acted as a control group who were not asked the question at all. One week later the dependent variable was measured - without seeing the film again they answered ten questions, one of which was a critical one randomly positioned in amongst the ten questions, asking 'Did you see any broken glass? Yes or no?'. Although there was no broken glass it was expected that some might be seen if the leading question of a week ago had changed the memory of the event to seem worse than it was.

Results

Verb	Mean estimate	Response	Smashed	Hit	Control	Probability of seeing broken glass with speed estimate			
						Verb	1-5 mph	6-10 mph	11-15 mph	16-20 mph
Smashed	10.46 mph	Saw broken glass	16	7	6	Smashed	.09	.27	.41	.62
Hit	8.00 mph	Did not see glass	34	43	44	Hit	.06	.09	.25	.50

Discussion

The authors conclude that the results show that the verb 'smashed' not only increases the estimates of speed, but also the likelihood of seeing broken glass that was not present. This indicates that information from the original memory is merged with information after the fact, producing one distorted memory. This shift in memory representations in line with verbal cues has received support from other research.

EVALUATION

Methodological: A well operationalised and controlled experiment, but lacks the ecological validity of having real, involved witnesses.

Theoretical: The research supports the idea that memory is easily distorted and has implications for eyewitness testimony in court.

Links: Interference and forgetting in memory, practical applications of memory, laboratory experimentation.

Developmental Psychology

Early socialisation

Cognitive development

Later socialisation

Sociability in infancy

- Sociability in new-borns is the tendency to seek interaction with other human beings.
- Sociability functions to draw adults' attention as a pre-requisite for developing specific attachments to care-givers.
- Human babies seem innately geared to respond to humans and play an active role in social interactions with them. Such innate tendencies are shown in new-born's perceptual and communicative abilities.

SIGHT

- Fantz (1961) claimed that very young infants prefer looking at stimuli that resemble human faces and that this preference is probably innate.
- Despite much controversy over this conclusion, many different types of evidence support the idea that the human face does have a special significance for new-borns. Babies as young as 9 minutes old will look at a *moving* picture of a normal face more than a moving picture of a scrambled face; and the focal length of a new-born is 21 centimetres - roughly the distance between the faces of a parent and a child held naturally.

SMELL

- MacFarlane (1975) found ten day old babies preferred contact with a pad that had been in contact with their own mother's breast rather than another mother's breast.

SOUND

- Condon and Sander (1974) found that babies as young as 12 hours old would synchronise their body movements in time with human speech (in a similar way to adults) far more than with tapping sounds or just disconnected vowel sounds. While the reliability of their frame-by-frame microanalysis of sound films has been questioned, their study has received support.
- DeCasper and Fifer (1980) found that learning sensitivity to parental speech probably begins pre-natally. In their study, mothers read aloud the same story many times over the last 3 months of their pregnancy and one day after birth their babies sucked more on a teat to hear the sound of their mother's voice rather than that of a stranger.

SOCIAL TENDENCIES IN PERCEPTION

CRYING

- Wolff (1969) suggested that crying is an important form of early communication and that parents can usually distinguish between hunger, pain and anger cries. More recent research has even suggested that listeners can distinguish between the crying of normal babies and those at risk from developmental problems.
- Crying produces signs of physiological anxiety in listeners and even milk flow in mothers, and prompts parental action.

SOCIAL TENDENCIES IN COMMUNICATION

SMILING

- Ahrens (1954) claimed infants have an innate tendency to smile at features that resemble a human face. From the age of one month an infant will smile at just two eye dots on an oval shape, but as the infant gets older more accurate representations of a face are required to elicit the smile.
- Smiling does seem to be innate, since it occurs automatically without external stimulation, often during REM sleep, even in blind infants. True 'social' smiling (in response to another's smile), however, only starts at two and a half months of age, and becomes a major reinforcer for adult interaction and communication.

TURN-TAKING

- Trevarthen (1969) proposed that even very young infants show pre-linguistic 'turn-taking' interactions with their parents, stopping activity while the parent is speaking, and responding afterwards.
- Meltzoff and Moore (1977) found that interaction in the form of imitation of adult facial expressions could be shown by new-born babies, for example imitation of an adult sticking out a tongue occurred on approximately 31% of occasions. This finding has not always been replicated, however.

EVALUATION

There is some disagreement between researchers over the causes of children's sociability that reflects a nature-nurture debate in this area.

- On the nature side, researchers such as Trevarthen and Meltzoff have argued that infants are born with innate capabilities to socially interact with human beings in particular.
- On the nurture side, learning theorists would argue that any behaviour exhibited by an infant that the adult recognises (perhaps mistakenly) as resembling a social response is paid attention to and positively reinforced - leading to that behaviour being shown again. An action may not have any innate 'meaning', but by the adult attributing intention to a child's actions and acting appropriately, the child itself will eventually come to understand the meaning of its own behaviour. This view of social development is one proposed by Vygotsky.

Attachment in infancy

WHAT IS MEANT BY ATTACHMENT?
- An attachment is a strong, long lasting and close emotional bond between two people, which causes distress on separation from the attached individual.
- Psychologists have been particularly interested in the development of first attachments in infancy, since they appear to have important consequences for later healthy development, especially concerning later relationships.

HOW DOES IT DEVELOP?
Attachment in infancy occurs gradually over a sequence of phases:

- Pre-attachment phase — 0-3 months — Infant preference for humans over other objects is shown by preferential looking and social smiling.
- Indiscriminate attachment phase — 3-7 months — Infant can distinguish between people and allows strangers to handle it.
- Discriminate attachment phase — 7-9 months — Infant develops specific attachments to certain people and shows distress on separation from them. Avoidance or fear of strangers may be shown.
- Multiple attachment phase — 9 months onward — Infant becomes increasingly independent and forms other bonds despite the stronger prior attachments.

HOW DO WE KNOW AN ATTACHMENT HAS FORMED?
Attachment can be tested via the 'Strange Situation' method, developed by Ainsworth et al (1971), where the mother and child are taken to an unfamiliar room and subjected to range of timed, increasingly stressful (for an attached child) set of scenarios, such as
- a stranger is introduced to the child in the presence of the mother
- the mother leaves the infant with the stranger
- after the mother returns and re-settles the infant, it is left alone
- a stranger enters and interacts with the lone infant
- mother returns again and picks up baby

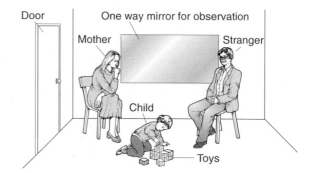

WHAT DIFFERENT KINDS OF ATTACHMENT ARE THERE?
Ainsworth et al (1978) discovered three main types of infant attachment using the Strange Situation, which occurred in various proportions:

Type A - Anxious-avoidant or **detached** (approximately 23% of sample)
The infant ignores the mother, is not affected by her parting or return, and, although distressed when alone, is easily comforted by strangers.

Type B - Securely attached (approximately 65% of sample)
The infant plays contentedly while the mother is there, is distressed by her parting, is relieved on her return, and, although not adverse to stranger contact, treats them differently from the mother.

Type C - Anxious-resistant or **ambivalent** (approximately 12% of sample)
The infant is discontented while with mother, playing less, is distressed by her parting, is not easily comforted on her return and may resist contact by mother and stranger.

WHAT CAUSES DIFFERENCES IN ATTACHMENT?
Parental sensitivity - Ainsworth et al (1978) suggested that secure attachment is dependent upon emotionally close and responsive mothering, whereas insecure attachments result from insensitive mothers. Although other factors are involved, the effects of maternal sensitivity have been supported.

Infant temperament - Researchers, such as Kagan (1982) suggest innate differences in infant temperament and anxiety may cause certain kinds of parental reaction and attachment.

Family circumstances - Attachment type may vary over time and setting with social and cultural environmental conditions, e.g. if a family undergoes stress (Vaughn et al, 1979).

Reliability of classification - Strange Situation methodology has been criticised and other attachment types proposed, e.g. type D.

THEORIES OF ATTACHMENT

PSYCHOANALYTIC
Freud believed that infants become attached to people who satisfy their need for food at the oral stage. Oral gratification causes drive reduction, which is experienced as pleasant. While Freud was right that attachment is important for later development, his drive theory and idea that attachment is due to food has not been supported.

LEARNING THEORY
Learning theory suggests that attachment should occur as parents become associated with pleasant stimuli, such as food and comfort, via classical conditioning. Harlow and Harlow (1969), however, showed that rhesus monkeys had an innate preference to form attachments to surrogate mothers who provide contact comfort rather than food.

ETHOLOGICAL
Bowlby (1951), influenced by ethological studies on imprinting, suggested infants were genetically programmed to form attachments to a single carer (the mother), within a critical time period. While Bowlby's ideas on attach-ment were important, research indicates that multiple attachments can be formed, within a sensitive time period according to Rutter (1981).

COGNITIVE
Schaffer (1971) points out that infants usually form attachments
- once they can reliably distinguish one care-giver from another.
- with the care-givers who stimulate and interact with them the most intensely.

Deprivation of attachment in infancy

BOWLBY'S MATERNAL DEPRIVATION HYPOTHESIS

Bowlby (1951) proposed that if infants were deprived of their mother (whom he regarded as their major attachment figure), during the critical period of attachment of the first few years of life, then a range of serious and permanent consequences for later development would follow. These included mental subnormality, delinquency, depression, affectionless psychopathy and even dwarfism.

Evidence for:
- Goldfarb (1943) studied children raised in institutions for most of the first three years of their lives, and found they later showed reduced IQ compared to a fostered control group.
- Bowlby (1946) studied 44 juvenile thieves and argued that their affectionless psychopathy was the result of maternal deprivation.
- Spitz and Wolf (1946) investigated infants in South American orphanages and found evidence for severe anaclitic depression in them.
- Harlow and Harlow (1962) researched the effects of social deprivation on rhesus monkeys. Deprived of an attachment figure, they interacted abnormally with other monkeys when they were eventually allowed to mix with them and were unable to form attachments to their own offspring after being artificially inseminated.

Evidence against:
- All the above studies had their methodological flaws, from failing to take into account the amount of environmental stimulation available in institutions, to generalising from animal studies.
- Rutter (1981), in 'Maternal Deprivation Reassessed', a thorough review of research in the area, concluded that Bowlby:
  1 was not correct in his ideas about monotropy (attachment to one figure only) or strict critical periods for attachment.
  2 failed to distinguish between the effects of deprivation (losing an attachment figure) and privation (never having formed an attachment).

POSSIBLE EFFECTS OF DEPRIVATION

SHORT TERM EFFECTS
- Symptoms of the 'Syndrome of Distress:
  1 Protest - the infant expresses their feelings of anger, fear, frustration, etc.
  2 Despair - the infant then shows apathy and signs of depression, avoiding others.
  3 Detachment - interaction with others resumes, but is superficial and shows no preferences between other people. Re-attachment is resisted.
- Temporary delay in intellectual development.

LONG TERM EFFECTS
- Symptoms of 'Separation Anxiety':
  1 Increased aggression.
  2 Increased clinging behaviour, possibly developing to the point of refusal to go to school.
  3 Increased detachment
  4 Psychosomatic disorders (e.g. skin and stomach reactions).
- Increased risk of depression as an adult (usually in reaction to death of an attachment figure).

EVALUATION

According to Rutter (1981), there are many sources of individual differences in vulnerability to the short and long term effects of deprivation, including:

- Characteristics of the child, e.g.
  1 Age - children are especially vulnerable between 7 months and 3 years (Maccoby, 1981).
  2 Gender - boys, on average, respond worse to separation than girls.
  3 Temperament - differences in temperament, like aggressiveness, may become exaggerated.

- Previous mother-child relationship - The infant's reaction to separation may depend upon the type of attachment, e.g. secure, anxious-resistant or anxious-avoidant (Ainsworth et al, 1978).

- Previous separation experience - Infants experienced in short term stays with (for example) relatives are more resistant to the effects of deprivation (Stacey et al, 1970).

- Attachments to others - Since Schaffer and Emerson (1964) revealed that multiple attachments are possible (in opposition to Bowlby's (1951) ideas), infants who are not deprived of all attachment figures manage the effects better.

- Quality of care - Research has revealed that both the short and long term effects of deprivation can be dramatically reduced by high quality care in crèches and institutions respectively.

- Type of separation - Some research has indicated that long term separation due to death or illness, if accompanied by harmonious social support, has less of a long term effect than separation due to divorce.

Privation of attachment in infancy

- According to Rutter (1981), the most serious long term consequences for healthy infant development appear to be due to privation - a lack of some kind - rather than to any type of deprivation/loss. However, in his review of the research, Rutter found that the many proposed adverse effects of privation were **not** always **directly** due to a lack of an emotional attachment bond, but often to a deficiency of other important things that an attachment figure may provide (e.g. food, stimulation or even family unity), but an orphanage or dysfunctional family may not.

MAJOR CONSEQUENCES OF PRIVATION AND THEIR PRECISE LIKELY CAUSES
Rutter (1981)

Intellectual retardation
Due to a deficiency of stimulation and necessary life experiences.

Developmental dwarfism
Due mainly to nutritional deficiencies in early childhood.

Affectionless psychopathy
Due to failure to develop attachments in infancy.

Anti-social behaviour/delinquency
Due to distorted intra-familial relationships, hostility, discord or lack of affection.

Enuresis
Bed-wetting is mainly associated with stress during the first six years.

MEDIATING FACTORS
Factors likely to affect the severity of privation effects include:
- **Type of childcare available** - orphanages, for example, which provide a high standard of care may reduce the effects of lack of stimulation or stress, but may still have a high turnover of staff that prevents attachments forming with the orphans.
- **The duration of the privation** - the longer the time delay before making an attachment, the greater the chance of failure to form an attachment and thus developing affectionless psychopathy. Although research unequivocally says that experiences at all ages have an impact it seems likely that the first few years do have a special importance for bond formation and social development.
- **Temperament and resilience of the child** - perhaps most importantly, there has been the repeated finding that many children are not excessively damaged by early privation, and that the effects of it can be reversed.

EVIDENCE FOR THE REVERSIBILITY OF PRIVATION EFFECTS

CASE STUDIES OF EXTREME PRIVATION
Freud and Dann (1951) studied six 3 year old orphans from a concentration camp who had not been able to form attachment to their parents. These children did not develop affectionless psychopathy, probably because they formed close attachments with each other (rather like the two twins raised in extreme privation studied by Koluchova, 1972), and despite developing a number of emotional problems, their intellectual recovery was unimpaired.

Such extreme case studies clearly involve many sources of privation, not just of attachment figures, but also indicate the strong resilience that children's development can show.

ISOLATED RHESUS MONKEYS
Novak and Harlow (1975) found that rhesus monkeys kept in social isolation from birth could develop reasonably normally if they were given 'therapy' by later being allowed to occasionally play with monkeys of their own age.

However, despite indicating the possibility of recovery from total social isolation, generalising the results from rhesus deprivation studies to human deprivation ignores the large differences between the two species.

ADOPTION STUDIES
Hodges and Tizard (1989) found that institutionalised children (who had not formed a stable attachment), adopted between the ages of two and seven, could form close attachments to their adoptive parents.

However, the children returned to their own families had more problems forming attachments and all the institutionalised children had problems with relationships outside their family.

Kadushin (1976) studied over 90 cases of late adoption, where the children were over five years old, and found highly successful outcomes, indicating that early privation does not necessarily prevent later attachment.

'Social and family relationships of ex-institutional adolescents' Hodges and Tizard (1989)

AIM

To investigate (longitudinally and with a matched comparison group of control children) whether experiencing early institutionalisation with ever-changing care-givers until at least two years of age will lead to long term problems in adolescence for adopted and restored children. Early studies by Bowlby (1951) and Goldfarb (1943a) found that there were many short and long term effects of the early institutionalisation of children, which were attributed to maternal deprivation or privation and were regarded as largely irreversible. However, later studies by Tizard and others on a group of adopted, fostered and restored children with early institutional experience showed that there were markedly less dramatic effects on intellectual and emotional development (probably due to improved conditions) but still difficulties in interpersonal relationships. The children were studied at age 4 and again at age 8, by which time the majority had formed close attachments to their parents, but showed, according to their teachers, more problems of attention seeking behaviour, disobedience, poor peer relationships and over-friendliness. The present study was conducted as a follow up study to see:

- If these children would continue to 'normalise' and lose further effects of early institutionalisation at age 16 or worsen with the stresses of adolescence.
- If adopted children would continue to do better than restored children by age 16, as earlier studies had indicated.

METHOD

Subjects:

All 51 children studied at age 8 were located, of which 42 were available to study at age 16. From these, 39 were interviewed: 23 adopted (17 boys, 6 girls), 11 restored (6 boys, 5 girls) and 5 in institutional care (3 boys, 2 girls). A comparison group of children who had not experienced institutionalisation was gathered for the **family** relationship study, matched, for example, in terms of age, gender, parental occupation and position in the family. Another comparison group of children who had not experienced institutionalisation was formed for the **school** relationship study from the classmate nearest in age of the same sex.

Procedure:

- The adolescents were interviewed on tape and completed the 'Questionnaire of Social Difficulty' (Lindsay and Lindsay, 1982).
- Mothers or careworkers were interviewed on tape and completed the 'A' scale questionnaire (Rutter et al, 1970).
- Teachers were asked to complete the 'B' scale questionnaire (Rutter et al, 1970) on the adolescent's behaviour.

RESULTS

- Institutionalised children differed in their degree of attachment to their parents in that
  a adopted children were **just as attached** to their parents as the comparison group
  b restored children were **less attached** to their parents than the comparison group and adopted children.
- Institutionalised children had **more problems** with siblings than the comparison group, especially the restored children.
- Adopted children were **more affectionate** with parents than restored children (who were less affectionate than the comparison group).
- No difference was found in confiding in, and support from, parents between institutionalised children and comparisons, although the former were less likely to turn to peers.
- Institutionalised children showed significantly worse peer relationships, were less likely to have a particular special friend, and were noted by teachers to be more quarrelsome and less liked by, and show more bullying of, other children.

EVALUATION

Methodological:

Longitudinal methods -	Many advantages and disadvantages, e.g. loss of subjects using this method.
Design -	Lack of control over this natural experiment, since children were obviously not randomly assigned to adoptive, restored and control groups, there always remains some doubt over the effect of the children's personality characteristics on the results.
Procedure -	Problems of self-report questionnaires and interviews as far as socially desirable answers or deception is involved on the subjects part, and experimenter expectation on the interviewer's part.
Data analysis -	A thorough statistical analysis was conducted on the results.
Ethical problems -	Of asking children and their guardians questions that might disrupt their interpersonal relationships, e.g. asking mothers if they loved all their children equally.

Theoretical: Implies that while Bowlby was wrong about many of the more dramatic effects of early institutionalisation, some long lasting effects on interpersonal relations do persist into adolescence. Further follow up study needs to be conducted to see if adolescent behaviours and feelings persist into adulthood, however. There are some important practical implications for adoption practices from this study.

Links: Child attachment, longitudinal studies.

Cross-cultural differences in child raising

CAUSES OF CROSS-CULTURAL DIFFERENCES IN CHILD RAISING

Cultural differences in child raising are usually due to either:

- **Environmental conditions**, e.g. during severe famines it is common for parents in some tribes in Uganda to either abandon their children or exchange them for money or food. Barry et al (1959) have found a correlation between child rearing practices and food accumulation.
- **Social norms**, e.g. the Mundugumor tribe of New Guinea studied by Mead (1935) treated their children with dislike and the Yanomamo of the Amazon studied by Chagnon (1968) produce aggressive children because of social norms of violent and warlike behaviour.

> **ENVIRONMENTAL AND CULTURAL INFLUENCES**
> ↓
> **PARENTAL STYLE OF CHILD-RAISING**
> ↓
> **CHILDREN'S ABILITIES AND BEHAVIOUR**

CROSS-CULTURAL DIFFERENCES DUE TO CHILD-REARING STYLES

ATTACHMENT

Using the Strange Situation method (Ainsworth et al, 1978), cross-cultural differences in types of attachment have been revealed.

	Type of attachment			Parental style
	Secure	Anxious-avoidant	Anxious-resistant	
U.S.A. Ainsworth et al (1978)	65%	23%	12%	Middle class American mothers with a tendency to spend a good deal of time interacting with their children at home.
ISRAEL (kibbutz) Sagi et al (1985)	37%	13%	50%	Children have contact with parents but mainly raised communally in a large group.
GERMANY Grossman et al (1985)	33%	49%	18%	A good deal of time spent with children at home but with a tendency to maintain a large interpersonal distance and wean offspring early from close contact.

However, according to Kagan et al (1978) there is a great deal of consistency across cultures (from Guatemalan Indians to African Bush People) in the onset of distress on separation from attachment figures (at around 7 months), as well as the onset of overcoming that distress (around 15 months). This possibly indicates the role of genetic influences underlying the effects of child-rearing techniques.

SOCIAL BEHAVIOUR

Independence - The raising of American children to be independent seems to start at birth. Whiting (1964) found that, unlike all the other cultures they investigated, babies in the USA do not usually sleep in the same bed or room as the parents. Harkness and Super (1992) suggest this difference in dependency is also reflected by the individualistic language that urban American parents use to describe their offspring's good points (e.g. intelligent, inquisitive) compared to the terms emphasised by rural Kenyans (e.g. dependable, respectful).

Social conduct - Goodnow et al (1984) found that in different cultures the parental expectations of appropriate social behaviour at different ages vary. Japanese mothers expect their children to be emotionally mature, compliant and polite earlier than American or Australian mothers, who in turn expect their children to be more socially skilled and verbally assertive at younger ages.

Whiting and Whiting (1975) revealed cross-cultural differences in parental punishment of aggression, although the effects of this punishment have been debated.

COGNITIVE ABILITIES

Cultural differences in child rearing influence children's cognitive abilities in many ways, e.g. by controlling the occurrence, frequency and acceptability of certain activities, as well as the responsibility given to the child (Feldman, 1994). Given the wide variation in stimulation received through different early child-rearing techniques, however, there is a remarkable degree of consistency in linguistic competence and intellectual development across cultures.

Language development - Schieffelin and Ochs (1983) found that while the parents of the Kaluli of Papua New Guinea rarely talk to their babies, their infants learn to speak their language to normal standards.

Intellectual abilities - Kagan et al (1980) found that infants of the Guatemalan Indians of San Marcos were kept inside their dark huts with little or no stimulation until they could walk. Although initially very quiet and intellectually retarded, they had become alert and bright by later childhood and had developed normal intelligence by adolescence.

Academic performance - Stevenson and Stigler (1992) found that the parental attitudes of American parents towards their children's education (such as not helping with homework or giving more house chores) seemed to be correlated with their offspring's poorer performance in reading and arithmetic compared to children in Taiwan and Japan.

EVALUATION

Cross-cultural studies on child-rearing are useful to shed light on the generalisability of western research in the area, the effects of alternative child raising techniques and the possible causes of those different techniques.

There is disagreement over exactly **how different** child-rearing methods are across cultures - Minturn and Lambert (1974) suggested that there are just as many differences **within** a culture in child rearing than between cultures, and different methodologies often reveal differing degrees of similarity.

Piaget's theory of cognitive development

Jean Piaget

- Jean Piaget, although a zoologist by training, was involved in the early development of intelligence tests. He became dissatisfied with the idea that intelligence was a fixed trait, and came to regard it as a process which developed over time due to biological maturation, and which adapted the child to its environment.
- Piaget was interested in the kind of mistakes that children make at different ages, thinking that these would reflect the cognitive progress they had made, and so spent many years studying children (especially his own) via the clinical interview method, informal experiments, and naturalistic observation.

Intellectual development occurs through <u>active interaction</u> with the world

Increased understanding only happens as the child actively interacts with and *discovers* the world, children do not passively receive their knowledge, they are *curious* and *self-motivated.*

Intellectual development occurs as a <u>process</u>

Piaget thought that children think in *qualitatively* different ways from the adult, we are not born with all our knowledge and understanding 'ready-made', but have to develop our intelligence in **stages**.

Individuals <u>construct</u> their understanding of the world

Through interaction, each individual has to **build** their own mental framework for understanding and interacting with their environment.

WHAT DOES THE CHILD BUILD?

HOW DOES THE CHILD BUILD?

SCHEMATA

A schema is an internal representation of a specific physical or mental action. It is a basic building block or unit of intelligent behaviour which enables the individual to interact with and understand the world. The infant is born with certain reflexive action schemata, such as sucking or gripping, and later acquires symbolic mental schemata. The schemata continue to develop and increase in their complexity and ability to let their owners function well in the world.

ASSIMILATION

This is the process whereby new objects, situations or ideas are understood in terms of the schemata the child already possesses. The world is 'fitted in' to what the child already knows.

ACCOMMODATION

This is the process whereby the existing schemata have to be modified to fit new situations, objects or information. The existing schemata are expanded or new ones are created.

OPERATIONS

In middle childhood, **operations** are acquired - these are higher order mental structures which enable the child to understand more complex rules about how the environment works. Operations are logical manipulations dealing with the relationships between schemata.

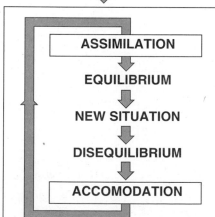

ASSIMILATION

EQUILIBRIUM

NEW SITUATION

DISEQUILIBRIUM

ACCOMODATION

A baby uses its innate feeding schema to suck on all nipples (mother's or baby bottle's).

The child can deal with the world.

The baby encounters a drinking beaker for the first time.

The baby's sucking schema is not appropriate - a big mess is made!

The baby has to modify its feeding schema so it can use all beakers (ie return to assimilation).

(Adapted from Gross, 1996)

Piaget's stages of cognitive development 1

Piaget proposed four stages of cognitive development which reflect the increasing sophistication of children's thought. Every child moves through the stages in a sequence dictated by biological maturation and interaction with the environment.

1 THE SENSORIMOTOR STAGE

(0 to 2 Years)

The infant only knows the world via its immediate senses and the actions it performs. The infant's lack of internal mental schemata is illustrated by;

- profound *egocentrism* - the infant cannot at first distinguish between itself and its environment.
- lack of *object permanence* - when the infant cannot see or act on objects, they cease to exist for the child.

Throughout this stage internal representations are gradually acquired until the **general symbolic function** allows both object permanence and language to occur.

Evidence for

Piaget investigated his children's lack of object permanence during this stage by hiding an object from them under a cover. At 0 to 5 months, an object visibly hidden will not be searched for, even if the child was reaching for it.
At 8 months the child will search for a completely hidden object.

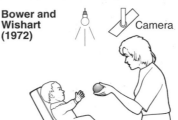

Bower and Wishart (1972)

Child offered object with lights on. Child begins to reach for object.

Evidence against

Bower and Wishart (1972) offered an object to babies aged between 1 to 4 months, and then turned off the lights as they were about to reach for it. When observed by infra-red camera, the babies were seen to continue reaching for the object despite not seeing it.
Bower (1977) tested month old babies who were shown a toy and then had a screen placed in front of it. The toy was secretly removed from behind the screen, and when the screen itself was taken away, Bower claimed that the babies showed surprise that the toy was not there.

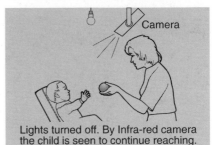

Lights turned off. By Infra-red camera the child is seen to continue reaching.

2 THE PRE-OPERATIONAL STAGE

(2 to 7 Years)

The child's internal mental world continues to develop, but

- is still **dominated by** the external world and the **appearance** of things.
- shows **centration** - the child only focuses on one aspect of an object or situation at a time.
- **lacks** the mental sophistication necessary to carry out logical **operations** on the world.

The pre-operational child, therefore, shows

- *class-inclusion problems* - difficulty in understanding the relationship between whole classes and sub-classes. The child focuses on the most visibly obvious classes and disregards less obvious ones.
- *egocentrism* - the difficulty of understanding that others do not see, think and feel things like you do.
- *lack of conservation* - the inability to realise that some things remain constant or unchanged despite changes in visible appearance. By only focusing on the most visible changes, the child fails to conserve a whole host of properties, such as number, liquid and substance.

Evidence for

Class-inclusion tests - if a child is shown a set of beads, most of which are brown but with a few white ones, and is asked 'are there more brown beads or more beads', the child will say more brown beads.

Piaget and Inhelder (1956) - demonstrated the egocentrism of pre-operational children with their 'Three Mountain Experiment'. Four year olds, when shown a mountain scene and tested to see if they could correctly describe it from different viewpoints, failed and tended to choose their own view. Six year olds were more aware of other viewpoints but still tended to choose the wrong one.

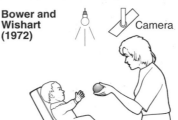

Three Mountain task — Doll — Child

Conservation experiments - Piaget tested for many different types of conservation. The child would fail in each case, since it lacked the necessary operations.

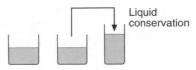

Liquid conservation

Evidence against

McGarrigle et al modified Piaget's class inclusion tasks to make them more understandable and appropriate. They first asked pre-operational children (with an average age of 6) a Piagetian type question - 'Are there more black cows or more cows?' They then turned all of the cows on their sides (as if asleep) and asked 'Are there more black cows or more sleeping cows?' The percentage of correct answers increased from 25% to 48%.

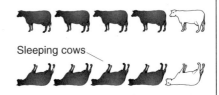

Sleeping cows

Hughes demonstrated that 3.5 to 5 year olds could de-centrate and overcome their egocentrism, if the task made more 'human sense' to them. When these children had to hide a boy doll from two policemen dolls (a task that required them to take into account the perspectives of others but had a good and understandable reason for doing so) they could do this successfully 90% of the time.

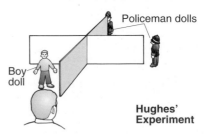

Policeman dolls
Boy doll
Hughes' Experiment

Piaget's stages of cognitive development 2

3 CONCRETE OPERATIONAL STAGE

(7 to 11 years)

At the concrete operational stage, the child's cognitive complexity allows it to

- carry out mental **operations** on the world - that is logical manipulations on the relationships between objects and situations. Two such operations are **compensation**, and **reversibility**.
- **de-centre** - that is more than one aspect of an object or situation can now be taken into account at the same time.

An important limitation on the child's thought at this stage, however, is that the mental operations cannot be carried out purely in the child's head - the physical (concrete) presence of the objects being manipulated is needed. Thus, although the conservation tests can be successfully completed, the child needs to see the transformation taking place.

Evidence for
Liquid conservation

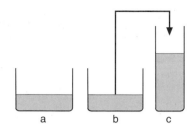

When liquid is poured from **b** to **c**, a concrete operational child can compensate for increasing height with decreasing width and can mentally reverse the pouring, therefore conserving liquid (realising that the amount of liquid remains the same).

Number conservation

When row **b** is spread out, the concrete operational child can realise that the number remains unchanged, despite the alteration in appearance.

Piaget conducted many tests of conservation on concrete operational children and found that their mental operations allowed them to think about problems in new ways.

Evidence against

McGarrigle and Donaldson (1974) Demonstrated that pre-operational children of between 4 to 6 years could successfully conserve if they were not mislead by demand characteristics into giving the wrong answer. McGarrigle and Donaldson therefore added an 'accidental transformation' condition where a 'naughty teddy' arrives and disarranges one of the rows. Under this condition more children (63%) could conserve number since the transformation was not meant to have been deliberately intended.

Row 1 ◯ ◯ ◯ ◯ ◯ Are there the same number?
Row 2 ● ● ● ● ● Answer = Yes

Naughty Teddy 'accidentally' disarranges row 2 to make it longer

◯ ◯ ◯ ◯ ◯ Are there the same number?
● ● ● ● ● Answer = Yes

4 FORMAL OPERATIONAL STAGE

(11 onwards)

At the formal operational stage, the child's mental structures are so developed and internalised that

- ideas can be manipulated in the head and reasoning/deductions can be carried out on verbal statements, without the aid of concrete examples.
- the individual can think about hypothetical problems and abstract concepts that they have never encountered before.
- the individual will approach problems in a systematic and organised way.

Evidence for
Transitive inference tasks -
the child can follow the abstract form of arguments, e.g.

if A > B > C, then A > C.

They can solve problems, such as 'Edith is fairer than Susan. Edith is darker than Lily. Who is the darkest?', *without* needing to use dolls or pictures to help them.

Deductive reasoning tasks -
problems, such as the pendulum task, where the child is given string and a set of weights and is asked to find out what determines the swing, are carried out logically and systematically.

Evidence against

Gladwin (1970) is one of many investigators who have questioned the appropriateness of Piagetian experimental tasks for testing non-western cognitive development. Often detailed investigation has found that formal operational thought has been acquired, but in a culturally specific manner. For example, the Pulawat navigators of Polynesia show complex formal operational thought when guiding their canoes at sea, yet will tend to fail standard western tests of cognitive development.

Evaluating Piaget's theory of cognitive development

THEORETICAL CRITICISMS

AGES

- Much research has seemingly demonstrated that children possess many of the cognitive abilities that Piaget outlined at ages much *earlier* than he expected.
- Often improving upon, or altering, the method of testing/assessing the child reveals their cognitive abilities better (see Bower, Hughes, McGarrigle, etc. below).
- In addition, Piaget seemed to have over-estimated people's formal operational ability - some research has even suggested that only one third of the population actually reach this stage.

CONCEPTS

- While Piaget's theory provides us with a detailed description of development, some have said that it does not really provide us with an explanation of it.
- Some of the concepts are vague, and the stages often show so much overlap (decalage) that development is perhaps better regarded as a *continuous process*.
- By focusing on the child's mistakes, Piaget may have over-looked important abilities that children do possess, or may have wrongly deduced the reason for their failure.

NEGLECTS

- Piaget neglected many important **cognitive** factors that could have accounted for the *individual differences* in development that children show, such as *memory* span, motivation, impulsiveness, practice, etc.
- Overall, in many researchers' view (e.g. Bruner, Light, etc.), he severely underestimated *social influences* on development. By concentrating on individual maturation and *self* construction of mental life, Piaget neglected
  a the role of society in facilitating and providing increased understanding,
  b the child's understanding of social situations (especially in Piaget's experimental situations), and
  c children's ability in and use of language at different ages.

METHODOLOGICAL CRITICISMS

INAPPROPRIATE TESTS

- A frequent criticism is that Piaget's experiments were *over-complicated* and *difficult to relate to*.
- By simplifying the tasks and ensuring that they made what Donaldson has termed 'human sense', researchers such as Bower and Wishart (1972) (with their object permanence experiment), and Hughes (1975) (with his 'Policeman Doll' experiment) have demonstrated cognitive abilities in children who would not be expected to show them.

DEMAND CHARACTERISTICS

- Even in fairly uncomplicated tasks, Piaget's experiments *ignored* the child's *social understanding* of the test, and may have led the child to give a socially desirable or expected answer instead of what the child really thought and understood.
- McGarrigle and Donaldson (1974) with their 'Naughty Teddy' Experiment, and Rose and Blank (1974) with their one question variation, both demonstrated significantly greater conservation rates in pre-operational children.

OVERALL METHODS

- Piaget's use of the clinical interview method, informal experimentation, and small sample sizes, *lacked scientific rigour*.
- Although these methods had their advantages, the generalised conclusions drawn from them may have been somewhat biased.

STRENGTHS

THEORETICAL IMPORTANCE

- Piaget's theory has received a lot of longitudinal, cross-sectional and cross-cultural *support* over many years, and while the theory has been subject to modification and criticism, many fundamental aspects of his theory are still accepted as valid contributions today.
- Many psychologists have taken Piaget's ideas far more rigidly than they were intended. Piaget modified his theory to take into account certain criticisms and hoped that one day it could be integrated with other theories that dealt with aspects of children's internal life that he had ignored (for example Freud's theory of emotional and personality development).

PRODUCTIVITY

- Piaget's ideas *generated* a huge amount of critical *research* which has vastly increased our understanding of cognitive development.
- Bruner and more socially orientated theorists have used Piaget's views as a 'spring board' to develop their own and to answer many of the issues raised by Piaget's research.

APPLICATIONS

- Piaget's views have had an important impact on *educational* practice - changing the way children are taught today and hopefully making education more effective and enjoyable.
- Piaget has also contributed to psychological theories of children's play and moral development.

'Asking only one question in the conservation experiment' Samuel and Bryant (1984)

AIM

To support, using a more detailed procedure and a wider age range of subjects, Rose and Blank's experimental criticism of Piaget's conservation studies. Piaget and Szeminska (1952) found pre-operational children (below the age of seven) could not conserve (realise that some properties, such as number, volume, and mass, remain the same despite changes in their physical appearance) by conducting experiments, whereby:

1 They showed 2 rows of counters and asked a pre-transformation question 'are there the same number in each row?' The answer was usually '**yes**'.

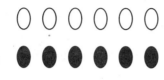

2 They then lengthened one of the rows and asked the (same) post-transformation question 'are there the same number in each row?' The answer given was then usually '**no**'.

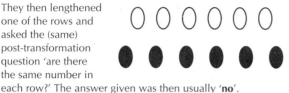

Piaget took the 'no' answer to mean that the children thought there were now a greater number of counters in the lengthened row and that these children could not conserve. However, Rose and Blank (1974) disagreed with this conclusion. They argued that Piaget had made a methodological error by imposing **demand characteristics** - when an adult deliberately changes something and asks the same question twice, children think that a different answer is **expected**, even though they may well be able to conserve. Rose and Blank (1974) conducted a study where they only asked one question (the post transformation one) to reduce these misleading expectations, and found that more children were able to conserve when they only had to make one judgement than when they had to make two in the standard Piagetian presentation.

Samuel and Bryant (1984) wanted to replicate this study on a larger scale using
• four age groups (5, 6, 7 and 8 year olds),
• three types of conservation test (number, mass, and liquid volume), and
• three ways of presenting the tests (standard Piagetian way, one judgement/question way, and fixed array with no visible transformation).

METHOD

Subjects: Independent measures design was used. 252 boys and girls were divided into 4 age groups (of 5, 6, 7 and 8 year olds).

Procedure: In each age group every child was tested 4 times each for conservation of number, mass, and liquid volume in one of three ways:

• The standard Piagetian way: (asking the pre- and post-transformation questions)

• The one judgement way: (asking only the post-transformation question)

• The fixed array way: (asking only the post-transformation question, ***without seeing*** the transformation)

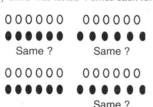

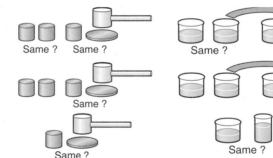

In all three methods of presentation, the 12 conservation tests each child experienced were systematically varied to prevent order effects. Two different versions of each type of conservation test were given to ensure the child could show a proper understanding of the concepts involved.

RESULTS

Mixed design analysis of variance and Newman-Kreuls tests showed that
• Children were significantly more able to conserve in the one judgement task.
  This supports Rose and Blank's (1974) experiment and criticism of Piaget's methods.
• Older children did significantly better than younger children in conservation.
  This supports Piaget's theory of cognitive development in general.
• The conservation of number task was significantly easier than the other tasks.
  Indicating support for Piaget's notion of decalage.

MEAN ERRORS OUT OF 12 CONSERVATION TESTS

Age	Standard	One judgement	Fixed Array
5	8.5	7.3	8.6
6	5.7	4.3	6.4
7	3.2	2.6	4.9
8	1.7	1.3	3.3

EVALUATION

Methodological: *Good methods* - The study used a control group, different tests of conservation, and different aged subjects.
Good data analysis - The data was extensively analysed to reveal its significance.

Theoretical: *Implications* - The study supports some of Piaget's notions and some of those of his critics.

Links: Child cognitive development. Research methods – demand characteristics.

Piaget and education

APPLICATIONS OF PIAGET'S THEORY TO EDUCATION
Piaget himself did not apply his theory to the classroom, and most of the following recommendations are what other researchers have proposed, based on Piagetian principles. Overall, Piaget's theory has applications for *when* and *how* to teach.

WHEN TO TEACH
- Because of Piaget's ideas on biological maturation and stages, the notion of '**readiness**' is important - children show qualitatively different kinds of thinking compared to adults, and should not be taught certain concepts until their underlying cognitive development has progressed far enough.

HOW TO TEACH
- Because of Piaget's emphasis on the individual child's self-construction of its cognitive development, education should be *student centred* and accomplished through **active discovery learning**.

CURRICULUM IMPLICATIONS
- Some researchers have suggested that, because of the notion of readiness, certain concepts should be taught before others or even in a specific *order;* for example conservation of number, followed by conservation of weight, followed by conservation of volume.
- New knowledge should be *built on pre-existing schemas*, which should be expanded through accommodation. Concrete operational children should, therefore, start with concrete examples before progressing onto more abstract tasks - an approach that has been adopted by the Nuffield Science curriculum.
- However, there should be a *balance* between accommodation (learning new concepts) and assimilation (practising and utilising those concepts).

THE ROLE OF THE TEACHER
- The role of the teacher in the Piagetian classroom is as a *facilitator*. Teachers should be involved in the indirect imparting of knowledge, not direct tuition, and should, therefore

  1 focus on the *process* of learning, rather than the end product of it.

  2 assess the *level* of the child's development, so suitable tasks can be set.

  3 choose tasks that are *self-motivating* for the child, to engage its interest and further its own development.

  4 set tasks that are *challenging* enough to put the child into *disequilibrium,* so it can accommodate and create new schemas.

  5 introduce abstract or formal operational tasks through *concrete* examples.

  6 encourage *active interaction* not just with task materials but with other children. In small group work children can learn from each other.

LIMITATIONS ON PROGRESS
- Piaget proposed that cognitive development could *not* be speeded up, because of its dependence on biological maturation.
- Piaget disagreed with Bruner over the ability of *language training* to advance cognitive reasoning, and studies by Sinclair-de-Zwart seem to support Piaget's view - pre-operational children were given training in the use of comparative terms, such 'long', 'short', 'thin' and 'fat', to help accelerate their ability to pass conservation tests. The training *failed* to improve their ability, presumably because the words were just verbal labels that could not be related to the necessary underlying concepts involved in conservation (they lacked the necessary operations, in Piaget's view).

CRITICISMS
- Criticisms of Piaget's applications to education have been made, both of the notion of readiness and discovery learning.
- Meadows (1988), in her review of the research, finds that 'the behaviours typical of different stages... can certainly be accelerated by training... Contrary to the predictions of the Piagetian account, training does produce improvement in performance which can be considerable, long-lasting and pervasive. A variety of training methods have been seen to succeed'.
- Brainerd (1983) has concluded that while 'self-discovery training can produce learning, it is generally *less* effective than tutorial training'.

Vygotsky's theory of cognitive development

VYGOTSKY'S APPROACH
- Vygotsky was a Russian psychologist whose ideas on cognitive development were very similar to Bruner's. Vygotsky focused on the importance of *social interaction* and *language* as major influences on children's development of understanding.

SOCIAL INTERACTION
- Vygotsky sees the whole process of cognitive development as being social in nature - *'we become ourselves through others'*.
- At first the child responds to the world only through its actions, but society provides the *meaning* of those actions through social interaction.
- Vygotsky illustrates this with the example of pointing - the child may reach towards an object and fail to grasp it, but the parent will *interpret* this as a pointing gesture.
- 'The original meaning to this unsuccessful grasping movement is thus imparted by others. And only afterwards, on the basis of the fact that the child associates the unsuccessful grasping movement with the entire objective situation, does the child himself begin to treat the movement as a pointing gesture. Here the function of the movement itself changes: from a movement directed towards an object, it becomes a movement directed towards another person, a means of communication, the grasping is transformed into pointing.' Vygotsky (1978)

INTERNALISATION AND LANGUAGE
- Cognitive development, therefore, proceeds, according to Vygotsky, as the child gradually *internalises* the meanings provided by these social interactions. The child's thinking and reasoning abilities are at first primitive, crude and do not involve the use of language, and so the greatest advance comes when we internalise *language*.
- Speech starts off as communication behaviour that produces changes in others, but when language becomes internalised, it converges with thought - *'thought becomes verbal and speech rational'* Vygotsky (1962). Language allows us to 'turn around and reflect on our thoughts' - directing and *controlling* our thinking, as well as communicating our thoughts to others.
- Eventually, language splits between these two functions as we develop an abbreviated inner voice for thinking with, and a more articulate vocabulary for communicating with others. Internal language vastly increases our powers of problem solving.

ZONE OF PROXIMAL DEVELOPMENT
- Because cognitive development is achieved by the *joint* construction of knowledge between the child and society, it follows that any one child's potential intellectual ability is greater if working in *conjunction* with a more expert person other than alone. Vygotsky defines the *zone of proximal development* (ZPD) as

'the distance between the actual developmental level as determined by individual problem solving and the level of potential development as determined through problem solving under adult guidance or in collaboration with more capable peers. The zone of proximal development defines those functions that have not yet matured but are in the process of maturation, functions that will mature tomorrow but are currently in an embryonic state. These functions could be termed the "buds" or "flowers" of development rather than the "fruits" of development'.

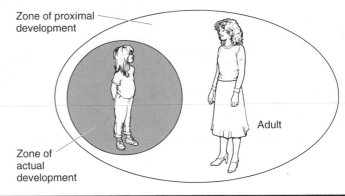

Zone of proximal development

Zone of actual development

Adult

VYGOTSKY AND EDUCATION
- Tharp and Gallimore (1988) propose the following definition of teaching according to Vygotsky's ideas *'Teaching consists in assisting performance through the ZPD. Teaching can be said to occur when assistance is offered at points in the ZPD at which performance requires assistance'* and go on to quote Vygotsky (1956) who said that teaching was only good when it *'awakens and rouses to life those functions which are in a stage of maturing, which lie in the zone of proximal development'.*
- Teachers should assist performance by working sensitively and *contingently* within the ZPD. Bruner developed this idea of contingency (responding appropriately and flexibly to the child's individual needs only when required) in his own work, and Wood and Middleton (1975) have investigated contingency by watching mothers help their children build a puzzle. The mothers showed contingency by offering different levels of help depending on how much difficulty the child was having.

Bruner's theory of cognitive development 1

Jerome Bruner was a cognitive scientist who provided valuable contributions to our understanding of cognitive development and its application to education. He agreed with Piaget that through active interaction with the world, the child could increase its underlying cognitive capacity to understand the world in more complex ways. Bruner differed from Piaget, however, in that he
- was more concerned with *how* knowledge was *represented* and organised as the child developed, and therefore proposed different *modes* of representation.
- emphasised the importance of *social* factors in cognitive development, in particular the role of language, social interaction and experience, which could pull the child towards better understanding.

MODES OF REPRESENTATION
- Bruner's theory is concerned with *ways* of *representing* or thinking about knowledge at different ages, not stages as such. Bruner proposed *three modes* of representation that develop in order and allow the child to think about the world in more sophisticated ways, but all exist in the adult (we do not lose these ways of thinking like in Piaget's stages).
- The modes are the enactive (0 to 1 years), iconic (1 to 6 years), and symbolic (7 years onwards).

THE ENACTIVE MODE
- This mode of representation is dominant in babies, who first *represent* or understand the world through their *actions*.
- Knowledge is, therefore, stored in *'muscle memory'* - for example, a baby may continue to move its arm to shake a rattle, even if the rattle has been visibly removed, since, for the baby, it was the action of the arm that caused the noise rather than the rattle itself.
- Similarly, when we learn to walk or ride a bicycle, knowledge is represented in our enactive mode - we cannot learn to ride based on people showing or telling us what to do.
- Bruner also points out that certain patients with temporal and occipital cortex brain damage can often not identify objects such as an egg by vision but must perform some kind of appropriate action, such as breaking and peeling it before they can name it.

THE ICONIC MODE
- This mode represents knowledge through visual or auditory *likenesses*, *images* or icons.
- Once a baby can represent the aforementioned rattle as a visual image in its iconic mode, the rattle can exist independently from its actions - the baby will have acquired what Piaget would have called object permanence.
- Once children are dominated by their iconic mode (from around 1 to 7 years of age) they can represent fairly large amounts of information - if you were asked how many windows you have in your house, you would probably summon up a visual image of your house to count them, but that image could be used to answer other questions too.
- However, children dominated by their iconic mode have *difficulty* thinking beyond the images, to categorise the knowledge or understand relationships between objects.

THE SYMBOLIC MODE
- This mode enables children to encode the world in term of information storing symbols, such as the *words* of our language or the numbers of mathematics.
- This allows information to be *categorised* and summarised so that it can be more readily *manipulated* and considered - the word 'furniture' allows us to think about and discuss the concept without having to imagine any or all of the different tables, chairs, sofas, etc. that we have experienced, or even to consider as yet unexperienced items of furniture. Numbers can also be used as abstract symbols, so we can perform calculations without being tied to physical amounts.
- The symbolic mode allows children to think beyond physical images and its superiority over the iconic mode has been demonstrated by Bruner and Kenney (1966).
- Bruner also investigated how information categorised by language can be better *organised* into *hierarchies*.

BRUNER AND KENNEY'S (1966) TRANSPOSITION TASK

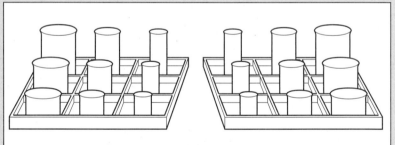

Reproduction task   Transposition task

- Five to seven year old children were familiarised with the position of nine plastic containers placed on a 3 x 3 grid. The containers were then scrambled and the children had to put them back in the original position (the reproduction task). Next the smallest and thinnest container was moved to an opposite corner, and the children were asked to 'make something like what was there before' (the transposition task).
- All children could perform the reproduction task fairly well. However, only the 7 year olds could perform the transposition task adequately. It appeared that the five year olds were dominated by the original image (their iconic mode), whereas the older children could translate the display into verbal rules (their symbolic mode), e.g. 'It gets taller going back and fatter going sideways' and could use these rules in the new ways.

Bruner's theory of cognitive development 2

THE ROLE OF LANGUAGE AND EDUCATION

Bruner stressed education and social interaction as the major motivators of cognitive development, and, in particular, proposed that society provides our language which gives us symbolic thought. Unlike Piaget, who thought that language was merely a useful tool which reflects and describes the underlying symbolic cognitive structures such as operations, Bruner believed that language *is* symbolic/logical/operational thought - the two are inseparable. According to Bruner, therefore, **language training** *can* speed up cognitive development, a suggestion that Piaget's theory rejects (since he believed that cognitive structures could only be developed through the child's individual maturation and interaction with the world).

LANGUAGE ACCELERATING DEVELOPMENT

- Francoise Frank (reported by Bruner, 1964) showed how the ability of pre-operational children to give the correct answer in liquid conservation tasks could be improved if they were encouraged to use and rely upon their linguistic descriptions (i.e. their symbolic mode) of the task.
- Frank reduced the visual (iconic mode) effect of the conservation changes by screening most of the beakers during the experiment. Once the children were less dominated by their iconic mode, they could concentrate on their verbal (symbolic mode) descriptions of what was happening, and were more able to conserve.
- Once the 5 and 6 year olds had used their language to solve the conservation task, they showed an increased ability to pass other non-screened conservation tasks. 5 year olds showed an increase from 20 to 70%.
  6-7 year olds increased from 50 to 90%.

Step 1 Show standard beakers with equal water and a wider beaker of the same height.

Step 2 Screen the beakers so the water level is hidden, but mark the level of the water on screen.

Step 3 Pour water from the standard beaker into the screened wider beaker.

Step 4 Ask the child, without it seeing the water 'which has more to drink or do they have the same?'
Result - in comparison with an unscreened pre-test there is an increase in correct answers:
4 year olds - increase from 0% to 50%
5 year olds - increase from 20% to 90%
6 year olds - increase from 50% to 100%
Children justify their response linguistically by saying for example 'You only poured it'.

Step 5 The screen is removed and:
4 year olds - all revert to pre-test answer of less water in the wider beaker, overwhelmed by the appearance of the water (iconic mode).
5-6 year olds - virtually all stick to the right answer, relying on their previous verbal justification (symbolic mode) 'You only poured it from there to there'.

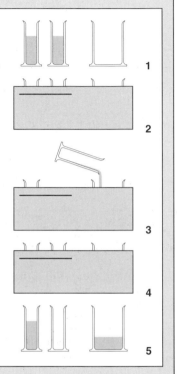

Sonstroem et al (1966) encouraged children who failed conservation of substance tests to use all of their modes of representation to increase their ability to conserve. The children who rolled the plasticine into a ball themselves (iconic mode) while watching their own actions (iconic mode) and verbally describing what was happening, e.g. 'it's getting longer but thinner' (symbolic mode) showed the greatest improvement in conservation.

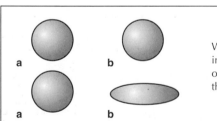

When the ball 'b' is rolled into a sausage, pre-operational children think there is more plasticine.

BRUNER AND APPLICATIONS TO EDUCATION

- Unlike Piaget who saw the role of the teacher merely as a facilitator for the child's own developmental maturation, Bruner argued that the teacher should **actively intervene** to help the child construct new schemas - instruction *is* an important part of the learning process. The teacher or 'more knowledgeable other' provides the 'tools' or 'loan of consciousness' required for the child to develop cognitively by providing structure, direction , guidance and support, not just facts.

Structure and direction

- Bruner proposed the **'spiral curriculum'** - material should be structured so that complex ideas can be presented at simplified levels first and then *re-visited* at more complex levels later on.
- Children should be made aware of the structure and direction of the subjects they study, and progression should proceed via an *active problem solving* process.

Guidance and support

- Bruner developed the idea of **'scaffolding'** - a kind of hypothetical support structure around the child's progression though a topic. The scaffolding allows the child to climb to the higher levels of development in manageable amounts by
  1 reducing degrees of freedom (simplifying the tasks)
  2 direction maintenance (motivating and encouraging the child)
  3 marking critical features (highlighting relevant parts or errors)
  4 demonstration (providing model examples for imitation)

The information processing approach to cognitive development

ASSUMPTIONS

- The information processing approach to cognitive development is a recent approach that aims to apply experimental cognitive psychological research from a number of areas, such as attention, perception and memory, to explain children's development of understanding.
- In the usual cognitive psychological style, children's minds can be regarded as computers that gradually develop in their ability to process information - to receive it, store it and use it appropriately. Just as the efficiency of a computer depends upon the speed of its processor, the amount of RAM it has to manipulate information at any one time and the sophistication of its software programs, so young children will, at first possess similar limited information processing abilities.

PROCESSING SPEED

- Young children are actually physically slower at transmitting information along neurones - as the brain matures, nerve fibres become myelinised and can transmit their electrical messages faster, thereby increasing their processing speed.

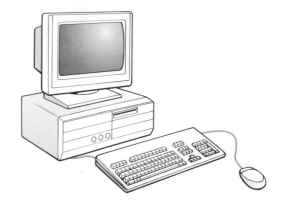

Siegler's (1978) balance beam tests show how children's ability to solve problems is directly related to the number of aspects of a problem they could recognise and combine at the same time. (Processing skill is needed to identify the aspects of the problem, processing capacity is needed to combine them at the same time).

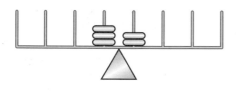

Five year olds only look at the weight. They can decide which way this balance will tip.

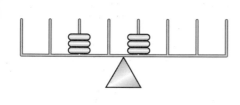

Nine year olds solve the problem by looking at weight, but if weight is equal they can take into account distance.

Thirteen to seventeen year olds can take into account the interaction of both weight and distance in making their decision.

PROCESSING CAPACITY

- Case (1992) proposes that young children have a limited 'mental space' or working/short term memory with which to hold and think about information - thus making it difficult to take into account more than one aspect of a problem at a time (Piaget called this centration, and argued that it led to conservation errors). As the child grows older, 'mental space' increases as
  a neural processing speeds up and
  b strategies for processing information become more automatic with practice and, therefore, need less conscious attention - thus freeing up 'mental space' for other work (rather like experienced drivers being more able to concentrate on other tasks while driving when their driving skills become automatic through practice).

Evidence

- Tests on short term memory capacity support the idea that processing capacity increases with age - people's ability to recall digits after hearing them just once improves with age (adults can recall around seven, plus or minus two).

PROCESSING SKILLS

- As the child grows and gains experience in the world, its skills for processing information (organising, categorising and problem solving) develop, becoming faster, more complex and flexible. More efficient strategies can be used, such as chunking and organising information, to improve short or long term memory, and heuristics or 'rules of thumb' enable problems to be solved more quickly.
- Fischer (1980) has developed a theory that shows how skills develop and, like many other researchers in the area, argues that different children will develop particular skills or talents in different 'domains' of ability depending upon their environmental experience. Domain skills may not be entirely dependent on environmental stimulation, however, since Baron-Cohen (1990, 1995) proposes that autism, now widely held to be a congenital disorder, is due to a lack of 'theory of mind' - the domain of mental representation and social understanding.

Evidence

- Chi (1978) found that children skilled at chess could remember patterns of chess configurations better than adults who were inexperienced at chess, indicating that domain skill rather than general capability was most important. In computer terms a more efficient program on a less powerful machine was more efficient.

The development of IQ test performance - nature approach

EVIDENCE FOR GENETIC CAUSES	EVALUATION

SELECTIVE BREEDING STUDIES

- Thompson (1952) selected rats that were 'maze-bright' or 'maze dull' by timing how long they took to negotiate a maze. By selectively breeding the two types of rats (only letting them breed with rats from their own group) Thompson found that the maze learning differences between the offspring of the maze-bright and maze-dull rats increased with the number of generations, until, by the sixth generation, the bright rats made approximately 80% fewer mistakes than the dull rats.
- Henderson (1970) found that the ability of rats to negotiate obstacles to find food would not always improve if their environmental conditions were enriched (as nurture orientated theorists would predict). However, the fact that some of the rats did show some improvement, indicates at least some interaction between genetic abilities and environmental experience.

- Cooper and Zubek (1958) found that there was no significant difference in the performance of selectively bred maze-bright and maze dull rats if they were both raised in either very deprived or enriching environmental conditions (which there should have been if maze learning was under genetic control). Studies of rats raised in enriched environments indicate that physiological changes in the synaptic connections of their brains occur as a result.
- In Thompson's (1952) experiment, it is important to note that only maze-learning was genetically transmitted, not the learning of other tasks.
- Studies on the selective breeding of rats are useful, since we can not selectively breed humans, but there are problems in generalising the results to humans.

GENETIC RELATEDNESS AND IQ

- Family resemblance studies on the heritability of IQ have been conducted on the assumption that the closer the genetic relationship between two people, the closer their IQs will be.
  However, it is equally likely that more closely related people will probably live together in very similar environments, and so the best evidence for genetic influences in this area is gained from studying the similarity of IQ between genetically identical subjects (monozygotic/identical twins) who have been raised in different environments, due to adoption for example (a high positive correlation between them would strongly support a large role for genetic factors in the development of IQ).
- Bouchard and McGue (1981) conducted a review of 111 world-wide studies on family IQ, ignoring studies which they claimed had methodological deficiencies, and came up with the following average correlations of IQ.
  The strongest evidence for genetic influences on IQ from these results is the finding that identical twins raised apart have more similar IQs than non-identical twins raised together.

	Average correlation
Identical twins reared together	.86
Identical twins reared apart	.72
Non-identical twins reared together	.60
Siblings reared together	.47
Siblings reared apart	.24
Cousins	.15

Bouchard and McGue (1981)

- Bouchard et al (1990) have continued this line of investigation in their Minnesota Twin Study, but have focused more on studying the IQ similarity of identical twins reared apart. From their intensive studies of the twins so far, they estimate that 70% of the variance in IQ scores are due to genetic inheritance, a larger estimate than that made by Bouchard & McGue (1981) in their earlier review.

Methodologically, studies on genetic relatedness and IQ have been subject to many criticisms, e.g. by Kamin (1977):

1 It is very difficult to control for environmental influences to arrive at an accurate estimate of the genetic contribution to intelligence. Even studying adoption cases is problematic, since:
  - Different environments can not be guaranteed - in some cases an effort has even been made to place the adopted children in similar family environments.
  - The infants may not have been separated exactly from birth and share the same womb experience anyway.
  - The self-selecting sampling techniques employed in studies such as Bouchard et al's (1990) Minnesota Twin Study have been accused of leading to an exaggeration of the similarities between separated identical twins.
  - The different types of IQ test used in the different studies, makes it hard to compare the results, since they are standardised in different ways.

2 The experimenter bias sometimes exhibited in this controversial area has led to:
  - The questioning of the validity of some findings, e.g. Cyril Burt's data on separated identical twins, which was used to support the claim that 80% of the variance in intelligence is genetically determined, but was thoroughly rejected by Kamin (1977).
  - An overly genetic interpretation of the data in some studies and a neglect of environmental influences, e.g. the noticeable differences in Bouchard & McGue's (1981) correlations between:
  a Identical twins reared together and identical twins reared apart (a difference of .14).
  b Siblings reared together and siblings reared apart (a difference of .23).
  In both cases, the genetic relatedness is the same and the differences are more attributable to environmental experiences.

The development of IQ test performance - nurture approach

EVIDENCE FOR ENVIRONMENTAL CAUSES   EVALUATION

EFFECTS OF EARLY PRIVATION ON IQ

If measured intelligence can be significantly reduced by environmental privation, then support is provided for the nurture approach.

- Sameroff and Seifer (1983) identified ten environmental factors, such as the mental health and educational level of the mother, the presence of the father, etc., each of which could lead to a loss of approximately 5 IQ points.
- Vernon (1965) in a cross cultural study revealed that children from disadvantaged backgrounds with little education and a poor home life scored lower on IQ tests, even on the spatial and non-verbal items.
- Many studies, e.g. Koluchova (1972) have shown that measured intelligence can be drastically reduced by extreme early environmental privation, but can also be dramatically improved, even to normal levels, by later normal or enriched conditions.

The dramatic recovery of IQ after extreme privation does seem to indicate the strong motivating effects of genetic influences. Correlational studies often neglect the possibility that genetic influenced behaviour can elicit different reactions - children with lower IQ may be rejected or abused by their parents or just cause their parents to give up attempts to educate them.

ENVIRONMENTAL ENRICHMENT AND IQ

If measured intelligence can be significantly increased through environmental enrichment, then support is provided for the nurture approach.

- Caldwell and Bradley (1978) devised the Home Observation for Measurement of the Environment (HOME) checklist, which is capable of measuring the quality of the home environment for children and its implications for intellectual development. Using the HOME checklist it has been found that factors like the emotional responsiveness and stimulation of the child by the parents are of key importance.
- Operation Headstart was an attempt by the government of the USA in 1965 to provide extra learning experiences for pre-school children from disadvantaged backgrounds. It produced some short lasting gains in IQ, but a longer term 'sleeper effect' in improved academic grades and attitudes to academic work (Collins, 1983).
- Scarr and Weinberg (1976, 1983) found that black children adopted from poor backgrounds and raised in white families of higher income and educational level showed an average IQ of 106 (110 if adopted within 12 months of birth) compared to a control group from a similar background who had an average IQ of 90.
- Skeels (1966) reports the case of 13 infant orphans who, with an average IQ of 64 were transferred to a special institution and given enriching interaction with older girls. By the age of seven they had gained an average of 36 points compared to a control group of orphans who remained in the orphanage and whose IQ dropped by an average 21 points from an original average of 86
- Lynn and Hampson (1986) have reported rises in the national average IQ of Britain (by 1.7), Japan (by 7.7) and the USA (by 3.0) over a 50 year period (1932-1982), which can not be accounted for in terms of genetic factors.
- Howe (1990) has argued that the degree of hard work and practice shown by children with exceptional abilities is often underestimated - even genius needs to be fuelled.

The nature approach would predict that if IQ is under largely genetic control then IQ scores should remain reasonably consistent over time. Jensen (1969) argued that projects like Headstart were a waste of time and resources since poor and minority children were genetically less able to take advantage of them. The strategies employed in projects like Headstart have been accused of

- not producing the long term effects they were designed for.
- being inappropriate for the children they were applied to.
- being overly focused on improving and measuring IQ.

However, Headstart did provide some long term gains and other intervention projects have been more successful.

Attempts at 'hothousing', or intensively educating children, can have negative effects on other areas of functioning and be stressful to the children.

EVALUATION OF NATURE-NURTURE DEBATE IN IQ DEVELOPMENT

All researchers in the area agree that both genetic and environmental influences interact in very complex ways - the genotype of an individual can only be expressed through a phenotype that is the product of genes building physical structures from environmental resources. The environmental influences on intelligence begin in the womb, indeed Denenberg et al have even shown that rats with inherited brain abnormalities which are transplanted into the wombs of healthy rats do better on learning tests than rats with the same abnormality raised in 'unhealthy' wombs. This indicates that the 'uterine environment can have long-term broad and beneficial behavioural effects' (Denenberg quoted in *New Scientist*, March 1998) and is important for the development of cognitive abilities.

The precise genes involved in intelligence have proven difficult to locate, perhaps due to the lack of funding provided for this social sensitive area of research in the Human Genome Project. However, Plomin (1997) has claimed to have discovered a gene called IGF2R which can account for 2% of the variation in IQ test results.

Plomin's finding reflects another major problem - that not only are IQ tests often lacking in reliability as measures of intelligence, but intelligence may not be a unitary phenomenon - some aspects may be under more genetic control than others. IQ tests do take into account some different 'kinds of intelligence' and the Minnesota Twin Study has found that, whereas verbal ability correlations between separated identical twins are high, the correlations for memory are lower and spatial ability are variable.

Moral development - the psychoanalytic approach

FREUD'S THEORY OF MORAL DEVELOPMENT

DEVELOPMENT

- Freud proposed that **moral feelings** come from the **superego** - that part of the psychic apparatus that develops as a result of the **Oedipus complex**.
- The Oedipus complex occurs in the phallic stage of psychosexual development and involves the child's feelings of attraction towards their opposite sex parent. However, because the **boy fears** that his father will **castrate** him and the **girl fears** that she will **lose** her mother's **love**, both end up identifying with their same sex parent.
- **Identification** involves internalising all the same sex parent's moral behaviour, and the superego is therefore an 'inner parent' rewarding good actions and punishing bad ones.

THE SUPEREGO

- There are two main aspects of the superego, the **conscience** and the **ego-ideal**.
- The conscience represents the **punishing** parent and imposes feelings of **guilt** for immoral thoughts or deeds, whereas the ego-ideal represents the **rewarding** parent and is responsible for feelings of **pride** and satisfaction for 'good' thoughts or deeds.

```
          SUPEREGO

  CONSCIENCE        EGO-IDEAL

  Imposes guilt     Imposes pride

  Represents the    Represents the
  punishing parent  rewarding parent
```

PREDICTIONS

- Moral behaviour will be fairly **consistent** across different situations, since the child internalises a **fixed impression** of its parent's morality during the Oedipus complex which becomes a permanent part of the personality.
- **Strength** of morality depends upon
  a the strength of the parent's morality, and
  b the **motive for identification** - Freud claimed that **males** have **stronger consciences** than females, because they identify out of a stronger motive (fear of castration rather than loss of love).
- **Greater wrong-doing** leads to **less guilt**. Since guilt is aggression directed against the self, **releasing aggression** via immoral acts leaves less to punish yourself with.

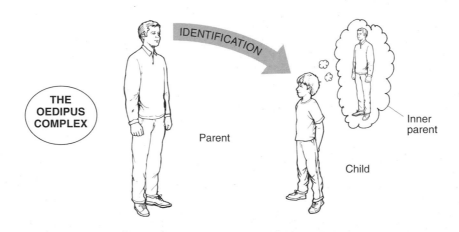

THE OEDIPUS COMPLEX

IDENTIFICATION

Parent

Child

Inner parent

EVALUATION OF FREUD'S THEORY OF MORAL DEVELOPMENT

- There is **little evidence** to support Freud's theory in general and the Oedipus complex in particular, especially the motives for identifying with the same sex parent. The superego, and thus Freud's view of morality, is therefore of **doubtful validity**.

- Cognitive developmental theorists have pointed out that morality does **not** stop developing after the phallic stage, but develops and matures from childhood to adulthood. Zahn-Waxler (1979) found moral feelings are shown by 18 month old children.

- There is no evidence to support Freud's view that women are morally inferior to men. **Hoffman**, in a review of the literature, found that if anything, **females** were slightly **more** able to **resist** temptation than males.

- Freud's **hydraulic theory** of an **inverse** relationship between moral behaviour and guilt has fallen into disrepute. **MacKinnon`s** (1938) study, however, does provide some evidence for Freud's ideas. Almost 100 subjects were given a difficult task to do, but were subtly given the chance to cheat. Around 50% did, and these **cheaters** usually felt **less guilty** than the non-cheaters. Furthermore, the cheaters showed strong feelings of restlessness and aggression during testing (perhaps letting out their pent-up aggression), and were more likely (than non-cheaters) to have received physical rather than psychological punishment as children.

- An internal personality based conscience implies moral consistency across a variety of moral situations (although Freud's notion of irrational behaviour does allow some inconsistency). Thus people who have internalised a strong superego, might be expected to be consistently honest across a variety of situations. **Hartshorne and May's** (1932) study, however, found that **cheating** was **fairly situation specific**, although a later re-analysis of the data did reveal a small significant amount of consistency in honesty.

Moral development - the learning theory approach

LEARNING THEORIES OF MORAL DEVELOPMENT

CLASSICAL CONDITIONING

- Explains **moral behaviour** in terms of **conditioned emotional responses**, formed in the usual classical conditioning manner.

  unconditional stimulus → unconditional response
  Shout/smack → **Anxiety**

  conditional stimulus **Immoral act** + unconditional stimulus **Shout/smack** → UCR **Anxiety**

  conditional stimulus **Immoral act** → conditional response **Anxiety**

- Repeated pairing of the conditional stimulus and unconditional stimulus will eventually cause anxiety just at the thought of an immoral act.
- According to **Eysenck,** the **timing** of the associations will produce different moral effects
  a **punishment before** immoral acts causes a sense of **conscience** (resistance to temptation),
  b **punishment after** immoral acts develops feelings of **guilt** (a sense of remorse).

OPERANT CONDITIONING

- Suggests that the development of moral behaviour depends upon the reinforcement consequences of a child's behaviour.
- The moral behaviours of a society will be **positively reinforced** (rewarded) by attention and praise when children show them, while immoral behaviours will usually be **punished** and so are less likely to occur again. Avoiding immoral behaviour will be **negatively reinforced** by threats of punishment.
- Positive reinforcement is usually **more effective** than punishment because
  a **rewards** give **information** about correct behaviour, a sense of **pride,** and the **motivation** to repeat the good behaviour.
  b **punishment** does not reinforce the correct behaviour, leads to **resentment, hostility** and **tolerance,** and may increase bad behaviour if that behaviour is used to gain attention.

SOCIAL LEARNING THEORY

- Suggests that children learn moral behaviour by **observing** and **imitating models** who behave in a moral way, especially if they see the model's behaviour positively reinforced and **expect** similar rewards.
- Observation of models who are punished for an immoral act will cause the child to experience **vicarious** (indirect) punishment, resulting in the child avoiding that particular behaviour.
- Generalised imitation may provide a better explanation of acquiring parental morals than Freudian identification.

SOLOMON ET AL (1968)

a Dog moves towards forbidden food

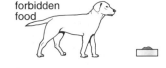

Dog swatted with newspaper

Dog resists food longer

CONSCIENCE

b Dog eats forbidden food

Dog swatted with newspaper

Dog eats food quickly, but shows guilt afterwards

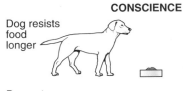

GUILT

EVALUATION OF LEARNING THEORIES OF MORAL DEVELOPMENT

The theories and their application to morality have received experimental support.
- **Aronfreed** (1963) found boys punished verbally **before** touching a forbidden toy were more able to resist touching it when the experimenter left the room than boys punished **after** touching it.
- **Solomon et al** (1968) found similar effects when punishing dogs before or after eating forbidden food. When starved and left alone with the food the dogs that had been punished before touching it resisted longer, while those punished afterwards showed more signs of 'doggy guilt'.
- However, the evidence gathered from non-human subjects is of doubtful generalisability, and social learning theory experiments often take place in artificial laboratory conditions.

These theories can account for moral inconsistency since morality is reinforced differently by different environmental situations.
- **Hartshorne and May** (1930) found that the consistency of immoral behaviour across different situations was not high.

Moral behaviour may be better explained in terms of children's compliance or conformity to adult norms and rules, rather than fixed learning. Kochanska and Aksan (1995) distinguish between committed compliance and situational compliance (where parents have to constantly prompt children to do as they are told).

Learning theories **underestimate cognitive** factors in moral development. Although the social learning approach has introduced cognitive aspects such as expectancies and internal reinforcement and punishment, the theory neglects the complexity and influence of moral reasoning on behaviour.
- For example, punishment can increase immoral behaviour if the individual is doing it for attention, whereas external reward can sometimes lead to a decrease in moral behaviour by undermining the intrinsic rewards for it (Lepper et al, 1973).

These theories do **not** take into account any developmental (qualitative) moral **progress**, but merely imply that children acquire more moral or immoral behaviour with age.

Moral development - the cognitive developmental approach

COGNITIVE DEVELOPMENTAL THEORIES

PIAGET'S THEORY

- Piaget proposed that moral development occurred in **stages** over time and that the level of **moral reasoning** a child showed reflected its underlying stage of cognitive development. Piaget suggested two main stages of moral development:

  1 **Heteronomous morality** - Shown by 5-10 year old children who regard morality as **obeying other people's rules** and laws. This thinking of this stage is typical of **pre-operational** thought and shows **moral realism** - rules and laws are understood as almost real and **fixed** things that are to be strictly obeyed or automatic punishment will follow (**immanent justice**). Immoral acts are judged by their **observable consequences** rather than intentions - a large amount of *accidental* damage is seen as worse than a small amount of *deliberate* damage.
  2 **Autonomous morality** - Shown by those above 10 years, who regard morality as **following their own set of rules**/laws. The thinking of this stage is typical of **concrete** and later **formal operational** thought and shows **moral relativism** - rules and laws are understood as social creations agreed by mutual consent and the **intentions** of actions can be taken into account.

- Piaget believes the moral thinking of an adult can be a mixture of heteronomous and autonomous morality, but the main shift from the former to the latter occurs when the child no longer shows egocentrism and is less dependent on the authority of adults.
- Piaget believes children can use moral principles before they can think about and justify them.

KOHLBERG'S THEORY

- Kohlberg attempted to produce a more detailed theory of moral development by presenting individuals of all ages with moral dilemmas in the form of short stories to solve.
- The dilemmas involved ten universal moral issues, such as the ethics of punishment, liberty and truth; and the reasoning used to justify the answer indicated the level of moral development.
- Kohlberg proposed six universal stages, reflecting three major levels of morality, which everyone progresses through in order.

Level	Stage	Moral reasoning shown
Pre-conventional	1 Punishment & obedience orientation.	Rules are kept to avoid punishment.
	2 Instrumental – relativist orientation.	'Right' behaviour is that which ultimately brings rewards to oneself.
Conventional	3 Good boy - nice girl orientation.	'Good' behaviour is what pleases others - conformity to goodness.
	4 Law & order orientation.	Doing one's duty, obeying laws is important.
Post-conventional	5 Social contract orientation.	'Right' is what is demo-cratically agreed upon.
	6 Universal principles orientation.	Moral action is taken based on self chosen principles.

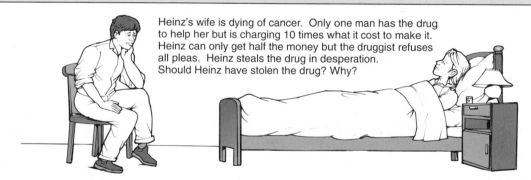

Heinz's wife is dying of cancer. Only one man has the drug to help her but is charging 10 times what it cost to make it. Heinz can only get half the money but the druggist refuses all pleas. Heinz steals the drug in desperation. Should Heinz have stolen the drug? Why?

EVALUATION OF COGNITIVE DEVELOPMENTAL THEORIES OF MORAL DEVELOPMENT

Piaget supported his theory of moral development by questioning children about their understanding of rules (in **games** like marbles) and by presenting them with **moral stories**, whereas Kohlberg presented people with **moral dilemmas**.

Kohlberg's dilemmas are criticised as
- **too difficult** for children to relate to,
- **too hypothetical**,
- **too culturally biased** and
- **too biased towards male** ideas of morality, such as justice, rather than female moral notions like caring, sympathy and responsibility (**Gilligan** 1982).

The theory **ignores** moral **feelings** and the **relationship** between a person's moral **thought** and **behaviour** - knowing what should be done does not always lead to doing it.
- **Bandura & McDonald** (1963) found children would imitate a model's immoral behaviour regardless of their level of moral development

Some of Kohlberg's ideas and studies have been successfully supported:
- **Longitudinally - Colby et al** (1983) studied 58 American males over 20 years and found they went through 4 of Kohlberg's stages.
- **Cross-culturally - Snarey** (1985) found evidence for Kohlberg's first 4 stages in many cultures. Cultures differ, however, in their moral priorities.
- **Cross-sectionally - Fodor** (1972) found that delinquents operated at lower levels of moral development than non-delinquents.

Some studies have found that stage six morality is rarely reached and that some people may actually **skip stages** or **revert** to earlier stages, which goes against Kohlberg's ideas. Eisenberg (1986) has found parallels with Kohlberg's stages in pro-social helping in dilemmas.

Gender development - terms and issues

How are gender identities developed - through nature or nurture?

→ **GENDER IDENTITY**

- Gender identity usually involves a correspondence between sexual identity and societies' appropriate gender role behaviour, but not always, e.g. transsexuals who believe they have been born in the wrong body.
- Gender identity usually influences sexual preference, but not always, e.g. homosexuality.

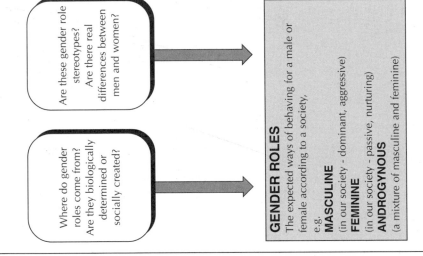

Where do gender roles come from? Are they biologically determined or socially created?

Are these gender role stereotypes? Are there real differences between men and women?

GENDER ROLES
The expected ways of behaving for a male or female according to a society,
e.g.
MASCULINE
(in our society - dominant, aggressive)
FEMININE
(in our society - passive, nurturing)
ANDROGYNOUS
(a mixture of masculine and feminine)

- Bem has investigated the content of gender roles in Western societies, but proposes that one individual can possess both masculine and feminine characteristics, and those who possess them both in equal measure are termed androgynous.

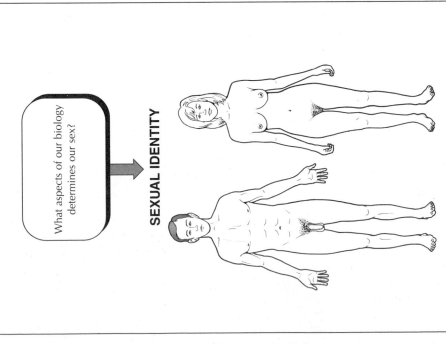

What aspects of our biology determines our sex?

→ **SEXUAL IDENTITY**

- Usually there is a correspondence between chromosomal sex (XX for female, XY for male), gonadal sex, and genital/physical appearance sex, but not always, e.g.
- **Adrenogenital syndrome** – causes chromosomal **females** who have been over exposed to male hormones to develop a **male-like external appearance.**
- **Testicular feminizing syndrome** – causes chromosomal **males** who are insensitive to testosterone to develop a **female external appearance.**

'The measurement of psychological androgyny' Bem (1974)

BACKGROUND

Psychologists and the general public have long regarded masculinity and femininity as opposite extremes of a continuum, so that people are either masculine **or** feminine. This dichotomy has neglected the possibility that people may show **both** masculinity and femininity (i.e. be androgynous), and that individuals who do not show both behaviours and behave in a very sex typed way may actually be restricted by their narrow behaviour.

AIM

The aim of this article is, therefore, to describe the development of the Bem Sex-Role Inventory (BSRI), a questionnaire designed to measure masculine, feminine and androgynous behaviour.

HOW DOES THE BSRI WORK?

The questionnaire includes masculinity and femininity scales, each containing 20 personality characteristics thought appropriate for a male or female to show, which those tested have to rate for how true they are of themselves (from 1, 'Never or almost never true', to 7, 'Always or almost always true'). The BSRI tells whether a person is masculine, feminine, or androgynous, by finding the difference between the masculinity and femininity scores, either by using a t-test or just subtracting the masculine from the feminine total (for a rough estimate).

- High negative scores on the test means a person is masculine typed.
- High positive scores on the test means a person is feminine typed.
- Low scores near zero mean the person is androgynous.

The questionnaire also contains a social desirability scale, composed of items neutral to each sex to make sure that those tested are not just generally agreeing with the test items regardless of whether they are masculine or feminine in nature.

HOW WAS THE BSRI CONSTRUCTED?

100 judges, 50 male, 50 female, rated 200 personality characteristics on a seven point scale for how desirable they were for either a man or a woman to show in American society. Twenty personality characteristics were selected for the masculinity scale and twenty for the femininity scale which were rated significantly more desirable for one sex rather than the other.

Twenty neutral items were selected from 200 personality characteristics which were found not significantly more desirable for one sex or the other. It appeared that both male and female judges agreed on which items were masculine, feminine or neutral.

PSYCHOMETRIC ANALYSIS OF THE BSRI

The BSRI was given to 444 male and 279 female introductory psychology students at Stanford University and also to 117 males and 77 females at the Foothill Junior College, in order to test the internal and external reliability, validity and discriminatory power of the questionnaire.

RELIABILITY

Internal consistency
- Was found highly reliable for all three scales.
- Masculinity and femininity scales were established as independent measures of gender identification.
- Subjects were not just agreeing with socially desirable traits regardless of whether they were masculine or feminine.

Test, re-test consistency
- The BSRI was given about one month later to a small sample of the original university students and a high correlation was achieved between the first and second tests.

VALIDITY

Concurrent validity
- Was tested by correlating the BSRI with two other tests which claim to measure gender roles. The correlations between them were not high.

DISCRIMINATORY POWER

Male subjects scored significantly higher on masculinity and were significantly more likely to be on the masculine side of androgyny compared to female subjects. Female subjects scored significantly higher on the femininity scale and were significantly more likely to be on the feminine side of androgyny compared to male subjects.

EVALUATION

Methodological: The BSRI does not take into account the fact that androgyny scores can be achieved by individuals who score very high or very low on both masculinity and femininity. The concurrent validity of the questionnaire was not high.

Theoretical: The BSRI has proven a useful research tool in distinguishing between different subjects and in investigating the positive and negative effects of gender behaviour.

The questionnaire is 'culture bound' due to the fact it was constructed on the basis of American views on the desirability of gender behaviour.

Links: Gender role identity. Psychometric testing. Reliability, validity and discriminatory power.

Gender development – psychological theories

COGNITIVE DEVELOPMENTAL THEORY

- Kohlberg (1966) argued that a child's **understanding** of its gender **develops** over time.
- The child classifies itself at around the age of three as male or female, and this **gender identity causes imitation** of appropriate masculine or feminine behaviour.
- Understanding of gender is complete at about 7, when the child realises that it remains **stable** over time and **constant** across situations.
- Bem proposes the idea of gender **schemas**.

EVIDENCE FOR THE APPROACH

Kohlberg (1966) questioned children aged around two or three about their understanding of gender. These children often **lacked**

- gender stability – thinking, for example, that they could become a mother **or** a father when they grew up, and
- gender constancy – illustrated, for example, by boys thinking that their gender could change if their hair grew long or they wore a dress.

CRITICISMS

- Many studies have shown that **gender** typical **behaviours** are shown by boys and girls at the age of **2 or less** (e.g. toy preference, Kuhn et al, 1978).
- Kohlberg's claim that gender constancy and stability only **start** at the age of **three** is contradicted by Money and Ehrhardt's finding that **gender reassignment** is **problematic after** this age.

SOCIAL LEARNING THEORY

- Proposes that gender identity/behaviour is **learnt** through **observation**, **imitation** and **behaviour shaping**.
- Gender role behaviour for both sexes is learnt automatically through observation of male and female social models (such as parents, peers, media characters, etc.) but the **performance** of the appropriate gender behaviour depends upon the reinforcement received (or expected) for it from society. Imitation causes gender identity.

EVIDENCE FOR THE APPROACH

There is evidence that society treats boys and girls in different ways:

- **Fagot** (1978) conducted **naturalistic observations** of parent/child interactions and found that boys were **encouraged** to be independent and active, girls to be dependent and passive.
- **Condry and Condry** (1976) **experimentally** showed that adult **perceptions** of, and reactions to, babies' behaviour change depending upon whether they think they are seeing a baby boy or girl.
- **Mead** (1935) proposed **cultural relativism** – gender roles depend upon the society, which supports the nurture rather than nature approach. Mead's study of New Guinea tribes found that men and women of the
  - **a** Arapesh – both showed stereotypically western 'feminine' characteristics,
  - **b** Mundugumour both showed stereotypical 'masculine' characteristics,
  - **c** Tchambuli showed the reverse of western stereotypical gender roles.

CRITICISMS OF THE APPROACH

- **Maccoby and Jacklin** (1974) reviewed a large number of studies on gender acquisition and concluded the **evidence for imitation** is very **mixed** – especially for young children, who often imitate **both** parents.

PSYCHOANALYTIC THEORY

- Freud suggested that the **Oedipus complex** could adequately account for the development of gender role behaviour (although he was less certain about the so called electra complex for girls).
- The successful **internalisation** of the **same sex parent**'s behaviour at the end of the Oedipus complex is crucial to the development of gender identity and sexual orientation. **Both** parents need to be present for this to occur.
- Freud would argue that gender identity is virtually **complete** by the age of **five or six**.

EVIDENCE FOR THE APPROACH

Freud's ideas have not received much experimental support, although Hetherington (1966) reports that the absence of the father before the age of four tends to make boys less masculine and females more awkward in their later interactions with men.

CRITICISMS

- Freud's theory has been criticised on many grounds, but especially for the electra complex and the notion of penis envy, even by other psychoanalysts such as Horney (1924).
- Many studies of children brought up by 'untypical' Freudian families, for example composed of single parents or homosexual/lesbian parents, have found that 'normal' gender role development occurs in virtually all cases.
- Freud's theory ignores the many other influences, both biological and social, that will affect a child's gender development.

Gender development – biologically based theories

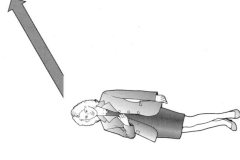

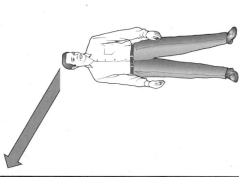

THE BIOLOGICAL APPROACH

- The biological approach proposes that the development of gender is dictated by **physiological processes** within the individual and occurs as **biological maturation** takes place.
- From an **evolutionary** point of view, the human male appears to have been equipped with greater physical strength, aggression and visuospatial ability, but lower sensitivity to pain (perhaps adapting them better for hunting/competition), whereas women seem to have evolved more regular activity levels and greater social sensitivity and verbal ability (perhaps adapting them better for more passive/nurturing behaviour).
- These supposedly natural behavioural tendencies are regulated by **hormone** levels – just as hormones trigger the physical changes of puberty, so they also affect the thoughts and behaviour of males and females. The hormone **testosterone** seems especially active in triggering the increased amounts of aggression and 'rough and tumble' play that males show even at young ages.

EVIDENCE FOR THE BIOLOGICAL APPROACH

- **Money** (1972) studied 25 girls with **adrenogenital syndrome** due to an overdose of male hormones while in the womb, and found that 20 of them showed **'tomboyish'** behaviour showing greater interest in outdoor activity and less in dolls, childcare and self adornment.
- **Imperato-McGinley et al** (1974) studied members of the **Batista family** who, due to a mutant gene, were born with the external features of (and grew up as) young girls, but **physically changed into men** at puberty. The large increase in testosterone at puberty activated a process that should have occurred during embryonic development and their vaginas healed over, their testicles descended, they grew full sized penises and became men - showing **masculine behaviour** (including marrying women).
- **Animal studies** have shown that female monkeys **given testosterone** show male monkey behaviour, such as increased aggressiveness, dominance and even sexual behaviour.

CRITICISMS OF THE BIOLOGICAL APPROACH

- Girls with adrenogenital syndrome may show more masculine behaviour because they look like males, and therefore may be **treated like males**, rather than because of the testosterone.
- The Batistas may have been able to adopt masculine behaviour more readily, despite being raised as girls, because of their **supportive environment**, rather than biological changes.
- The evidence of the link between testosterone levels and aggression is often correlational. Studies have shown that testosterone levels can increase **after** successful dominant behaviour.
- It is not legitimate to generalise from animal gender studies to human gender behaviour.

THE BIOSOCIAL APPROACH

- The biosocial approach moves **away from** the **direct** influence of **physiological** factors on gender behaviour and identity, and focuses on the **interaction** of biological and social factors:
  - a **Biological predispositions** for male babies to be more irritable and harder to pacify than female babies may lead to different **social reactions** from the caregivers around them. Male babies may, therefore, be treated as more independent and aggressive than female babies, and may become so.
  - b The **anatomy** (physical appearance) of males and females may serve as a **cue** for the **social labels** and expectations that society possesses for masculine and feminine behaviours.
  - c **Social factors** have a **greater influence** upon gender identity and behaviour than biological ones, but there may be a **critical** or **sensitive time period** to acquire gender identity.

EVIDENCE FOR THE BIOSOCIAL APPROACH

- **Money and Ehrhardt** (1972) studied girls with adrenogenital syndrome who were raised and treated as boys because of their male looking genitalia. If the mistaken classification was discovered and **corrected before the age of three**, then adjustment to the new gender usually proceeded without many problems. However, this was not the case after three years.
- **Money and Ehrhardt** (1972) also studied chromosomal males with testicular feminizing syndrome, which caused them to be raised as females due to their female external appearance. In the majority of all cases these individuals identified fully with their (female) role of upbringing regardless of their underlying biology.
- Cases of **sexual reassignment** for penis amputation and hermaphrodites have also supported the notion that social and psychological factors outweigh the influence of biological factors in the development of gender identities.

CRITICISMS OF THE BIOSOCIAL APPROACH

- There have been some cases which have **contradicted** the **critical age** of reassignment idea, such as the Batistas.
- Most of the studies supporting the biosocial approach involve individuals with **unusual biological conditions**, and so may **not** be **representative** of gender role development in the majority of the population.

The development of the self

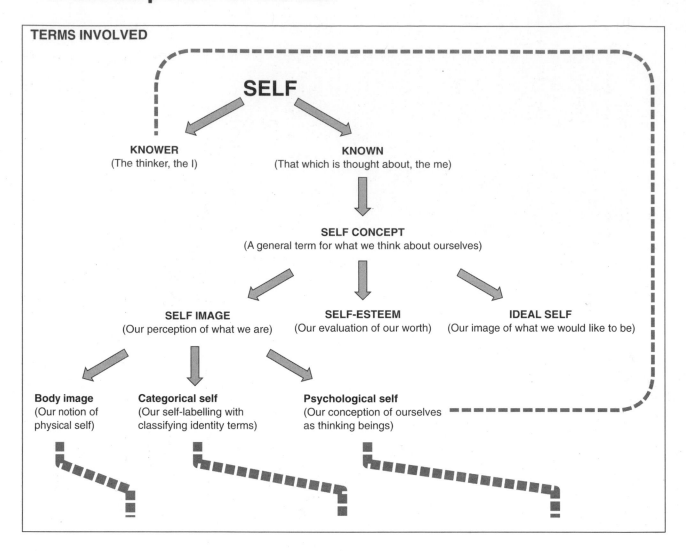

TERMS INVOLVED

SELF

KNOWER
(The thinker, the I)

KNOWN
(That which is thought about, the me)

SELF CONCEPT
(A general term for what we think about ourselves)

SELF IMAGE
(Our perception of what we are)

SELF-ESTEEM
(Our evaluation of our worth)

IDEAL SELF
(Our image of what we would like to be)

Body image
(Our notion of physical self)

Categorical self
(Our self-labelling with classifying identity terms)

Psychological self
(Our conception of ourselves as thinking beings)

SEQUENCE OF DEVELOPMENT

BODY IMAGE
- The first aspect of the self to develop - a recognition that we are **physically separate** from our environment.
- **Lewis & Brooks-Gunn** (1979) showed that by 20 months 75% of infants would touch their own nose if a mirror reflection showed it was coloured with rouge, thus demonstrating self recognition.
- The **body** image forms an important basis for self **labels**, identity and self-esteem (e.g. short, fat, ugly, etc.), especially during the body changes of adolescence.
- **Jersild** (1952) found that physical aspects of the self were the most commonly reported sources of dissatisfaction in adolescents.
- **Jones & Bayley** (1950) found that there were psychological conse-quences of early or late onset of puberty in males.

CATEGORICAL SELF
- The classifying labels start on a **physical** basis (gender is a first important one for the child, ethnic awareness comes a little later around 4-5 years).
- The categories become increasingly **social** in nature, especially as new social roles are recognised and gained (e.g. brother, child, pupil). Classification of **mental** attributes occurs later.
- **Erikson** (1963) suggests that adolescence is a time for **identity crisis**, and is a crucial time for developing new roles/self-conceptions.
- **Kuhn** (1960) asked the 7 and 24 year olds to list twenty answers to the question 'who am I?'. The 24 year olds gave twice the number of social roles (50%) compared to the 7 year olds (25%).

PSYCHOLOGICAL SELF
- At first the infant has *no* self-awareness of itself as a thinking being.
- By around 4 years the child can distinguish between its bodily self and inner thinking self (**Flavell**, 1977).
- The development of **language** provides the necessary tools to reflect upon and describe the psychological self and its attributes, starting from the basic use of 'I' and 'me' terms to language to describe mental aspects of the self such as intelligence, personality traits etc.
- Once a highly developed thinking self is achieved, the individual is better able to **evaluate** the (social) worth of categorical labels. This is when a sense of **self-esteem** starts to develop, depending on the positive or negative evaluation of, for example, being male, fat, intelligent, white, etc.

Theories on the development of the self concept

INDIVIDUAL BASED THEORIES OF SELF DEVELOPMENT

PIAGET'S COGNITIVE THEORY

Self image development

- The self image is merely a set of information organising schemas about the self. Self-schemata can be regarded as theories that we have about what we are like, and there is evidence that we pay more attention to information that fits these ideas and will act to be consistent with them (Markus and Sentis, 1982).
- As the child's cognitive framework for understanding the world develops, so will its self image schemas.
- The body image schema is the first to develop when object permanence is gained.
- Self categorising labels (daughter, sister, niece) become more understood as the child aquires operations & becomes less egocentric – seeing itself from others' point of view.
- Formal operational thought allows the child to think about itself in hypothetical ways (e.g. its ideal self.)

Self-esteem development.

- The child will be at first limited in its ability to evaluate its self worth until it has decentred enough to judge how others regard it.
- Formal operational thought allows the child to compare and evaluate itself in terms of social abstract norms and the ideal self. The problems of adolescence may often involve these comparisons.
- Coopersmith (1967), however, investigated children aged 10-12 and found no relationship between self-esteem and common norms such as physical attractiveness, height, social class, etc. Perhaps these children had not reached formal operational thought though.

FREUD'S PSYCHOANALYTIC THEORY

Self image development

- The child begins life as an unsocialised, primitive, biological Id - just the experiencing part (the 'I') that seeks gratification but has no notion of itself, time or the external world.
- The sense of the self existing in the world (the 'me') only comes about through the development of the ego, with its reality principle.
- Identification with the same sex parent during the Oedipus complex provides the child with many aspects of its self concept (gender role and morals) and provides it with the superego to evaluate itself.

Self-esteem development

- The development of the superego provides the child with its ideal self and internal standard by which to measure its self worth.
- The two aspects of the superego, the ego ideal and the conscience, give the child feelings of low or high self-esteem.

SOCIETY BASED THEORIES OF SELF DEVELOPMENT

Symbolic interactionism

- Symbolic interactionists view the self as a social construct, ach eved through the reactions (social feedback) of other people.
- Cooley termed this the 'looking glass self', suggesting that society's reactions act as a mirror for our identity - we react to society in the way we think they perceive us, and our actions in turn affect those perceptions.
- Research on self-fulfilling prophecy supports these ideas and Coopersmith's study found that the reactions of parents to their offspring was crucial for the development of high self-esteem.

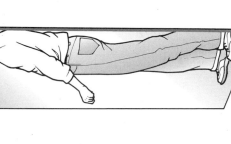

Role theory

- Goffman suggests that our self consists of a set of roles that we adopt and play in different situations, and although we may internalise some of these roles, the theory implies an incoherent self.

Social identity theory

- Social identity theory proposes we derive our identity and self-esteem from the groups we allocate ourselves to, and that we always seek to maintain positive self-esteem.

Phenomenological theory

- Roger's humanistic approach says that we strive for coherent self identity, and that the conditions of worth others place upon us or unrealistic ideal selves will give us negative self-esteem.

Social learning theory

- Traditional learning theory suggests that the 'self image' is merely a set of learnt behaviours from the social environment, although SLT adds the possibility of observational learning, imitation and cognitive awareness of these behaviours.
- This view does not regard the 'self' as a coherent whole.

Social Psychology

Social influence

Pro- and anti-social behaviour

Social relationships

'A study of prisoners and guards in a simulated prison' Haney, Banks, and Zimbardo (1973)

AIM
To demonstrate the situational rather than the dispositional causes of negative behaviour and thought patterns found in prison settings by conducting a prison simulation with 'normal' subjects playing the roles of guard and prisoner.

METHOD
Subjects: 22 male subjects selected (through personality assessment) from an initial pool of 75 volunteers based on their stability, maturity and lack of involvement in anti-social behaviour. They were mostly Caucasian, middle class, college students, who were strangers to each other and were randomly allocated to either prisoner or guard roles. Prisoners signed a consent document which specified that some of their human rights would be suspended and all subjects were to receive $15 a day for up to 2 weeks.

Apparatus: Prison - a basement corridor in Stanford University Psychology department converted into a set of 2 x 3 metre prison cells with a solitary confinement room (a tiny unlit closet), a 'yard' room and an observation screen (through which covert video and audiotape data recording could take place).
Uniforms - to facilitate role identification, guards were given khaki shirts and trousers, batons and reflecting sunglasses. Prisoners wore loose fitting smocks with identification numbers, no underwear, a lock and chain around one ankle, and a nylon stocking cap to cover their hair.

Procedure: The procedure, as with the apparatus, was designed to establish 'functional equivalents' for the experience of prison life.
* Prisoners were arrested by real police outside their houses by surprise, taken to a real police station for finger-printing and processing, and were then driven blindfolded to the mock prison (where they were stripped naked, 'deloused', and dressed in prisoner's uniform). Prisoners remained in the 'prison' 24 hours a day and followed a schedule of work assignments, rest periods, and meal/toilet visits.
* Guards worked only 8 hour shifts, and were given no specific instructions apart from to 'maintain a reasonable degree of order within the prison necessary for its effective functioning' and a prohibition against the use of physical violence.

RESULTS
The effects of imprisonment were assessed by video and audio tape observation of behaviour and dialogue, self-report questionnaires, and interviews. The experiment had to be terminated after 6 days, instead of the intended 14, because of the pathological (abnormal) reactions shown by both prisoners and guards.

* **Effects on prisoners** - subjects showed what was termed the 'Pathological Prisoner Syndrome' - disbelief was followed by rebellion which, after failure, was followed by a range of negative emotions and behaviours. All showed passivity (some becoming excessively obedient) and dependence (initiating very little activity without instruction). Half the prisoners showed signs of depression, crying, fits of rage, and acute anxiety, and had to be released early. All but two of those who remained said they would forfeit the money if they could be released early.

The experimenters proposed that these reactions were caused by a loss of personal identity, emasculation, dependency, and learned helplessness brought about by the arbitrary and unpredictable control, and the norms and structures of the prison system.

* **Effects on guards** - subjects showed what was termed the 'Pathology of Power' - huge enjoyment of the power at their disposal (some worked extra time for no pay, and were disappointed when the study was over) led to the guards abusing it and dehumanising the prisoners. All prisoners' rights were redefined as privileges (going to the toilet, eating, and wearing eye-glasses became rewards), and punishment with little or no justification was applied with verbal insults. Although not all guards initiated aggressive action, none contradicted its use in others.
The experimenters proposed that these reactions were caused by a sense of empowerment legitimised by the role of 'guard' in the prison system.

EVALUATION
Methodological: Lack of ecological validity - A role play simulation lacks 'mundane realism' and may produce artificial results. The experimenters admit factors, such as the lack of physical violence, and minimum duration of the sentence, limit the generalisability of the simulation, but point out that most of the functional equivalents of the prison system were implemented and that most of the subjects' excessive reactions went beyond the demands of the role play (prisoners called each other by their ID numbers in private, and guards showed aggression even when they thought they were not being observed).

Data analysis - Was mostly qualitative rather than quantitative.

Ethical problems - 1 The study was ethically approved beforehand - perhaps the dramatic and disturbing results cause the ethical objections, but these came from the subjects not the experimenters.

2 The subjects had signed an informed consent document, but were unaware that they would be arrested in public and of exactly how realistic their imprisonment would be.

3 The experiment was terminated early and debriefing and assessment of the subjects took place weeks, months and years afterwards.

Theoretical: The research provides support for social psychological explanations of behaviour, has wide ranging implications for the usefulness and ethics of existing penal systems, and has been used to facilitate our understanding of the psychological effects of imprisonment.

Links: Social influence - particularly power, leadership, obedience (see Milgram) and conformity.

Social power

DEFINITION

Social power refers to the influence a person has to change another's thoughts, feelings, or behaviour. There are many sources of power, many ways in which it can work and many effects it can have on those who have it and those who yield to it.

NORMS OF POWER

Power relations are embedded in the hierarchical nature of society. Zimbardo et al's (1973) prison simulation experiment showed how the role of prison guard and the power that went with it could be readily assumed by subjects selected on the basis of their normality. Clearly, the norms of guard power (operating from coercive and legitimate power bases) can be readily understood (although exaggerated by media portrayal) and internalised by anyone.

THE IMPACT OF POWER.

According to **social impact theory** (Latane, 1981), the strength of influence felt by a target is determined by three factors:
- The **strength** (or importance) of the influencer,
- The **number** of influencers,
- The **immediacy** (or closeness) of the influencer/s.

Increases in each of the above factors will cause the power of influence to increase, while decreases in these factors (or an increase in the target's strength or number) will have the opposite effect. For example, you are more likely to be influenced by several very important people standing in front of you, than by one unimportant person talking over the telephone.

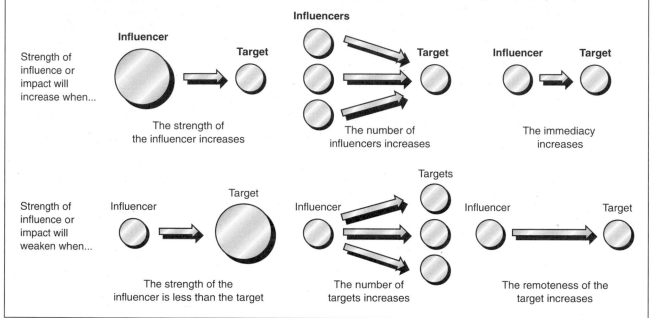

TYPES OF POWER

Raven and others have identified six different (although they can operate simultaneously) sources or *bases of power*:

1 Reward power
This influence is based on the ability to provide what others **want** or to remove what they do not want. Many people possess this source of power (e.g. parents, employers, friends), but note that they offer many different types of reward (e.g. love, money, approval). This power only works as long as the rewards can be given by the influencer and are wanted by the receiver.

2 Coercive power
This involves the ability to **punish**, by inflicting some form of negative stimulus (e.g. disapproval, ridicule, pain) or by removing pleasant stimuli (e.g. affection, wages). This power base requires constant supervision, since it produces negative feelings and attitudes in its victims who only tend to comply behaviourally to demands rather than really accepting them.

3 Referent power
This is the influence a person has because they are **respected** or admired. The target wishes to identify with (be like) the influencer and is more likely to follow their wishes. Role models and idols have this power, but only maintain it as long as they are liked or respected.

4 Legitimate power
This is where the target accepts the **norms** (probably internalised) that the influencer should have (has the right to) influence over them. The legitimacy of the power obviously depends on the situation - we accept that a referee can tell us what to do in a football match, but not outside of that situation.

5 Expert power
The power an influencer has because the target believes they possess **superior knowledge** in a desired area. We are thus at the mercy of our doctor's advice in matters of health, and at the mercy of garage mechanics when our cars need servicing.

6 Informational power
One person or a group of people, expert or otherwise, can have power if they provide socially accepted **information**. This ties in with the social reality hypothesis and Festinger's social comparison theory (we look to others to know how to react in certain situations).

Theories of leadership

Leadership is 'the process of influencing group members towards achieving group goals' Kagan (1991).
A leader can be said to be the person who possesses the greatest influence (power) over the group members.
Leadership research has focused on two interrelated issues - the emergence and effectiveness of leaders. Over the years three approaches have aimed to explain who will become a leader and what makes a leader effective.

PERSONALITY TRAIT APPROACH

The first approach to leadership was the trait approach or 'Great man' approach (Carlyle, 1841), whereby researchers attempted to isolate the characteristics, either mental or physical that would determine who emerged as the leader.

- Randle (1956) gave psychological tests to and interviewed 1427 executives from 27 companies in the USA, and identified thirty traits which distinguished good from bad or mediocre leaders. The most important traits appeared to be drive, intelligence, and motivation.
- Mann (1959) reviewed over 100 studies which attempted to correlate leadership with personality characteristics, but only found weak evidence for leaders being more intelligent, extrovert, dominant, and sensitive than non-leaders.
- Shaw (1976) also found only weak generalisations from his review, indicating that, on average, leaders tended to have greater amounts of intelligence, relevant knowledge, sociability, popularity, motivation, initiative, and persistence.

Different leaders will tend to have different traits and skills and will, therefore, be effective for different reasons.

Personality traits associated with successful leaders operate from different power bases, e.g. intelligence and greater relevant knowledge provides informational and expert power, sociability and popularity provide referent and reward power, dominance leads to legitimate and coercive power.

- Lewin et al (1939) investigated the effectiveness of three leadership styles, autocratic, democratic, and laissez-faire, and found that, overall, the democratic leadership was most effective for morale, co-operation, consistency of work, and quality. Autocratic leadership leads to greater quantity, but poorer morale & consistency of work. However this study may have been biased by democratic American researchers.

The trait approach lost favour, however, since

a the studies often relied on studying existing leaders who may have acquired some of the traits from their experience of leadership, e.g. relevant knowledge, popularity, dominance, etc., rather than prior possession of the traits leading to their emergence as leaders.
b no strong consistent and conclusive leadership traits emerged, different studies produced different lists of characteristics, indicating that perhaps situational factors determine who becomes a leader, and that different groups may give rise to different types of leader.

SITUATIONAL APPROACH

The situational approach aimed to discover the conditions under which anybody could emerge as and become an effective leader.

1 Role theory

- Goffman suggests roles are like parts in a play - anybody can slot into them, therefore, anybody can become a leader if they adopt the leader's role. The role may be adopted informally, through natural emergence, or artificially through appointment.
- Bales (1955) used the leaderless group discussion technique and found that groups regarded leaders as the ones who fulfilled one of two major roles in the group:
  a Task leader role, which was concerned directly with the job at hand, and
  b Socio-emotional leader role, which supported the group in their attempts to reach the goal.

● = emergent leader's position.
○ = other group members
— = lines of communication.

2 Informal emergence

- Hamblin (1958) showed experimentally how a crisis situation would often lead to the emergence and acceptance of a leader, compared to a non-crisis situation.
- Leavitt (1951) showed how anybody could emerge as a leader and take on the responsibilities if placed in a situation where they were at the centre of a communication network. Those subjects placed in communication networks, such as the wheel or chain, tended to accept the challenge and act like leaders, sending more messages, making fewer errors and solving problems more quickly. They were also recognised as leaders by the rest of the group. Leadership may, therefore, become a self-fulfilling prophecy.

3 Formal appointment

- Bell and French (1950) randomly picked individuals from groups of navy recruits and assigned them the leadership role of 'acting petty officer' over their colleagues. They found that they were not only accepted as leaders by their groups, but were also retained in that position.

While accepting that most people could emerge as a leader under certain circumstances, it should be noted that some people are more likely to emerge as leaders under those same circumstances than others, due to having better 'qualifications' to meet the needs of the situation.

INTERACTIONIST APPROACH

The overall function of the leader is to enable the group to achieve its goals, but of course different groups have different goals and will, therefore, require different leadership skills. An effective leader is, therefore, the group member most able to facilitate the group's success - the right person, in the right group at the right time. Different leaders will emerge in a football team, a business, or a gang of hell's angels because of the specialist skills they possess.

- Fiedler (1971) proposed a contingency theory of leadership effectiveness - leaders were identified as either task orientated (autocratic and concerned with getting the job done) or relationship orientated (concerned with happy and productive workers) by measurement on the 'least preferred co-worker scale', and it was found that task orientated leaders were most effective in easy or difficult situations, while relationship orientated leaders were most effective in moderate situations.

Milgram's study of obedience (1963) 1

PROCEDURE

Subjects were led to believe that the experiment was investigating the effects of punishment on learning. The subjects were tested one at a time and were always given the role of teacher (through a fixed lottery). The subject saw his apparent co-subject (in reality an actor) strapped into a chair with electrodes attached to him, since he was to be the 'learner'. The subject ('teacher') was told the shocks would cause no permanent tissue damage and was given a trial shock of 45 volts. The subject then started the experiment in the shock generator room next door by testing the learner over an intercom, and was told by the experimenter (the authority figure) to administer increasing levels of electric shock for each wrong answer (which the actor gave often). The experiment finished when either the subject refused to continue (disobeyed the experimenter's request), or had reached the maximum shock on the scale

AIM

To investigate how far people will go in obeying an authority figure.

(450 volts). The subject was then fully debriefed as to the real nature of the experiment, re-introduced to the learner in a friendly way and reassured that no damage had been done since the learner had not really received any shocks at all!
In the basic set-up of the experiment the subject received feedback reactions from the learner he was 'electrocuting' only by a thump on the wall at 300 volts followed by no further reply, but in a later condition vocal feedback was given (this was standardised by the use of a tape recording). Milgram decided to conduct many variations of the study to determine the key factors that were responsible for the obedience.

APPARATUS

Two rooms in the Yale Interaction Laboratory were used - one for the learner containing an 'electric chair' and an answering device, the other for the teacher and experimenter with an electric shock generator.
The generator did not actually give shocks to the learner, and was used to measure the dependent variable of obedience. It was a convincing machine with a row of 30 switches that ranged from 15 volts to 450 volts in increments of 15 volts, and was marked with descriptive terms of the shock effects - ranging from 'slight shock' through to 'Danger: severe shock' and 'XXX'.

THE SUBJECTS

They were 40 males between the ages of 20 and 50 from a range of occupations, and were drawn from the New Haven area. They were obtained by newspaper ad's for participation in a study of learning at Yale University and were paid $4.50 just for turning up.

VOCAL FEEDBACK CONDITION

At **75 volts** moans/groans.
At **150 volts** requests to be excused from the experiment.
At **195 volts** yelled 'Let me out! My heart's bothering me'
At **285 volts** agonised scream
At **300 volts** kicked the wall and begged to be released.
At **315 volts** no further responses.

THE EXPERIMENTER

He was 31 years old, dressed in a grey laboratory coat, and appeared somewhat stern and impassive through the experiment. If at any point the subject showed reluctance to administer the shock, he would command them to continue with standardised prompts ranging from 'please continue' to 'You have no other choice, you *must* go on'.

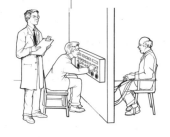

THE LEARNER

An actor was required to play the role of the learner - an Irish-American, 47 year old accountant who appeared mild-mannered and likeable.

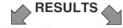
RESULTS

Levels of obedience expected

Psychology students and professional colleagues were asked what percentage of subjects would administer the highest degree of shock (450 volts) - the answers ranged from 1 to 3, with a mean of 1.2.

Subjects' realisation of shock effects

In the post-experimental interview the subjects were asked "How painful to the learner were the last few shocks that you administered to him?". The mean response was 13.42 out of 14 - 'extremely painful' on the scale.

Behavioural reactions to the study

'In a large number of cases, the degree of tension reached extremes that are rarely seen in sociopsychological laboratory studies. Subjects were observed to sweat, tremble, stutter, bite their lips, groan and dig their fingers into their flesh. These were characteristic rather than exceptional responses to the experiment. One sign of tension was the regular occurrence of nervous laughing fits. Full-blown, uncontrollable seizures were observed for 3 subjects. On one occasion, we observed a fit so violently convulsive that it was necessary to call a halt to the experiment. In the post experimental interviews, subjects took pains to point out that they were not sadistic types, and that the laughter did not mean they enjoyed shocking the victim'. Milgram (1963).

The percentages of those who continued to the maximum shock level:

65% Remote victim condition. The victim in a separate room and no feedback until a bang on the wall at 300 volts. No subject stopped before 300 volts.

62.5% Vocal feedback condition. With the verbal protestations, screams, wall pounding, and ominous silence after 300 volts. Only a few stopped before 300 volts.

92.5% Two teacher condition. The subject was paired with another teacher (a confederate) who actually delivered the shocks while the teacher only read out the words.

47.5% Shift of setting condition. The experiment was moved to a set of run down offices rather than the impressive Yale University.

40% Proximity condition. Learner moved into the same room so the teacher could see his agonised reactions.

30% Touch proximity condition. The teacher had to force the learner's hand down onto a shock plate after he refused to participate after 150 volts.

20% Absent experimenter condition. The experimenter has to leave and give instructions over the telephone. Many subjects cheated and missed out shocks or gave less voltage than ordered to.

10% Social support condition. Two other subjects (confederates) were also teachers but soon refused to obey. Most subjects stopped very soon after the others.

Milgram's study of obedience 2

DISCUSSION - FACTORS EXPLAINING OBEDIENCE

THE IMPACT OF THE INFLUENCES
Social impact theory (Latane) - explains factors that might have affected the obedience:
- The impact of the **experimenter on the subject** - The experimenter was close (immediate) and important to the subject. When the experimenter gave instructions over the telephone, obedience decreased. When the number of teachers was increased and they disobeyed the experimenter, the impact of his power and authority was diffused.
- The impact of the **learner's distress on the subject** - The subject was at first not in close proximity to the learner - when the consequences of his shocks were made more immediate (when the learner was brought into the same room) obedience decreased. When there were two teachers, and the naive subject only had to read out the questions, the naive subject felt even less individually responsible and obedience increased.

THE SOCIAL SITUATION
- Subjects were bound by a **social contract**, the **norms** of being involved in research are that the subjects do what they are requested to do. Subjects had volunteered, which caused a sense of obligation.
- The location of respectable Yale University added **legitimate power** to the situation (obedience decreased when the location was moved)

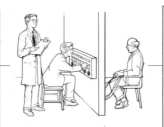

THE APPARATUS
Subjects showed **momentum of compliance** - once they began obeying, they found it hard to justify stopping, since:
- the switches only went up in 15 volt increments
- the subject had little time to think (they had to give the shock within 5-6 seconds)

THE AUTHORITY FIGURE
The experimenter as the authority figure possessed **legitimate** and **expert power**, representing scientific authority and **taking responsibility** for the consequences of the obedience. The grey laboratory coat represented the power that **uniform** has in our society. Bickman (1974) showed this; when an experimenter was dressed in a guard's uniform and told passers-by to pick up paper bags or give a coin to a stranger there was 80% obedience, compared to 40% when the experimenter was dressed 'normally'.

THE SUBJECT
Those who gave the highest levels of shock tended to have stronger authoritarian characters and seemed more prone to blame the subject than themselves for the obedience. However, the scale of the obedience suggests that this is a type of behaviour that **anybody** could show - what Arendt has called the **banality of evil**. Milgram suggests that when faced with commands from legitimate authority figures we lose our sense of responsibility for our own actions, and become the agents of others' wishes (the state of agency).

DISCUSSION - EVALUATION OF THE RESEARCH PROCEDURE

EVALUATION OF THE METHODOLOGY
- **Well controlled experiment** - the procedure was well standardised (even the feedback from the learner was tape-recorded) while different variables were carefully manipulated to see the effect on obedience (which was accurately operationalised as the amount of voltage given).
- **Subjects were male and volunteers** - a self-selecting sample, but overall 636 subjects were tested during the 18 different variation studies. Women have been found to show similar levels of obedience, and cross-cultural studies have found equal or higher levels (85% in Germany, 80% in Jordan).
- **Realism of experiment** - Orne and Holland (1968) have argued that the subjects did not really think that the learner would come to harm. They suggest that the subjects are involved in a '**pact of ignorance**' with the experimenter and obey in much the same way as a member of a magician's audience will comply and put their head under the guillotine which has just split a cabbage head in two! Psychologists such as Aronson (1988) have suggested that the experiment is an artificial test of obedience and therefore **lacks 'mundane realism'** or ecological validity. Milgram argues that while there are important differences between experimental and real life obedience, there is a fundamental similarity in the psychological processes at work - especially the process of agency. **Hofling et al's** (1966) study found that 21 out of 22 nurses obeyed an unknown doctor's telephone instructions to administer twice the normal dose of a drug that was clearly labelled with warnings against such an action. The obedience was shown under **real life** hospital conditions.

EVALUATION OF THE ETHICS
Against the study
Baumrind (1964) criticised the study as being unethical since:
- It caused distress to the subjects. One had a seizure and all of the subjects could have suffered psychological damage.
- Milgram deceived the subjects as to the true nature of the experiment, and, therefore, did not receive their informed consent.
- Milgram's study abused the right of subjects to withdraw from a psychology study - those wishing to leave were told to continue.

For the study
Milgram defended himself on ethical grounds by pointing out:
- The methodology was not unethical since the results obtained were completely unexpected, and although the subjects appeared uncomfortable with their obedience, Milgram concluded that 'momentary excitement is not the same as harm'.
- Subjects could have left, they were not physically restrained.
- All subjects were fully debriefed and reassured. They were shown that the learner was completely unharmed and had not received any shocks. A follow up opinion survey conducted a year later found that 84% were 'glad to have been in the experiment', 15% were neutral, and only 1.3% were 'sorry or very sorry to have been in the experiment'. Around 80% of the respondents said there should be more experiments like Milgram's conducted, and around 75% said they had learnt something of personal value from their experience. The subjects were also examined by a psychiatrist one year after the study who found no signs of harm.

Studies of conformity

CONFORMITY DEFINITIONS AND TYPES

Definition: 'Yielding to group pressure' Crutchfield (1962). According to Aronson (1976) the pressure can be real (involving the physical presence of others) or imagined (involving the pressure of social norms/expectations). Kelman (1958) suggests that the yielding can take the form of

- compliance - A change in behaviour without a change in opinion (just going along with the group),
- internalisation - A change in both behaviour and opinion (the group's and your own opinions coincide), or
- identification - The individual changes their behaviour and opinions to identify with the influencing group.

CONFORMITY STUDIES

JENNESS (1932)

Asked subjects to estimate the number of beans in a bottle, first individually and then as a group. When asked individually again, the subjects showed a shift towards the group's estimate rather than their own. This was rather a simple experiment, however.

SHERIF (1935)

Asked subjects to estimate how far a spot of light in a completely dark room moved. Sherif kept the point of light stable, but due to the autokinetic effect illusion (caused by small eye movements) each individual reported fairly consistent estimates that often differed from other subjects.
However, when subjects were put in groups, their estimates converged towards a central mean, despite not being told to arrive at a group estimate and despite denying that they had been influenced by the others in post experimental interviews.

ASCH (1951, 1952, 1956)

Asch wanted to test conformity under non ambiguous conditions and, therefore, devised a very simple perceptual task of matching the length of a line to one of three other comparison lines. The task was so easy that control subjects were correct 98% of the time. In the experimental condition only one real (naive) subject was tested, but was surrounded by six confederates of the experimenter, who were also supposed to be subjects but had been told beforehand to all give the same wrong estimate on 12 out of the 18 trials. The only real subject was second to last to give their estimate, and was, therefore, faced with either giving their own opinion or conforming to the group opinion on the critical trials.

Out of 123 naive subjects tested, the average rate of conformity was 32%. 75% conformed at least once, 25% not at all and 5% conformed on every trial.
Asch conducted variations to identify factors influencing conformity, such as:

- increasing the group size - Asch found little increase above 3 or 4, although other studies have found that larger groups will increase conformity but at a decreasing rate.
- providing support for the subject - when Asch provided an ally that agreed with the naive subject's estimates, conformity dropped to 5.5%. It seems that the unanimity of the group is important. If the ally changed to the group's estimates, then the naive subject would often follow suit.
- increasing the difficulty of the task - when the comparison lines were made closer in length, the rate of conformity increased.
- when the naive subject could write down their response, conformity dropped.

Even subjects that did not conform, felt strong social pressure to do so. One was heard to exclaim 'I always disagree - darn it!', and on being debriefed, commented 'I do not deny that at times I had the feeling "to heck with it, I'll go along with the rest"'.

Direction that answers were given in

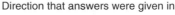

Only real subject

Test card

CRUTCHFIELD (1954)

Crutchfield tested for conformity without physical presence by placing subjects in individual cubicles with electronic display boards which supposedly let each subject know what the others had answered. In fact, he allowed each subject to believe they were the last to answer and presented them with uniformly wrong group answers on half the tasks.
Crutchfield tested over 600 subjects using a variety of stimuli such as Asch's line comparison tests, obviously incorrect factual statements, and personal opinions. He found 30% conformity in Asch's line test, 46% conformity to the suggestion that picture of a star had a larger surface area than a circle (when it was a third smaller), and 37% agreement to the statement 'I doubt that I would make a good leader' (which none agreed to when asked on their own).

CRITICISMS OF CONFORMITY STUDIES

- Artificiality - the above studies mostly reflect conformity under laboratory conditions, with meaningless stimuli.
- The high conformity found may only reflect the norms prevalent in the USA in the 1950s. Replications have found widely varying rates of conformity in more recent times and when the studies have been conducted cross culturally.

Theories of conformity

CRUTCHFIELD'S CONFORMING PERSONALITY THEORY (1955)
After Crutchfield had tested his subjects for conformity, he also gave them a number of personality and I.Q. type tests, and found, for example, that those subjects who conformed the most typically
- were less intellectually competent - perhaps they were more open to the expert power of others
- had less ego strength - perhaps making them less confident in their own opinion
- had less leadership ability - perhaps making them less able to assert their own opinion
- were more narrow minded / Authoritarian - perhaps inclining them stick to the majority answer

However, if conforming personalities exist, then they should conform in a variety of situations, but McGuire (1968a) has found inconsistency of conformity across different situations.

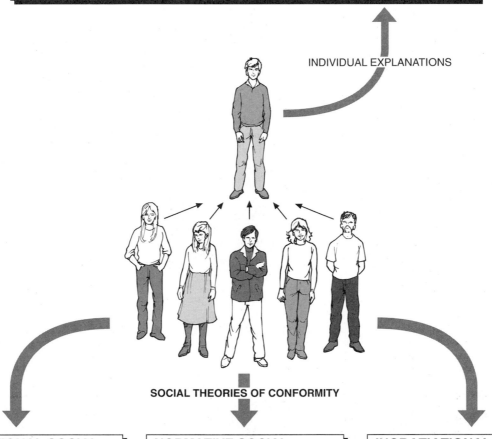

INDIVIDUAL EXPLANATIONS

SOCIAL THEORIES OF CONFORMITY

INFORMATIONAL SOCIAL INFLUENCE
Deutsch and Gerard (1955) have suggested that one motive for conformity is based on the **need** that everyone has **for certainty**.
When individuals are placed in ambiguous/**uncertain conditions**, they are more likely to refer to others to know how to react (Festinger called this **social comparison**).
Under these conditions, other people possess informational or **expert power** and individuals may show **internalisation** conformity - both their behaviour and opinions coincide with the group's.

Informational influence explains the conformity found in Sherif's study and much of the conformity in Asch's tasks - especially when the difficulty of the task was increased. A few of Asch's subjects seemingly experienced perceptual distortion, but the majority believed that the group's judgement was superior.

NORMATIVE SOCIAL INFLUENCE
Deutsch and Gerard (1955) have proposed that another motive for conformity is based upon the **need** for **social acceptance** and **approval**.
When individuals are put into a potentially **embarrassing situation**, such as disagreeing with the majority, they are faced with a **conflict** between their own and others' opinions.
Under these conditions other people have **reward** or **coercive power** which may lead individuals into **compliance** - publicly agreeing with the group, but privately maintaining their own opinions.

Normative influence explains some of Asch's conformity results, especially in the private answer variation. Some of his subjects reported private disagreement with the groups answers, commenting 'If I'd been the first I probably would have responded differently'.

INGRATIATIONAL SOCIAL INFLUENCE
Mann (1969) suggested a third motive for conformity, based upon the **desire** to **join a particular social group**.
When individuals are given the opportunity to conform to a particular group's opinions, they will **actively** take it to become more **like** the group.
Under these conditions, members of the target group may possess **reward** and **referent power** and their acceptance of the individual may lead to **identification** conformity - wholeheartedly coinciding with the group's behaviour and opinions.

Ingratiational influence may have its basis in Freudian identification, and is supported by social identity theory (which suggests that individuals gain their self esteem from groups they allocate themselves to).

Collective behaviour - group behaviour

GROUP BEHAVIOUR
A group is usually a fairly small collection of individuals who possess a common identity, structure, communication network, and a shared set of interests or goals. Research discussed here will focus on **intra-group** behaviour - the effects of groups upon member's thinking and behaviour **within** a group

GROUPTHINK
Janis (1972) coined the term 'groupthink' to describe 'a deterioration of mental efficiency, reality testing, and moral judgement that results from in-group pressures'. Poor groupthink decisions are made by groups that are isolated, intolerant of dissent, and lacking in impartial leadership - all of which rules out realistic alternatives.

BRAIN STORMING
Brainstorming in groups increases creativity and error detection, but is less efficient in terms of man hours of work.

GROUP POLARISATION
Stoner (1961) found group discussion led to more extreme decisions than individual decision making. Through a process of social comparison, members tend to shift ever further towards the average initial direction of the group until a clear group norm is reached. Kerr (1981) found the best indicator of a jury's final verdict was the majority consensus of its first poll.

GROUP THINKING

CONFORMITY
Groups exert a powerful influence upon members in the form of norms of behaviour. Groups often possess various roles which guide intra-group behaviour and facilitate communication.

SOCIAL LOAFING
When individuals work with others on a **shared task**, social loafing can occur (individuals put in less effort than they would alone) even on a simple task like tug-of-war (Ringlemann, 1913) or group shouting (Latane et al, 1979).

GROUP BEHAVIOUR

SOCIAL FACILITATION
Social facilitation refers to **the effect that the mere presence of other people has on our performance**. The effect can be either:
Positive - increasing/facilitating our performance, or
Negative - decreasing/inhibiting our performance.

Performance appears to be **facilitated** by the presence of others when **easy** or **well known tasks** are attempted, but **inhibited** when **difficult** or **challenging tasks** are undertaken. Social facilitation research has focused on:
The coaction effect - when people are working individually but side by side on similar tasks, and
The audience effect - when a group of people are watching an individual performing a task.

RESEARCH ON THE COACTION EFFECT
- **Triplett (1898)** - found children working **in pairs** could reel in a fishing rod significantly faster than on their own.
- **Allport (1920, 24)** found **simple** tasks, such as crossing out all the vowels on a sheet of newspaper, were performed more efficiently than **difficult** tasks, such as multiplication tests and problem solving activities, when subjects were tested in coacting groups.

RESEARCH ON THE AUDIENCE EFFECT
- **Michaels et al (1982)** - found good pool players showed an **increase** in shot accuracy by 9%, whereas poor players showed a **decrease** of 11% when watched by an audience.
- **Bell and Yee (1989)** - found skilled karate kickers performed well when tested in front of an expert audience and on their own, whereas **unskilled** karate kickers performed significantly *fewer* kicks in front of the audience.

THEORIES OF SOCIAL FACILITATION
- **Arousal Theory - Zajonc (1960, 66)** suggests the **mere presence** of others puts us into a state of **physiological arousal**, which **always energises behaviour** - whether it be correct (easy task) or incorrect (difficult task) behaviour.
- **Evaluation apprehension theory** - individuals feel they are under evaluation whenever they are with others, which may motivate them to **compete** or make them become **self-conscious** and **anxious**.
- **Distraction conflict theory** - Baron (1986) suggests performance is affected by **attentional conflict** between the task and others. Well known/simple tasks, being more automatic, require **less attention** and so will be less distracted by the presence of others, whereas difficult tasks require more attention, so are more open to disruption.

Collective behaviour - crowd behaviour

CROWD PSYCHOLOGY
Crowds are larger groups of people, typically with less clear lines of organisation and communication between members, and often gathered together on a transitory basis.

Crowd psychology has largely focused on the nature of crowd action - whether it is
- wild, unruly and irrational, involving a loss of identity, or
- purposeful, rule governed and rational (i.e. understandable in terms of precipitating factors or the crowd's identity and goals).

LOSS OF CONTROL AND RATIONALITY

COLLECTIVE UNCONSCIOUS THEORY
Le Bon's (1895) book *The crowd* typified this theoretical approach, arguing that individuals in a crowd lose their conscious individual personalities to the primitive, animalistic, spirit of the crowd. Individuals in a crowd descend 'several rungs in the ladder of civilisation', showing impulsive, irritable, highly suggestible and overly emotional behaviour, and an incapacity to reason.

DEINDIVIDUATION
Zimbardo and other researchers suggest that individuals may lose their sense of individual identity and control over behaviour in a crowd for many social psychological reasons - such as sensory overload, arousal, anonymity, and reduced self awareness. These factors may lead to loosened inhibitions and, therefore, uncharacteristic behaviour not in line with usual internal standards.

EMERGENT NORM THEORY
Turner and Killian (1972) explain the behavioural contagion often shown by crowds by proposing that the collective action of crowds is triggered off by the first people to show a clear pattern of behaviour. These actions define the norm of behaviour - the social reality of what is permitted, since, according to social comparison theory, people in a crowd are uncertain how to react and look to others for information. Thus, if the emergent norm becomes 'applauding the performance', 'run for the fire escape', or 'throw bricks', then crowd members blindly follow the established pattern.
Conformity to emergent norms and behavioural contagion can occur without conscious realisation, as in cases of mass psychogenic illness

THE POLITICS OF 'WILD MOB' THEORIES
Explanations of mobs as being unruly and irrational serve the political purpose of denying that crowd action can be caused by legitimate social concerns. It should not be forgotten that the majority of crowds are peaceful and are gathered together for the rational purpose of enjoyment.

RULE-GOVERNED AND RATIONAL

THE SOCIAL CONDITIONS FOR RIOTS
Most psychologists agree that crowds do not riot without reason. Schneider (1988) gives 4 conditions necessary for a riot to occur:
1   A long standing suppressed impulse of hostility (often due to perceived social injustice/oppression).
2   A precipitating incident (e.g. the beating of Rodney King in the Los Angeles riots).
3   The translation of impulse into behaviour (this usually occurs as the incident and anger it causes focuses and energises behaviour).
4   The relaxation of usual inhibitions against violence (mostly due to anonymity and social sanction as rioting becomes normative).

SOCIAL IDENTITY THEORY
Reicher (1982a) argues that traditional crowd psychology ignores the social causation of crowd behaviour and regards only individuals as capable of directly planned and rational behaviour. Reicher used social identity theory and the St Paul's riot in Bristol to show how crowd behaviour was not wild and irrational, but defined and directed by the group identity assumed by the individuals. Violence was spontaneous and uniform (e.g. collective brick throwing), but governed and limited by the aims of being a member of the St Paul's community (crowd aggression was directed at the police only and restricted to the St Paul's geographic area). Rather than wild, mindless mob violence, the crowd directed traffic flow through the area and families did their shopping while the riot was in progress.

NORM THEORY
Marsh (1978) has found that regularly occurring crowds develop implicit roles and norms that guide and regulate behaviour. From studying football crowds on the terraces, Marsh distinguished and named different groups among the crowd of supporters (e.g. 'novices', 'rowdies', and 'nutters') each with their own identities, rules, and constraints on behaviour. Football hooliganism is not as wild and undirected as it is reported to be.

RATIONALITY OF EXTREME CROWD BEHAVIOUR
Even panic stampedes to escape from fires can be seen as rational competitive responses in the social conditions they take place in. However, overly calculating and rational theories do underestimate the effects of fear and confusion on the ability to reason in crowds.

Following or resisting influence

FOLLOWING INFLUENCE

THE DEGREE OF INFLUENCE ACHIEVED

Kelman (1958) identified three forms of social influence that seem to reflect the **degree** of change that the influence has on the target as well as the **motives** for the change;

- **Compliance** - people change their behaviour, but **not** their private opinions, attitudes or emotions.
- **Internalisation** - people change their behaviour **and** thoughts - they come to think as the influencer/s want them to think.
- **Identification** - people change their behaviour and thoughts to become more like somebody or to join a group they really admire or respect. Identification implies a more general and complete change in behaviour and may involve stronger feelings of commitment.

THE PSYCHOLOGICAL EFFECTS OF YIELDING TO POWER.

- **Behavioural commitment** - continual behavioural compliance to the demands of others may actually lead to a change in thinking - internalisation. Continually behaving in a way that contradicts your beliefs causes dissonance (feelings of uneasiness) and since thoughts/attitudes are more readily altered than past actions, the individual may come to believe in what they are doing.
- **Momentum of compliance** - starting off with small amounts of compliance may gradually lead to greater amounts as it becomes harder to justify stopping in the light of your past behaviour.
- **Loss of responsibility** - being continually under the power of others may lead to learned helplessness (Seligman): losing feelings of control, responsibility, self-efficacy, and self-esteem.

REASONS FOR FOLLOWING

- **Achieving goals** - both personal needs and group goals are achieved by yielding to social influence. Most societies only function effectively because people conform to social norms of interaction or obey social hierarchies.
- **Group identity** - social groups provide us with information about ourselves and our environment (informational social influence), and are a source of self-esteem and comfort (normative social influence).
- **Socialisation** - personality differences can account for following social influence - Crutchfield found evidence for a conforming personality type, while Rotter (1973) has proposed that those who yield to outside influences may have an external locus of control. However, most research supports the idea that every member of a society learns their culture's norms of power.

RESISTING INFLUENCE

TYPES OF INFLUENCE RESISTANCE

- **Independent behaviour** - involves the true rejection of social influence to behave in accord with one's own internal attitudes, regardless of whether they coincide with the influencer's or not.
- **Anticonformity** - involves resisting social influence by refusing to behave as wished or behaving in the opposite way (Willis, 1963). This behaviour is still affected by society however.

EXAMPLES OF RESISTING SOCIAL INFLUENCE

- **Independence in conformity and obedience experiments** -
  Although disobedience in Milgram's (1963) experiment was low (around one third refused to give the maximum shock), Asch's (1951) conformity experiment showed higher rates of resistance (only 5% conformed on every trial, 25% did not conform at all).
  Resistance in these experiments was significantly increased by having social support - just one ally in Asch's study lowered conformity from an average of 32% to 5%, two other teachers disobeying in Milgram's experiment lowered obedience to 10%.
- **Rebellion** - Gamson et al (1982) found that around 97% of groups showed dissent and 50% completely rebelled to unfair requests from authority figures - probably because groups provide a greater opportunity for dissent to be expressed and discussed, and social support to justify and implement rebellion.
- **Minority influence** - Moscovici (1976) argues minority groups can break majority consensus through adopting a consistent position.

REASONS FOR RESISTING SOCIAL INFLUENCE

- **Psychological reactance** - Brehm (1966) argued that perceived constraints on freedom lead some to resist in order to assert their freedom - telling people they are not allowed to do something is often a good way of getting them to do it!
- **Socialisation** - The society the individual is raised in can affect the level of independence. Higher rates of obedience have been found in Germany and Japan, but lower rates in France. Berry (1966, 1967) discovered that Eskimos who live in an individual hunting society where self reliance is highly valued, showed more independent behaviour than members of the Temmi of Africa whose agricultural society is more socially integrated.

'Cognitive consequences of forced compliance' Festinger and Carlsmith (1959)

AIM

To investigate 'what happens to a person's private opinions if he is forced to do or say something contrary to that opinion'. Festinger (1957) proposed a theory of cognitive dissonance which states that the greater the dissonance (disagreement or contradiction) between two opinions held by the same person, the greater the pressure to reduce it through changing one of the opinions, unless there is a very good corresponding reason for the disagreement. It follows, therefore, that:

* 'If a person is induced to do or say something contrary to his private opinion, there will be a tendency for him to change his opinion so as to bring it in line with what was done or said.' For example, if a person is induced to say that a boring experiment was interesting, there will be dissonance between
  a the persons opinion that the experiment was boring and
  b the knowledge that they have said it was interesting. They will thus be motivated to reduce the dissonance by persuading themselves that the experiment was in fact fairly interesting (changing the opinion because the behaviour cannot be undone).
* 'The larger the pressure to elicit the overt behaviour (beyond the minimum needed to elicit it), the weaker will be the above mentioned tendency'.
  For example, if a person is given $20 to say a boring experiment was interesting (a large pressure, and a good reason to hold dissonant opinions) there will be less of a tendency to change their opinion to think the experiment was interesting than if they are only given $1 (not a good reason for holding dissonant opinions).

METHOD

Subjects: 71 male psychology students participating as a requirement of the course.

Design: Laboratory experiment, independent measures design, 20 subjects were used in each condition. The independent variable was the size of reward for saying a boring experiment was interesting (the degree of justification for opinion change) manipulated in two conditions $1 and $20.
The dependent variable was how enjoyable the boring task was rated (to measure the amount of opinion change produced).
A control condition was used to measure how enjoyable the task was with no contradictory statement or payment.

Procedure: Subjects were asked to participate in an hour of very boring activities (emptying and filling a tray with spools and continuously turning 48 pegs in a board) and were then allocated to one of three conditions:
a Control condition - waited 4 minutes

b $1 condition - were asked to tell a waiting subject in the next room (in fact a confederate) that the experiment they had just completed was very enjoyable, exciting, and interesting for a payment of $1.
c $20 condition - were asked to tell a waiting subject in the next room (in fact a confederate) that the experiment they had just completed was very enjoyable, exciting and interesting for a payment of $20.

All subjects were then interviewed by another researcher (supposedly involved in research unrelated to the previous experiment) who, unaware of which condition the subject had been in, asked subjects to rate how enjoyable the experiment was, how worthwhile to themselves and science it was, and how willing they would be to participate in another similar experiment. Measures were also taken of how convincing and persuasive the subject was in convincing the confederate that the experiment was enjoyable etc.

RESULTS

* Subjects rated the task as significantly more enjoyable (at the P< 0.03 level) in the $1 condition compared to the $20 condition.
* Subjects' willingness to participate in a similar experiment was slightly significantly higher (at the P< 0.15 level) in the $1 compared to $20 condition.
* Subjects rated the task as slightly significantly more scientifically important (at the P< 0.08 level) in the $1 condition compared to $20 condition.

* There was no significant difference in the subjects' ratings of how much they had learnt from the experiment between the $1 and $20 conditions.
* There was no significant difference in the subjects' attempts to persuade the confederate of the experiment's enjoyability between the $1 and $20 conditions.

EVALUATION

Methodological:

Procedure - A well standardised and convincing procedure was used to direct subjects' attention away from the true purpose of the experiment. Those who were suspicious of the experimental set up were discarded in the analysis of data. The opportunity sample (male psychology student biased), however, was not particularly representative.

Data analysis - t-tests were used on attitude scales which are usually taken to represent ordinal level data, and one tailed tests would have been more appropriate to the hypotheses under investigation.

Ethical problems - Deception was employed, unpleasant dissonance was induced, and subjects were asked to lie.

Theoretical: The research provides reasonable, although not dramatic, support for the effect of dissonance on attitude change. However, there are theoretical debates over what causes dissonance (freedom of choice, commitment or personal responsibility), and whether self-perception theory may account for the findings.

Links: Social influence, social cognition, and attitude change.

Pro-social behaviour

DEFINITIONS

PRO-SOCIAL BEHAVIOUR
'Behaviour that benefits others or has positive social consequences.' (Staub, 1978)
This definition is concerned with the consequences not the motives of pro-social behaviour.

HELPING BEHAVIOUR
'Behaviour that intentionally helps or benefits another person.' (Bar-tal, 1976)

ALTRUISM
'Helping another person for no reward and even at some cost to oneself.' (Krebs and Miller, 1985)

ALTRUISM

THE DEBATE OVER ALTRUISM
There is a long standing philosophical and psychological debate over whether pure altruism is possible.

Those who argue against altruism point out that there are always physical or psychological rewards, either intrinsic (such as self-esteem, satisfaction, etc.), or extrinsic (such as social approval, money, etc.), behind any intentional act of helping. At a more fundamental level, apparently altruistic acts have been explained by sociobiologists in terms of the genetic 'rewards' of self sacrificing behaviour.

This position of 'universal egoism' is almost irrefutable, however, for one can always think of rewards for an act of help but cannot guarantee that these rewards were the basis of the helper's intentions.

Those who think humans are capable of true altruistic behaviour, suggest that it is governed more by impulsive, *emotional* factors rather than cool, rational thought processes. Research into altruism in humans has therefore mainly focused on the role of emotional arousal and empathy.

EMOTIONAL AROUSAL
Piliavin et al (1981) suggest that the plight of others, especially in emergency conditions, can cause such emotional arousal in the bystander that it could lead to an impulsive, non-rational desire to give help.

However, the emotional arousal triggered in the bystander that provokes this urge is experienced as unpleasant, and thus helping serves to reduce it.

For this reason, the helping can be seen as selfishly motivated - reducing the unpleasant arousal and avoiding the guilt of not helping is seen as rewarding - and so arousal can become just another factor in the analysis of costs and rewards for helping.

EMPATHY
Empathy involves the desire to reduce another person's distress (rather than your own distress as a watching bystander). Coke et al (1978) have experimentally demonstrated that the emotion of empathy will increase helping behaviour, but its altruistic status is less clear.

Empathy involves the bystander taking on the perspective of the victim and, therefore, vicariously experiencing the distress of others. However, this interpretation could still involve selfishness, since the motive is based on thinking 'what if this happened to **me**?'.

Alternatively, people who feel empathy for others may feel saddened by the victim's plight and help in order to raise their own mood (Cialdini et al, 1987).

Batson, however, suggests that empathy involves a genuine desire to reduce other people's distress rather than our own. In a cleverly designed study, Batson et al (1981) found that empathetic observers would volunteer to receive electric shocks in the place of another, even if they could easily reduce their own distress at seeing the other person given shocks by leaving the experiment or putting less effort into a test that required a high score in order to let the observer swap places with the victim.

'Good Samaritanism: an underground phenomenon?' Piliavin, Rodin, and Piliavin (1969)

BACKGROUND

Social psychologists were prompted into investigating helping behaviour by the case of Kitty Genovese (a woman stabbed to death over a period of 30 minutes in front of 38 unresponsive witnesses). Most studies were conducted under strict laboratory conditions, using non-visual emergency situations. The main theories of helping behaviour involved diffusion of responsibility and the economic analysis of costs and rewards for helping.

AIM

To investigate, under real life conditions, the effect on the speed and frequency of helping, and the race of the helper, of
- the type of victim (drunk or ill)
- the race of the victim (black or white)
- the presence of helping models (present or absent)
- the size of the witnessing group

METHOD

Design

Field experiment

Independent variables (4):
- Type of victim (drunk or ill)
- Race of victim (black or white)
- Presence of helping models (present or absent)
- Size of the witnessing group

Dependent variables recorded:
- Frequency of help
- Speed of help
- Race of helper
- Sex of helper
- Movement out of area
- Verbal comments

Subjects

New York subway travellers between 11am and 3 pm, approximately 45% black, 55% white, mean of 8.5 bystanders in critical area, opportunity sample.

Situation

Non stop 7.5 minute journey in subway carriage

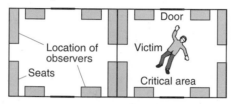

Procedure

4 teams of 4 researchers
- female who recorded reactions
- 2 males one acting victim one model

Victims - 3 white, 1 black, all aged between 26-35, dressed and acted identically. Instructed to collapse after 70 seconds and remain on floor until helped.
Model instructed to help 70 seconds after collapse until end if no other help.

103 trials conducted in total, of which: 38 involved drunk victim (smelt of alcohol and carried a bottle in paper bag). 65 involved sober victim carrying a cane.

RESULTS

1. Frequency of help was impressive - overall 93% helped spontaneously (before the model), 60% of which involved more than one helper. Help was so spontaneous that the model's effect could not be properly studied.

2. No diffusion of responsibility was found with group size.

3. A victim who appeared ill was more likely to receive help than one who appeared drunk. There was 100% help for the cane victim (of which 65 out of 68 trials involved spontaneous help) but 81% help for the drunk victim (of which 19 out of 38 trials involved spontaneous help). Help was also offered more quickly for the cane victim (a median of 5 seconds compared to 109 second delay with the drunk victim).

4. There was a tendency for same race helping to be more frequent, especially in the drunk condition.

5. Men were significantly more likely to help the victim than women.

6. The longer the emergency continued without help being given:

   a The less impact the model had on the other bystanders.

   b The more likely bystanders were to leave the area.

   c The more likely it was that observers would discuss their behaviour.

DISCUSSION OF RESULTS

Unlike earlier studies of helping behaviour, bystanders were continuously and visually presented with the emergency situation, making it difficult to ignore.

Immediate situations decrease diffusion of impact.

The Arousal: Cost-Reward Model proposes that the decision to help depends upon the costs and rewards of helping versus not helping. Therefore, less help for drunk victim since costs of helping are high (perhaps dangerous), costs of not helping are low (no blame), and rewards are low (probably less gratitude).

Less costs of helping same race in terms of public censure, more witness arousal empathy with victim.

Less cost for men in terms of ability to physically help.

Arousal: Cost-Reward Model argues that bystander arousal produced by the plight of others can be reduced by leaving the area or rationalising the decision not to help (e.g. by regarding the victim as undeserving) if help is not given.

STRENGTHS OF STUDY

- High ecological validity - study took place under naturally occurring conditions.

- Highly standardised procedure

- Yielded a lot of detailed data.

- Proposed a theoretical explanation to account for levels of helping in all conditions of the experiment.

WEAKNESSES OF STUDY

- Methodological weaknesses - conditions are under less strict control in field experiments than laboratory experiments. Insufficient trials conducted in some conditions of the experiment to yield reliable data, e.g. there were fewer drunk victims, only 8 black cane carriers.

- Ethical weaknesses - deception, lack of consent, no debriefing, and the production of anxiety and or inconvenience for the bystanders are all ethically problematic.

The situational determinants of helping behaviour

THE REACTIONS OF OTHERS

Pluralistic ignorance - if several people are present and nobody shows signs of concern or action, then the situation may be socially defined as 'in need of no action'. This is a form of informational social influence, bystanders look to each other to know how to react.

Latane and Rodin (1969)

Subjects sitting in a waiting room went to help a female experimenter (they had heard fall over next door) more often and more quickly when alone than when in the company of a confederate of the experimenter who did nothing.

Latane and Darley (1968)

Subjects completing a questionnaire in a waiting room that began to fill with smoke were more likely to report the smoke when alone than when in a group of three (despite being unable to see clearly after 6 minutes!).

Aaarrhh!!!!!

THE NUMBER OF BYSTANDERS

Social impact theory (Latane, 1981) suggests that a diffusion of responsibility occurs when many witnesses are present - the impact of a victim's plight is felt less strongly for each subject and so more witnesses can actually mean less helping.

Darley and Latane (1968)

Individual subjects, who were meant to be discussing social problems with other participants in separate cubicles over an intercom system (to prevent embarrassment), heard one of the group (in fact a tape recording of a confederate - there were no other real participants) explain that he was prone to have seizures when under stress - and later proceeded to have one! The experimenters measured the percentage who helped within 4 minutes.

When the subject thought there were:

a 2 in the group, 85% intervened.
b 3 in the group, 62% intervened.
c 5 other subjects, 31% intervened.

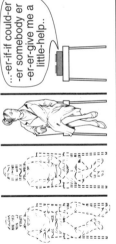

...-er-if-if could-er -er somebody er -er-give me a little-help...

THE NORMS OF SOCIETY

Different social norms or expectations to help in certain situations may influence helping behaviour. Most societies conform to norms of reciprocity (help is given to those who are likely to return the favour); social responsibility (helping dependent others, e.g. beggars); and neighbourliness (helping those who live locally). However, norm theory does not predict which norms will be conformed to when there is a conflict between them, e.g. helping a beggar who is dependent but not likely to reciprocate the favour.

ENVIRONMENTAL LOCATION

Help is less likely to be given in built up urban areas than more rural areas, perhaps because of stimulus overload (Milgram, 1970), greater risks due to crime levels or the more impersonal environment of largely populated areas.

AMBIGUITY

Help is more likely to be given in clear-cut and emergency situations.

THE PROXIMITY OF BYSTANDERS

Social impact theory (Latane, 1981) suggests that as the remoteness between the bystander and victim increases (the greater the distance between them), the less directly responsible the bystander will feel. Someone requesting donations in front of you is more likely to be helped than someone asking by telephone.

Piliavin et al's (1969) subway studies revealed that help was offered just as frequently on crowded subways as uncrowded ones, suggesting that it is more difficult to refuse help in an immediate, face-to-face, non-remote situation, such as the enclosed space of a subway.

Factors affecting the decision to help

INFORMATION PROCESSING OF EMERGENCIES

Latane and Darley (1970) proposed an information processing explanation of helping behaviour that identifies several stages involved in the decision making process of whether to help another.

Is the situation needing help **NOTICED**?

— NO → **HELP NOT GIVEN**

YES ↓

Is the situation **DEFINED** as an emergency?

— NO →

YES ↓

Does the potential helper **TAKE RESPONSIBILITY**?

— NO →

YES ↓

Does the potential helper decide **HOW** to help?

— NO →

YES ↓

Does the potential helper **ACT** upon the chosen way to help?

YES → **HELP GIVEN**

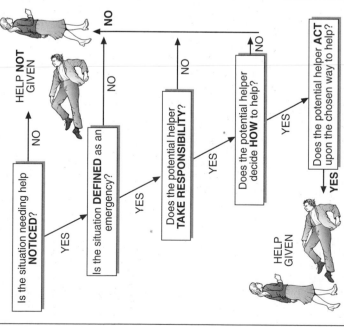

COSTS AND REWARDS OF HELPING

Exchange theory - Proposes that the decision to help is made on rational grounds, by calculating the profits of intervening. If the costs of helping (e.g. loss of time, money, health) outweigh the rewards (e.g. praise) then help is unlikely. Experiments support this theory, but it may be over-rationalistic, ignoring the emotions aroused by the distress of victims.

		Costs of helping victim	
		LOW	HIGH
Costs of not helping victim	HIGH	Direct help	Indirect or no help
	LOW	Help depends on norms	No help

Arousal: cost-reward model - Piliavin et al (1981) suggested different kinds of helping situation may cause different motives for helping: 'one kind is triggered by quick, non-rational emotional arousal in response to emergencies, the other kind is influenced more by the potential helper's analysis of the costs and benefits of helping'

THE COSTS OF HELPING IN DIFFERENT SITUATIONS
THE COST OF TIME

Darley and Batson's (1973) 'Good Samaritan' study operationalised the cost of time for subjects by telling them that they were either on time, behind schedule or ahead of schedule to deliver a talk in the next building on the 'Good Samaritan'. Of those who had plenty of time to reach the building 63% helped a man in the corridor on the way who was slumped in a doorway, compared to 45% of those who were on schedule and 10% who thought they were late.

THE COST OF HELPING DIFFERENT VICTIMS

Piliavin et al tested helping behaviour for different victims by having confederates collapse in subway trains under different conditions. When the confederate

- had a walking cane, help occurred quickly and frequently
- had a bottle and smelt of alcohol, help occurred slowly and less frequently
- had (fake) blood dribbling from their mouth, help occurred frequently but indirectly

The costs of helping and not helping were different in each condition.

NATURE OF BYSTANDER

Personal factors affecting the decision to help include
- the past reinforcement history of the individual for helping behaviour plus internalised norms
- the level of moral development reached
- the personality of the individual (those who are emotionally empathetic may help more)
- similarity to the victim (the greater the similarity, the greater the help given)
- the individual's relationship to the victim (greater helping if genetically related or friend)
- the mood of the bystander (good moods lead to more help)

Aggression - social learning theory of aggression

SUPPORTING EVIDENCE

Bandura et al (1963) allowed one group of children to watch an adult model perform certain aggressive acts with an inflatable 'Bobo doll' which were unlikely to occur normally, such as throwing the doll up in the air, hitting it with a hammer and punching it while saying things like 'pow' and 'boom'. When these children were left in a playroom with the inflatable doll, they frequently imitated the same acts of aggression, compared to a control group who had not seen the model and showed none of the behaviours.

Bandura (1965) used a similar experimental set-up, but showed different consequences for the model's aggression to three groups of children. One group saw the model's aggression being rewarded, one group saw the model being punished for the aggression, and another group saw no specific consequences.

When allowed to enter the playroom, the children who had seen the model punished showed less imitative aggression than the other two groups. However, if all the children were offered rewards for doing what the model had done, all groups showed high levels of imitation.

The children in the model punished group had clearly learnt the aggression by observation, but had not shown their potential to imitate it because they expected negative consequences.

SOCIAL LEARNING THEORY AND AGGRESSION

Social learning theory was developed mainly by Bandura and Walters, and suggests that aggression is **learnt** from the environment (rather than being an inner drive) through reinforcement and the process of **modelling**. Modelling involves learning through the **observation** of other people (models), which may lead to **imitation** if the behaviour to be imitated **leads to desirable consequences**.

Bandura distinguished between the learning of aggressive behaviour and the performance of it. Aggression may be learnt from models through observation, but the likelihood of it being imitated depends on the perceived consequences of the model's aggression - if a child sees a model's aggression being rewarded, this acts as vicarious (indirect) reinforcement for the child who will proceed to imitate it. If the child sees aggression in others punished then, although the behaviour is learnt, it is less likely to be imitated.

Models can be parents, peers or media characters (thus this theory has implications for the portrayal of violence on television).

EVALUATION
Methodological faults

Bandura's social learning theory laboratory experiments have been accused of being overly **artificial** (hitting a Bobo doll is not the same as inflicting aggression on a real person) and of inducing **demand characteristics** (the children may have believed that they were meant to behave aggressively).
However, other experimental studies have demonstrated that children are more likely to hurt other children after viewing violent behaviour (Liebert and Baron, 1972).

Theoretical faults

The theory neglects the role of innate factors in aggression. However, social learning theory does provide a more credible explanation of the transmission of violent behaviour than the traditional behaviourist view of learning, and has investigated the types of models and behaviours that are most likely to be imitated.

IMPLICATIONS FOR REDUCING/CONTROLLING AGGRESSION

The implication of social learning theory is that if aggressive behaviour is not observed or reinforced in a society, then it will not naturally occur.

However many examples of aggression already frequently occur in the great majority of societies, and so the theory would be more realistically applied to reducing aggression.

This could be achieved by ensuring that aggression is not reinforced, or that negative consequences are seen to follow it. The direct punishment of aggression raises problems though, since it may itself be perceived as an aggressive act that is socially approved of - indeed research consistently demonstrates that 'aggression breeds aggression'. Munroe and Munroe (1975) found cross-culturally that childhood aggression is highest in societies whose families highly punish their children for showing aggression.

Social learning theory would suggest that media violence should be dramatically reduced.

'Transmission of aggression through imitation of aggressive models' Bandura, Ross, and Ross (1961)

AIM
To demonstrate that learning can occur through mere observation of a model and that imitation can occur in the absence of that model. More specifically:
- Children shown aggressive models will show significantly more imitative aggressive behaviour than those shown non-aggressive or no models.
- Children shown non-aggressive, subdued models will show significantly less aggressive behaviour than those shown aggressive or no models.
- Boys should show significantly more imitative aggression than girls, especially with the male rather than female aggressive model.

METHOD
Subjects: 72 children, 36 boys and 36 girls, aged 37-69 months (with a mean age of 52 months) were used.

Design: Laboratory experiment, in which the independent variable (type of model) was manipulated in three conditions:
- Aggressive model shown
- Non-aggressive model shown
- Control condition, no model shown

The dependent variable was the amount of imitative behaviour and aggression shown by the children.

A matched pairs design was used with 24 children (12 boys and 12 girls) assigned to each condition, with an effort made to match subjects according to pre-existing levels of aggression. In addition to the above manipulations, in the experimental conditions:
- Half the subjects observed a same sex model.
- The other half observed opposite sex models.

Procedure: In the experimental conditions children were individually shown into a room containing toys and played with some potato prints and pictures in a corner for 10 minutes while either:
- The non-aggressive adult model (either male or female) played in a quiet and subdued manner for 10 minutes, or
- The aggressive model distinctively aggressed against a 5 foot inflated Bobo doll by **a** sitting on it and repeatedly punching it on the nose, **b** striking it on the head with a mallet, and **c** throwing it up in the air and kicking it around the room. The aggressive model also uttered verbally aggressive statements such as 'sock him in the nose', 'throw him in the air' and 'pow', as well as two non-aggressive statements - 'he keeps coming back for more' and 'he sure is a tough fella'.

All children (including the control group) were then individually taken to a different experimental location and subjected to mild aggression arousal by being stopped from playing with some very attractive toys. This arousal took place in order to give all groups an equal chance of showing aggression and also to allow the group shown the non-aggressive model to demonstrate an inhibition of aggressive behaviour.

All children were then shown into another room which contained both aggressive toys (e.g. a 3 foot high Bobo doll, a mallet, dartguns, and a tether ball) and non-aggressive toys (e.g. a tea set, dolls, and colouring paper), and were observed through a one-way mirror for 20 minutes.

Observers recorded (with inter-scorer reliabilities of .90 correlation coefficient) behaviour in the following categories:

- **Imitation behaviour of aggressive model**:
  a physical aggression, e.g. sitting on the doll and repeatedly punching it on the nose.
  b Verbal aggression, e.g. 'sock him' or 'pow'.
  c Non-aggressive speech, e.g. 'he sure is a tough fella'.
- **Partial imitation behaviour of aggressive model**, e.g. mallet aggression against other objects or sitting on the Bobo doll without punching it.
- **Non-imitative physical and verbal aggression**, e.g. just punching the Bobo doll, physical aggression with other objects and verbal non-imitative remarks 'shoot the Bobo' or 'horses fighting, biting'.
- **Non-aggressive behaviour**, e.g. non aggressive play or sitting quietly.

RESULTS
1. Children in the aggressive model condition showed significantly more imitation of the model's physical and verbal aggression and non-aggressive verbal responses than children who saw the non-aggressive model or no model at all in the control condition.
2. Children in the aggressive model condition usually showed more partial imitation and non-imitative physical and verbal aggression than those who saw the non-aggressive model or no model at all, but not always to a significant degree.
3. Children in the non-aggressive model condition showed very little aggression, although not always significantly less than the no model group.
4. Children who saw the same sex model were only likely to imitate the behaviour significantly more in some of the categories. For example, boys would imitate male models significantly more than girls for physical and verbal imitative aggression, non-imitative aggression and gun play; girls would imitate female models more than boys for verbal imitative aggression and non-imitative aggression only, but not significantly.

EVALUATION
Methodological:

Procedure -	Not completely standardised presentation of model's behaviour (later experiments used videotape presentation)
Artificiality -	Bizarre acts of aggression were shown and imitated against a Bobo doll, not a real person.
Ethical problems -	Aggression was induced in, and taught to, children. Exposure to an adult stranger's aggression may have been frightening for the children.

Theoretical: The research provides reasonable support for the social learning theory idea that behaviour can be acquired through observation rather than direct personal experience, and that reinforcement is not required for learning to occur. This study has important implications for the effects of media violence on children.

Links: Social learning theory, aggression, socialisation, gender differences.

Frustration-aggression theory of aggression

SUPPORTING EVIDENCE

Experimental evidence
Barker et al (1941) found that children frustrated by being kept waiting a long time before they were allowed to play in a room full of attractive toys were more aggressive and destructive (throwing the toys against the wall and stamping on them) than a second control group of children who were not frustrated.

Correlational evidence
Hovland and Sears (1940) found a significant correlation between economic frustration (measured in terms of the price of cotton) and displaced aggression on scapegoats (measured in terms of the number of lynchings of blacks) in the southern states of America between 1882 and 1930.

REFINEMENTS OF THE THEORY
Studies have demonstrated that the greater the degree of frustration, the greater the likelihood of aggression. Frustration is increased by being **thwarted**

- **close to achieving the goal**
  Harris (1974) manipulated the variable of frustration by having confederates push into bus stop, cinema, and supermarket checkout queues either in front of **a** the second person in line (high frustration) or **b** the twelfth person (lower frustration). Verbal aggression was greater in the high frustration condition.

- **unexpectedly**
  Kulick and Brown (1979) led subjects involved in telephoning for charity donations to believe that they could expect either a high or low degree of success. When they actually gained no donations at all. those subjects with the greatest expectations were more frustrated and showed more aggression - slamming the phone down harder and speaking more harshly.

- **without good reason**
  In the same study, those subjects who were given legitimate reasons for donation refusal were less aggressive than those who were not.

FRUSTRATION-AGGRESSION THEORY
In proposing their frustration-aggression theory, Dollard et al (1939) suggested that:
> **'...aggression is always a consequence of frustration and, contrariwise... the existence of frustration always leads to some form of aggression.'**

Dollard et al's theory was an attempt to link the Freudian notion of aggressive drives to the behaviourist's ideas of stimulus-response interactions. According to the frustration-aggression theory, aggression is an **innate drive response** to frustrating external **stimuli** from the environment.
The frustrating stimuli can be any **social** conditions that thwart our satisfaction, such as poor housing, unemployment, etc.
The aggressive response can take many forms - such as overt aggressive behaviour against the cause of frustration, or indirect release through **displacement** of aggression onto scapegoats or even aggressive fantasy.

EVALUATION
Dollard et al's extreme version of the frustration-aggression hypothesis has now been rejected by research showing that

- **aggression is not always caused by frustration**
  There are many other social factors and theories that can explain the occurrence of aggression without frustration. Social learning theory argues that aggression may be caused by imitating other's - especially if their aggressive behaviour was positively reinforced; while conformity theory would suggest that aggression is caused by following the norms or expectations of the group.

- **frustration does not always lead to aggression**
  Frustration can lead to a range of responses, not just aggression, for example despair or depression (Seligman). **Berkowitz** (1968) suggested that frustration causes anger or a 'readiness' to aggress, but argues that aggression will only result if there are aggressive cues or provocative stimuli in the environment. Berkowitz and Le Page (1967) found, for example, that frustrated individuals showed greater aggression if they were in the presence of guns than neutral objects (the weapons effect).

IMPLICATIONS FOR REDUCING/CONTROLLING AGGRESSION
According to the original theory, since aggression is regarded as a drive response, the energy associated with it can not be destroyed and must be released in some form. There are, therefore, two implications:

- **Prevent or reduce frustration** in the first place, e.g. by improving economic conditions, but of course there will always be frustrations of some sort as long as resources are limited.

- **Control the expression of aggression** by finding harmless ways of displacing it, such as through vigorous exercise, sport or even through watching violent T.V. (emotional **catharsis**). The concepts of drive reduction and displacement have fallen into disrepute, however, through lack of experimental support.
  According to Berkowitz's modification of the original model, one major implication for the reduction of aggression is through the control of aggressive stimuli such as guns. As Berkowitz comments, weapons not only allow violence but can stimulate it as well: 'The finger pulls the trigger, but the trigger may also be pulling the finger'.

Social and environmental factors influencing aggression

OVERCROWDING

Overcrowding is a popular social psychological explanation of aggression in, for example, highly populated inner city areas.

McCain et al (1980) found that more crowded prisons experienced higher amounts of aggressive and disruptive behaviour, although Freedman et al (1975) found no significant correlation between population density and aggression in areas of New York City.

Calhoun (1962) conducted a famous study on overcrowding in rat populations and found that the rats developed many different anti-social behaviours, including indiscriminate 'berserk' attacks on females and juveniles, and even cannibalism.

EVALUATION

However the precise causes of aggression in these circumstances are difficult to isolate - inner city areas have many problems that could act as stimuli for aggression, such as increased poverty, competition, drug abuse, crime etc. Some social psychologists suggest that invasion of personal space may be the key factor.

IMPLICATIONS FOR REDUCING/ CONTROLLING AGGRESSION

A rather obvious recommendation would be to increase the volume of space per individual in crowded areas. Careful architectural design and planning could ease congestion. This is an especially important application of research, given the increasing incidence of 'road rage' in Britain.

DEINDIVIDUATION

Deindividuation occurs when an person is no longer identified as an individual. It can therefore occur

- when surrounded by large numbers of others, i.e. in crowds, or
- when clothing makes individual identification difficult or impossible, i.e. when in uniform or disguise.

Deindividuation of the aggressor can lead to a loss of inhibitions and an abdication of personal responsibility, making aggression more permissible or easily expressed. Deindividuation of the victim of aggression can lead to dehumanisation and a disregard of their individuality and rights as a human being.

EVALUATION

Zimbardo (1970) found hooded subjects gave twice the level of electric shock to a victim than those with normal clothes and name tags.
Some psychologists would argue that deindividuation is really only a social factor that facilitates the expression of aggression rather than being a fundamental cause of it.

IMPLICATIONS FOR REDUCING/ CONTROLLING AGGRESSION

Introduce measures to increase individual identity in crowds - football grounds achieve this through identity cards and video surveillance.

CONFORMITY TO NORMS

Research indicates that aggression can be produced and shaped through conformity to norms of aggression in society. Different groups in society may produce different norms of aggression both in terms of when aggression should be expressed and how it should be expressed.

Marsh (1978) studied the norms of aggression involved in football hooliganism - violence was expected by the group in order to save face, but was controlled by being expressed in a ritualised way (comparable to the aggressive rituals in animals studied by ethologists such as Lorenz). Once a rival fan had been kicked to the floor and been made to bleed, the combat was finished - anyone going excessively further than that was described as a 'nutter', a clear deviant from the group norm.

Anderson (1994) has discovered similar norms governing predominantly teenage violence in inner cities of the USA, which revolve around the expectations of receiving 'respect'.

EVALUATION

Theories like conformity to norms imply that aggression is under the control of conscious and rational (in terms of the social situation) thought processes. However, many environmental factors (such as pain or heat) that contribute towards aggression probably operate at a more primitive level.

IMPLICATIONS FOR REDUCING/ CONTROLLING AGGRESSION

Group norms already control the expression of aggression. To reduce the level shown would involve changing the expectations of the group. Norms of aggression do vary enormously from one culture to another, so change is a possible if a lengthy possibility.

Non-social approaches to aggression

THE PHYSIOLOGICAL APPROACH TO AGGRESSION

GENETIC CAUSES

Researchers have argued that the possession of an extra 'Y' chromosome is more likely to make males aggressive. However, the research is mixed, and XYY chromosomes are too rare to explain all aggression.

Other researchers point out that aggression could be passed through the genes (the selective breeding of rats has supported this idea), indeed Johnson et al (1972) have demonstrated that rat aggression against frogs is governed by a genetic time switch, frog-killing does not start until rats are 50 days old.

Evaluation

Physiological findings are in-complete and reductionist. Generalising animal findings to human behaviour is questionable.

Reduction of aggression

Only genetic testing or gene therapy would provide any possibility of controlling the genetic contribution to aggression. However, this raises many practical and ethical problems.

BIOCHEMICAL CAUSES

Some suggest that male aggressiveness is due to high levels of testosterone. Studies of criminals with a history of violence have shown them to have higher levels of testosterone compared with non-violent criminals.

Hormonal changes in women before menstruation can produce aggressive behaviour (Floody, 1983), although this finding is not universal.

Evaluation

It is difficult to know whether increased levels of testosterone are a cause or effect of the violence. Dominant but non-aggressive criminals also have higher levels (Ehrenkranz et al, 1974), suggesting that aggression may not be the only effect.

Biochemicals and hormones, as well as substances like alcohol or drugs, have variable effects on behaviour.

Reduction of aggression

Castration of violent sexual offenders has produced dramatic decreases in aggression, although the studies have not always been well controlled.

NEUROPHSIOLOGICAL CAUSES

Neurophysiologists have identified many areas of the brain involved in aggression, in particular the temporal lobe and limbic system. It even seems that different structures within the brain may be responsible for different types of aggression - Bard (1928) removed parts of cat brains to produce 'sham rage' (the signs but not the attack behaviour of aggression), while Moyer (1976) claimed to have identified areas involved in predatory aggression.

It seems that injury to these areas of the brain responsible for aggression can sometimes lead to excessive and uncontrollable violence - Charles Whitman, a man who shot 38 people, was later found to have had a temporal lobe tumour.

Evaluation

Isolating precise areas responsible for aggression is to oversimplify the massive interconnectedness of the brain. Delgado (1967) stimulated the aggression centres of monkeys by remote control and found that their aggression was not indiscriminate but directed according to their position on the dominance hierarchy - showing the influence of the reasoning parts of the brain.

Reduction of aggression

Brain surgery could have a calming effect on aggressive patients, but the disastrous past use of lobotomisation should warn us against such drastic measures.

THE DRIVE THEORY APPROACHES TO AGGRESSION

THE PSYCHOANALYTIC APPROACH

Freud proposed that aggression was a manifestation of the death instinct, Thanatos, which seeks our own destruction. However to prevent aggression being directed against ourselves, it is displaced outwards onto others - in Freud's opinion we must destroy others if we are not to destroy ourselves.

Freud argued that aggressive urges build up in the hydraulic, closed energy system of the mind and must be released in some form. Those who are over-controlled about expressing their aggression may eventually cause an uncontrollable and spontaneous outburst to occur (Megargee).

Evaluation

Hydraulic drive theories of aggression have been substantially rejected, and scientific support is lacking for many other aspects of psychoanalytic theory.

Reduction of aggression

Catharsis and sublimation, e.g. in sports, could provide a safe outlet for aggressive impulses.

THE ETHOLOGICAL APPROACH

This considers the evolutionary function of aggression - to allow animals to defend themselves and to compete for food and mates. Ardrey suggests animals have a 'territorial imperative' - the desire to obtain and defend territory to secure access to food and mates. Aggression is thus a highly adaptive behaviour.

However, it is also an extremely risky behaviour to indulge in since it is returned by other organisms and may result in death before genes have been passed on. For this reason, animals have evolved behaviour rituals that aim to:

- Settle potentially aggressive disputes between competitors for food, dominance and/or mates before resorting to damaging violence.
- Allow animals to 'signal surrender' to halt combat before further serious damage or death is incurred by one or both competitors (appeasement rituals).

According to Lorenz, aggression is an innate hydraulic drive that will discharge itself spontaneously if no suitable target for aggression is in the environment.

Evaluation

Red dear stags attempt to resolve conflicts over mating rights by indulging in roaring contests - the loudest one wins; while wolves will attempt to threaten off others through raised hackles, growling, and snarling. Lorenz argued that humans also attempt to resolve conflict through intimidation and threats. Rats and dogs expose their bellies as appeasement responses, humans beg and cry. However, unrestrained aggression does occur in animals such as chimpanzees.

Reduction of aggression

Lorenz argued that aggression has to be released in ritualised ways. Guns and weapons should be removed, since they interfere with ritual expression.

Explanations of individual, social, and cultural diversity in pro-and anti-social behaviour

DIVERSITY

INDIVIDUAL DIVERSITY

There are large differences *between* individuals in levels of aggression and helping behaviour, but reasonable consistency *within* individuals over time. Aggression is a trait that especially shows a high correlation between childhood and adulthood - on a par with the stability of intelligence over time.

SOCIAL DIVERSITY

Different sections within a society will often show varying levels of aggression. Boys, for example, are found to be consistently more aggressive than girls in virtually all societies.

Males show more direct and 'chivalrous' types of helping behaviour than females. Those living in inner cities may show less helping and more aggression, while those in low socio-economic groups may be exposed to more environmental causes of aggression.

CULTURAL DIVERSITY

Cultures show wide differences in aggression and helping behaviour.

The Arapesh of New Guinea were described by Margaret Mead (1935) as gentle, kind, co-operative, and generous. Children from traditional Maori, Aboriginal, and Blackfoot Native American cultures have all scored high on pro-social behaviour, while children on Israeli kibbutzim continue to co-operate on joint tasks, even when individual achievement is rewarded (Moghaddam et al, 1993).

Cross-cultural tests on attitudes to helping illustrate differences too - Hindu Indians tend to see helping as a universal obligation compared to Americans who consider the giving of help as more dependent upon factors like the nature of the help needed, the economic costs and benefits of helping and the closeness of the relationship to the victim.

On the negative side however, Mead (1935) also described another New Guinea tribe, the Mundugumor, who were ruthless, uncaring, selfish and aggressive. Chagnon (1974) studied the Yanomano of the Upper Amazon, an extremely fierce people whose society is in an almost constant state of warfare and where up to a third of males die violent deaths.

Amongst the more industrialised countries, the USA shows significantly higher levels of homicide, rape and violent crime than most European countries.

EXPLANATIONS

PERSONALITY TRAIT

Individuals may possess more aggressive personality traits due to genetic factors (significantly higher correlations in aggressiveness have been found between identical twins than non identical), or individual reinforcement history.

Research has found mixed support for altruistic personality traits - Hartshorne and May (1928) concluded that helping was more situation specific, although later studies disagreed.

PHYSIOLOGY

Individual differences in aggression could result from damage to the temporal lobe or limbic system of the brain, or differences in testosterone hormone levels.

ENVIRONMENTAL TRIGGERS

Social frustrations and overcrowding can trigger higher levels of aggression. Stimulus overload can reduce helping.

PHYSIOLOGY

Predisposing genetic and hormonal factors could account for higher levels of male aggression.

SOCIAL LEARNING

Could account for higher levels of aggression in boys than girls. Fagot (1978) observed that parents encouraged and reinforced more aggressive behaviour in boys than girls.

SOCIALISATION

The most supported explanation of cultural variations in pro- and anti-social behaviour involves childhood learning and/or conformity to norms of aggression in society.

Cultures that disapprove of violence produce less aggression, even if surrounded by aggressive neighbours, e.g. the Amish society in America. Similar findings occur with helping behaviour, which is higher in Israeli children in kibbutzim than nearby cities.

Whiting and Whiting (1975) found greater childhood helping behaviour in cultures whose children are involved in family responsibilities, chores, and sibling raising (e.g. Kenya and Mexico) than cultures whose children are paid for contributions to family life (e.g. USA).

ENVIRONMENTAL INFLUENCES

Different cultures will be exposed to different levels of environmental triggers for aggression. Turnbull (1972) found that the Ik mountain people of Uganda, who live in extreme poverty due to very scarce environmental resources, are extremely selfish, cruel, and uncharitable.

PHYSIOLOGY

While biological influences should not be ignored (e.g. Bolton, 1973, has linked hypoglycaemia to homicide among the Qolla people of the Andes), the huge cross-cultural variations in pro- and anti-social behaviour indicate a greater role for learning factors.

The influence of the media on pro-and anti-social behaviour

LABORATORY EXPERIMENTS ON MEDIA VIOLENCE
Bandura's experiments showed that aggression could be learnt and imitated from live, filmed or cartoon models.
Liebert and Baron (1972) found that children who had watched a violent programme were more likely to hurt another child. However laboratory studies may produce artificial results.

CORRELATIONS ON MEDIA VIOLENCE
Eron (1987) found a significant positive correlation between the amount of aggression viewed at age 8 and later aggression at age 30.
Phillips (1986) has found correlations between highly publicised incidents of aggression, such as murder cases or boxing matches, and the number of corresponding incidents in society at large.

NATURAL EXPERIMENTS ON MEDIA VIOLENCE
Joy et al (1986) measured children's levels of aggression in a Canadian town one year before and after television was introduced, and found a significant increase compared to the non significant increases in towns that already had television.

FIELD EXPERIMENTS ON MEDIA VIOLENCE
Parke et al (1977) showed juvenile delinquents in the USA and Belgium either violent or non-violent television for a week in their homes. Aggression was greater for the violent TV group especially in those children who had previously shown higher levels.

OBSERVATIONAL LEARNING
Violent behaviour could be learnt by observation and imitated if rewarding.

DISINHIBITION
Watching aggression could reduce inhibitions about behaving aggressively as it is seen as socially legitimate.

AROUSAL
Aggressive emotional arousal or excitement from watching aggression may lead to real violence.

DESENSITISATION
Watching aggression may lead to an increased acceptance or tolerance of it in society.

NEGATIVE EFFECTS (OF MEDIA VIOLENCE)

MEDIATING FACTORS
- The personality of the viewer. The effects of TV violence often depend on what the child brings to the screen.
- The amount of exposure to media violence.

HOW MIGHT THE MEDIA INFLUENCE BEHAVIOUR ?

NO EFFECT
Howitt and Cumberbatch (1974) analysed 300 studies concluding that TV violence has no direct effect on children's behaviour.
Freedman (1984, 1986) argues that although there is a small correlation between levels of viewing and behaving aggressively, the causal connection is very weak.

POSITIVE EFFECTS OF MEDIA VIOLENCE

INOCULATION
Watching antisocial violence could provide the opportunity to discuss its immorality or to see it come to no good (the 'baddie' loses).

CATHARSIS
According to Freud's ideas, watching violence could provide a relief from pent up aggression, as it is released through emotional sympathy.

STUDIES ON THE CATHARTIC EFFECT OF TV VIOLENCE
Feshbach and Singer (1971) claimed that children shown aggressive programs over a 6 week period showed *less* aggressive behaviour than those who saw non-violent TV. However, this study has been accused of methodological flaws, and more recent studies have not replicated or have found the opposite findings.

POSITIVE EFFECTS OF PRO-SOCIAL MEDIA

POSITIVE ROLE MODELS
Just as aggression could be learnt from aggressive media models, so pro-social role models could also provide a basis for observational learning and imitation - especially if their behaviour produces rewards such as public praise, social respect etc. (the 'goodie' always wins in the end).

STUDIES ON THE EFFECTS OF PRO-SOCIAL TV
Sprafkin et al (1975) found over 90% of children chose to help a puppy instead of personal gain after watching a program that involved helping ('Lassie'), while Baron et al (1979) found children were more co-operative after watching the 'The Waltons'.
Hearold (1986) analysed approximately 200 studies and concluded that pro-social television has around twice the effect on children's behaviour than anti-social television.

Differences in relationships

DIFFERENT TYPES OF RELATIONSHIP

RELATIONSHIP TYPES

Liking
The affection felt for casual acquaintances

Companionate love
The affection for those with whom our lives are deeply entwined

Passionate love
A state of intense physiological arousal/ absorption in another

(Berscheid and Walster 1978)

MARRIAGE RELATIONSHIP TYPES

Symmetrical
Husband and wife both have jobs, housework and role behaviour is not sex-typed, little leisure time together

Parallel
Husband is the wage-earner, housework is sex-typed, and little time is spent together

Differentiated
Both work, although the husband's job is emphasised. Housework is sex-typed, and most leisure time is spent together

Reversed
Wife is the main wage-earner, housework is not sex-typed, relationship is very companionate

Johnson et al (1992)

DIFFERENCES IN RELATIONSHIP EFFECTS

Relationships are one of the most powerful causes of happiness and unhappiness in people's lives according to self reports. Baron and Byrne (1997) report the following positive and negative effects involved in relationships:

- Married people report being happier and healthier than those who are single (Steinhauer, 1995), although the gap is closing - unmarried men are happier now than in the past, while married women are less happy (Glenn and Weaver, 1988).
- Passionate love tends to decrease over time (Tucker and Aron, 1993), and, while women are more satisfied with a marriage if they continue to feel sparks of passionate love, male satisfaction does not seem affected by it (Aron and Henkemeyer (1995).
- Both men and women are more satisfied if they show companionate love - sharing activities and ideas, laughing together, etc..
- Single and divorced people are significantly more likely to suffer from mental disorder than married people.
- The breakdown of relationships can have negative effects upon more than just the couple - more than a third of children in the USA have divorced parents and the possibility of long term negative effects on their lives because of it (Friedman et al, 1995).

Evaluation

It is difficult to account for the differences in happiness and mental health between those who are married and those who are single. It is possible that lasting relationships provide social support to overcome difficulties, but it is also likely that unhappy or mentally disordered people have more difficulty getting married.

CROSS-CULTURAL DIFFERENCES IN RELATIONSHIPS

Moghaddam et al (1993) point out many differences between western and non-western cultures that can profoundly affect the nature of relationships. The following table illustrates some of these differences and incorporates Hui And Triandis's (1986) 'individualistic' and 'collectivistic' dichotomy as well as Hsu's (1983) distinction between 'continuous' and 'discontinuous' societies.

WESTERN CULTURES

1 are **individualistic** - emphasising the individual, their goals, rights attitudes and needs. As a consequence there is
   - a focus on the study of first acquaintance, close friendship and intimate partnerships between two people
   - a strong social norm of monogamous relationships
   - an emphasis of choice in relationships due to
     a the western lifestyle of high mobility and easy long distance communication, giving greater availability of relationships.
     b the notion of romantic love - that choosing a perfect match to love deeply is necessary to fulfil one's own needs
   - a tendency for relationship interactions to be more governed by individual, economic based resource allocation and voluntary reciprocity (the returning of favours based on individual responsibility)

2 are **discontinuous** - youth and progress are emphasised and change regarded as important and inevitable. Consequently
   - there may be an increase in the preference for, and study of, temporary relationships
   - rules in relationships may be less important, since, if they are broken, the relationships can be left and others found.

NON-WESTERN CULTURES

1 are **collectivistic** - emphasising the group, its decisions, attitudes and needs, and one's duties towards it. As a consequence, there is
   - more emphasis on long-term kinship and social group relationships, often involving more than two people
   - a higher frequency of polygamous relationships
   - a lack of choice in relationships due to
     a more stationary lifestyles, leading to less availability
     b obligations to family and social norms. Marriage is supposed to take into account the wishes of others and is frequently arranged
   - a tendency for relationship interactions to be more governed by group need or equality based resource sharing and obligatory reciprocity (the returning of favours as an important social responsibility)

2 are **continuous** - showing a concern for heritage, customs, tradition, and respect for the wishes of one's elders. Consequently:
   - change is viewed with suspicion, perhaps leading to greater stability in relationships
   - rules in relationships are strictly and formally adhered to because of the need to maintain long-term stable relationships.

Evaluation

- The research on western relationships has seriously restricted implications for non-western societies, and has neglected certain kinds of relationships in western society, e.g. the more collectivistic relationships of rural communities, and relationships with family members.
- There is a tendency to assume that western relationships are superior due to ideological dogma. However, cross-cultural study of relationships points out reasons for their frequent failure in western societies - the individualistic values of independence, satisfaction of personal needs and personal control inherently conflict with the intimacy, sharing and compromise demanded by relationships, making them more difficult to maintain. In collectivistic societies, the norms of dependency, sharing, and lack of personal control aid the maintenance of relationships. Gupta and Singh (1982), for example, found that newly weds in India, who married out of love, reported more intense feelings of love than those from arranged marriages. However, this pattern had reversed after five years and became more exaggerated after ten years.

Factors influencing the formation of attraction

SITUATIONAL FACTORS

PROXIMITY

This factor refers to the physical or functional distance between individuals, what Kerckoff (1974) called our field of available', and suggests that the smaller the distance separating individuals, the greater the chance of attraction taking place. This factor is necessary for other influences, for example

- those who live near us are more likely to share our beliefs, social class, education etc. (see similarity)
- we have to be close to somebody in order to reward them (see learning theory)
- proximity allows increased exposure, which leads to familiarity (see familiarity)

Evidence

Festinger et al (1950) studied student friendship patterns in university campus housing and found that the students were most friendly with those living next door, less friendly with those living two doors away and least friendly with those living at the end of the corridor. Bossard (1931) found that couples in Chicago who lived within one block of each other were more likely to get married than those who lived two blocks apart, whereas Clarke (1952) found that more than 50% of people marrying in Colombus Ohio lived within walking distance of each other.

Evaluation

Proximity provides the minimum conditions necessary for attraction to start and maintain itself, but note that too close a proximity can invade our personal space and make us feels uncomfortable until our relationship has developed – the better we know someone the closer we allow them!

EXPOSURE AND FAMILIARITY

Zajonc investigated the 'mere exposure effect', which suggests that, all other things being equal, people prefer stimuli that they have seen more often. Close proximity clearly increases the chance of repeated exposure, which may lead to familiarity and a sense of trust.

Evidence

Zajonc et al (1971) asked subjects to evaluate photos of strangers and found that those strangers, who appeared more often than others were rated more positively. This effect has also been found for repeated exposure of music, paintings, and political candidates. Segal (1974) studied police cadets who were assigned to their rooms and classroom seats alphabetically, and found that they were more likely to rate someone as a friend who was close in the alphabet to them. Newcomb (1961) conducted a two year study of liking patterns in rented accommodation. The best predictor of liking in the second year was familiarity.

Evaluation

Repeated exposure may give a greater chance that negative characteristics will be found in other people or that boredom or stimulus satiation may occur, in which case the proverb 'familiarity breeds contempt' may be supported. Most research however has supported the link between familiarity and attraction.

PERSONAL FACTORS

SIMILARITY

Although, ideally, we would want the most attractive person possible, in reality we tend to be attracted by similarity – not just of looks, but also of beliefs, attitudes and values ('birds of a feather flock together'). Rubin (1973) suggested similarity is rewarding because we are more likely to agree with similar people, which leads to more joint activities and confidence in ourselves and our opinions, and facilitates communication.

Evidence

Griffit and Veitch (1974) studied 13 males who spent 10 days in a nuclear fall-out shelter, and concluded that those who were the most similar liked each other the best by the end.
Cann et al (1995) found attraction was greater towards a stranger who had similar attitudes. However, agreement that the same joke was funny had the strongest effect on attraction.

Evaluation

Winch (1955) has argued that in some cases **complementarity** is more important than similarity in determining the formation of attraction (i.e. 'opposites attract'). Snyder and Fromkin (1980) suggest that we dislike people who are too like us, as we like to see ourselves as unique. Rosenbaum (1986) proposed that although similar attitudes do not have much effect on liking, we are repulsed by dissimilar attitudes. This idea is not well supported.

PHYSICAL ATTRACTIVENESS

A strong research finding is that people are not only drawn towards those who are *physically* attractive, but see these people as *psychologically* attractive as well – having a whole host of other positive traits (such as popularity, warmth, generosity etc.).

Evidence

Dion (1972) using photographs of 7 year old children found that attractive children were less likely to be thought of as anti-social than unattractive children.
Walster et al (1966), using the 'computer dance' procedure, found the most important factor in determining whether a woman would be asked for a second date was her physical attractiveness, regardless of the man's.

Evaluation

Physical attractiveness is not absolute or objective ('beauty is in the eye of the beholder'), and can be influenced by a number of characteristics, such as

- culture – Garfield (1982) found that different cultures have different conceptions of beauty, and even in the same culture norms of attractiveness will vary
- gender – in 'western cultures' men seem to be more attracted by physical beauty, whereas women's preferences are not predominantly physical – Sigall and Landy (1973) found that the physical attractiveness of the male's partner increased his status in the eyes of other males, whereas the reverse was not true for women
- context – The perception of a person's beauty can change with circumstances – those who disagree with us may lose their physical appeal. Efran (1974) found good looking criminals received more lenient sentences *unless* their looks were involved in the crime

RECIPROCAL LIKING

A more subtle form of similarity is that we like people who like us. Aronson proposed the reward-cost principle, which states that we will be attracted to those who like us and consistently make positive comments about us, as opposed to those who do not (presumably because it increases our self esteem).
Aronson and Linder's (1965) 'gain-loss' theory is somewhat less obvious – we like people *more* who start off by disliking us and then change their mind, than we do those who liked us all along, and the same theory applies for those who start off by liking us and then change to dislike.

Evidence

Aronson and Linder (1965) found experimental support for the 'gain-loss' theory by letting subjects overhear (a confederate's) opinions of them. When the confederate of the experimenter started off by stating negative things about the subject and then switched to positive things, the subject rated the confederate more positively.

Evaluation

In general our liking depends upon how much we respect the opinions and motivations of the people who praise us. If the praise is seen as false flattery, then dislike occurs.

Social psychology - theories of relationships

ECONOMIC THEORIES

- Researchers such as Homans and Blau explain relationships in terms of economic transactions - an assessment of the costs and rewards involved in interacting with others.
- **Exchange theory** - suggests that the attraction of others depends upon the profit they provide for us - the rewards of interacting with them (e.g. stimulation, money, love) minus the costs (e.g. effort, time, money) - relative to the profits of other relationships.
- **Equity theory** - proposes that participants in a relationship seek a fair (equitable) return of rewards in proportion to their initial investment in their relationship (the rewards that they bring to it).

Relationship formation and maintenance

- Exchange and equity theories predict that relationships will be maintained when
  - **a** both partners are satisfied with their 'comparison levels' of rewards (the agreed ratio of costs and rewards) in their current relationship (Thibaut & Kelley, 1959)
  - **b** the comparison level for alternative relationships is low
  - **c** the costs of leaving the relationship are high
  - **d** partners are similar in their ability to reward each other

Relationship breakdown

The theories predict relationship breakdown when
  - **a** one or both partners are dissatisfied with their comparison levels of rewards
  - **b** the comparison level for alternative relationships is high (there are better relationships elsewhere)
  - **c** the costs of leaving the relationship are low (one or both partners are able to leave the relationship with little loss)
  - **d** partners are not similar in the ability to reward each other

Evaluation of theories

- It is difficult to quantify all psychological costs and rewards in a relationship to test the theories.
- However, just using the variable of physical attraction, Murstein (1972) found couples in intimate relationships were more likely to be equally attractive.
- The theory is rather 'mercenary', not dealing with emotions which can over-ride the calculation of profit in relationships.
- The theory is derived from the values of capitalistic societies.
- The theory may not apply to certain relationships, e.g. family.

LEARNING THEORY

- Byrne and Clore (1970) use the learning theory principles of classical and operant conditioning to explain attraction in terms of
  - **a** a conditioned emotional responses
  - **b** the consequences of interpersonal behaviour
- The reinforcement an individual provides depends upon what basic human needs they can satisfy for the other person, such as the need for resources (e.g. food), love, sex, etc.

Relationship formation and maintenance

- Theory predicts relationships will be maintained if
  - **a** partners are associated (by classical conditioning) with pleasant stimuli and life experiences such as successful careers or happy domestic environments
  - **b** partners positively reinforce each other with pleasant stimuli such as interaction, sex, presents, etc.

Relationship breakdown

- Theory predicts relationship breakdown when
  - **a** partners are associated with unpleasant life experiences, such as unemployment, poverty, etc. (classical conditioning)
  - **b** partners do not reinforce each other with pleasant stimuli (boredom) or inflict more negative than positive stimuli on each other (operant conditioning)

Evaluation of theory

- The theory links well with the economic theory notions of cost and rewards.
- Veitch & Griffith (1976) found the attraction shown towards a stranger depended upon whether he was associated with good or bad news.
- The theory realises that relationships are influenced by more than two people.
- Some relationships exist despite very few rewards and the giving, not just receiving, of reinforcement (due to the norm of reciprocity) is regarded as important.

COGNITIVE THEORY

- Heider (1958) proposed balance theory, which argues that people strive for 'cognitive consistency' in their liking and disliking of others, and are motivated to achieve balanced relationships.

Relationship formation and maintenance

- A cognitive triad is a pattern of relationships involving three people. The triad will be balanced, and consistent relationships maintained, if the multi-plication of the signs leads to a '+'.

A balanced triad where relationships are consistent.

– = negative feeling
+ = positive feeling

Ex-boyfriend
Boyfriend + Girlfriend

Relationship breakdown

- Unbalanced liking patterns are due to inconsistent attitudes in relationships and produce unpleasant 'cognitive dissonance' that people are motivated to reduce by changing their attitudes.

An unbalanced triad where the relationships are causing cognitive dissonance

Ex-boyfriend
Boyfriend + Girlfriend

Evaluation of theory

- Aronson & Cope (1968) found subjects liked a professor more when he showed hostility towards a graduate who had previously upset the subject.
- The theory realises that relationships are influenced by more than two people.
- The triad models only involve three people and ignore the strength of liking.

EVOLUTIONARY THEORIES

- Sociobiological theorists, such as Dawkins (1989), aim to account for attraction and relationships by looking at the evolutionary survival functions of it.

Relationship formation and maintenance

- Friendship and affiliation has probably evolved due to the advantages of increased protection and hunting efficiency that groups provide.
- Male-female bonds may have evolved to help care for helpless human infants. As the brain and head size of babies increased, they had to be born at earlier and less developed stages. The extra care required would involve both parents and attachment bonds that kept them together would be selected by evolution because of the increased survival rate of their offspring.

Relationship breakdown

- Unfaithfulness may be genetically advantageous for both sexes:
  - **a** **The male** optimal method of passing on genes is to mate with many females, since they cannot guarantee the offspring are their own and produce many gametes.
  - **b** **Females** produce and invest in a limited number of eggs, and so mating with a male of better genetic quality without discovery, will make their offspring fitter as well as receiving care from the current partner.

Evaluation of theories

- The theories propose that there are conflicting evolutionary tendencies to bond yet cheat, which perhaps explains the difficulty of maintaining intimate relationships.
- Pair bonding in humans may only have evolved to last long enough to provide care for helpless human infants.
- These ideas have ethical implications - what is natural is not necessarily moral.

The breakdown of attraction

- In addition to providing theories that explain the breakdown of relationships, social psychologists have identified the important factors and processes that are involved.

FACTORS LEADING TO BREAKDOWN OF RELATIONSHIPS

ENVIRONMENTAL FACTORS

PHYSICAL ENVIRONMENT
- **Distance** - Relationships involving a lack of proximity are difficult to maintain due to the lack of reinforcement, ability to share activities and intimacy, plus the inevitable extra costs involved (links with learning and exchange theories).
- **Hardship** - Lack of resources may cause frustration and aggression which may be directed at the partner (links with frustration-aggression theory). Negative emotions produced by hardship may become associated with the partner (by classical conditioning).

SOCIAL ENVIRONMENT
- **'Field of availables'** - The greater the number and quality of alternative partners in a social environment, the greater the comparison level for alternatives (this links with exchange theory).
- **Family and friends** - Competition for intimacy and attention or dissimilarity of attitudes and beliefs between one partner and the friends and/or family of the other partner (this links with cognitive balance theory) can cause problems.

INTER-PERSONAL FACTORS

BOREDOM
- **Lack of stimulation** - Unhappiness due to lack of stimulation and reinforcement (this links with learning theory) can lead to break-up in itself or by facilitating unfaithfulness by increasing the appeal of alternative relationships (this links with exchange theory).
- **Reduction in stimulation** - Sex is one of the most powerful reinforcers, but its frequency rapidly declines during the first four years of a relationship (Udry, 1980). However, 41% of married couples still have sex twice a week compared to 23% of single people.

CONFLICT
Only 1.2% of married couples report never having disagreements (McGonagle et al, 1992). Important factors in conflict are:
- **Rule-breaking** - Argyle and Henderson (1984) found the breaking of implicit rules of trust and intimacy were major factors in relationship break-down.
- **Compromise difficulties** - the discovery of differences over time reduces similarity, and the time-commitment of relationships reduces an individual's ability to achieve goals and indulge hobbies.
- **Conflict maintenance** - The tendency to respond in equally negative and destructive ways perpetuates conflict.

INDIVIDUAL FACTORS

BACKGROUND
According to Duck (1988) relationships are more likely to breakdown between individuals who:
- **Differ in demographic background** - perhaps due to dissimilarity of cultural attitudes and expectations.
- **Marry very early** - either in their relationship (due to lack of time for compatibility assessment) or in terms of age (due to lack of coping skills).
- **Have experienced a lack of relationship commitment** - either in their family or personal life.
- **Come from lower socio-economic or education levels.**

SOCIAL SKILLS
Baron & Byrne (1997) suggest lack of social skills can influence breakdown:
- **Coping strategies** - couples who differ in the way they cope with stress are less satisfied with their relationship (Ptacek & Dodge, 1995).
- **Conflict avoidance** - more men than women believe that avoiding conflict is a legitimate way of dealing with it. This can lead to a perpetuation of conflict and a lack of resolution.
- **Emotional expressiveness** - those unable to express emotions are less happy in relationships (King, 1993).

PROCESSES INVOLVING THE BREAKDOWN OF RELATIONSHIPS

DUCK'S STAGES IN PERSONAL RELATIONSHIP BREAKDOWN

INTRA-PSYCHIC PHASE
personal assessment of costs and rewards

DYADIC PHASE
confrontation and negotiation with partner

SOCIAL PHASE
involvement and use of social network

GRAVE DRESSING PHASE
retrospective analysis and public distribution of break-up story

CONFLICT
Rusbult and Zembrodt (1983) categorised four methods of dealing with relationship dissatisfaction.

CONSTRUCTIVE

VOICE Try to resolve problems	LOYALTY Wait for improvement
EXIT Leave relationship	NEGLECT Distance self from relationship

ACTIVE — PASSIVE

DESTRUCTIVE

The nature, origins, and transmission of prejudice in society

---

THE NATURE OF PREJUDICE - WHAT IS IT?

DEFINITION: 'Prejudice is an attitude (usually negative) towards the members of some group, based solely on their membership of that group'. Baron & Byrne (1991).

Prejudice is literally pre-judgement, having an attitude (relatively permanent disposition) towards something or somebody that is not necessarily based on an accurate assessment of that object or person. Prejudice is a central (major) attitude, and like all attitudes it has cognitive, affective and behavioural components.

Cognitive - the way we think about things. This component refers to the categorisation of information (putting people in categories) and our beliefs concerning members of those categories. This part is concerned with the process and effects of stereotyping.

Affective - the feelings involved in the attitude. In prejudice the feelings concerning the above thoughts/cognitions are strong feelings of either hostility or liking (prejudice can be for or against something or somebody).

Behavioural - the action taken, how we actually behave towards people and objects, sometimes based on the way we think and feel about them.

In psychology the cognitive and affective components are termed 'prejudice' and the behavioural component 'discrimination'.

SOCIAL/HISTORICAL AND ENVIRONMENTAL CONDITIONS
The social conditions in any society, such as the allocation of **scarce resources**, are the product of historical processes, often influenced by past prejudice/discrimination.

THE ORIGINS OF PREJUDICE AND DISCRIMINATION

PSYCHOLOGICAL PROCESSES
Psychological processes and theories such as **stereotyping, social identity theory, intergroup conflict theory**, and **scapegoating** will act on environmental conditions to produce prejudice.

PREJUDICE AND DISCRIMINATION IN SOCIETY
At any one time a society will contain many prejudices in the form of:

Social stereotypes
Standard, over-generalised images of a group, often with negative contents.

Discriminatory norms
Expected ways of behaving towards the objects of discrimination.

Institutionalised prejudice
Where prejudiced stereotypes and norms become ingrained into a society's structure.

Studies by Clark and Clark (1947) and Hraba and Grant (1970) show how self-esteem in children can be based on socially learnt values regarding their skin colour. As society changes, so do the values and self-esteem.

THE SOCIAL TRANSMISSION OF PREJUDICE WITHIN A SOCIETY

CONFORMITY THEORY
- New members of society can acquire existing prejudice through conformity to norms of discrimination. Conformity is especially powerful if individuals grow up in a **non-conscious ideology** - not even knowing that there are other ways of behaving.

Evidence
Minard (1952) found coal miners conformed to norms of prejudice above ground but norms of co-operation below. **Pettigrew** (1959) found conformity to prejudice in the USA.

Evaluation
Conformity does account well for the transmission of pre-existing prejudices, but can not account for their origin.

NEW MEMBERS OF SOCIETY

SOCIAL LEARNING THEORY
- Discrimination in society could also be acquired by the social learning theory processes of **observation** and **imitation**. An individual will learn acts of discrimination from those around, but will be more likely to demonstrate those behaviours if they expect positive consequences (e.g. social approval or increased self-esteem.)

Evidence
Bandura's (1963) Bobo doll study showed how children could learn and demonstrate aggressive behaviour just by observation.

Evaluation
A good theory that can explain both the acquisition and demonstration of prejudice and discrimination within a society.

The origins of prejudice - social group explanations

STEREOTYPING

- As Pennington (1986) notes, stereotyping involves
  a **categorising** people into groups based on visible **cues**, such as gender, nationality, race, religion, bodily appearance, etc.
  b assuming **all** members of a group share the **same characteristics**.
  c **assigning individuals to these groups** and presuming they possess the same characteristics based on little information other than their possession of the noticeable trait or cue.
- While stereotyping is an **in-built cognitive process**, it is important to realise that the **cues** seen as important to categorise (e.g. gender, skin colour, religion, etc.) and the **content** of the stereotype itself (e.g. personality traits) are not fixed, but historically determined and **changeable** over time.
- Stereotypes serve to **exaggerate** the **similarities within groups** ('those people are all the same') and exaggerate the **differences between groups** ('they are not like us').
- Stereotyping, therefore, literally involves **pre-judging** an individual, and, although it serves the important **functions** of categorising and generalising knowledge, it can lead to **unrealistic perceptions**, and **inter-group hostility**.

Evidence
- Karlins et al (1969) showed how the content of stereotypes concerning 'Americans' and 'Jews' changed over a 40 year period - the former seeming to become more 'materialistic' and the latter appearing to be less 'mercenary', for example.
- Many studies have shown how stereotyping can lead to prejudice, e.g. Buckhout (1974) and Duncan (1976).

Evaluation
- McCauley & Stitt (1978) propose that stereotypes are now best regarded as **probabilistic beliefs**. People are asked to estimate what percentage of a group would possess certain characteristics, and this is compared to the estimate for people in general, to arrive at a diagnostic ratio.
- Although the contents of stereotypes are usually derogatory, and stereotyping accounts for the **thinking** in prejudice, it does **not** explain the **strong negative emotions** nor all the discriminatory **behaviour** shown in society.

INTERGROUP CONFLICT THEORY

- According to Sherif, the prejudice in society is caused by:
  a The existence of groups
  b **Competition** between those groups
- Conflict exists between groups because each group will struggle to obtain limited resources. Sherif argued that competition will always provoke prejudice, and conducted a field study to investigate this idea.

Evidence
- Sherif et al (1961) conducted a field study in Robbers' Cave State Park in America. Two groups of 11 boys were created and a tournament was set up between them that was sufficient to produce fighting and name calling.
- The basis of many wars has been resource competition.

Evaluation
- Tyerman and Spencer's (1983) study on groups of boy scouts showed that competition is not always sufficient to cause conflict and discrimination.
- Sherif's study was ethically dubious given that its goal was to deliberately create prejudice and fighting over penknives was involved.

THE PROCESS OF STEREOTYPING

Intra group similarities in characteristics are exaggerated

Inter group differences are exaggerated

Intra group similarities in characteristics are exaggerated

Individual allocated to group based on visible cues

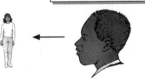

MINIMAL GROUP THEORY

- Minimal group theory suggests that merely dividing people into groups is sufficient to cause prejudice to occur between them. Tajfel and Turner (1979) explain this phenomena in terms of their social identity theory (SIT), which proposes that
  a people allocate themselves to groups and gain their identity from those groups
  b people need to feel good about themselves and, therefore, seek positive self-esteem
  c people will want to feel they are in the best group and will, therefore, act to make it so, even if that means putting other groups down

Evidence
- Tajfel et al (1971) conducted a study on Bristol schoolboys, who they assigned to meaningless groups, in some cases completely randomly by the toss of a coin. Tajfel found that the individual members would not only allocate more points to their own group members but would often maximise the difference between the groups - even if it meant their own group receiving fewer points overall.

Evaluation
- Tajfel's results have received cross-cultural confirmation, but his experiments have been accused of artificiality and demand characteristics. The study may only reflect the norms of competition found in many societies - co-operative societies may not show the minimal group effect (Wetherall, 1982).

SCAPEGOATING THEORY

- Scapegoating theory has its roots in Dollard et al's frustration-aggression theory, which argues that socially **frustrating conditions** such as economic depression and unemployment **leads to aggression**.
- According to the theory, this aggression needs to be **displaced** and **blame** allocated, so a **scapegoat** is found - usually a **minority** 'out-group' which is in a less powerful position to defend itself.

Evidence
- Weatherley (1961) found that anti-Semitic subjects (those prejudiced against Jews), who were frustrated by being insulted, were later more aggressive in their descriptions of people with Jewish sounding names. However, it should be noted that verbal prejudice does not always show itself in discriminatory behaviour as LaPiere (1934) found.
- The scapegoating of minorities in times of economic hardship has been historically documented world-wide.

Evaluation
- This theory links well with intergroup conflict theory by elaborating on another effect of competition, the frustration it can provoke.
- The theory accounts for the fluctuations of prejudice and discrimination over time, reflecting changing economic conditions.

'Experiments in intergroup discrimination' Tajfel (1970)

AIM

To illustrate a fundamental cause of intergroup discrimination - the mere categorisation of people into groups. Tajfel proposed that because of the frequent competitive behaviour shown by groups in our society, individuals do **not** just learn to conform to **specific** prejudices, but learn a **general** tendency (a '**generic norm**') to categorise people into ingroups and outgroups ('us' versus 'them') and to act in favour of their own ingroups. This generic norm of discriminating against the outgroup soon comes to operate automatically in any group situation, **without**

- any individual interest reasons for the discrimination
- any previous attitudes of hostility or dislike towards the outgroup
- any need for negative attitudes to develop before the discrimination occurs

Tajfel aimed to support the above theory that people will automatically discriminate without any prior prejudice merely by being put into groups, by testing the effect of categorisation on children's behaviour without the effect of any pre-existing attitudes or self interest.

EXPERIMENT ONE
METHOD

Subjects: sixty-four, 14 and 15 year old schoolboys, previously acquainted with each other, tested in groups of eight at a time.

Procedure: All subjects took part in a study that they were told tested visual judgement, involving estimating the number of dots on a screen. The boys were then informed that they would be divided into groups such as 'over-estimators' or 'under-estimators' (supposedly based on their performance, but in fact at random) and were asked to participate in a task where they had to allocate reward and penalty points (that would later be translated into real money at a rate of 1 tenth of a penny per point) to other boys.

Each boy was then individually told which group they were in and tested in isolation from the others. Each received a booklet of matrices that showed how they could allocate different combinations of rewards and penalties to boys from the groups, but it was made clear that
- they would **not know** the **identities** of the boys they were allocating points to, **only** whether they were members of the **same group** as themselves (ingroup) or of the **other group** (outgroup)
- they would **never** be **allocating** points **to themselves** - their points would be determined by the actions of every other boy in the same way

Each matrix consisted of 14 combinations of rewards or penalties, with the top and bottom row points always going to the member of one of the groups. Six types of matrix, with differing combinations of rewards and penalties, were each presented with three different group choices, e.g.

1 Between **two ingroup** members:

| Rewards for member 36 of 'overestimators' | 1 | 2 | 3 | 4 | 5 | 6 | 7 | 8 | 9 | 10 | 11 | 12 | 13 | 14 | Choice | 8 |
| Rewards for member 23 of 'overestimators' | 14 | 13 | 12 | 11 | 10 | 9 | 8 | 7 | 6 | 5 | 4 | 3 | 2 | 1 | example | 7 |

2 Between **two outgroup** members:

| Rewards for member 42 of 'underestimators' | 1 | 2 | 3 | 4 | 5 | 6 | 7 | 8 | 9 | 10 | 11 | 12 | 13 | 14 | Choice | 7 |
| Rewards for member 15 of 'underestimators' | 14 | 13 | 12 | 11 | 10 | 9 | 8 | 7 | 6 | 5 | 4 | 3 | 2 | 1 | example | 8 |

3 Between an **ingroup** and an **outgroup** member:

| Rewards for member 36 of 'overestimators' | 1 | 2 | 3 | 4 | 5 | 6 | 7 | 8 | 9 | 10 | 11 | 12 | 13 | 14 | Choice | 14 |
| Rewards for member 42 of 'underestimators' | 14 | 13 | 12 | 11 | 10 | 9 | 8 | 7 | 6 | 5 | 4 | 3 | 2 | 1 | example | 1 |

In each matrix, subjects had to choose just one of the two point combinations for the group members (typical example choices are shown above).

RESULTS

Subjects could adopt one of three strategies: maximum ingroup profit, maximum fairness, or maximum generosity to outgroup. It was found that
- in choices between two ingroup members, or two outgroup members, the strategy of maximum fairness was usually adopted, but
- in choices between a member of the ingroup and outgroup a strategy nearer maximum ingroup profit was significantly shown.

EXPERIMENT TWO
METHOD

Subjects: forty-eight, 14 and 15 year old schoolboys, previously acquainted with each other, tested in three groups of sixteen at a time.

Procedure: Subjects were again randomly divided into two groups, supposedly based upon their preferences for the paintings of Klee and Kandinsky, and were given new matrices consisting of 13 combinations of rewards or penalties to further test ingroup favouritism choices.

Between an **ingroup** and **outgroup** member:

| Rewards for member 17 of 'Klee group' | 7 | 8 | 9 | 10 | 11 | 12 | 13 | 14 | 15 | 16 | 17 | 18 | 19 | Choice | 19 | 19 | 7 |
| Rewards for member 25 of 'Kandinsky group' | 1 | 3 | 5 | 7 | 9 | 11 | 13 | 15 | 17 | 19 | 21 | 23 | 25 | example | 25 | 25 | 1 |

RESULTS

Subjects could adopt one of three intergroup strategies: maximum ingroup profit, maximum joint profit, or maximum difference in favour of the ingroup. Subjects significantly tended to adopt the strategy of **maximum difference in favour of the ingroup** e.g. 7 / 1 at the expense of maximum ingroup profit, e.g. 19 / 25

EVALUATION

Methodological:
Artificiality - Groups are rarely meaningless.

Theoretical: The research opposes previous beliefs that competition was necessary and sufficient to produce prejudice.

Links: Prejudice. Self identity and self-esteem

The origins of prejudice - authoritarian personality theory (Adorno et al, 1950)

DEFINITION

- The authoritarian personality is a type of person whose **personality traits** predispose them to be prejudiced to minority 'out' groups, such as ethnic or racial minorities.
- They are preoccupied with power, being submissive to authority figures but hostile and contemptuous towards people of lower status.
- They are intolerant of uncertainty and are inflexible in their beliefs and values - which are very conventional. These characteristics predispose them to strictly categorise people into 'us' and 'them' groups, and see their own group as superior to other groups.

WHY ARE THEY LIKE THIS?

EXPLANATIONS

- The authoritarian personality has usually experienced a very harsh and disciplinarian upbringing from their parents.
- This enforces a very rigid, 'black and white', rule following style of thinking, making them very intolerant of ambiguity.
- The authoritarian personality also has strong **unconscious** feelings of hostility towards the parents, but **displaces** these negative feelings onto safer targets - minority 'out' groups.
- People with authoritarian personalities also tend to be strict parents and, therefore, indirectly raise authoritarian offspring.

WHAT IS IT?

The Authoritarian personality

WHAT EVIDENCE IS THERE FOR IT?

CRITICISM

- There are two main types of criticism:
  1 Methodological - the F-scale is worded so that agreement to all statements means authoritarianism, but this may lead to *acquiescence response set* - the tendency to agree rather than disagree with opinions.
  2 Theoretical -
    a Much of the theory is based on debatable Freudian concepts.
    b Hyman and Sheatsley (1954) found that lower educational level was probably a better explanation of high F-scale scores than fixed authoritarian personality traits.
    c Personality trait explanations cannot account for sudden and widespread changes in prejudice across a whole society.
    d The F-scale only deals with right wing politics.

EVIDENCE

- Adorno et al developed and administered personality questionnaires to measure authoritarian personality traits. The most famous questionnaire was the **F-scale** (measuring Fascism or anti-democratic views), which indirectly measured general prejudiced tendencies. The more statements the individual agreed with, such as 'Obedience and respect for authority are the most important virtues a child can learn' or 'People can be divided into two distinct classes, the weak and the strong', the more authoritarian they were deemed to be.
- Much research has supported the authoritarian personality type (Christie and Cook, 1958), and studies have confirmed many predictions based upon it - i.e. that authoritarian personalities are more likely to obey authority figures and support harsher sentences as a jury member.

WHAT CRITICISMS ARE THERE?

TWO OFFSHOOT THEORIES

DOGMATISM

- Rokeach (1960) developed a dogmatism scale that measured closed-mindedness, inflexibility, and authoritarian characteristics, regardless of political ideology. Thus dogmatic or authoritarian characters can occur to either the left or the right of the political spectrum.
- Unfortunately, Rokeach's scale also suffered from acquiescence response set.

TOUGHMINDEDNESS AND RADICALISM

- Eysenck (1954) showed how authoritarian/dogmatic tendencies could be combined with political ideology by proposing two interacting personality dimensions:
  1 Toughmindedness vs. tendermindedness (toughmindedness is the equivalent of authoritarianism/ dogmatism).
  2 Radicalism vs. conservatism (the equivalent of left vs. right wing)

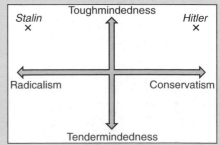

The reduction of prejudice

METHOD OF REDUCTION   **EXAMPLES**   **EVALUATION**

EDUCATION

Educating children with notions of tolerance and providing them with an insight into the causes and effects of prejudice can help reduce prejudice and discrimination according to a number of theories.
Conformity to norms theory would argue that education is necessary to prevent a 'non-conscious ideology' forming in communities where prejudice is so accepted it becomes an unquestioned norm.
Social learning theory suggests prejudice should be seen to be punished and tolerance rewarded if imitation in children is to be produced.

EXAMPLES

Jane Elliot conducted the 'blue eyes-brown eyes' study on her classes to teach them what it felt like to be the victim of prejudice (just based on eye colour). Interviews with the children as adults revealed that the study had inoculated them against discriminatory behaviour.
Public campaigns by minority groups, such as the 'Black is Beautiful' movement, had lasting effects on public awareness of racial issues in the USA.

EVALUATION

Education can reduce prejudice if it is carried out at a social level and is seen to be unacceptable by the majority in society.
Education has its greatest effect on the young. If adults 'are compelled to listen to information uncongenial to their deep-seated attitudes, they will reject it, distort it, or ignore it' (Aronson, 1992).

EQUAL STATUS CONTACT

Meeting members of other social groups can reduce prejudice by reducing the effect of stereotypes. This occurs as
- intergroup similarities are perceived (they are like us)
- outgroup differences are noted (they are not all the same)

Contact only changes group stereotypes if
- it is between individuals of equal status
- individuals are seen as representative of their group

EXAMPLES

Racial de-segregation studies have had some success.
Deutsch and Collins (1951) - found desegregated public housing increased inter-racial 'neighbourly activities' which were shown by 39% and 72% of the white housewives in the two desegregated housing projects but by only 1% and 4% of those in the two segregated projects. There was evidence that racial group perceptions changed dramatically for some, as one white housewife commented 'I started to cry when my husband told me we were coming to live here. I cried for three weeks... Well all that's changed... I see that they're just as human as we are... I've come to like them a great deal'.
Star et al (in Stouffer et al, 1949) found that 93% of white officers and 60% of enlisted men reported getting along 'very well' with the black troops they were fighting with in World War Two (everyone else said 'fairly well').

EVALUATION

Sherif, in the Robber's Cave study, found inter-group contact alone was insufficient to reduce prejudice between competing groups. Equal status contact only acts to reduce prejudice at an interpersonal level and does not counter the prejudice of group stereotypes (individuals are seen as 'exceptions to the rule'), if inequality at a social level makes true equal status contact impossible.
Stephan (1978) reviewed desegregation studies and found no significant reduction in prejudice or increase in black children's self esteem.
Star et al's study revealed that improved racial relationships in desegregated troops were not always generalised to interactions outside of fighting conditions, for example one white soldier commented 'they fought and I think more of them for it, but I still don't want to soldier with them in garrison'.

SUPER-ORDINATE GOALS

Star et al concluded that 'efforts at integration of white and coloured troops into the same units may well be more successful when attention is focused on concrete tasks or goals requiring common effort'. Making groups work together to achieve 'super-ordinate goals' (goals that cannot be achieved by groups working separately) is likely to reduce prejudice according to
- intergroup conflict theory - super-ordinate goals reduce the competition that causes prejudice.
- social identity theory - working together may merge 'in' and 'out' groups to one whole in-group identity.

EXAMPLES

Sherif et al (1961) significantly reduced intergroup hostility between two groups of children, the 'Eagles' and the 'Rattlers', by providing 'super-ordinate goals' in the last phase of their 'Robber's Cave' experiment.
Aronson et al (1978) used the 'jigsaw technique' with mixed race classroom groups. Each child received a part of the whole assignment and was dependent on the other children in the group to perform well in it. Inter-racial liking and the performance of ethnic minorities was increased.

EVALUATION

Inter-personal liking in these studies is not always generalised to social groups as a whole. When children leave their jigsaw classrooms they may return to a prejudiced family or society.
Superordinate goals cannot always be set up between all groups and failure to achieve them may result in worse prejudice.

SOCIAL POLICY

Political and social measures can act to reduce institutionalised discrimination through
- ensuring political power sharing
- providing equal opportunities legislation
- affecting the media (which maintains and perpetuates unequal stereotypes)
- encouraging 'one-nation' in-group perception
- targeting areas of economic frustration

EXAMPLES

The Supreme Court case of Brown vs. Board of Education in 1954 started the desegregation of public schools in the USA. Power sharing in South Africa ended Apartheid policies there.
Bogatz & Ball (1971) found that white children in the USA who watched mixed race TV programs like 'Sesame Street' developed more positive attitudes towards blacks and Hispanics.

EVALUATION

Policies like desegregation must be equally applied and regarded as inevitable and socially supported - half-hearted measures often cause more disruption.
There is a danger that discrimination will just shift to more subtle forms.

Comparative Psychology

Reproductive Strategies

Kinship and social behaviour

Behaviour analysis

Concepts, approaches, and theories in comparative psychology

WHY STUDY NATURAL ANIMAL BEHAVIOUR?

Psychologists such as Lea (1984) suggest that the study of natural animal behaviour has enabled them to

- **understand other species** - to practically aid in managing, training or conserving other animals
- **use the same methodology to study humans** - to benefit from the naturalistic observational techniques developed from studying behaviour in the wild

- **gain a greater theoretical understanding of human behaviour** - by using the same evolutionary and ethological ideas and concepts devised to explain the development and function of animal behaviour
- **gain indirect knowledge of human behaviour** - by directly generalising the results of studies on animals to humans

THE THEORY OF EVOLUTION

Charles Darwin's claim that humans evolved from other animals provided the starting point for comparative psychology. The basic principles of evolutionary theory are

Charles Darwin

- **genetic mutation and phenotype variation** - during reproduction genetic mutation and chromosome variation occurs, which affects the physiology and behaviour of the offspring
- **adaptation** - some genetic mutation and chromosome variation results in changes of physiology and behaviour that allows an organism to adapt itself better to its particular environment (ecological niche)
- **selective pressure** - those aspects of the environment that favour certain characteristics of animal physiology and behaviour over others
- **natural selection** - individuals with adaptive physiology and behaviour will be more likely to survive in their environment and compete successfully with other members of their species who do not have the same advantage
- **fitness** - increased survival chances and competitiveness means an increased likelihood of producing more offspring, who will also possess the favourable genetic mutations (survival of the fittest)
- **evolution** - species develop from other species, genetically and physically, over very long periods of time (though not necessarily in a smoothly continuous way). A species exists when the genetic variation of a group becomes different enough from the species it evolved from to prevent reproduction occurring with it

ETHOLOGY

Ethology is a branch of zoology and ethologists such as Tinbergen (1951) aim to study animal behaviour in the natural environment to reveal its

Nico Tinbergen

- **immediate cause** - i.e. what in the environment triggers the behaviour
- **development over the animals life cycle (its ontogeny)** - i.e. is the behaviour the result of the biological maturation of instincts, environmental learning, or a mixture of both
- **survival function** - i.e. why has the behaviour evolved, what evolutionary advantages does it provide or might it have provided to the possessors' evolutionary ancestors.
- **development within the species (its phylogeny)** - i.e. how did the behaviour evolve into its present form over generations

The 'classical ethologists', such as Lorenz and Tinbergen, used evolutionary theory, detailed natural observations, and field studies to investigate how a species' behaviour adapted it to its environment. Modern ethology built upon this pioneering work by expanding the number of species studied; taking more into account the animals' social environment (social ethology); applying its methods to human behaviour (human ethology); incorporating some laboratory experimentation; and eventually adopting sociobiology as its explanatory basis for function.

SOCIOBIOLOGY

E.O. Wilson

- Sociobiology is the theoretical system applied to social ethology, and, unlike previous approaches, examines the evolution of social behaviour in terms of the survival consequences it has for the genes each animal possesses. Genes are regarded as the fundamental unit of evolution, their 'purpose' is merely to replicate copies of themselves. Behaviour evolves not for the good of the species or even the individual, but for the good of the genes. According to Dawkins (1976) all animals are merely 'survival machines' to carry our 'selfish genes' and the more adaptive their physiology and behaviour, the greater their fitness (ability to produce offspring that will themselves pass on copies of their genes).
- By focusing on genes, the idea of inclusive fitness and the social co-evolution of evolutionary stable strategies between and within species, sociobiologists such as Wilson, Hamilton, Trivers, and Dawkins have been able to explain many aspects of human and non-human social behaviour (including altruism, a topic that presented many problems to previous explanatory theories).
- Sociobiology has extended its theoretical basis to incorporate the idea of cultural evolution and the interaction it might have with genetic evolution. Here the concept of the 'meme' has been proposed - an **idea** or concept that forms the basic **unit** of cultural evolution, which replicates itself from one **mind** to another and is subject to the same evolutionary pressures and laws as genes.
- Sociobiological theory has proposed some powerful arguments for the origin of animal and human behaviour, but has been criticised theoretically and ethically, so its ideas should be applied with caution.

The nature of sexual reproduction

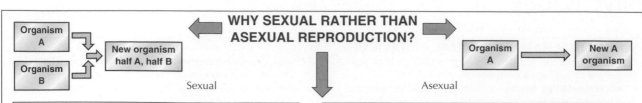

WHY SEXUAL RATHER THAN ASEXUAL REPRODUCTION?

Organism A + Organism B → New organism half A, half B

Sexual

Organism A → New A organism

Asexual

DISADVANTAGES OF SEXUAL REPRODUCTION

1 Only **half copies** of genes are reproduced in each offspring (compared to whole, exact copies with asexual reproduction).
2 Sexual reproduction is **far more costly** than asexual reproduction in terms of
   • **energy** - to locate, defend, and mate with another
   • **risk of damage** - location, defence, and mating activities all present a considerable risk of damage, due to visibility to predators or aggression from competitors or even mates
   • **risk of failure** - males, in particular, may not only fail to secure a mate, but cannot guarantee the offspring are their own and may raise other male's offspring (cuckoldry)

ADVANTAGES OF SEXUAL REPRODUCTION

1 Sexual reproduction provides greater genetic variability in offspring that will better adapt some of them to survive change in the physical and biological environment.
   • Producing genetically variable offspring allows evolutionary adaptation to **inter-species competition** - individuals stand a better chance of staying ahead in the '**genetic arms race**' against evolutionary development in predators, prey and parasites.
   • Producing genetically variable offspring **reduces sibling competition** for the same environment (which may occur in genetically identical asexual reproducing organisms).
2 The sexual reproduction process gives **genetic advantages** of
   • aiding in DNA repair
   • preventing maladaptive mutations affecting all offspring
   • allowing the easier expression of favourable recessive genes

HOW TO SEXUALLY REPRODUCE?

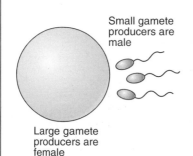

Small gamete producers are male

Large gamete producers are female

1 Produce gametes that will fuse with other gametes to produce offspring capable of becoming a mature organism to pass on its own genes.

2 Adopt a strategy to maximise the chance of gamete fusion or offspring survival, i.e. have many offspring or ensure a few live to mate themselves.

Abandon care of offspring to mate more often

Care for fewer offspring to help them survive

GAMETE FUSION STRATEGY

Invest in gametes
by devoting resources to provide a few large, hardy and long lasting gametes. These 'investing' egg producers are 'females' who must be careful not to waste their costly gametes.

Compete with gametes
by producing many small, mobile, cheaply resourced and short lived gametes and competing to fuse these to gametes with resources. These 'parasitic' sperm producers are 'males'.

ZYGOTE SURVIVAL STRATEGY

Invest in parental care of offspring
by contributing either before or after birth, energy for defending offspring or providing material resources for offspring.

Abandon care of offspring
by leaving them defence-less or with the other parent (winning the 'race to desert'), so greater effort can be devoted to further zygote production

MATING EFFORT/INVESTMENT + **PARENTING EFFORT/INVESTMENT**

REPRODUCTIVE INVESTMENT

THE CAUSES OF DIFFERENT LEVELS OF REPRODUCTIVE INVESTMENT

The reproductive investment (mating + parental effort) shown by the male and female of a species is determined by an interaction of
1 **biological factors** - such as anisogamy (different sized gametes in males and females) and evolved physiology (e.g. the gestation of the offspring inside the female for mammals but outside for frogs)
2 **environmental factors** - such as the climate or levels of food resources and predators

THE CONSEQUENCES OF DIFFERENT REPRODUCTIVE INVESTMENT

Different levels of reproductive investment in the male and female of a species have many consequences for
1 **sexual selection behaviour**, e.g. mate competition or choice
2 **mating systems** and social organisation
In many species it is often the **female** who shows the greatest degree of reproductive investment, since, due to anisogamy, she starts by investing more in her gametes.

The consequences of sexual reproduction - mating systems and tactics

A mating system is 'the way in which male and female sexual behaviours interact in a species'. Each sex will try to maximise its reproductive success, and this will usually lead to conflict as each tries to impose their optimal strategy on to the other. Due to anisogmy (differential investment in gametes) the male's initial optimal strategy is to mate with as many females as possible, since he produces many low cost sperm, whereas the female's optimal strategy is to carefully choose mates who offer the best genetic or material investment, so as to not waste the resources she has invested in each egg.

The mating system is the outcome of this struggle and is determined by a number of factors such as

- **environmental resources** - the distribution of resources required by the most-investing sex determines whether the least-investing sex can control these resources and, therefore, impose their preferred mating system.

- **evolved physiology** - the evolution of mating systems can only proceed from past physiological adaptations, for example, once internal female fertilisation or gestation has evolved, male paternity becomes far less assured and female investment becomes greater.

- **strategies of others** - every individual must survive within the social competitive environment of its own species, and so its mating strategy must compete with the mating strategy of other members of its species, both of the same and different sex.

Mating systems enormously affect the social organisation of a species, e.g. patterns of parental care, social structure, etc. Emlen and Oring (1977) distinguished between 4 main types of mating system - polygyny, monogamy, polyandry, and promiscuity. Although the majority in a species may adopt a system, some may adopt other mating strategies.

POLYGYNY

Where males have a number of mates in a breeding season, but females usually have only one mate.

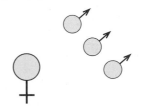

- **Resource defence polygyny:** depends upon whether environmental resources can be defended - if they are clumped, and therefore defensible, males can seek to control them through territoriality. Orian's (1969) polygyny threshold model proposes that if a male has a territory of sufficient quality, it will be worth a female joining a group of other females already in it, rather than seeking a single male with a poorer quality territory. Male honey guide birds defend territory with honeycombs, into which they only allow females.
- **Female group defence polygyny:** depends upon females clumping together for defensive reasons (e.g. female gorillas), or for hunting reasons (e.g. lionesses), and males competing to defend the group. This is in male interests, since successful defence means greater access to females and so greater reproductive success. It is in female interests since they only mate with dominant males who will pass on their reproductive success to the offspring.
- **Male quality polygyny:** depends upon female selection of the male with the best reproductive qualities, such as courtship display ability, regardless of resource or female grouping.

POLYANDRY

Where females have a number of mates in a breeding season, but males usually only have one mate.

This system is very rare since it only arises when

- males abandon their initial optimal strategy to mate many times. This may occur when males are unable to control female required resources, and conditions favour females asserting an advantageous strategy of multiple matings.
- females, find it advantageous to mate more than once to gain, for example, more male resource offerings, parental care, or genetic variability for their offspring.

An example is the American spotted sandpiper, where the females are larger, hold the territory, and lay eggs for many males to take care of.

MONOGAMY

Where both the male and the female only usually mate with a single member of the opposite sex, either in a single breeding season (serial monogamy) or for life.

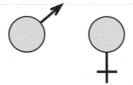

Monogamy is fairly rare since it only arises when the rewards of male parental care outweigh those of male polygynous mating (the usual male optimal strategy) and there are no further advantages for females to re-mate. These conditions are likely to occur when, for example,

- **harsh environmental or predatory conditions** mean that male care is essential for offspring survival. Males who leave to mate again, are unlikely to have any offspring that survive, e.g. both male and female herring gulls are needed to protect offspring from predators.
- **the polygyny threshold is not reached** due to similar territory quality for all males - meaning it is not advantageous for females to share a territory with others.

PROMISCUITY

Where multiple matings are made by both males and females.

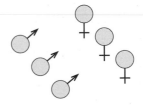

This system is fairly common and arises when

- males adopt their optimal strategy of multiple matings
- females mate more than once to gain previously mentioned (under polyandry) advantages, plus certain social group based advantages, such as encouraging sperm competition, preventing infanticide by confusing paternity, or reducing the stress of denying male mating which may lead to aborted offspring. An example are chimpanzees, where the females mate with many males. The females care for the young and the males show tolerance towards the young due to uncertain paternity.

The consequences of sexual reproduction - mate competition

This involves **competition between members of the less-investing sex** to fuse their gametes with members of the most-investing sex. Due to anisogamy, the male of a species contributes less biological resources to their gametes and so (unless providing significant parental care of the zygote) is **usually the less-investing sex**. Competition, therefore, usually occurs between males to copulate with investing females. To ensure gamete fusion and reproductive success, competition takes place before and after copulation.

PRE-COPULATION COMPETITION

COMPETITION TO LOCATE/ATTRACT MATES

Usually takes the form of signalling by the less-investing sex to compete in finding or attracting the more-investing sex. This often incurs costs of energy and risk of predation, since signalling and searching can be conspicuous and time consuming. For example, the flashing illuminous displays of fireflies and species specific birdsong.

COMPETITION TO ACCESS MATES

Aggressive competition to access and defend mates can occur on

- a short term basis just before copulation - usually when oestrus occurs for a limited time period and/or at the same time in all females, e.g. combat between deer stags during the mating season for control of the harem (Clutton-Brock et al, 1982).
- a long term basis - usually when oestrus is more variable over time or less synchronised amongst females, e.g. defence of the pride by lions.

COMPETITION FOR RESOURCES

This usually involves aggressive competition between members of the less-investing sex to control resources required by the more-investing sex, such as foraging areas or safe nesting sites, e.g. bull elephant seals compete for safe birthing beaches that the females will seek out, Grouse compete to hold 'leks' (mating sites).

EVALUATION

Studies have confirmed the prediction that the above competition methods will lead to evolutionary selection pressures for the less-investing sex to develop

- greater size and combat physiology, e.g. the males of many species (deer, seals, apes) are larger than the females and have evolved greater aggressiveness and weapons such as antlers and tusks. In the rare cases where males are the more investing sex, the females tend to be larger and more aggressive.
- intra-sexual defensive displays to defend territories or resolve combat. In some birds more singing and more songs predict the better defence of territory. Red deer stags will attempt to resolve contests by bellowing - the loudest wins.

POST-COPULATION COMPETITION

SPERM COMPETITION

In species where the female mates with many males, competition may occur as later males seek to displace previous male sperm, e.g. blackwinged damselfly males have evolved a penis designed to remove previous sperm before depositing their own. A male dunnock will peck the cloaca of his mate if another male has been found nearby, causing her to eject the intruder's sperm.

POST-COPULATION GUARDING

Competition to ensure the female does not mate with another male after copulation can take many forms:

- Remaining attached until fertilisation - some stick insects remain in copula for 79 days to prevent other mating attempts. However, this reduces the opportunity for the males to mate again.

- Remain nearby to protect - this allows the possibility of other mating by the male, but also increases the possibility for the female. This strategy depends upon the number of other males and females around.
- Provide post-copulation anti-mating measures, for example some species of snake and insect will plug the female's genital opening after mating, whereas certain male butterflies leave an anti-aphrodisiac chemical on the female to deter other males.

INFANTICIDE

When new single males take over a group of females, they may sometimes kill the offspring of previous male mating in order to bring the female out of lactation and into oestrus more rapidly, e.g. this occurs in lion prides (Schaller, 1972) and Langur monkeys (Hrdy, 1979).

EVALUATION

It is important to remember that male strategies co-evolve with female strategies.

- In the case of male anti-sperm measures, this may be in the female's best interests, since multiple mating increases the risk of predation and the inconvenience of persistent male mating attempts - female dungflies have been seen to drown in dung pats because of repeated male efforts to hold them down to mate.
- In the case of infanticide, this is clearly not in the female's interest, having already invested so heavily in resources and care for the offspring. In these cases, females may fight to protect their offspring from new males or may evolve other strategies such as false oestrus to confuse paternity.

The consequences of sexual reproduction - mate choice

Mate choice involves the ways in which the **more-investing sex** (usually female) **chooses members of the less-investing sex** (usually male). It is important for the more-investing sex to choose well, since they have **more to lose** if they mate with poor genetic material. Choice can be made **passively** by assuming that the less-investing mate has already demonstrated reproductive qualities by winning the intra-sexual competition to gain access to the more-investing sex. However, there are a number of good reasons why the investing sex may play a more **active** role in selecting an appropriate mate:

REASON FOR CHOICE

ENSURING THE CORRECT SPECIES

Since the more-investing sex (usually female) has more to lose from mating with the incorrect species (offspring will not be produced or may be infertile), they must evolve species discrimination. Members of the less investing sex (usually males with high numbers of 'low cost' gametes) often have much less to lose from inappropriate mating and may, therefore, show less discrimination - mating with the wrong species or even with inanimate objects.

CHOOSING MATES WITH MATERIAL OFFERS

The most-investing sex will be more likely to select mates who can offer some material contribution or other investment to the development of the offspring, such as food, nest sites, territory, or parental care.

CHOOSING MATES WITH GENES FOR HIGH REPRODUCTIVE SUCCESS

The more-investing sex will be more likely to select mates who show physical characteristics or traits associated with reproductive success.

There is disagreement, however, over whether the selected traits are

- real indicators of good genes - selected by females to produce 'macho' sons also capable of high reproductive success because of the favourable traits, such as greater strength, the 'good genes' provide
- arbitrary indicators - selected by females to produce 'sexy sons' who will also show these arbitrary traits and be selected themselves because of it, perhaps leading to runaway selection pressures on the 'sexy' trait to become ever more exaggerated
- indicators of parasite resistance - selected by females to gain genes for healthy offspring

CONSEQUENCES OF CHOICE

EVOLUTION OF COURTSHIP SIGNALS

Species-specific signals evolve, often from displacement behaviours shown by the species which become stereotyped, ritualised, and 'emancipated' from their original functions, e.g. species specific bird calls and visual displays such as the head toss of male ducks in their courtship rituals.

EVOLUTION OF COURTSHIP GIFTS

Selection pressure will lead to the evolution of, for example, food gifts or nest building, e.g. male hangingflies offer dead insects as a food gift to the female, with the size of the gift corresponding to the length of time spent in copulation. Some insects wrap up their food gifts to prolong the time allowed in copulation and an insufficient gift may result in failed sperm transfer, or even consumption by the female.

EVOLUTION OF COURTSHIP CHARACTERISTICS

Some selected characteristics are specifically linked to survival advantages (good genes), e.g. female moorhens choose small fat males to better incubate their eggs.

However, selection pressure will sometimes lead to the evolution of greater exaggeration of the physical characteristics associated with reproductive success until the costs of the trait outweigh the fitness benefits. Thus, the less-investing sex will develop courtship signals that are ever more loud, large, long lasting or intricate.

Anderson (1982) showed that male long-tailed widowbirds were selected by females upon the length of their tails. Peacocks are selected based upon the magnificence of their tail displays.

EVALUATION

Trivers' parental investment theory predicts sex role differences in mate competition and choice, but can also predict sex role reversals in behaviour if the male becomes the more investing sex, e.g. in mormon crickets, the male provides very valuable food resource contributions for the offspring, and so it is the females who compete (and in fact have evolved to be larger than the males) and the males who choose.

Parental care of offspring

Since producing copies of genes which can survive to pass on further copies, is the primary aim of evolution, survival of offspring is very important.

WHY CARE?

HIGH INTRA-SPECIES COMPETITION

High levels of competition **within a species** for the same environmental niche, will mean parents who invest more parental care in raising sizeable and skilled offspring, will promote their survival.

Oystercatchers have to learn the skills of opening shellfish from their parents if they are to survive independently.

HARSH PHYSICAL ENVIRONMENT

Parental care may be vital to the survival of offspring in environmental conditions which are poor in resources or climatically harsh.

Penguins in the Antarctic have to intensively care for their young if they are to survive the extreme cold.

HIGH INTER-SPECIES COMPETITION

Parental care may also be vital to the survival of offspring when a species has a high number of predators.

Many species of herbivorous mammals, such as wildebeest, have to closely guard their young from predators.

HOW MUCH CARE?

NONE
Some species produce such vast numbers of offspring that parental care is both unnecessary and impossible.

ONE PARENT
When intra- and inter-specific competition is moderate, and physical conditions are reasonable, one parent is sufficient for care.

BOTH PARENTS
When intra- and inter-specific competition is high, and physical conditions are unfavourable, both parents are required.

WHICH ONE CARES?

FEMALE
The most common single provider amongst species.

MALE
The most common 'deserter' of parental care amongst species.

THEORIES OF PARENTAL CARE CHOICE

There are many theories to explain which sex provides the parental care in a species, including:

- **The sex that has already invested the most** - Female investments in their offspring are usually greater than the male's due to anisogamy (more highly resourced gametes) and, in internally fertilised species, gestation. Death of offspring will, therefore, cost females more in lost time and energy compared to males.
- **The sex with parental certainty** - Ridley (1978) pointed out that females have the certainty that half the offspring's genes are their own, whereas males, especially in internally fertilising species, have no such guarantee that the offspring are theirs rather than earlier or later mating males.
  With external fertilisation, it seems easier for males to be more sure that it is their sperm fertilising the eggs in their presence. Indeed, the males of many species of fish (who see fertilisation of the eggs occurring 'before their eyes') show paternal care of the offspring.
  However, studies have shown that paternity can sometimes be just as uncertain in externally fertilising species, due to sperm competition, and that in some species the strategy of male caring, even if some of the offspring are not their own, may lead to more surviving offspring than males who mate with many but care for none.

- **The sex that loses the 'race to desert'** - Dawkins and Carlisle (1976) proposed that parental care may be dictated by the order of gamete release, i.e. the order in which eggs and sperm are released determines which sex can leave first after mating and leave the care of the offspring to the other. With internally fertilising species, the male can clearly leave the potential offspring after depositing his sperm inside the female, whereas in external fertilising species the female can leave her eggs for the male to fertilise afterwards (thus the higher proportion of male carers in fish). However, in external fertilisers where gamete release occurs simultaneously, around 80% of the care is still carried out by the male.
- **The sex that lives nearest the embryos** - Williams (1975) suggested the association hypothesis which proposes that the sex which finds itself living in closest proximity to the embryos after fertilisation will care for them. Gross and Sargent (1985), in a review of all the parental care theories, found this the most supported one. Thus, male stickleback fish care for the young (and even chase away the female) since they have already invested heavily in defending a territory and building a nest that it would not be advantageous to abandon.

Parent-offspring conflict

CAUSES OF PARENT-OFFSPRING CONFLICT

Trivers (1974) pointed out that according to the sociobiological theory of the 'selfish gene', although parents and offspring are obviously genetically related, they only possess 50% of their genes in common, and so some degree of conflict of interests will occur between them. Parents will want to invest in the survival of many offspring, both present and future, whereas each offspring is primarily interested in its own survival.

WEANING CONFLICT

In order to invest equally in all offspring, the parent will want to reserve care resources (of time, energy, etc.) for future offspring and only give each current offspring the minimum care necessary for its survival. Once this is done, it is in the parents' interests to stop caring (wean the infant) and start producing a new set of young.

Offspring, however, are expected to demand more investment than the minimum to receive the extra, although diminishing, benefits of parental care until

- they are large enough to better feed themselves, rather than rely on the parent to do so
- they need to become independent to raise their own offspring
- their selfishness leads to a greater genetic cost in lost siblings (who also share copies of their genes)

There will, therefore, be a time when offspring are demanding more care than the parents are willing to provide - the weaning conflict. Herring gulls deliberately crouch in their nest to hide their size to get extra parental care.

Hinde (1977) showed that weaning occurs in rhesus monkeys at around 15 weeks, when the parent will actively encourage the infants independence.

Tutin (1979b) observed immature chimpanzees frequently attempted to interfere with their mother's copulation (in 340 out of 1070 observed mating encounters).

Nash (1978) observed that older female baboons were more likely to show longer parental care than younger female baboons who had more chances to reproduce again.

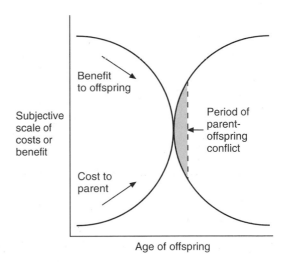

Parent-offspring conflict
adapted from Trivers (1974)

FEEDING CONFLICT

Feeding conflict occurs between parents and their offspring throughout the duration of parental care, weaning conflict occurs towards the end of parental care.

Offspring are often adapted to demand more food than the parent is willing to give them and may even evolve ways to manipulate their parents to gain extra attention. For example the exaggerated gaping and begging signals shown by chicks in a nest or the exaggerated crying of human infants.

INFANTICIDE

Infanticide is a fairly common occurrence in species such as lions and langur monkeys, where adult males gaining control of a harem of females will kill the offspring of previous males in order to bring the females back to their reproductive cycle more quickly.

Infanticide of an animal's own offspring, as might well be expected, occurs only rarely, and when it does occur it is always in the parent's rather than the offspring's interest. Some species are capable of adjusting their brood size to environmental conditions. When conditions are plentiful, larger brood sizes can be produced and cared for, whereas when conditions are harsher, less offspring are produced to ensure parental care is sufficient. However, 'if food supplies take a turn for the worse, parents may stop feeding the weakest of a litter, eat it, or feed it to its siblings (Polis, (1981)' quoted in Lea (1984)

SIBLICIDE

When siblings fight for resources, some offspring may be damaged or perish. This may increase the other siblings' fitness if the extra care they gain outweighs the genetic loss of the related sibling. However, siblicide will usually reduce the parents fitness. Spotted hyena babies fight within the den while the mother hunts for food. The pups bite each other, wounding or killing their siblings so they cannot go outside to be fed by the mother when she returns. Competition occurs most frequently between siblings of the same sex, and, while this may be advantageous to the surviving siblings, the parents have no choice in the matter and probably lose in fitness because of it.

However, parents of some species ignore siblicide, or even show behaviours that may encourage it to a certain extent, e.g. egrets lay eggs at one or two day intervals, instead of at the same time,

thereby allowing older siblings to have a size advantage over younger offspring - often producing a runt of the litter. It is in the parent's interest to do this since, if food becomes scarce, it enables the strong offspring to survive and the weak to perish, saving time and energy for the parent.

Mock and Ploger (1987)- demonstrated that the asynchronous hatching of cattle egrets was the most efficient parental strategy - by artificially manipulating brood ages, they found equally aged young fought too much and demanded too many parental resources.

Competition for food depends on the number of siblings - blue tits gape and beg vigorously for food, because a litter may consist of ten or more chicks, whereas the two or three chicks of herring gulls are less frantic in their begging competition.

Imprinting

EXAMPLES

Konrad Lorenz noticed the way ducklings and goslings followed their mother after birth, and found that if he allowed greylag goslings to see him rather than their mother in the first day after hatching, then they would follow him around.

Lorenz experimentally demonstrated that the goslings preferred him to their natural mother, and argued that it was different from traditional learning in a number of ways.

Lorenz termed this rapid attachment and following behaviour 'imprinting' and argued that it was different from traditional learning in a number of ways.

LORENZ'S VIEW OF IMPRINTING

SPECIES-SPECIFIC

Lorenz (1937) believed that imprinting:

- only occurred in certain precocial species (where the young have highly developed senses and independent mobility at an early stage), such as geese and ducks.
- had a survival function specific to these species, since the more dependent offspring of altricial species did not require it.

FUNCTION

- Lorenz suggested that the main function of imprinting was to enable the offspring to become rapidly attached to the parent. This is achieved by learning to discriminate between objects based upon their movement, colour, sound, and shape. In this way, offspring learn to recognise their parents from other environmental stimuli and will follow them.

INNATE

Lorenz (1937) proposed that

- imprinting was an innate, genetically determined instinct or species-specific behaviour.
- the environmental sign stimuli were fairly general aspects of size, shape, and movement.
- the instinctual fixed action pattern response was following.
- this kind of learning occurred in the absence of reinforcement.

CRITICAL PERIOD

- Lorenz believed that imprinting was governed by a genetic 'time switch' and, therefore, it had to occur within a critical period of time if it was to happen at all.
- Hess (1958) found the 'peak' critical period for imprinting in goslings and ducklings was between 12 to 17 hours. Although imprinting could occur before and after this time, it became increasingly unlikely.

IRREVERSIBLE

- Lorenz suggested that imprinting that occurred during the critical period was permanent and could not be reversed by later experience.
- Lorenz found that the greylag geese which imprinted upon him later tried to mate with humans, in preference to members of their own species, as adults.

EVALUATION

Subsequent research has revealed that imprinting

- occurs in many different animals, such as species of sheep, dogs, fish, primates, and even human beings.
- is involved in many different types of behaviour (not just following parents), such as acquiring food and territory preferences, or communication signals.

EVALUATION

Lorenz and others realised that the rapid attachment of imprinting had many short and long term functions.

- Short term - offspring protection (by preventing separation from the parent) and survival skills tuition.
- Long term - the acquisition of later species-specific behaviours, e.g. bird song, parenting style, and appropriate choice of mate. Harlow socially deprived rhesus monkeys and found they showed abnormal mating and parenting behaviour as adults.

EVALUATION

- Imprinting probably involves some kind of genetically determined 'template' that specifies what kind of characteristics the offspring should regard as its parent (Lea, 1984). Because the characteristics seem so approximate, errors in imprinting can occur as Lorenz demonstrated.
- Although there is no reinforcement, the strength of imprinting increases with the amount of exposure to the 'parent' and possibly the amount of effort taken to follow it (Hess, 1958).

EVALUATION

- Sluckin (1961) found that chicks kept in isolation during the 'critical period' could still imprint afterwards. This led to him proposing the idea of a 'sensitive time period' - a time when learning was most likely to occur in natural conditions.
- The imprinting period comes to an end either as the chicks become more selective in their responses (Guiton, 1958), or develop a fear response to unknown objects after imprinting (Hinde, 1956).

EVALUATION

- Guiton (1966) showed that imprinting was not permanent by imprinting ducklings on chickens or even yellow rubber gloves. In both cases the ducks attempted to mate with other ducks when older.
- Studies on different species support the idea that imprinting is reversible but can leave strong preferences in adult life.

LATER VIEWS ON IMPRINTING

Genetic explanations for apparent altruism

THE PROBLEM OF ALTRUISM

Apparent altruism refers to the way in which some animal behaviour seems unselfish - providing a service to another individual at a cost to the helper. Sociobiological evolutionary theory argues that true altruistic behaviour should not occur since those who help others at a cost to themselves are less likely to survive to pass on their altruistic genes, compared to selfish individuals.

Research shows that instances of 'true altruism' are only likely to occur on a non-voluntary or mistaken basis, due to deception or exploitation by a parasitic recipient, e.g. birds that are deceived into caring for cuckoo eggs. For this 'true altruistic' behaviour to continue, the costs must not be so great as to wipe out all those who possess the genes for it.

Where a species has evolved apparently altruistic behaviour that seems costly to the organism, research has indicated that there is either
- a **genetic reward** in terms of **survival for copies of genes possessed by the organism** (e.g. kin 'altruism') or
- a **long term reward** for the **organism** involved (e.g. delayed reciprocal 'altruism')

KIN 'ALTRUISM'

The most common instances of extremely self sacrificing behaviour occur towards genetically related individuals.

Examples:

Care of offspring - parental care involves many costs to the parent in terms of biological resources (e.g. egg investment, gestation, and lactation in mammals), time and effort (e.g. feeding) and danger (e.g. competition for resources and offspring defence). Parents are not the only kin altruistic providers of offspring care. However, since 'nest helpers' are found in some species where offspring stay with their parents to help raise further parental offspring. Mumme (1992) found that Florida scrub jays have sibling helpers who increase the chances of later offspring surviving to 60 days by five times.

Warning signals - are often altruistic, since they can attract the attention of predators to the caller while increasing the survival chances of those warned. Warning calls made by species that live in social groups containing many genetically related individuals will increase their genetic fitness. Caution must be used when ascribing kin altruistic motives, since some species, such as Belding ground squirrels, emit different kinds of warning call - one in response to goshawks which produces a confusing group dash for cover (selfishly disguising the caller), another in response to coyotes which immediately attracts the attack towards the caller (Sherman, 1985).

Eusocial insects - such as ants, termites, and some species of bee and wasp contain workers that help raise offspring and even sacrifice their lives to defend them, despite being unable to reproduce themselves.

Explanation

Since the 'aim' of evolution is to replicate copies of genes, organisms should be expected to be 'helpful' towards individuals who share partial copies of their genes - their relatives. Close relatives, like full brothers or sisters, who share half our genes can, therefore, be regarded as 'offspring equivalents' and so self-sacrificing behaviour that saves the lives or increases the fitness of many relatives may be phenotypically altruistic yet genotypically selfish (Barash, 1982).

If altruistic genes allow a sufficient number of relatives sharing copies of your genes to survive, then individual self-sacrificing behaviour will result as an evolutionary stable strategy - an individual will have made a genetic gain if the self sacrificing behaviour saves at least two brothers or eight cousins. Hamilton(1964) used the term 'inclusive fitness' to describe the overall genetic gain made by individuals who show kin altruistic behaviour towards those sharing part or whole copies of their genes.

DELAYED RECIPROCAL 'ALTRUISM'

Under certain conditions individuals of a species will help another **unrelated** individual at some **short term cost** if there is a high probability of a **long term return** of the favour.

Examples:

Baboon coalitions - Packer (1977) found that pairs of young male baboons without mates would co-operate together to gain access to the dominant male's partner. One distracts the dominant male (risking damage) while the other mates with the partner. The distracting baboon's seemingly altruistic behaviour exists since the favour may be returned by the other baboon in the future, providing at least some chance of reproductive success.

Vampire bat feeding - Wilkinson (1984) found that vampire bats living in groups would regurgitate blood to genetically unrelated individuals who had not managed to feed, since the favour was likely to be returned if the donors themselves were unsuccessful in feeding in the future.

Explanation

Delayed reciprocal 'altruism' only evolves as an evolutionary stable strategy if individuals can recognise each other and impose sanctions upon cheats who do not return favours. Axelrod and Hamilton (1981) used game theory analysis of the prisoner's dilemma to show that a long term 'tit-for-tat' strategy (starting co-operatively and then following the last person's behaviour of helping or cheating) would enable altruistic helping to emerge as an evolutionary stable strategy without constant abuse of reciprocation.

Sociality - why live in groups? 1

LOCALISATION OF RESOURCES
A species may live in social groups merely because of the localised clumping of resources, such as food and shelter/birthing sites, or mate availability around these environmental resources.

INTRA-SPECIES ADVANTAGES
A group may bestow advantages on individuals within a species, such as providing protection against the physical environment, e.g. heat retention in huddles of penguins; providing social structure to prevent continual damaging intra-specific aggression, e.g. dominance hierarchies and social appeasement responses; or providing aid in the rearing and education of the young.

INTER-SPECIES ADVANTAGES - SOCIAL DEFENCE AGAINST PREDATORS

Increased vigilance
'More eyes' provide a greater ability to detect predators and allow more time to indulge in activities other than vigilance.
Warning can be transmitted to others through following the fleeing behaviour of the one who spots the predator or through alarm calls. Powell (1974) found that groups of ten starlings reacted faster to a model of a hawk than a single starling, despite the much greater time it individually spent in vigilance. Kenward (1978) found that goshawk success at capturing pigeons was approximately 80% for solitary pigeons but 10% for flocks of over twenty.
Species like the mongoose show organised turn-taking vigilance.

Dilution
Large numbers of prey present at any one time dilute the effect of predators by overwhelming their consumption capacity.
Simultaneous group breeding in large numbers prevents the continual predation that non-simultaneous breeding would produce by providing predators with a long time to pick off offspring. This is literally safety in numbers, since predators do not physically have enough time to consume large numbers.
Adelie penguins simultaneously jump into the sea in large groups, since their predators, tiger seals, then only have time to capture one or two before the group escapes.

Dilution Effect in Penguin Predation

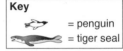

Number of prey | Poor penguin strategy ... Good penguin strategy

Time

Key
 = penguin
 = tiger seal

SOCIAL GROUPS MAY PROVIDE ANTI-PREDATOR BENEFITS IN A VARIETY OF WAYS, FROM PASSIVE SAFETY TO TACTICAL STRENGTH IN NUMBERS

Co-ordinated escape tactics
Groups of fleeing prey can benefit from the confusing effect of numbers on predators or can adopt co-ordinated escape tactics such as tight swarming and explosion from the point of attack in birds and fish

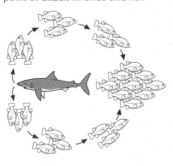

Selfish herding
Hamilton (1971) in 'Geometry for the selfish herd' pointed out that those who are on the inside of a sizeable group are less likely to be caught by predators than those on the outside.

Co-ordinated defence
Groups of prey can adopt defensive tactics unavailable to single individuals such as the mobbing of predators by birds, the collective defensive attack of bees, wasps and ants, or the circular defensive pattern of musk oxen against wolves.

Sociality - why live in groups? 2

INTER-SPECIES ADVANTAGES - SOCIAL CO-OPERATION IN FORAGING/HUNTING

Location of food

Groups may provide 'many eyes' and therefore detect food more readily, or, if separate foraging excursions are made, successful individuals can communicate the location of food on their return either

- incidentally, e.g. in cliff swallows who follow successful foragers on their way back to the source of prey
- deliberately, e.g. through the communication dance of honeybees

Increased capture rate

Social co-operation in hunting can increase capture rates through the use of tactics unavailable to individuals, for example,

Spotted hyenas attacking wildebeest calves were successful on 15% of 74 attempts on their own, but successful 74% of 34 attempts when working in pairs. This was due to the fact that one hyena could distract the mother wildebeest while the other attacked the defenceless calf (Kruuk, 1972).

Lionesses adopt group tactics to compensate for their lack of speed and stamina, such as a multi-directional stealthy approach to prey or charging at groups of prey to encourage the weaker members of it to break away from the safety of the herd.

SOCIAL GROUPS MAY AID FORAGING AND HUNTING IN A NUMBER OF WAYS

Increased capture size

The use of social co-operation and greater numbers to tackle larger prey has been noted in many species, for example,

Lions - Schaller found that groups were twice as successful in hunting than individuals and could tackle larger prey such as adult buffalo, which individuals would be unable to tackle alone.

Hyenas - adjust their prey to group size, hunting small Thompson's gazelles when alone but zebra in packs.

Army ants - use strength of numbers to attack prey many times their collective size, such as cockroaches.

Increased capture defence

Groups of predators are more likely to protect their prey from other predators, from both the same and other species, in large numbers. This is especially adaptive where many predators feed on the same type of prey, e.g. the various carnivores (lions, hyenas, etc.) preying on the herbivores (antelope, zebra, etc.) of the African plains.

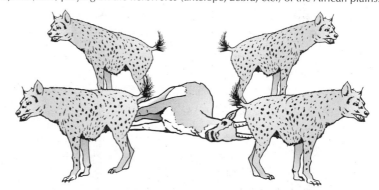

DISADVANTAGES OF SOCIAL GROUPING/CO-OPERATION

- Competition for resources - larger groups may mean less food, mates, space, etc. per individual, or less for certain individuals if a strict dominance hierarchy exists. Less food may mean less offspring and greater aggressive intra-specific competition.
- Increased risk of parasites and disease - large social groups present an increased opportunity for parasite and disease transfer. In large groups of cliff swallows, parasites can reduce the survival chances of the young by 50%. Increasing numbers also leads to greater pollution of the environment.
- Increased risk of reproductive failure - due to possible inbreeding, cuckoldry, misdirected female parental care, or infanticide. Brown and Brown (1989) found that brood parasitism (getting another to parent your offspring) in cliff swallows increased with group size.
- Increased chances of detection - greater numbers make groups more conspicuous, large numbers of prey draw the attention of predators, while a large number of predators reduces the chances of making surprise attacks.

However, note that where social co-operation has evolved, it is usually because evolutionary success does not favour group disadvantages over group advantages.

Signalling systems - function and evolution

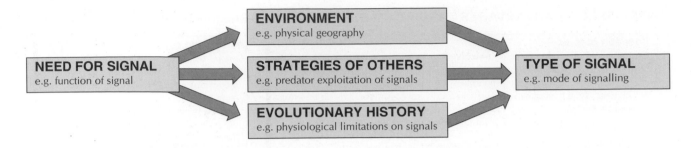

ENVIRONMENT
e.g. physical geography

NEED FOR SIGNAL
e.g. function of signal

STRATEGIES OF OTHERS
e.g. predator exploitation of signals

TYPE OF SIGNAL
e.g. mode of signalling

EVOLUTIONARY HISTORY
e.g. physiological limitations on signals

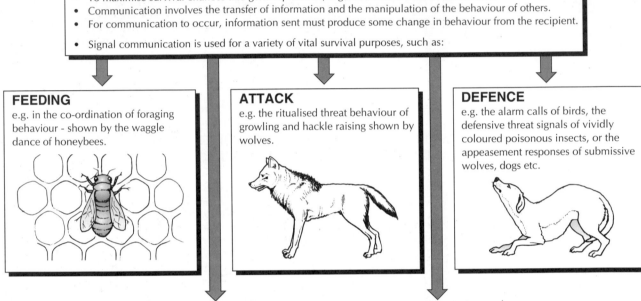

THE FUNCTION OF SIGNALS
- Signals are a basic form of non-linguistic communication.
- To maximise survival chances and gene replication, organisms must often communicate.
- Communication involves the transfer of information and the manipulation of the behaviour of others.
- For communication to occur, information sent must produce some change in behaviour from the recipient.

- Signal communication is used for a variety of vital survival purposes, such as:

FEEDING
e.g. in the co-ordination of foraging behaviour - shown by the waggle dance of honeybees.

ATTACK
e.g. the ritualised threat behaviour of growling and hackle raising shown by wolves.

DEFENCE
e.g. the alarm calls of birds, the defensive threat signals of vividly coloured poisonous insects, or the appeasement responses of submissive wolves, dogs etc.

SOCIAL ORGANISATION
e.g. the status signals of posture shown by the dominant wolves, monkeys etc. in dominance hierarchies, or the greeting signals shown between group members of social species (such as the eye-brow flash recognition response in humans).

REPRODUCTION
e.g. the mating fitness displays of competing male peacocks, or the location and readiness pheromone signals emitted by some female moths to attract mates.

THE EVOLUTION OF SIGNALS
Visual communication displays often evolve from behaviours shown in feeding, body maintenance or movement, and become increasingly stereotyped and divorced from their original function as they become used for communication, e.g. mallard duck courtship displays appear to have originally evolved from feather preening movements.

The use of behaviour for signalling often starts through approach-avoid conflicts between competing males, or in courtship when communication of intent becomes important for survival - a male may risk damage in a fight, but needs to compete; he risks an aggressive rejection from a female, but needs to mate to pass on his genes. Under these stressful conditions, hesitation in intention movements or displacement activity (behaviour unrelated to the present situation) may act as signals - which will become more effective if presented in clear stereotyped and ritualised ways. Thus the mallard duck, caught in a dilemma over whether to approach or avoid a female duck, may have started preening himself as a displacement activity in his anxious state of indecision. This would have acted as a signal for the female to know his intentions (and so stay or approach the male if interested or remove herself if not).

Communication can co-evolve between the sender and the receiver by acting directly on the nervous system, e.g. sign signals automatically triggering fixed action patterns of behaviour (see Tinbergen's (1952) study of the stickleback).

Signalling systems - modes of signalling

MODE OF SIGNAL	ADVANTAGES	DISADVANTAGES	EXAMPLES
TACTILE SIGNALS	1 High certainty that the message will be received due to intimacy of contact.	1 Extremely limited in range. 2 Fairly limited in the amount and complexity of information.	• Herring gull chicks peck at the beaks of their parents to stimulate feeding behaviour. • Bonobo chimpanzees signal conciliation through sexual touching behaviour.

SOUND SIGNALS	Allow communication to occur 1 over long distances 2 past physical obstacles 3 quickly 4 in the absence of light 5 in a detailed and complex way since much information can be sent in sound waves 6 multi-directionally - good for reaching many receivers	Sound waves, however 1 lack directional control, and are, unfortunately, easily detected by predators. Some calls seem designed to minimise the chances of location by predators 2 are costly in terms of energy to produce them and are short lasting (fade quickly) 3 may distort over distance	• Humpback whale song has an extremely long transmission range. • Bird warning calls are effective since they transmit the message very quickly and to many receivers simultaneously. • Bird mating songs are efficient signals since they convey enough detail to distinguish one species from another and can be received by other through obstacles such as thick foliage. • Dolphin clicks and whistles can transmit information through very murky water. • Human language - the most detailed form of communication, is capable of transmitting an infinite variety of messages.

CHEMICAL SIGNALS	1 Long-ranging 2 Long-lasting 3 Do not require the continued presence of the sender 4 Fairly discrete - some signals are only detectable by members of the same species 5 Transmits messages past physical objects and in the dark	1 Fairly slow in delivering information 2 Relatively limited in complexity of information sent 3 Difficult to control direction and duration, due to wind conditions, for example	• Moth pheromones can be detected and followed by the male from several kilometres away. • Cats, dogs, and rabbits mark their territory with chemicals in their urine or faeces, or even rub their scent glands against objects. The scents act as territory signals without the continual presence of the animal itself and are fairly long lasting. • Ants communicate primarily through chemical signals ranging from alarm to trail following signals.

VISUAL SIGNALS	1 Fast 2 Fairly large amounts of information can be sent 3 Directional 4 Can be long lasting and energy efficient, e.g. body markings	1 Limited range 2 Blocked by obstacles 3 Requires light 4 Visible to predators	• Birds use colourful mating displays that visually indicate the sexual fitness of the signaller. • Squid are capable of sending different visual messages in the form of colour patterns on different parts of their body, sometimes simultaneously in different directions to different receivers. • Wasp coloration sends a continuous warning to predators.

'The curious behaviour of the stickleback' Tinbergen (1969)

WHY STUDY THE STICKLEBACK?
- The stickleback is an ideal animal for laboratory study, since it is easy to capture in large numbers, tame (not frightened by experimentation, probably because of its protective spines), hardy, and small enough to thrive in small tanks of water.
- The stickleback is ideal for studying instinctual behaviour since it readily shows it in a very noticeable and intriguing way.

COURTSHIP & REPRODUCTIVE BEHAVIOUR
The stickleback mating cycle follows an unchanging ritual and naturally occurs in early spring in shallow, fresh waters.

Territorial behaviour: Each male stakes out and defends a territory from any intruder, male or female, and builds a tunnel-like nest of weeds in a shallow pit. The male then changes colour from grey to red and bluish white and begins courtship.

Reproductive behaviour:

First stage - Male swims towards a female in his territory in a series of zigzags. The female notices and swims towards the male with her head up exposing her belly swollen with eggs.

Second stage - Male turns and swims towards his nest and is followed by the female. The male makes rapid, thrusting, sideways movements towards the nest entrance.

Third stage - The female enters the nest and the male prods her tail base with rhythmic thrusts causing her to lay eggs. The female then exits the nest and the male slides in to fertilise the eggs, then chases the female away and looks for another (repeating the process up to four times before his mating impulse subsides).

Fourth stage - The male guards the nest from all predators and other sticklebacks (regardless of gender) and fans water over the eggs with his fins to oxygenate them. The eggs require more oxygenating every day, which the male provides, until just before hatching. Once hatched, the male keeps the brood together for a day or so.

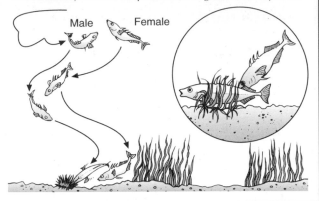

SIGN STIMULI
Investigation of the stickleback's behaviour revealed that fixed action patterns of behaviour were instinctively triggered by 'sign stimuli' - certain aspects of an object rather than the whole object, for example

- **Redness** - having noticed that the red colour of other males (or even the red of a postal van 100 yards away) initiated attack behaviour in male sticklebacks, models were constructed of different colours to measure their ability to elicit attack - red models were most assaulted.
  Redness also initiates following behaviour in females, who will follow a red model wherever its leads - even into a non-existent nest if the model is thrust into sand.
- **Shape** - the swollen belly of the female initiates male courtship behaviour, even if shown a male swollen with food.
- **Prodding** - the female response of egg laying can be triggered by prodding of her tail base with a glass rod, even if the male has been previously removed before her eyes.

DRIVES
Since it was noted that response to sign stimuli were only shown in the breeding season, Tinbergen studied the internal drives of behaviour and discovered:

- **Drive cycles** - stickleback drives wax and wane in cycles. Each cycle runs its course in succession, e.g. fighting drives, followed by nest building urges, followed by courtship drives, followed by parental care.
  Nest building will not occur (even if materials are available) until territory has been defended, courtship will not begin (females will be driven off) until the nest is built.
  If the nest pit is filled by the experimenters, the stickleback will dig it again and will continue to do so if it is repeatedly filled until the nest building urge overwhelms and the nest is constructed on a flat surface.
  Hormonal changes probably cause inner drives - castrating male sticklebacks removes the first stages of mating but has no effect on parental care (eunuch fish care for eggs).
- **Drive conflict** - the interaction between drives is important since the presence of a female stickleback in the male's territory provides the sign stimuli for both attack and mating. This conflict of drives was shown to be the cause of the male zigzag movements - the 'zig' reflects the male's attack drive to approach (and is more pronounced when the defence drive is strong), the 'zag' reflects the mating drive to lead the female (and is more exaggerated when the sex drive is strong).
- **Displacement activity** - when two drives are present in equal amounts and intensely conflict with each other (e.g. the attack and retreat drives in fighting male sticklebacks), a third behavioural drive is often activated as an outlet - a 'displacement activity' (fighting males will suddenly show the irrelevant, head down behaviour of nest digging). This was confirmed by attacking male sticklebacks with a model of another male.

EVALUATION
Tinbergen states that while other animals should be investigated to discover comparisons of any significance (they have found examples of displacement activity in starlings too), the in-depth study of the stickleback was necessary for a complete understanding of all its instinctual behaviour and how those behaviours interact with each other. Mammals show more flexibility in behaviour due to learning, but important instinctual influences probably underlie much of human behaviour (for example human conflict, neuroses, and sex life).

Links: Ethological approach, experimentation, reproductive behaviour, parental care, instinct, signalling communication, ethics of animal experimentation.

'Forty years of rhesus research' Rawlins (1979)

AIM
The article in *New Scientist* aims to describe:
- the history of the oldest continuously maintained primate colony in the world, Cayo Santiago, and
- some of the findings it has produced on rhesus monkey behaviour.

At the time of writing the colony had existed for forty years.

HISTORY
- Cayo Santiago is a 15.5 hectare island located off the coast of Puerto Rico.
- It functions as a laboratory in the field to study rhesus monkey social organisation and development.
- It was set up by Carpenter and Bachman in 1939 to allow long-term observations of rhesus monkey behaviour and to provide a supply of animals for biomedical research.
- 450 rhesus monkeys (plus 14 gibbons that later became aggressive and had to be removed) were released and, after 18 months of fighting, they had organised themselves into 6 social groups.
- Social, sexual, dominance, and travelling behaviour were studied, as well as various aspects of their biology.
- The removal of 490 monkeys during the Second World War for research on disease, plus problems maintaining supplies to the island, meant research had stopped by 1944, leaving only 200 monkeys.
- In 1956 Altmann reintroduced census and marking of the 150 surviving colony members and produced an important paper on rhesus social organisation and behaviour.
- In 1970 Sade ended the random capture of the monkeys for biomedical research and allowed the intact groups to remain undisturbed - increasing the potential for long term naturalistic studies.
- When the article was written in 1979, there were 610 monkeys, in 6 social groups ranging in size from 53 to 139, that were trapped, marked, and genetically tested just once a year. Many fruitful lines of research were developing.

FINDINGS
- The rhesus monkeys showed annual cycles of behaviour - the mating season lasting from July to December, the birthing season from January to June.
- They also showed daily rhythms - feeding at first light, resting and grooming during the midday heat, feeding and playing in the afternoon, and finally returning to the trees to sleep in the evening.
- Grooming was found to serve the function of removing parasites, and reflected the dominance hierarchy of the group.
- Each social group was composed of 2 to 4 matrilines of adult females, their adult daughters, and their offspring.
- The adult males of each group arrived from other troops, since all juvenile males left their troop of birth when mature (at 3 or 4 years) never to return. It was, therefore, the male rhesus that prevented inbreeding, or 'stirred the genetic pot'.
- Social order (and thus access to resources such as food) was maintained by dominance hierarchies and ritualised threat and appeasement behaviour, which, by minimising damaging fighting, was adaptive for both strong and weak monkeys.
- Adult males usually held the highest rank and whole female matrilines had a social rank.
- Within matrilines the youngest daughter and offspring outranked all older sisters but not their mother.
- Male juveniles entering a new troop usually worked their way up from the bottom of the male hierarchy.
- Despite individual differences in aggression amongst the troops, all 6 groups showed the same general social structure.
- Rhesus monkeys were found to be aware of who they were genetically related to.

EVALUATION
Methodological: **Strengths of the field laboratory** - the island habitat is ideal for accurate observation which would be very difficult in the wild. It allows detailed longitudinal studies of rhesus society over generations. The capture allows easy identification and tracking of genetic relationships allowing the study of paternity and female reproductive strategies - again very difficult to accomplish in the wild. The 'open air' laboratory also functions as a reserve for the species and allows comparisons to be made with pure laboratory and wild observations.

Weaknesses of the field laboratory - The early random removal of monkeys probably disrupted the natural social structure and behaviour of the colonies - as did the artificial feeding of the animals with supplies and the yearly trapping. There are ethical problems with the capture of wild rhesus monkeys for study.

Theoretical: The findings are of very limited generalisability to human behaviour, although ethologists are not necessarily concerned with making such comparisons.

Applications: The research has implications for aiding the survival of rhesus monkeys.

Links: Social and reproductive behaviour in animals. Research methods.

Learning in the laboratory - classical conditioning

Classical conditioning is concerned with **learning by association**, and refers to the **conditioning of reflexes** - how animals learn to **associate new stimuli with innate bodily reflexes**. The principles of classical conditioning were first outlined by **Pavlov**, and were then adopted by behaviourists, such as Watson, who attempted to use them to explain how virtually all of human behaviour is acquired. Pavlov was a physiologist who, while studying the salivation reflex, found that the dogs he was using in his experiments would sometimes start salivating before the food had reached their mouths, often at the sight of the food bucket. Clearly the dogs had learnt to **associate new external stimuli** (such as sights and sounds), with the **original stimulus** (food) that caused the salivation reflex. In a series of thorough and well controlled experiments, Pavlov found many new stimuli could be associated with reflexes and went on to introduce special terms for, and investigated many aspects of, the conditioning process.

Pavlov's apparatus

Bell Food

Salivation recording device

Dog in harness

Salivation tube connected to dog's cheek

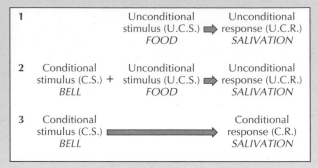

1 Unconditional stimulus (U.C.S.) ➡ Unconditional response (U.C.R.)
   FOOD *SALIVATION*

2 Conditional stimulus (C.S.) + Unconditional stimulus (U.C.S.) ➡ Unconditional response (U.C.R.)
   BELL *FOOD* *SALIVATION*

3 Conditional stimulus (C.S.) ➡ Conditional response (C.R.)
   BELL *SALIVATION*

ASPECTS AND PROCESSES OF CLASSICAL CONDITIONING

TIMING

The law of temporal contiguity
Pavlov found that for associations to be made, the two stimuli had to be presented close together in time. If the time between the presentation of the C.S. (bell) and the presentation of the U.C.S. (food) is too great, then learning will not occur.

Variations in contiguity
There are different ways to present the C.S. and U.C.S. together.
- **Forward conditioning** - involves presenting the C.S. (bell) just before and during presentation of the U.C.S. (food), producing the strongest learning.
- **Backward conditioning** - is where the C.S. (bell) is presented after the U.C.S. (food), but produces very little learning.
- **Simultaneous conditioning** - is where the C.S. (bell) and U.C.S. (food) are presented at the same time.
- **Trace conditioning** - involves presenting and removing the C.S. (bell) before the U.C.S. (food).

DURATION

Reinforcement
The learning link will last as long as the U.C.S. (food) is occasionally re-presented with the C.S. (bell).
It is the reflex-based U.C.S. which acts as the reinforcer and strengthens the learning link.

Extinction
If the C.S. (bell) is continually presented without the U.C.S. (food), then the C.R. (salivation) will gradually die out or extinguish.

Spontaneous recovery
If a period of time is left after the C.R. has extinguished, then the C.R. will be exhibited again if the C.S. is presented.

Inhibition
The fact that the C.R. can show spontaneous recovery at a later date after extinction shows that the C.R. does not fade away, but has been actively inhibited by the non-presentation of the U.C.S.

FLEXIBILITY

Generalisation

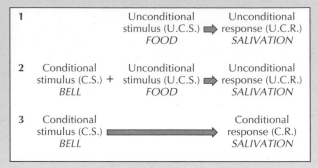

Amount of salivation

A B C D E Tones

Pavlov found that the C.R. could be triggered by stimuli which resembled the original C.S. - the closer the resemblance the greater the C.R., e.g. if the original C.S. bell had a tone of C, then the dogs would salivate to a lesser degree to tones of B and A.

Discrimination

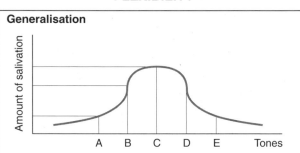

Amount of salivation

A B C D E Tones

By only presenting the U.C.S. with the original C.S., discrimination from the similar C.S.s occurs.

Higher order conditioning
Once the C.S. is reliably producing the C.R., the C.S. acquires some reinforcing properties itself - a new C.S. can be associated with the original C.S., until the new C.S. will also produce the C.R.

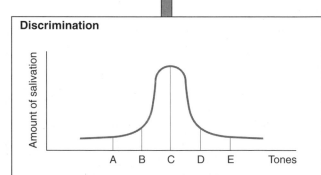

Learning in the laboratory - operant conditioning

THE BASIC THEORY

Operant conditioning involves learning through the consequences of behavioural responses. The principles of operant conditioning were first investigated by **Thorndike**, and were then thoroughly developed by the famous behaviourist Skinner, who applied them to explain how many aspects of human behaviour are acquired. Thorndike studied the way cats would learn to escape from his puzzle box by **trial and error**. Cats did not immediately acquire the desirable escape behaviour, but gradually increased in their ability to show it over time. Nevertheless, Thorndike found that any response that led to desirable consequences was more likely to occur again, whereas any response that led to undesirable consequences was less likely to be repeated - a principle which became known as the **Law of Effect**.

However, as with classical conditioning, the law of contiguity applies - associations between responses and consequences have to be made close together in time for learning to occur.

Thorndike's puzzle box

Cats had to emit the response of pulling the string inside the box to release the catch on the door to provide escape (a pleasant consequence). Time to escape decreased with each trial (the number of times the cat was put back in the box).

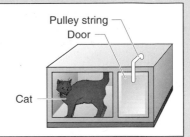

Skinner box

Rats had to press a lever to receive a food pellet, which would increase the likelihood of the lever pressing response reoccurring.

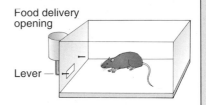

ASPECTS OF REINFORCEMENT

CONSEQUENCES

Positive reinforcement
This increases the likelihood of a response by providing pleasant consequences for it, e.g. food.

Negative reinforcement
This increases the likelihood of a response that removes or provides escape from unpleasant consequences, e.g. stopping an electric shock.

Punishment
This decreases the likelihood of a response being repeated if it is followed by inescapable negative/unpleasant consequences, e.g. an electric shock.

Secondary reinforcement
Secondary reinforcers are those that are associated with naturally occurring primary reinforcers (e.g. food, water, warmth, etc.), for example money, tokens, or parents.

FREQUENCY

Schedules of reinforcement
Continuous schedules - involve reinforcing every response made.
Partial schedules - involve reinforcing responses in varying frequencies to affect response and extinction rates, for example:
- *Fixed ratio schedule* - reinforcing a fixed number of responses (e.g. a food pellet for every ten lever presses in a Skinner box).
- *Variable ratio schedule* - reinforcing an average number of responses (e.g. a food pellet on average every ten lever presses, sometimes after 8 sometimes after 12 presses).
- *Fixed interval schedule* - reinforcing after a fixed amount of time (e.g. a food pellet for a lever press each minute in a Skinner box).
- *Variable interval schedule* - reinforcing after an average amount of time (e.g. a food pellet on average each minute, sometimes after 50 seconds sometimes after 70.

Extinction
If the response is not reinforced, it will gradually die out or extinguish.

FLEXIBILITY

Generalisation

Skinner found animals would make responses that resembled the originally reinforced response - a pigeon reinforced for pecking a red key, would also peck (although less frequently) at an orange or pink key.

Discrimination

Occurs by only reinforcing the original response.

Behaviour shaping
By reinforcing responses that increasingly resemble a desired end behaviour in a step by step manner, very complex behaviour can be built up from simple units.
The first responses are reinforced until perfected and then reinforcement is withheld until the behaviour is refined to the next desired behaviour.

Learning in the natural environment

CRITICISMS OF LABORATORY STUDIES OF LEARNING

The behaviourist theories of learning clearly identified important processes of learning under the controlled conditions of the laboratory, and their findings have had many practical applications to education, animal training, and behaviour therapy. There are, however, important criticisms of the behaviourist's approach to learning and the conclusions they drew from their experiments, for example:

- **Lack of ecological validity** -the investigation of learning in the laboratory and the testing of animals with unnatural tasks, such as lever pressing, may have distorted or ignored the natural and innate learning abilities shown by animals.
- **Neglect of differences in learning ability between species** - by focusing on just a few species, such as rats or pigeons, and generalising the results to all animals, the behaviourists not only ignored the differing cognitive influences on learning that different species show (e.g. the ability of humans and higher mammals to learn by observation and imitation), but importantly neglected the innate abilities in learning that every species will have evolved to better adapt themselves to their environmental niche.

Ethologists, therefore, aimed to study animal learning in the natural environment to see how the interaction of innate ability and environmental experience adapted animals to their environments.

INNATE BIASES IN LEARNING ABILITY

Ethologists would argue that animals have 'built-in' biases in natural learning ability, which they have evolved to better adapt themselves to their environment. The laws of learning are, therefore, not the same for all species, for example:

- Garcia and Koelling (1966) found that rats which were given a novel tasting solution and made to feel sick up to *3 hours* afterwards, would still learn to associate the two events and avoid that solution on future occasions, even after *only one* such trial in some cases. It, therefore, seems likely that rats have evolved a highly sensitive learning capability between taste and sickness, especially since this sensitivity makes 'evolutionary sense' - it aids survival.
- Honey bees are genetically prepared to learn the scent of a flower (only one association needed) but are less prepared to learn the colour (three associations) or form (over twenty associations).
- Lorenz (1935) demonstrated an increased learning sensitivity to particular stimuli can occur at *certain times* in an animal's life, when it is most important to acquire this learning. In his studies of imprinting he found that goslings will form strong attachments to moving, conspicuous objects in their environment during the first hours after hatching, and will follow and stay close to this object.
- Marler (1971) has also demonstrated that song birds acquire much of their particular song behaviour by listening to other birds during a certain time period in early life, and if they are deprived of this early experience they cannot learn it later. Thorpe showed chaffinches learn the regional dialect for their songs.
- Seyfarth et al (1980) showed that juvenile vervet monkeys probably inherited their alarm calls but learned to refine them over time.

FORAGING

Foraging is the seeking and acquisition of food from the environment. While the seeking of food is obviously guided by instinct, learning plays an important role in adjusting foraging behaviour to the fluctuating frequency and location of environmental resources. For example, Krebs et al (1972) found that great tits would learn to search for food in particular types of hiding places where they had previously discovered meal worms. Natural learning in foraging behaviour can be seen in

- **optimal foraging strategies** - Krebs et al (1978) found that blue tits will adopt the optimal foraging strategy of visiting alternative feeding sites equally until they learn which is reliably the more productive. Honey bees will modify their nectar load in proportion to the distance they have to travel; and Heinrich (1979), in his book *Bumblebee Economics,* found that learning was involved in foraging for nectar. Its seems that each bee learns to specialise on gathering nectar from a particular type of flower depending upon the frequency and location of that flower and the specialities of other bees. Learning is also demonstrated in their pattern of foraging, flowers are not re-visited before they have had a chance to replenish their nectar.
- **refining feeding techniques** - while bears will hunt for fish naturally, they learn and refine their particular techniques of catching the fish.
- **tool use** - chimpanzees learn to strip twigs or use long grass to collect termites, while Japanese macaques have learnt to extract sweet potatoes mixed with sand by placing them in water and eating what floats. This ability was culturally transmitted to other colonies of macaques.

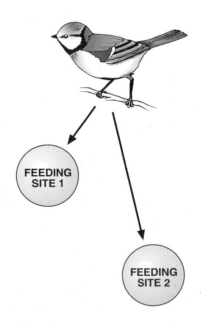

FEEDING SITE 1

FEEDING SITE 2

Homing behaviour

Homing involves learning to locate home sites/territories after absence
Homing can involve returning to home sites after short term forays for food, or the longer term and longer distance journeys involved in migratory behaviour. It seems that homing ability involves a range of innate and learnt abilities in interaction with each other.

INSTINCTUAL INFLUENCES

The initiation of migratory behaviour is largely under instinctual control. Migration evolved to cope with the differing environmental locations of food, warmth, and mating sites which would often be influenced by seasonal variation. Some species have, therefore, developed an instinctual behavioural tendency to migrate in a certain direction at a certain time, that seems to be triggered by environmental cues, such as temperature and day length, rather than experience or imitation. For example:

- European warblers appear to have internal genetic cues to migrate - some fly south to the Mediterranean, others to southern parts of Africa. When kept in a laboratory cage with constant daylength, these birds become restless in the spring and autumn. Those who migrate the furthest are restless the longest, and they even move towards the end of the cage nearest the direction of travel (Slater, 1985).

- Young European starlings will migrate in a fixed south-westerly compass direction to their normal wintering areas. Even if captured en route and displaced several hundred miles south, they will continue in an off-course Southwest direction, rather travelling Northwest to counteract the course change.
- Monarch butterflies travel northwards and southwards across North America with the changing seasonal temperatures.

However, although instinctual impulses can explain the initiation and general directional movement of migration, they do not account for the precise location of original home sites on the return journey - clearly learning is required for this.

Tinbergen & Kruyt (1938)

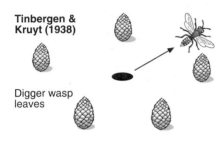

Digger wasp leaves

Experimenters move landmarks

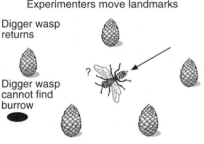

Digger wasp returns

Digger wasp cannot find burrow

LEARNING OF LANDMARKS

The precise location of home sites can be explained by experience - animals simply learn landmarks on the way out and 'reverse the order on the way back' (Ridley, 1995). For example:

- Tinbergen and Kruyt (1938) showed how digger wasps learn the environmental landmarks surrounding their burrow very fixedly before leaving. If these landmarks are moved in a systematic way, the wasp will search for the burrow in the wrong place. Watson found gulls show a similar fixedness of learning when approaching their nest sites.
- Most wild fowl are thought to learn their migratory route through following adults; while cuckoos, who migrate individually, apparently learn it themselves. Salmon learn the chemical traces of the river water they were born in, so they can later return to it to breed, sometimes after travelling vast distances.

Although learning can account well for the short range location of home sites, it is a less satisfactory explanation of the very long range homing behaviour seen in migration. Surely the amount of route information memorised over sometimes thousands of miles after just one such journey is enormous - and this all needs to be recognised in reverse on the return journey. Even if this does occur, it does not account for the ability of some animals to reach home after having been blown or moved 'off course'. This has led researchers to investigate whether true navigational ability is found in animals.

TRUE NAVIGATIONAL ABILITY

Perdeck (1958) found that although juvenile European starlings would migrate according to a general compass direction, adult starlings had developed navigational skills and could adjust their flight if their starting position was artificially moved to the south. True navigation, as opposed to route learning, should only be suspected, however, if animals are taken to completely unfamiliar locations and still manage to find their way home. Although the existence of true navigation has been debated by researchers such as Baker (1984), the following studies indicate it exists, in some birds at least:

- Kenyon and Rice (1958) sent albatrosses by air from Midway Island to various points in the North Pacific, such as Japan, the Philippines, and Hawaii, and found that 14 out of 18 homed successfully (the furthest albatross in the Philippines travelled 4,120 miles in 32 days).
- Walcott and Schmidt-Koeng (1973) showed that homing pigeons could successfully find their way home if released from a variety of unfamiliar sites, even when transported under anaesthesia or in rotating cages to prevent them from learning the route on the way out, or if fitted with translucent lenses that prevented them identifying visual landmarks from the air unless they were very close to them.

True navigation seems to be an innate ability that improves with practice.- Matthews (1972) found that visual landmark learning ability in pigeons bore no relation to their success in homing, in fact there was a slight negative correlation between the two abilities. However, homing pigeons have long been recognised to improve their ability if allowed to practice and explore their home site from the air.

There is still confusion over how animals navigate - humans achieve it through possessing a compass and a map to tell them where they are. Researchers have identified a number of possible sources for the 'compass' in animals, for example pigeons use the position of the sun in the sky, plus an internal clock to make allowances for its change throughout the day, to give them their direction (Hoffman, 1953, altered this internal clock by artificially changing the pigeons day/night light cycles and found predictable navigational errors occurred). Under cloudy conditions, pigeons seem to be able to detect magnetic direction (attaching magnets to their head will ruin their navigation if the sun is not visible) and many creatures including pigeons, bees, and migratory fish have been found to possess magnetite particles in their bodies.

Natural animal language

WHAT IS LANGUAGE?

Language is a form of communication which is distinct from signalling in many ways. Hockett (1960) and Aitchison have proposed various design criteria to define language, which involve aspects of its particular function, structure, and delivery.

- **FUNCTION** - language should allow
  interchangeability - the ability of the possessor to send and receive messages
  semanticity - the use of symbols to stand for or refer to objects, situations, events, concepts, etc.
  displacement - communication about things not currently present
  productivity - the creation of an infinite variety of new messages/meanings
  prevarication - the creation of conversation about things that have not happened, e.g. fiction or lies
  learnability and transmission - the acquisition of language and transferral to the next generation
  reflexiveness - the ability to use language to talk about language

- **STRUCTURE** - the form of language should show
  arbitrariness - the symbols used do not have to resemble the objects they stand for
  specialisation - the linguistic behaviour has developed only for communication
  duality and organisation - the language should be divisible into subcomponents which can be combined
  structure dependence - the possession of grammatical rules for combining units of language

- **DELIVERY** - the language should enable messages to be transmitted in the following ways
  spontaneously - the sender can initiate language at will and does not have to wait for triggers
  turn taking - communicators alternate conversational turns
  feedback - the user can hear the message it sends

HONEY BEES

Research by von Frisch (1967) revealed that honey bees communicate information about the distance and direction of food sources from the hive through the form of dance on the honeycomb that they perform upon returning from a foraging expedition. Distance is indicated by the speed of the dance and waggling of the abdomen, direction by the angle of the dance relative to the sun and gravity. More recent research by Kirchner and Towne (1994) using robotic honeybees and laser analysis of sound vibrations has revealed that both sound and dance are needed to communicate information about the location of food.

The honey bee dance certainly fulfils many language criteria, such as interchangeability, semanticity, and displacement, but has limited productivity and no prevarication, structure dependence, etc.

BIRD SONG

Marler (1970) proposed that some bird song shows certain functional and physiological similarities to human language. The chaffinch, for example, has at least 15 distinct calls for different functions and transmit regional dialects to its offspring.

EXAMPLES OF NATURAL ANIMAL LANGUAGE?

Some animal communication may be sophisticated enough to fulfil some of the criteria for language.

VERVET MONKEYS

Seyfarth and Cheyney (1980) identified three alarm calls in vervet monkeys which stand for distinct types of predator:
- Eagle call - caused vervets to look skywards and run for bush cover.
- Leopard call - caused listening vervets to look around them and climb trees.
- Python call - caused vervets to scan the floor area around them.

These calls show interchangeability, semanticity, and a degree of learnability and transmission (young vervets modify their calls by watching adults). However, productivity is very limited.

DOLPHINS

Dolphins communicate through a variety of squeaks, whistles and clicks, often in the ultrasonic sound range. The meanings of these sounds seem fairly specialised within particular dolphin groups - Bright (1984) recorded the sounds made by a dolphin being captured and played them to other members of the captive's social group. They turned and fled, whereas the same sounds played to a different group of dolphins only produced curiosity (indicating learnability and semanticity, for example). Bastian (1965) claims that captive dolphins which were separated from, but able to hear, each other, were able communicate complex information about training to each other by sound alone.

Teaching human language to non-human animals 1

STUDY		EVALUATION

TEACHING LANGUAGE TO PRIMATES

STUDY	RESULT	EVALUATION
GUA Kellogg and Kellogg (1933) raised the chimpanzee Gua with their own child attempting to teach spoken English.	**No speech** production at all. **Comprehension** of approximately 70 words.	An effort to teach human speech that was doomed to failure, due to the lack of appropriate vocal apparatus in primates.
WASHOE Gardner and Gardner (1969) taught the female chimpanzee Washoe American Sign Language (ASL).	**Semanticity** - comprehended and used over 130 distinct signs by the age of 4. **Productivity** - generalised signs to similar situations, called a swan 'water bird'. **Transmission** - taught signs to her children and other chimpanzees.	Four year old human children would have acquired around 3000 words. Terrace accused experimenters of unconsciously cueing the production of signs indicating imitation rather than understanding of meaning.
SARAH Premack and Premack (1972) taught the female chimpanzee Sarah a language using plastic symbols in certain orders.	**Semanticity** - understood link between plastic symbols and what they stood for. **Grammatical structure comprehension** - could understand grammatically complex instructions.	Showed a lack of spontaneity. Showed a lack of productivity - failed to construct new grammatical sentences not previously reinforced.
LANA Rumbaugh (1977) taught the chimpanzee an artificial language of symbols (Yerkish) on a computer keyboard.	**Productivity** - invented 'finger bracelet' for a ring, 'green banana' for a cucumber. **Grammatical structure** - understood word order difference between 'Tim groom Lana' and 'Lana groom Tim'.	Lana could monitor and correct the signs she typed into the computer by watching a screen that displayed them, perhaps indicating reading ability.
KOKO Patterson (1978) taught the gorilla Koko American Sign Language, using operant conditioning and modelling.	**Productivity** - e.g. created self description 'red, mad gorilla' and insult 'dirty toilet'. **Reflexiveness** - e.g. 'good sign Michael'. **Displacement** - e.g. apologised for biting 3 days before. **Prevarication** - lied and joked.	Terrace proposes that apes do not spontaneously initiate conversation, they merely respond to stimuli they have been reinforced for, or imitate. However, Koko often initiates requests and signs to herself and her dolls when alone.
NIM CHIMPSY Terrace (1979) taught the male chimpanzee Nim American Sign Language using operant conditioning and modelling.	**Grammatical structure** - there is some evidence that Nim showed two word order 'pivot grammar' similar to young human children (ie put the verb first in a two word utterance in 83% of cases.	Terrace argued that Nim only produced language behaviour without understanding of meaning, rarely produced more than two word utterances and did not develop turn taking interaction.
KANZI Savage-Rumbaugh (1988) studied the bonobo chimpanzee Kanzi, who spontaneously learnt language (Yerkish) by using a computer lexigram (a 'speaking' keyboard of language symbols) by observation.	**Displacement** - discusses events and makes requests over the telephone. Will ignore an orange in his presence if asked to fetch one from elsewhere. **Grammatical understanding and use** - uses two word grammatical ordering of verb before action.	Probably the most successful attempt. Very careful double blind testing conditions were employed, and all studies were videotaped. Kanzi is regularly tested under ecologically valid conditions (travelling through woodland each day).

'Teaching sign language to a chimpanzee' Gardner and Gardner (1969)

BACKGROUND

- One way to investigate whether another species might be able to learn human language is to try and teach it. Chimpanzees, being regarded as intelligent and sociable animals (although strong and occasionally difficult to handle), are regarded as good subjects for this kind of study.
- Past attempts at teaching chimps vocal language, e.g. Hayes and Hayes (1951) with the chimpanzee Vicky, failed because of the chimpanzee's inappropriate vocal apparatus. Since chimpanzees employ a variety of gestures in their natural environment, the aim of the study was to see if a chimpanzee could be taught American Sign Language.

METHOD

Design: a longitudinal case study of one chimpanzee.

Subject: Washoe (named after the county where the University of Nevada was situated) was a wild caught female chimpanzee aged between 8 and 14 months in June 1966 when the study began. Although Washoe was at first very young and dependent, it was decided to work with a chimpanzee so young in case there was a critical time period for language acquisition.

Equipment: trainers able to communicate in American Sign Language (ASL), a gestural language used by the deaf, were required. Although some ASL gestures are symbolically arbitrary, others are quite representational or iconic (they resemble what they stand for). Finger spelling was avoided as far as possible. Since ASL is currently used by humans, comparisons of young chimpanzee and human performance could be made. Washoe was always in the company of the researchers during her waking hours, all of whom used ASL in their games and activities with her.

Procedure: training methods made use of
imitation - past researchers noted that chimpanzees naturally imitated visual behaviour, so the researchers repeatedly signed in Washoe's presence. Washoe would readily imitate gestures but not always on command or in appropriate situations at first, so correct and exaggerated gestures were repeatedly made as prompts until Washoe emitted the correct sign. Routine activities, such as bathing, feeding, and tooth-brushing also helped produce (delayed) imitation.
babbling - Washoe's spontaneously emitted gestures were encouraged and shaped into signs by indulging in appropriate behaviour.
instrumental conditioning - tickling was used as a reinforcer to shape more accurate signs by withholding it until a clearer version of the sign was shown.

RESULTS

- **Measurement:** detailed records of daily signing behaviour were kept until 16 months, when their increasing frequency made such record keeping difficult. From 16 months, new signs were recorded on a checklist when three different observers noted a sign occurring in the correct situation without specific prompting. A sign was said to have been acquired when it was correctly used without prompting at least once a day for 15 consecutive days.

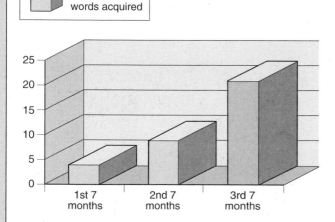

N°s. of new words acquired

(bar chart: 1st 7 months, 2nd 7 months, 3rd 7 months; y-axis 0 to 25)

- **Vocabulary:** thirty signs met the above criteria by the end of the twenty-second month, plus four more which occurred on more than half the days of a 30 consecutive day period. Four new signs were shown in the first 7 months, nine signs during the next seven months and 21 during the following seven months.

- **Differentiation:** Washoe's signing became more context and object specific over time, even showing the ability to distinguish between the use of 'flower' (originally used for all smells) and 'smell'

- **Transfer:** Washoe spontaneously generalised signs acquired in one context to other contexts, e.g. 'picture' to all pictures, 'dog' to unknown dogs, etc.

- **Combinations:** Washoe used signs in combination once she had 8 to 10 signs at her disposal. Some combinations were shown spontaneously, before they had been used by the researchers, e.g. 'gimme tickle' or 'listen dog'.

EVALUATION

Methodological: The training and testing conditions were not ideal (although controlled tests were being developed) and there are many practical problems with trying to teach chimpanzees language (they get distracted and frustrated).

Theoretical: There are many problems involved in deciding whether Washoe was acquiring language. She seemed to be showing semanticity, displacement, and productivity (creativity) but did not show structure dependence (no grammatical word order - although this was not reinforced by the researchers).

Ethics: The research has implications for the rights of apes, if they can talk should they not be given human rights?

Links: The debate over animal language. The use of animals as subjects. The ethics of testing animals.

Teaching human language to non-human animals 2

TEACHING LANGUAGE TO CETACEANS

Herman et al (1984) taught dolphins a symbolic language in two forms:

- **Akeakamai** - was taught an artificial, visual language of signs based on gestures and movements of the trainers' arms.
- **Phoenix** - was taught an artificial acoustic language based on computer generated whistling noises.

Each dolphin was taught a specific set of rules for combining the symbols of the language.

Herman et al were only interested in testing the linguistic comprehension, not production, of the dolphins.

RESULTS

Semanticity - could obey instructions to manipulate certain objects if the instructions were phrased in linguistic sounds or signs used to represent those objects.

Productivity - responded appropriately to grammatically specific and completely new combinations of words.

Displacement - followed instructions to search for objects in places hidden from view, and could even signal that an object was not present if asked to search for something that had not been placed in the pool.

EVALUATION

The majority of all attempts to teach dolphins language focus on comprehension rather than production.

TEACHING LANGUAGE TO PARROTS

Pepperberg (1983) has taught the African Grey Parrot, Alex, English spoken language through observation of human models communicating in social situations.

Selective reinforcement is also used, whereby correct responses are rewarded by the object being discussed and by verbal praise.

RESULTS

Semanticity - Alex uses language to show understanding of whether one object is the same or different from another.

EVALUATION

The primary focus of Pepperberg's studies is to investigate the cognitive abilities of the parrot rather than just language.

CONCLUSIONS

- **Productivity vs. comprehension** - there is a large debate over how important the production of language is compared to its comprehension. Dolphin studies were geared towards comprehension, and Savage-Rumbaugh sees it as the most important aspect of language.
- **The importance of grammar** - as it became increasingly clear that apes could produce language, some researchers, e.g. Terrace, began to emphasise how they produced it. Apes have demonstrated comprehension of fairly complex grammatical sentences and show two word pivot grammar in their production, but have not progressed much further. However, word order is not always consistent in human language (e.g. Finnish) or language use (deaf people make word order errors).
- **Comparative abilities** - the speed and extent of language and grammar acquisition in other animals, however, is far slower than in humans. A human child at age four is more linguistically competent than any other older animal.
- **Comparative physiology** - for some researchers 'the big question has been: do chimpanzees have the architecture in the brain that supports language?' (Hopkins of the Yerkes Primate Centre, cited in *New Scientist*, January 1998). Many think not, especially for the grammatical aspects of language, however, recent research by Gannon et al has discovered that

17 out of 18 chimpanzee brains they examined, showed development of the planum temporale (PT) on the left side of the cortex. In humans the PT is in the middle of an area involved in language comprehension, and this asymmetry of the brain was previously thought to be unique to humans.

- **Objectivity of research** - many would argue that the attachments researchers in this area develop to their subject matter and their tendency to show anthropomorphism to animal behaviour, distorts the objectivity of their studies, leading to over-exaggerated findings. Ape researchers in particular, however, would argue that close interaction and support is necessary to teach a language to any animal.
- **Alternative explanations** - Terrace argues that language-like behaviour in apes merely reflects ever increasing sophistication of operant conditioning responses to gain reward, not understanding of the meaning of those responses. The case of 'Clever Hans' a horse that seemingly understood language and could perform mathematical equations shows how easy it is to be mislead about animal abilities. All the horse had learnt was to detect the unconscious facial cues given by the trainer (out of relief when the right answer had been reached) for the reward of food. The majority of animal language researchers disagree with Terrace's view of ape language, however.

Evolutionary explanations of human behaviour

AGGRESSION

Lorenz generalised the evolutionary functions of animal aggression (mainly defence and competition) as well as its release mechanism (hydraulic drive theory) and form of expression (ritualisation) to human aggression. Ardrey (1967) argued that humans also show similar territorial behaviour to animals, and the same gender differences (males are usually more aggressive because they have to compete for females). While emphasising the same underlying evolutionary influences, Lorenz did note that human culture (in the form of weapons) did make humans a distinctly violent species.

PARENTAL CARE

Bonding - evolutionary explanations of imprinting and bonding in other animals (e.g. attachment for protection, food, and the development of necessary social behaviour) were applied to humans by Bowlby (1951).
Parent-offspring conflict - different evolutionary investment goals in parents and offspring explain many aspects of human parent-child interaction (e.g. baby crying, smiling, sibling competition, etc.). Evolutionary theory would predict more frequent child abuse by non-related careers, e.g. step parents or foster parents.

PHOBIAS

Seligman (1971) suggested that humans, like animals, have evolved evolutionary biases in learning. For example, humans seem 'biologically prepared' to learn fear responses to naturally dangerous objects or situations (e.g. heights, the dark, spiders, and snakes) more readily than non-dangerous natural phenomena.

EXAMPLES OF EVOLUTIONARY EXPLANATIONS OF HUMAN BEHAVIOUR

HELPING BEHAVIOUR

Like other social animals that live in groups for extended periods of time (e.g. dolphins, monkeys, or vampire bats), humans seem to have evolved not only kin altruistic behaviour but also delayed reciprocal altruism.

COMMUNICATION

Morris (1967) has argued that many aspects of non-verbal 'body language' communication are governed by evolutionary instinctual factors comparable to those shown in other species. Many facial expressions are recognised cross-culturally, e.g. expressions of emotion (Ekman, 1982) or the human 'eyebrow flash' recognition response (Eibl-Eibesfeldt, 1975). Some have suggested that 'motherese', the simplified style of speech which parents use with infants, has evolved.

ATTRACTION

Evolutionary theory provides explanations for why human relationships occur (to provide sufficient care for helpless young), why unfaithfulness may occur (to maximise genetic quality for females or transmission for males) and why relationships break down (after infants have grown to become independent). It also predicts gender differences in attraction (women have evolved to prefer power and status, men to prefer youth and beauty).

EVALUATION OF EVOLUTIONARY EXPLANATIONS

ADVANTAGES

- The study of evolutionary processes places human behaviour in an important environmental and historical **context**.
- The knowledge of evolutionary **processes** gained from studying animals can be usefully applied to human evolution.
- The evolutionary **functions** of behaviour discovered in animals (especially animals close to us on the evolutionary scale) may cast light on, or be generalised to, human behaviour.
- Animal findings may show how human behaviour is **distinct** or special.
- Evolutionary findings tend to counterbalance the nurture approach - showing how learning can be subject to genetically evolved biases.

DISADVANTAGES

- It is wrong to assume that behaviour must always have evolved for a particular purpose, it may be just a by-product or left-over of evolution. To give a famous dinosaur example - Tyrannosaurus Rex arms did not evolve to be so small for a reason, they were left over from evolutionary ancestors that walked on all fours.
- It is wrong to assume adaptation is an optimal solution - evolutionary adaptation always builds on past adaptation, which may not be an ideal base.
- 'Armchair adaptionism' (Lea, 1984) - it is easy to think up theoretical speculations or stories to explain evolutionary function, rather than rely on empirical research. Evolutionary theory may produce contradictory theories for the same behaviour.
- Evolutionary theory is reductionist and may be seen as overly deterministic. Other levels of explanation are necessary, e.g. social/psychological.
- Evolutionary explanations of human behaviour tend to underestimate or ignore the learning capabilities of humans which influence behaviour. Sociobiologists have, however, introduced the notion of the 'meme' - the basic unit of cultural evolution. Memes are ideas that replicate themselves from mind to mind and may even over-ride the influence of genetic evolution on behaviour, e.g. the meme for 'killing oneself to reach a higher plain of existence' that has occasionally been popular in certain cults.
- Evolutionary explanations may over exaggerate similarities between species due to anthropomorphism - a tendency to project human traits onto animals, e.g. saying a cat that is rubbing itself against your legs (probably to mark its territory) 'loves' you.
- Sociobiological ideas may be misunderstood or misapplied, e.g. to justify eugenic or capitalist politics (the latter may even have influenced sociobiological theory).

Biopsychology

Cortical functions

Awareness

Motivation and emotion

Methods of investigating brain function - measurement

MEASURING/OBSERVATIONAL TECHNIQUES

DIRECT RECORDING OF NEURONAL ACTIVITY

Microelectrodes are inserted into single neuronal cells and record their electrochemical activity, e.g.
Hubel and Wiesel measured the activity of single neuronal cells in the visual cortex of monkeys. By keeping the head still, various visual stimuli could be presented to different areas of the retina to discover both the area the cell represented and the stimuli it most responded to.

EVALUATION

Advantages

- Extremely precise - a very accurate way of investigating the living function of brain areas.

Disadvantages

- Very time consuming - an extremely large number of neurones occupy even a tiny area of brain.
- Too focused - it neglects the interactions between nerve cells that are responsible for brain functions.
- Invasive method - it, therefore, produces ethical problems, especially if applied to humans.

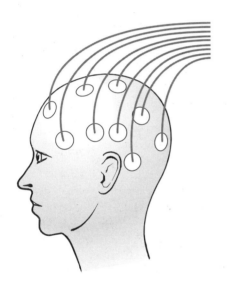

EXTERNAL RECORDING OF BRAIN ACTIVITY

Aims to detect brain activity from measurements made at the surface of the skull, e.g.

- electroencephalograms (EEG) - electrodes are attached to areas of the scalp, and the electrical activity of the brain beneath that they detect is amplified to reveal the frequency of the 'brain wave'. The frequency is the number of oscillations the wave makes in a second and ranges from 1-3 hertz (delta waves) to 13 hertz or over (beta waves).
- evoked potentials - record the change in the electrical activity of an area of brain when an environmental stimuli is presented or a psychological task is undertaken.

Electrooculargrams (EOG) measure electrical activity of eye movements, whereas Electromyograms (EMG) record activity from muscles to measure tension or relaxation.

EVALUATION

Advantages

- Non-invasive techniques - no alteration or intervention makes these methods of measuring brain activity more natural and ecologically valid.
- Practically useful - these methods can distinguish between levels of sleep and different types of subject, e.g. brain damaged, epileptic, those with Alzheimer's disease, etc.

Disadvantages

- Crude measure - the activity of millions of neurones is measured and averaged. The techniques indicate the activity level but not the precise function of the neurones involved.

SCANNING TECHNIQUES

1. **STILL PICTURES** - detailed three dimensional or cross-sectional images of the brain can be gained by the following non-invasive techniques:
   a. **Computerised Axial Tomography** (CAT scan) - is produced by X-ray rotation.
   b. **Magnetic Resonance Imaging** (MRI scan) - where magnetic fields are rotated around the head to produce an extremely detailed picture.

2. **DYNAMIC PICTURES** - moving coloured images of brain activity levels in different parts of the brain over time can be gained by invasive techniques such as:
   a. **Positron Emission Tomography** (PET scan) - which detects the metabolism level of injected substances (e.g. glucose) made mildly radioactive to show which parts of the brain are most active (using up energy) over a period of time.
   b. **Single Positron Emission Tomography** (SPET scan) - gives more detailed images.

EVALUATION

Advantages

- Detailed knowledge - scans can gain information about the brain structure and function of conscious patients, some while they are performing psychological tasks.

Disadvantages

- Non invasive scans - do not give information about activity, only physiology.
- Invasive scans - require the injection of mildly radioactive substances.

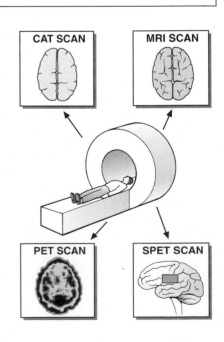

Methods of investigating brain function - alteration

ALTERATION/EXPERIMENTAL TECHNIQUES

ACCIDENTAL DAMAGE

Researchers use these natural experiments to compare the alteration in psychological functioning with the location of damage (by scan, surgery or autopsy). Damage may be caused by

- **strokes/tumours** - e.g. blood clot damage has revealed much about the location of motor, sensory, and linguistic functioning in the brain.
- **head trauma** - e.g. a railroad construction accident blew a 3 foot long metal rod through Phineas Gage's left frontal lobe in 1848, changing his personality to make him impulsive and irritable.
- **virus** - e.g. the virus herpes simplex damaged the temporal lobe and hippocampus of Clive Wearing causing anterograde amnesia.

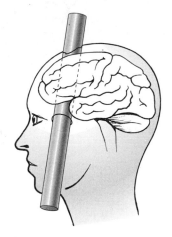

EVALUATION
Advantages
- The altering damage occurs 'naturally' so there are less ethical problems compared to other methods.

Disadvantages
- Lack of precision - the exact extent of damage is not controllable and may be difficult to assess.
- Comparison problems - comparison of the functioning in the individual before and after the damage is less objective, since it is often based on retrospective accounts of previous behaviour and abilities.
- Confounding variables - other non-physical effects of the damage may be responsible for behavioural differences. Social reactions to Phineas Gage's physical deformity may have affected his personality.

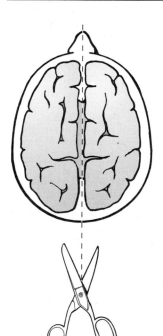

DELIBERATE DAMAGE
ABLATION/LESION STUDIES - aim to investigate function by removing areas of the brain or destroying links between areas. Some of the psychological functions investigated have included
- **Motivation** - ablation studies on the hypothalamus of rats have caused disrupted eating behaviour.
- **Aggression** - removing the amygdala of some animals has reduced their aggression.
- **Memory** - Lashley removed large portions of rat brains to find the location of memory.
- **Consciousness** - Sperry cut the corpus callosum of epileptic patients, producing a 'split mind'.
- **Psychopathology** - prefrontal lobotomy was performed on mental inmates to control behaviour.

EXPERIMENTAL EXPOSURE EFFECTS - aim to influence brain physiology by using environmental distortion or deprivation. Common examples are found in perceptual studies, e.g. Blakemore and Cooper's study of the visual cortex of cats exposed to an environment of vertical lines.

EVALUATION
Advantages
- Greater control - greater precision in the location of damage and the ability to compare behaviour before and after alteration leads to higher certainty over the effects of the damage.

Disadvantages
- Ethical problems of intervention - the deliberate change of behaviour is radical and irreversible.
- Non-human findings - may not be legitimately generalised to humans due to qualitative differences.
- Plasticity - the brain is a very flexible system which can compensate for damage. Removing one part of it will only show the performance of the rest of the system, not necessarily the missing part.

STIMULATION OF THE BRAIN
ELECTRICAL STIMULATION - aims to stimulate brain areas with microelectrodes to reveal their function through behavioural change. Examples include
- animal studies - Delgado stimulated areas of the limbic system to provoke aggression in monkeys and inhibit aggression in a charging bull (while standing in front of it!) by remote control.
- human studies - Penfield stimulated areas of the cortex in patients undergoing brain surgery and found locations that would produce body movement (primary motor cortex), body sensations (primary sensory cortex), memories of sound (temporal lobe) and visual sensations (visual cortex).

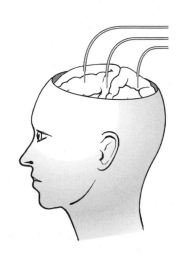

EVALUATION
Advantages
- Less harmful - the aim is to stimulate the brain rather than damage it (therefore more ethical).
- More valid - stimulation seems a better way of investigating the 'living' function of brain areas.

Disadvantages
- Invasive technique - the techniques still involve surgical operation, which can be risky.
- Interconnectedness - it is not easy to know exactly how far the stimulation has spread to other areas and the behaviour produced may not be natural, indeed it is often more stereotyped.

Localisation of brain function - exterior structure

LEFT SIDE VIEW OF BRAIN

FRONTAL LOBE OF CORTEX
- Involved in planning, initiative, and voluntary motor control. The frontal cortex is a very highly developed area in humans compared to other animals.
- Micro-electrode stimulation of the primary motor cortex produces twitches of movement in body parts.
- Damage causes lack of insight, loss of primitive reflex suppression, behavioural inertia (lack of spontaneity, and initiative), and an inability to adjust behaviour to make it appropriate to the situation.

PARIETAL LOBE OF CORTEX
- Involved in sensing and monitoring of body parts.
- Micro-electrode stimulation to the primary sensory cortex produces sensations in various parts of the body.
- Contains many sensory association areas, such as the visual association area necessary for object recognition (damage does not cause blindness but visual agnosia - the inability to recognise the identity of whole objects by sight). Also integrates information from different sensory areas to enable cross-modal matching (e.g, pairing up the sight and sound of an object).

Primary motor cortex
Strip involved in movement of body parts

Primary sensory cortex
Strip involved in sensation of body areas

Lateral Sulcus
Fissure dividing temporal from frontal and parietal cortex

Central Sulcus
Fissure dividing frontal and parietal cortex

Broca's area
Area involved in the production of language

Angular gyrus
Area involved in written language comprehension

Primary auditory area
Area involved in the analysis of sound

Primary visual area
Area involved in the analysis of visual stimuli

Wernicke's area
Area involved in language comprehension

Brain stem
Link between nervous system and brain

Cerebellum
Involved in balance and storage of motor movements

Left side view

TEMPORAL LOBE OF CORTEX
- Contains important areas for hearing, language and memory.
- Micro-electrode stimulation of the temporal lobe association areas produces 'dream-like' memories of events.
- Damage to specific brain areas in and around the edge of the temporal lobe produces specific deficits in language. Damage to Broca's area leads to motor aphasia (the disruption of spoken language production), damage to Wernicke's area leads to receptive aphasia (disruption to the comprehension of language) and damage to the angular gyrus disrupts reading comprehension.

OCCIPITAL LOBE OF CORTEX
- Contains the visual cortex and primary visual area.
- Micro-electrode stimulation of the primary visual cortex produces flickering patterns of light and colour.
- Damage to the visual areas of the cortex on one side of the brain will produce visual sensory neglect for objects in the visual field of the opposite side. Thus, damage to the right visual cortex will result in no visual conscious awareness of the left side of an object - people so affected will draw only the right hand side of a clock face or eat only the right half of food on their plate.

Localisation of function - cross-sectional structures

THALAMUS

- Acts as a relay station at the top of the brain stem to link information from the senses to the cortex.
- The thalamus monitors and relays commands to control the autonomic nervous system via nerves and the pituitary gland.

HIPPOCAMPUS

- Plays an important role in memory.

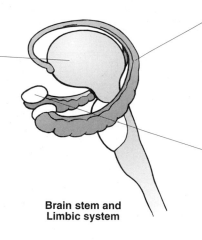

Brain stem and Limbic system

AMYGDALA

- Connected to the basal ganglia, septum, hippocampus, and other structures to form the LIMBIC SYSTEM which regulates, for example, emotion and memory.

HYPOTHALAMUS

- Plays an important role in motivation, homeostasis, and emotional arousal.
- Although tiny, it contains many areas with specialised functions, e.g. appetite control (by the ventromedial and lateral hypothalamus) and sexual behaviour (by the posterior hypothalamus).

CROSS-SECTION OF BRAIN (left side view)

CEREBRUM

- The two cerebral hemispheres have a thin surface layer, called the cortex, which is concerned with complex mental activities such as learning, thinking and consciousness.

RETICULAR ACTIVATING SYSTEM

- Regulates levels of arousal from sleep to attention.
- Acts as a filter for external stimuli, arousing higher levels of the brain if attention is demanded.

CORPUS CALLOSUM

- A thick mass of fibres that interconnect and allow communication between the two cerebral hemispheres.

PITUITARY GLAND

- Releases many hormones and regulates the endocrine system. It is linked to and controlled by the hypothalamus.

PONS

- Involved in sleeping, dreaming and waking.
- It is an important area of integration for nerve fibres to and from the body.

MEDULLA

- Controls the vital involuntary functions of breathing, heart rate, blood pressure, etc.
- It is the site of cross-over for nerves from one side of the body to the opposite side of the brain.

CEREBELLUM

- Co-ordinates balance and voluntary muscle activity involved in fine, precise movement.
- Also acts as a repository for the enactive (muscle) memory for fine motor skills.

Localisation of function - the cerebral hemispheres

LATERALISATION AND ASYMMETRY OF BRAIN FUNCTION

Most functions of the brain are contralaterally controlled - the sense information and functions of one side of the body are received and controlled by the hemisphere on the **opposite side of the brain**. Thus, touch, sound, and sight (but not smell) information received from the right side of the body is processed in the left hemisphere, which also controls right hand side body movements. Many functions are, therefore, duplicated in both hemispheres. However, there are some differences (asymmetries) in function between them.

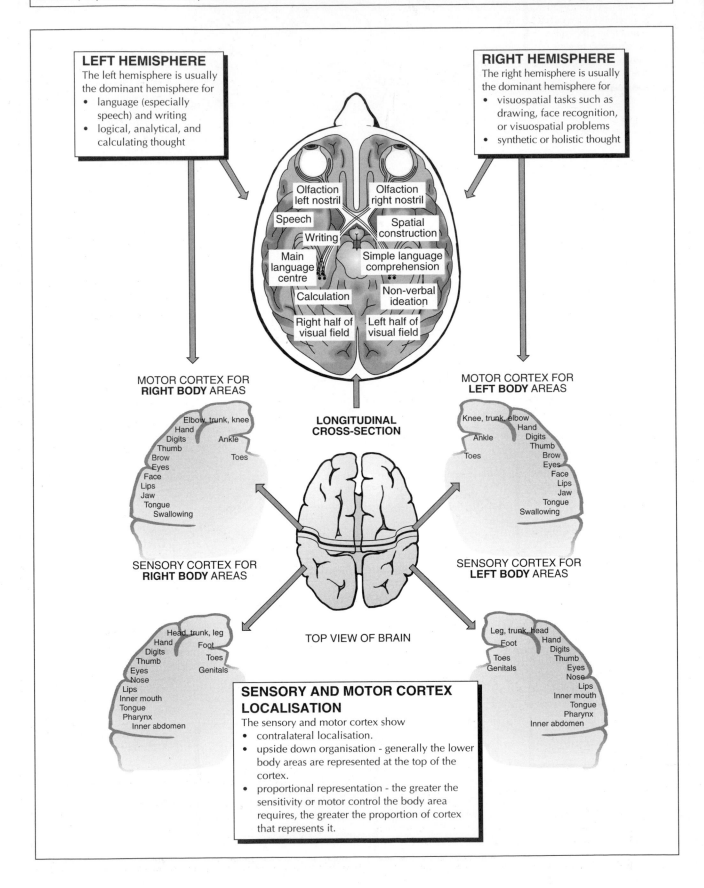

LEFT HEMISPHERE

The left hemisphere is usually the dominant hemisphere for
- language (especially speech) and writing
- logical, analytical, and calculating thought

RIGHT HEMISPHERE

The right hemisphere is usually the dominant hemisphere for
- visuospatial tasks such as drawing, face recognition, or visuospatial problems
- synthetic or holistic thought

Olfaction left nostril

Olfaction right nostril

Speech

Spatial construction

Writing

Main language centre

Simple language comprehension

Calculation

Non-verbal ideation

Right half of visual field

Left half of visual field

LONGITUDINAL CROSS-SECTION

MOTOR CORTEX FOR **RIGHT BODY** AREAS

Elbow, trunk, knee
Hand
Digits
Thumb
Brow
Eyes
Face
Lips
Jaw
Tongue
Swallowing
Ankle
Toes

MOTOR CORTEX FOR **LEFT BODY** AREAS

Knee, trunk, elbow
Hand
Digits
Thumb
Brow
Eyes
Face
Lips
Jaw
Tongue
Swallowing
Ankle
Toes

SENSORY CORTEX FOR **RIGHT BODY** AREAS

Head, trunk, leg
Hand
Digits
Thumb
Eyes
Nose
Lips
Inner mouth
Tongue
Pharynx
Inner abdomen
Foot
Toes
Genitals

TOP VIEW OF BRAIN

SENSORY CORTEX FOR **LEFT BODY** AREAS

Leg, trunk, head
Hand
Digits
Thumb
Eyes
Nose
Lips
Inner mouth
Tongue
Pharynx
Inner abdomen
Foot
Toes
Genitals

SENSORY AND MOTOR CORTEX LOCALISATION

The sensory and motor cortex show
- contralateral localisation.
- upside down organisation - generally the lower body areas are represented at the top of the cortex.
- proportional representation - the greater the sensitivity or motor control the body area requires, the greater the proportion of cortex that represents it.

'Hemisphere deconnection and unity in conscious awareness' Sperry (1968)

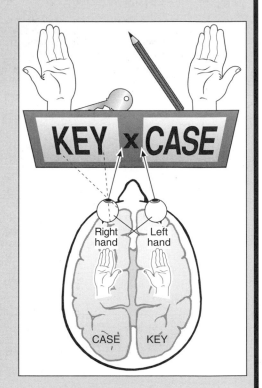

AIM

To present studies investigating the behavioural, neurological and psychological consequences of surgery in which the two cerebral hemispheres are deconnected from each other by severing the corpus callosum. Sperry uses these studies to argue that the 'split brain' shows characteristics during testing that suggest each hemisphere

- has slightly different functions
- possesses an independent stream of conscious awareness and
- has its own set of memories which are inaccessible to the other

METHOD

Subjects: A handful of patients who underwent hemispheric deconnection to reduce crippling epilepsy.

Design: A natural experiment. Severing the corpus callosum prevents communication between the left and right hemispheres.

Procedure: Since each hemisphere receives information from, and controls the functioning of, the opposite side of the body, the capabilities of each can be tested by

- presenting visual information to either the left or right visual field when the subject is focusing straight ahead. If this is done at fast speeds (about 1 tenth of a second) the eye does not have time to move and re-focus. Thus information presented to the left visual field, will be received by the right hemisphere of the brain
- presenting tactile information to either the left or right hand behind a screen (to remove visual identification). Thus tactile information from objects felt by the right hand will be received by the left hemisphere.

RESULTS

Visual stimuli presented in one visual field at a time

- Objects shown once to a visual field are only recognised if presented again in the same visual field, not the other - implying different visual perception and memory storage for each hemisphere.
- Objects presented in the right visual field, and therefore received in the left hemisphere, can be named verbally and in writing, indicating the presence of speech comprehension and production as well as writing ability.
- Objects presented in the left visual field, and therefore received in the right hemisphere, can <u>not</u> be named verbally or in writing, but can be identified through pointing, indicating that the right hemisphere has language comprehension but not speech or writing.
  These tests imply that the two hemispheres of the brain have different abilities and functions.

Different visual stimuli presented simultaneously to different visual fields

- If different visual stimuli are presented simultaneously to different visual fields, e.g. a dollar sign to the left, a question mark to the right, and the subject is asked to draw with the left hand (out of sight) what was seen, the subject draws the stimuli from the left visual field (the dollar sign). If asked what the *left hand has just drawn*, the subject's verbal, left hemisphere replies with what was seen in the right visual field (the question mark).

- If two related words are simultaneously presented to the different visual fields, e.g. 'key' to the left and 'case' to the right, the left hand will select a key from amongst a variety of objects, whereas the right hand will write what it saw in the right visual field (a case) without being influenced by the meaning of the word in the left visual field.

Tactile stimuli presented to different hands

- If an object has been felt by the left hand only, it can be recognised by the left hand again but cannot be named by the subject or recognised by the right hand from amongst other objects.
  These tests imply that one side of the brain does not know what the other side has seen or felt.

Tests of the non-dominant right hemisphere

- The left hand can pick out semantically similar objects in a search for an object presented to the left visual field but not present in the search array of objects, e.g. a watch will be selected in response to a picture of a wall clock. The left hand can sort objects into meaningful categories.
- The right brain can solve simple arithmetical problems (pointing out the correct answer) and is superior in drawing spatial relationships.
- The right brain appears to experience its own emotional reactions (giggling and blushing in embarrassment at a nude pin up presented to the left visual field) and can show frustration at the actions of the left hemisphere.

EVALUATION

Methodological: *Validity* - Being a natural experiment there is a lack of control over variables - in particular the subjects' mental abilities may have been atypical before the operation.

Theoretical: There do seem to be functional asymmetries between the hemispheres. However, research has revealed many individual differences - the above findings appear most typical of right-handed men. It should not be forgotten that the left and right hemispheres share many functions and are highly integrated.

Applications: The research has implications for helping patients with brain damage.

Links: Cortical functions, consciousness, psychosurgery.

Neurophysiology of perception

LIGHT ENTERING THE EYE

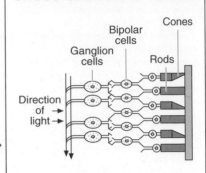

Lens (focuses image)
Cornea (bends light)
Image upside-down on macula of retina
Blind spot
Object
Pupil (regulates level of light entering eye)
Optic nerve leaving eye for brain

INNER EYE RETINAL AREA

Macula (cone rich area for focused precise vision)

Rod rich area

Patterns of light entering the eye are focused by the lens to form an upside down image on the retina. Stimuli focused onto the macula produce the sharpest images. The retina contains two types of photosensitive detection cells that convert light energy into nerve impulses:

- Cones - are fewer in number than rods, are sensitive to colour, and are mostly densely packed at the macula (providing greater sharpness or acuity of vision).
- Rods - respond to brightness only and are far more sensitive to weak illumination.

CROSS-SECTION OF RETINA

Cones
Bipolar cells
Ganglion cells
Rods

Direction of light →

With the aid of horizontal and amacrine cells, ganglion cells gather information from their receptive fields of rods and cones. Information gained from approximately 127 million rods and cones is summarised to 1 million ganglion cells.

VISUAL PATHWAYS THROUGH THE BRAIN

Stimuli from the left visual field is detected by the right hand side retinal surfaces, the optic nerves of which travel to the right hand side of the brain. The opposite occurs for stimuli from the right visual field

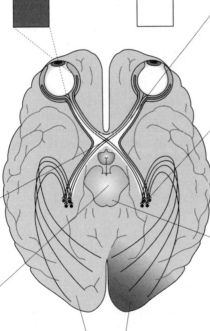

Optic chiasm
Optic nerve fibres cross at this point.

Thalamus
Located at the top of the brain stem.

UNDERSIDE VIEW OF THE BRAIN

Optic nerves
Relay sensory stimuli from retinal surfaces to areas of the brain responsible for vision

Lateral geniculate nucleus
A relay centre for visual information. Sends information on to the primary visual cortex

Superior colliculus
This is involved in perceiving 'where' objects are by locating stimuli in the visual fields and orienting the head to focus on them.

Primary visual cortex
Often termed the striate visual cortex, this area is involved in perceiving 'what' objects are. The primary visual cortex is required for conscious perception, since damage to it does not destroy all perceptual abilities, but produces 'blindsight' (non-conscious visual abilities).

GANGLION RECEPTIVE FIELDS

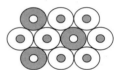

◉ Centre 'on'/surround 'off' cell

◉ Centre 'off'/surround 'on' cell

There are different types of ganglion cells. Some are activated by stimulation to the centre of their receptive field, but are inhibited by stimulation to the surrounding area, others show the opposite pattern of activation. These patterns of activation allow edges to be more easily detected at higher levels of the visual system.

STRIATE VISUAL CORTEX

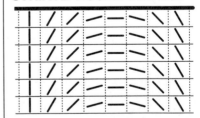

Hubel and Wiesel (1962) found the striate visual cortex shows hypercolumns of cells that respond to lines of the same orientation. Simple cells only respond to lines in a particular part of the visual field, complex cells respond to lines wherever they occur.
Other visual areas may contain hyper-complex cells that respond to even more precise visual stimuli.

Evaluation of neurophysiological findings

THE LIMITATIONS OF NEUROPHYSIOLOGICAL FINDINGS

- Neurophysiology often explains the hardware and function of different parts of the brain but often **ignores** the effect of **environmental experience** upon it. Some studies have looked at this issue, however, such as Blakemore & Cooper's (1970) exposure of animals to environments of vertical lines, and the effect of this on the striate visual cortex.
- Physiological explanations have not dealt with the **'mind body' problem** - they do not say how the physical structure and activity of the brain gives rise to the apparently non-physical conscious sensations and experience of mental life.
- There are many **limitations** of some of the **methods** used to identify brain activity, e.g. electrical stimulation of the brain may have a spreading activation effect to other areas (see methods of investigating brain function).
- The idea that neurophysiological explanations are sufficient to explain psychological functioning is dubious. In the case of visual perception, for example, Marr (1982) pointed out that the **aims** and **cognitive processes** of vision had to be considered rather than just the hardware. Indeed, once the processes by which perception occurs have been identified, the psychologist could change the hardware from the brain to a computer's circuits. There is, however, the possibility that vision could only be achieved by the complex biological hardware of the brain, but on the other hand, this biological complexity may also make a clear and useful explanation of perception impossible if the functions are spread in a parallel way over millions of neurones.

- Focusing just on the physiology of the brain may lead researchers to ignore the important implications that **psychological** research and theory has for the functions of brain areas. Hubel and Wiesel's 'bottom-up' description of feature detection in the cells of the visual cortex only focused on the 'input' from the retina, and thus ignored the 'top-down' influences of past experience and expectation that many psychologists such as Gregory (1970) have long pointed out. Recent investigations of the neural activity of cells that respond to the input of visual stimuli are now stressing the importance of the brain's background state of activity - 'It seems that the output of an individual neurone also depends on what the brain happens to be thinking about at the time' (McCrone, cited from *New Scientist*, December 1997). Maunsell and Treue (1996), for example, found the visual movement detection cells of monkeys would show increased activity to moving dots that they had been trained to pay attention to, compared to dots they could see but were not 'interested' in.

Integration of cortical areas devoted to speaking a written passage

Retinal information sent to the primary visual cortex is analysed to detect the lines and curves of letters in the text. Words are distinguished in the angular gyrus and transformed into a form that can be recognised and interpreted for meaning by Wernicke's area. Once the written passage has been understood and held in memory, Broca's area is involved in the formation of spoken words and the motor cortex initiates the physical production of them.

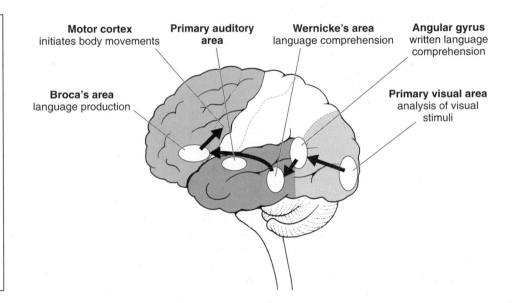

Motor cortex initiates body movements

Primary auditory area

Wernicke's area language comprehension

Angular gyrus written language comprehension

Broca's area language production

Primary visual area analysis of visual stimuli

ARGUMENTS AGAINST LOCALISATION OF FUNCTION

- **Localisation is not always clear cut**. In the case of brain asymmetry, for example, there are many variations in the location of function in the two cerebral hemispheres between male and female subjects and left and right handed subjects. The findings usually reported on the location of cerebral functioning are most representative of right-handed, male subjects.
- **The brain shows 'plasticity'**. According to some researchers, the brain is very flexible and can physically adjust the location of function if brain damage occurs (e.g. the recovery of language in children with left cerebral hemisphere damage), or specialisation to environmental conditions is required (e.g. blind Braille readers show an increase in the sensory cortex surface area devoted to the right forefinger, compared to non-Braille readers and their own left forefingers).
- **The brain is hugely integrated**. There are many different brain areas involved in abilities such as vision (Maunsell and Newsome, 1987, proposed there were at least 19 visual areas in macaque monkeys) and research needs to focus on how these areas **interact** together to produce function. The diagram above shows how just some of the areas involved in language interact in a simple task. Researchers such as Lashley believe in holism - that many functions are distributed across the whole brain. Lashley (1929) destroyed virtually all parts of rat brains in varying amounts to find the location of memory, and concluded that the 'law of mass action' applied -memory loss is related to the amount of damage inflicted upon a rat brain, not the location of it. Neuroscientists are currently accepting the view that the brain is a very dynamic system and that activity in one area of the brain is influenced by the background activity of the rest of the brain. We must 'stop thinking of neurones as if they are exchanging messages... most of the 5000 input lines to the average brain cell are actually parts of feedback loops returning via neighbouring neurones, or those higher up the hierarchy. Barely a tenth of the connections come from sense organs or mapping levels lower in the hierarchy. Every neurone is plumbed into a sea of feedback' (McCrone, cited in *New Scientist*, December, 1997)

The nervous and endocrine systems

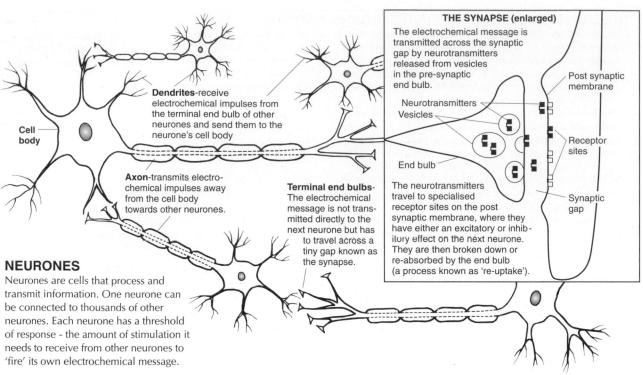

Dendrites-receive electrochemical impulses from the terminal end bulb of other neurones and send them to the neurone's cell body

Cell body

Axon-transmits electro-chemical impulses away from the cell body towards other neurones.

Terminal end bulbs- The electrochemical message is not trans-mitted directly to the next neurone but has to travel across a tiny gap known as the synapse.

THE SYNAPSE (enlarged)
The electrochemical message is transmitted across the synaptic gap by neurotransmitters released from vesicles in the pre-synaptic end bulb.

Neurotransmitters
Vesicles

End bulb

Post synaptic membrane

Receptor sites

Synaptic gap

The neurotransmitters travel to specialised receptor sites on the post synaptic membrane, where they have either an excitatory or inhib-itory effect on the next neurone. They are then broken down or re-absorbed by the end bulb (a process known as 're-uptake').

NEURONES

Neurones are cells that process and transmit information. One neurone can be connected to thousands of other neurones. Each neurone has a threshold of response - the amount of stimulation it needs to receive from other neurones to 'fire' its own electrochemical message.

THE NERVOUS SYSTEM

The nervous system is made up of 10-12 billion neurones of 3 main types:
- **Sensory neurones**, which respond to external stimuli such as touch and light.
- **Motor neurones**, which carry messages to muscles, organs or glands.
- **Association neurones** (by far the most common type), which transmit and integrate information between other neurones.

The nervous system includes:
- The **central nervous system** (CNS) which consists of the brain and spinal cord.
- The **peripheral nervous system** (PNS) which consists of 43 pairs of peripheral nerves whose function is to link the senses to the CNS and the CNS to the muscles and organs. The PNS functions through two main systems:
  1. The **somatic nervous system** - this allows communication and voluntary interaction with the outside world via the sensory and motor neurones.
  2. The **autonomic nervous system** - this connects the CNS to internal glands, organs and involuntary muscles in order to regulate internal processes without conscious control. It has two branches that interact to govern many aspects of behaviour, e.g. homeostasis:
  a The sympathetic branch - prepares the body for action by increasing heartbeat, breathing, blood sugar levels, and adrenaline release.
  b The parasympathetic branch - acts to conserve and restore body energy when relaxed.

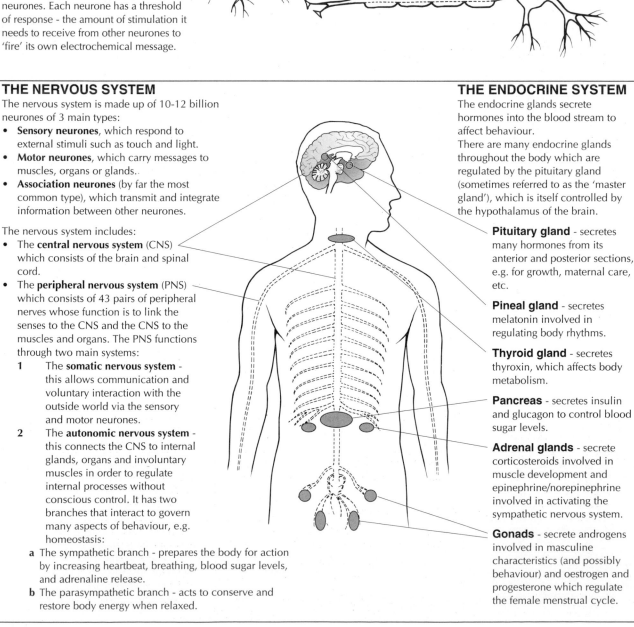

THE ENDOCRINE SYSTEM

The endocrine glands secrete hormones into the blood stream to affect behaviour.
There are many endocrine glands throughout the body which are regulated by the pituitary gland (sometimes referred to as the 'master gland'), which is itself controlled by the hypothalamus of the brain.

Pituitary gland - secretes many hormones from its anterior and posterior sections, e.g. for growth, maternal care, etc.

Pineal gland - secretes melatonin involved in regulating body rhythms.

Thyroid gland - secretes thyroxin, which affects body metabolism.

Pancreas - secretes insulin and glucagon to control blood sugar levels.

Adrenal glands - secrete corticosteroids involved in muscle development and epinephrine/norepinephrine involved in activating the sympathetic nervous system.

Gonads - secrete androgens involved in masculine characteristics (and possibly behaviour) and oestrogen and progesterone which regulate the female menstrual cycle.

Neurotransmitters, drugs and their effects

NEUROTRANSMITTERS AND THEIR EFFECTS

Neurotransmitters are the body's natural chemical messengers that transmit information from one neurone to another in the brain.

NEUROTRANSMITTER	EFFECTS	EVALUATION
• ACETYLCHOLINE (ACh)	• Excitatory effect at synapse with voluntary muscle, causing contraction. • Role in hippocampus of brain in memory consolidation.	• Curare blocks ACh from receptor sites causing muscular paralysis. • Loss of ACh producing neurones in Alzheimer's disease may cause memory loss.
• DOPAMINE	• Mainly inhibitory - involved in voluntary movement, learning, arousal, and feelings of pleasure.	• Deficiency causes Parkinson's disease, over activity is involved in schizophrenia
• GAMMA-AMINO BUTYRIC ACID (GABA)	• Mainly inhibitory - involved in motor control and anxiety.	• Valium increases GABA and has a calming effect on anxiety.
• NOREPINEPHRINE	• Excitatory - involved in the experience of a range of emotions and acts as a hormone to stimulate sympathetic nervous system.	• Injections cause accelerated heart rate which may be labelled as certain emotions. Deficiencies are involved in depression.
• SEROTONIN	• Mainly inhibitory - involved in sleep, arousal levels and emotional experience.	• Deficiencies can lead to mood, anxiety, and sleep disorders.

DRUGS AND THEIR EFFECTS

DRUG	EFFECTS	EVALUATION
• ALCOHOL	• Short term - depressant effect - lowers social inhibitions, reaction time, co-ordination, memory, and alertness. • Long term - produces many negative physical conditions, e.g. cirrhosis, memory loss, tolerance, dependence, addiction, and withdrawal symptoms.	• Possibly increases the sensitivity of neurones to the inhibitory neurotransmitter GABA.
• AMPHETAMINE	• Short term - stimulant effect - increasing alertness and arousal, giving an experience of increased energy and confidence. Large amounts lead to amphetamine psychosis - symptoms similar to paranoid schizophrenia, e.g. hallucinations. • Long term - produces 'crash' after-effects of fatigue and depression, which worsen with continued use. Tolerance and psychological dependence result with lengthy use.	• Originally used in the army to increase the stamina and confidence of soldiers. It has effects similar to epinephrine on the central nervous system. • Helps asthmatics, narcoleptics, and hyperactive children.
• COCAINE	• Short term - stimulant effect - involving short but intense feelings of energy, confidence, euphoria, and pain dulling. • Long term - produces 'crash' after-effects and many negative physiological effects on respiratory and circulatory system with continued use.	• Increases the firing rate of norepine-phrine (giving energy) and dopamine (giving euphoria) producing neurones. The depletion of these neurones probably leads to the crash experience.
• MDMA (Ecstasy)	• Short term - fairly mild, but long lasting effects of increased confidence, euphoria, and elation. Possibility of dehydration leading to convulsions and death.	• Increases serotonin effects by blocking its re-absorption by the synaptic end bulb. Continued use has lasting effects on brain biochemistry.
• HEROIN	• Short term - short but extremely intense feelings of euphoria, followed by longer pain dulling effects. • Long term - produces tolerance, addiction, and very severe withdrawal symptoms.	• Heroin powerfully binds with the brain's natural pain-killing enkephalin and endorphin receptor sites. Naloxone nullifies its effect.
• LSD	• Short term - produces vivid hallucinations, which can become frightening (a 'bad trip'). • Long term - can cause later flashbacks. No psychological or physical dependence is produced.	• Blocks serotonin receptor sites, reducing serotonin's effect (thus possibly reducing the inhibition of acytlcholine in cells involved in the initiation of dreaming).

States of awareness

	PSYCHOLOGICAL EXPERIENCE	PHYSIOLOGICAL CORRELATES

WAKING STATES

CONSCIOUS AWARENESS

PSYCHOLOGICAL EXPERIENCE	PHYSIOLOGICAL CORRELATES
• **Alertness** - involves open-eyed active consciousness with the full ability to concentrate on a task.	• Electroencephalograph (EEG) measurement shows beta waves (13 hertz or above).
• **Relaxation** - involves a passive but awake conscious experience, although the eyes may be shut.	• EEG measurement shows alpha waves (8 to 12 hertz). Electromyograms (EMG) show muscle relaxation.

ALTERED CONSCIOUS AWARENESS

PSYCHOLOGICAL EXPERIENCE	PHYSIOLOGICAL CORRELATES
• **Hypnotic trance** - involves a waking but passive state of awareness, resembling sleep, with an increased responsiveness to outside suggestion. May involve a division of conscious awareness.	• EEG shows brain waves associated with waking states, e.g. alpha waves. EMG shows physiological changes associated with relaxation. Electrooculogram (EOG) shows eye movements.
• **Meditation** - involves a relaxed but focused mental state that can lead to altered perceptions of reality.	• EEG shows alpha waves and even theta waves. Heart and respiration rates can be significantly decreased.

SLEEP STATES

NON-REM SLEEP

Sleep involves a series of stages:	EEG	EOG	EMG
• **Stage 1** - Lightest stage of sleep. Easily awakened.	Theta waves (3-7 hertz)	Slow rolling eye movements	Muscles relaxed but active
• **Stage 2** - Light sleep. Fairly easily awakened. Some responsiveness to external and internal stimuli (name calling produces K-complex activity).	Theta waves, sleep spindles, K-complexes	Minimal eye movement	Little muscle control
• **Stage 3** - Deep sleep. Difficult to awaken. Very unresponsive to external stimuli.	Delta waves (1-2 hertz) 20-50% of the time	Virtually no eye movement	Virtually no muscle movement
• **Stage 4** - Very deep sleep. Very difficult to awaken. Very unresponsive to external stimuli.	Delta waves over 50% of the time	Virtually no eye movement	Virtually no muscle movement

REM SLEEP

	EEG	EOG	EMG
• It is difficult to awaken people from rapid eye-movement (REM) sleep. If woken, individuals report vivid dreaming far more often than if woken from non-REM sleep (Dement and Kleitman, 1957).	High levels of mixed wave activity	Rapid eye movement reflecting dream content	Muscles in a state of virtual paralysis

ATYPICAL SLEEP STATES

PSYCHOLOGICAL EXPERIENCE	PHYSIOLOGICAL CORRELATES
• **Lucid dreaming** - involves the experience of feeling consciously in control of dream activity. This can occur spontaneously, although some claim to be able to produce the state at will.	• EEG, EOG and EMG measurements indicate REM sleep. Some researchers have been able to indicate their lucid dreaming state to external observers through pre-arranged eye movement signals.
• **Sleep-walking** - involves 'involuntary' physical activity while asleep. The sleep-walker can be difficult to awaken.	• Sleep-walking usually occurs during stage 3 or 4 deep sleep, often in the first three hours of sleep.
• **Narcolepsy** - inappropriate daytime sleepiness, sometimes involving a sudden desire to fall asleep or cataplexy (sudden short lived muscle weakness or paralysis in response to emotional arousal).	• Physiological measurement reveals that narcoleptics can show significantly frequent 'Sudden Onset REM Periods', where REM sleep occurs very quickly after falling asleep. • Cataplexy may be linked to REM sleep paralysis.

Body rhythms

	PSYCHOLOGICAL EXPERIENCE	PHYSIOLOGICAL CORRELATES
CIRCANNUAL RHYTHMS (Rhythms lasting about a year)	• Many behaviours in animals vary over a yearly cycle, such as hibernation, mating, and migration. • Some humans show seasonal affective disorder - a strong variation in mood over the year, usually involving depression during the winter months.	• A key regulator of physiology and behaviour in yearly cycles is light level. Darkness stimulates the pineal gland to produce melatonin - a hormone involved in controlling energy levels and mood. • However, many environmental and psychological factors can lead to winter depression, e.g. weather.
INFRADIAN RHYTHMS (Rhythms lasting longer than 24 hours)	• The infradian rhythm of menstruation in women occurs over a 28 day cycle and is associated with the behaviour changes of pre-menstrual syndrome (PMS). • The psychological effects occur around 5 days before menstruation in some women and can include mood change, irritability, dizziness, and changes in energy levels and eating habits.	• The menstrual cycle in women, although internally regulated, can be quite variable at first and is open to modification by external stimuli - such as light levels (indicating a role for melatonin) and the presence of other women (frequent interaction with particular women can cause synchronisation of menstruation, possibly due to chemical scents). • Not all women experience PMS however.
CIRCADIAN RHYTHMS (Rhythms lasting about 24 hours)	• Circadian rhythms determine our alertness and activity levels during the day and night. • Altering activity patterns over the 24 hour physiological cycle, for example through shift work or travel across time zones, can have an effect on behaviour, e.g. jet lag - feeling tired or over-active at the wrong time of day. • Some circadian rhythms, such as body temperature, will adjust over time to new activity patterns, indicating modification by external cues.	• Humans show physiological changes over a 24 hour cycle in hormone levels, body temperature, and heart, respiration and metabolic rate. • The human internal body clock is regulated by the suprachiasmatic nuclei of the hypothalamus that seems to naturally work on a 25 hour cycle (demonstrated by Siffre's cave study) but adjusts the circadian rhythms to the duration of daylight through monitoring light levels at the retina.
ULTRADIAN RHYTHMS (Rhythms lasting less than 24 hours) **Diurnal (day) rhythms**	• Individuals seem to vary in their activity levels, some being more alert and receptive to information in the morning, others in the evening. • Horne and Osterberg (1976) used their 'Morningness-Eveningness' questionnaire to confirm this distinction, although research findings on the effect of time of day upon performance have been mixed.	• Morning types seem to reach their physiological peak (as measured by body temperature, metabolic rate, etc.) earlier than evening types, indicating perhaps a 'phase advance' in their circadian rhythms (Marks and Folkhard, 1985). • However, these variations could be the result (rather than the cause) of the subject's lifestyle and activity levels during the day.
Nocturnal (night) rhythms	• The stages of sleep are cycled through around 5 times per night in the following way: **Relaxation to first cycle** - may involve hypnagogic experiences, e.g. dream images or falling sensations. **First cycle** - descent to deep stage 4 sleep (which lasts approx. 40 minutes), ends with a short REM period. **Second cycle** - gradual descent to deep stage 4 sleep (approx. 30 minutes), ends with a short REM period. **Third cycle** - Mostly stage 2 sleep, followed by up to 40 minutes of REM sleep. **Fourth cycle** - Around an hour of stage 2 sleep, followed by around an hour of REM sleep. **Fifth cycle** - Stage 2 sleep followed by a shorter REM period or waking (possibly with hypnagogic experiences). The level of dreaming and alertness is determined by when during the cycles a person is awoken.	• Night darkness identified at the retina causes the suprachiasmatic nuclei of the hypothalamus to trigger melatonin production in the pituitary gland. • Melatonin in turn stimulates the raphe nucleus to produce serotonin to trigger the activity of the reticular activating system (responsible for the sleep cycle). 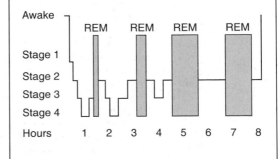

Theories of the function of sleep

SLEEP DEPRIVATION - IS SLEEP NEEDED?

ANIMAL STUDIES:
- Jouvet (1967) deprived cats of sleep by putting them on a floating island in a pool of water so that when they fell asleep they fell in and woke up. The cats developed abnormal behaviours and eventually died.
- Rechtschaffen et al deprived rats of sleep. They had all died after 33 days.

HUMAN STUDIES:
- Psychological effects - increased desire to sleep, difficulty sustaining attention (however, problem solving is less impaired), delusions, and depersonalisation.
- Physiological effects - minor changes, such as problems with eye focusing, but no significant major adverse effects. Sleep after deprivation is not cumulative (not much longer than usual), although more time is spent in REM sleep (a REM rebound effect). However, sleep deprivation studies are not indefinite.

THEORIES OF SLEEP FUNCTION

RESTORATION THEORY
Oswald (1966) suggests that the function of sleep, especially REM sleep, is simply to restore bodily energy reserves, repair the condition of muscles and cells and to allow growth to occur. Sleep could also aid psychological recovery.

Evaluation
For:
- Longer sleep (particularly stage 4) occurs after large amounts of physical exercise, and in growing children (REM occupies 50% of sleep in babies, 20% in adults).
- Growth hormones are released during stage 4 sleep, deprivation of which causes physical problems such as fibrositis.
- Sleep is greater after periods of stress and improves mood.

Against:
- Sleep duration is not reduced with lack of exercise.
- Deprivation of REM sleep does not produce significantly adverse effects.
- REM sleep involves an increase in energy expenditure and blood flow which *inhibits* protein synthesis.

MEMORY CONSOLIDATION THEORY
Empson and Clarke (1970) propose that sleep, especially REM sleep, facilitates the reinforcement of information in memory.

Evaluation
For:
- Subjects exposed to information before sleep remember less in the morning if deprived of REM sleep rather than non REM sleep.
- Perhaps more REM sleep occurs in younger humans because they have more to learn.

Against:
- There is little evidence against the theory, but memory consolidation can occur without sleep.

SLEEPING TO DREAM
Sleep may occur because the dreams that take place in it have important functions (see dream theories).

EVOLUTIONARY THEORY
All mammals sleep (the porpoise even shuts down one side of its brain at a time to do so), although the length of time varies according to the species. Given its universal nature and the fact that this unconscious and defenceless state seems a dangerous behaviour to show, sleep probably has an important evolutionary survival function, possibly to
- conserve energy when food gathering has been completed or is more difficult (e.g. at night), and/or
- avoid damage from nocturnal predators or accidents by remaining motionless.

Meddis (1975) suggests the duration of sleep a species shows depends upon its food requirements and predator avoidance needs.

Evaluation
For:
- Lions (which have few predators and meet their food needs in short bursts) and squirrels (who have safe burrows) sleep longer.
- Cattle (which have many natural predators) and shrews (which have high metabolic rates) sleep very little.

Against:
- Some evolutionary arguments suggest that animals who are highly preyed upon need to sleep little to keep constant vigilance for predators, however others suggest the opposite - that they need to sleep longer to keep them away from harm by remaining motionless.

Theories of the function of dreaming

THEORIES OF DREAM FUNCTION

CRICK AND MITCHISON'S REVERSE LEARNING THEORY

Crick and Mitchison (1983) argue that dreaming can be regarded as the **random** and **meaningless by-product** of the bombardment of the cortex with random stimulation from the brain stem during REM sleep, to serve the biological function of **clearing the brain** of useless or maladaptive information.

Evaluation
For:
- The two mammals that do not show REM sleep (the dolphin and spiny anteater) have abnormally large cortexes, perhaps to contain the useless memories they are not able to unlearn.

Against:
- The theory lacks detail over exactly how 'useless' information is identified and 'unlearned', and also neglects the apparent meaningfulness of many dreams.

REPROGRAMMING THEORY

Evans (1984) suggests that REM sleep is required by the brain to update itself in the light of new information received **during the day**, and that dreams are the interpretation of this assimilation.
Foulkes (1985), however, proposes that dreams reflect the way our cognitive systems organise and reprogram the stimuli received from random brain activity **during REM sleep**.

Evaluation
For:
- Subjects given unusual tasks before sleep, spend longer in REM sleep.

Against:
- If dreams interpreted the processed information so logically, why would dreams be so strange and incoherent?

WISH FULFILMENT

Freud suggested that dreams were the disguised expressions of unconscious desires and impulses. The recalled manifest content of the dream has been disguised by the dream censor through methods like symbolism to protect our conscious self from the anxiety provoking latent (hidden) meaning of the dream.

Evaluation
For:
- Many researchers have agreed that dreams are meaningful.

Against:
- There is little empirical evidence for Freud's theory in general and little reason for dream meanings to always be disguised.

HOBSON AND McCARLEY'S ACTIVATION SYNTHESIS THEORY

Hobson and McCarley (1977) propose a biological theory which regards dreams as the **meaningless** result of **random brain activity**. The activation part of the theory involves the random firing of giant cells in the reticular activating system (triggered by the presence of acetylcholine) which activates the sensory and motor areas of the brain during REM sleep. The synthesis part of the theory involves the attempt of higher parts of the brain to organise and make sense of the random activity producing the semi-coherent dreams we experience.

Evaluation
For:
- The theory has biological support and explains how the content of dreams could be influenced by particular areas of brain activation (balance areas may produce dreams of flying) or external stimulation while asleep (water splashed on a sleeper's face can be incorporated into their dreams).

Against:
- Foulkes (1985) proposes that dreams are **meaningful** interpretations of REM random brain activity in the light of our cognitive systems' organisational abilities. Dreams reflect the way we interpret information, relate it to past experience and help us prepare for situations not yet encountered. Hobson and McCarley have come to agree with this view that dreams can be meaningful.

PROBLEM SOLVING

Cartwright proposes that dreams are a meaningful way of considering worries or problems from conscious everyday life. Dreams may use metaphors (but are not deliberately disguised as Freud thought) and may provide solutions for problems.

Evaluation
For:
- Subjects given problems before sleep are more likely to solve them realistically if REM sleep is uninterrupted.

Against:
- There is little other evidence for the theory and most problems can be more quickly solved while awake.

'The relation of eye movements during sleep to dream activity: an objective method for the study of dreams' Dement and Kleitman (1957)

AIM

Aserinsky and Kleitman found a relationship between rapid eye movement (REM) during sleep and reports of dreaming. Dement and Kleitman aimed to provide a **more detailed** investigation of how objective, physiological aspects of rapid eye movement relate to the subjective, psychological experience of dreaming reported by subjects, by testing whether

- significantly **more dreaming** occurs **during REM sleep** than non-REM sleep under controlled conditions.
- there is a **significant positive correlation** between the objective length of **time** spent **in REM** and the subjective **duration of dreaming** reported upon waking.
- there is a significant **relationship** between the **pattern of rapid eye movements** observed during sleep and the **content** of the **dream** reported upon waking.

METHOD

Subjects: 7 adult males and 2 adult females - 5 of which were intensively studied, 4 of which were used to confirm results.

Design: Laboratory experimentation and observation.

Procedure: Subjects slept individually in a quiet dark laboratory room after a normal day's activity (except that alcohol and caffeine were avoided during the days before testing). Electrodes were connected near the eyes to register eye movement and on the scalp to measure brain waves during sleep - these were the objective measures of REM sleep. Subjects were awoken at various times during the night (fairly evenly distributed across the average sleeping time of the subjects) by a loud doorbell noise, and immediately reported into a recording device whether they had been dreaming and the content of the dream before any contact with the experimenter (to avoid bias). Subjects were never usually told whether their eyes had been moving before being awoken. Dreaming was only counted if a fairly detailed and coherent dream was reported - vague impressions or assertions of dreaming without recall of content were not counted.

STUDY ONE

Subjects were awoken in one of four different ways during either REM or non-REM sleep, and were compared to see if they had been dreaming.
- 2 subjects were awoken randomly
- 1 subject was awoken during 3 REM sleep periods followed by 3 non-REM periods, and so on.
- 1 subject was awoken randomly, but was told he would only be awoken during periods of REM sleep
- 1 subject was awoken at the whim of the experimenter

STUDY TWO

Subjects were awoken either 5 or 15 minutes after REM sleep began and were asked to decide whether the duration of their dream was closer to 5 or 15 minutes.
The length of the dream (measured in terms of the number of words in their dream narratives) was also correlated to the duration of REM sleep before awakening.

STUDY THREE

Subjects were awoken as soon as one of four patterns of eye movement had occurred for 1 minute, and were asked exactly what they had just dreamt.
- Mainly vertical eye movements
- Mainly horizontal eye movements
- Both vertical and horizontal eye movements.
- Very little or no eye movement

RESULTS

Generally, REM periods were clearly observed in all subjects and distinguished from non-REM sleep periods. REM sleep periods occurred at regular intervals specific to each subject (although on average occurring every 92 minutes) and tended to last longer later in the night.

STUDY ONE

Regardless of how subjects were awoken, significantly more dreams were reported in REM than non-REM sleep.
When subjects failed to recall dreams from REM sleep, this was usually early in the night.
When subjects recalled dreams from non-REM sleep it was most often within 8 minutes after the end of a REM period.

STUDY TWO

Subjects were significantly correct in matching the duration of their dream to length of time they had shown REM sleep for both the 5 minute periods (45 out of 51 estimates correct) and 15 minute periods (47 out of 60 estimates correct).
All subjects showed a significant positive correlation at the $P< 0.05$ level or better between the length of their dream narratives and duration of REM sleep before awakening.

STUDY THREE

There was a very strong association between the pattern of REMs and the content of dream reports.
- The 3 vertical REM periods were associated with dreams of looking up and down at cliff faces, ladders, and basketball nets.
- A dream of two people throwing tomatoes at each other occurred in the only mainly horizontal REM period.
- 21 periods of vertical and horizontal REMs were associated with dreams of looking at close objects.
- 10 periods of very little or no REMs were associated with dreams of looking at fixed or distant objects.

EVALUATION

Methodological: Dreams may be recalled easier in REM than non-REM sleep because the latter is a deeper stage of sleep - perhaps dreams occur in deeper sleep, but are more difficult to recall from it.

The study used a limited sample, mostly men, therefore showed a lack of generalisability.

Theoretical: The research provides support for the idea that dreams can be studied in an objective way. This then opens up areas of research for the effect of environmental stimuli on dreaming.

Links: Sleep and dream research. Laboratory studies.

The brain physiology of arousal and sleep

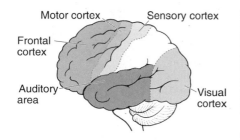

Motor cortex Sensory cortex
Frontal cortex
Auditory area
Visual cortex

CORTEX
All cortical structures show neural activity during waking that decreases with the onset of non-REM sleep. During dreaming REM sleep, however
- the frontal cortex is deactivated - reducing self awareness and planning which may account for the lack of realisation that one is dreaming, the lack of control over what is dreamt, and increased acceptance of bizarre dream content.
- areas of the cortex associated with sensory and motor functioning are active.

SUPRA-CHIASMATIC NUCLEUS
Regulates body rhythms in line with environmental light levels. When darkness is detected, messages are sent to the pineal gland. Removal of this structure in hamsters randomises their sleep-waking patterns.

THALAMUS
Acts as the relay station for arousal to various cortical structures during waking or REM sleep

PINEAL GLAND
On receiving light information from the supraschiasmatic nucleus, the pineal gland releases the hormone melatonin, which is thought to stimulate the production of serotonin, possibly in the raphe nucleus.

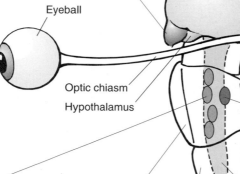

Eyeball

Optic chiasm
Hypothalamus

LOCUS COERULEUS
The locus coeruleus releases norepinephrine. It may cause arousal by increasing sensitivity to environmental stimuli.

RAPHE NUCLEUS
The raphe nuclei release serotonin and may be involved in causing sleep, since their destruction causes sleeplessness.

RETICULAR ACTIVATING SYSTEM
Regulates arousal levels from sleep to focused attention.
Acts as a filter for external stimuli, arousing higher levels of the brain if attention is demanded.
Moruzzi and Magoun (1949) found that
- stimulating the RAS awoke sleeping cats
- damage of the RAS in cats caused coma.

PONS
Involved in attention, sleeping and dreaming.
Some pontine cells are involved in the muscular paralysis of REM sleep (Jouvet found that their removal caused cats to act out their dreams). Other neuronal cells in the pons show rapid firing just before the onset of REM sleep

MEDULLA
Controls the vital involuntary functions of breathing, heart rate, blood pressure, etc. It is thought to play a role in the physiological changes of sleep.

PHYSIOLOGY AND BIOCHEMISTRY OF SLEEP
Hobson and McCarley proposed a neurological model of how dream activity is initiated. They suggest that there are two types of neuronal cells in the brain stem that control dreaming, which can be termed REM-ON and REM-OFF cells.
When the **REM-OFF cells** are **active**, they produce serotonin which **inhibits** the production of acetylcholine in the **REM-ON cells**.
When the **REM-OFF cells** are **inactive**, the serotonin **inhibition** of acetylcholine ceases and the **REM-ON cells activate dreaming**.
Pappenheimer et al isolated a substance known as Factor S from the cerebrospinal fluid of sleep deprived goats that caused rats and rabbits to fall asleep when injected with it. Seven millionths of a gram of Factor S (a muramyl peptide) was later extracted from 3000 litres of *human* urine and proved powerful enough to provide 500 doses - each capable of inducing 6 hours of NREM sleep when injected into rabbits.

The nature and applications of hypnosis

CHARACTERISTICS OF HYPNOTISED SUBJECTS

The word 'hypnotism' is derived from the Greek for sleep - 'hypnos'. However, there are distinct differences between the two phenomena.

Hypnosis is characterised by a number of behaviours:

- **Relaxation and suspension of planning** - hypnotised subjects sit quietly and do not seem to plan or initiate activity. Control is given over to the hypnotist.
- **Suggestibility** - hypnotised subjects will respond to suggestions and obey instructions with little sign of inhibition, even if the request is normally unusual or impossible to do.
- **Atypical behaviour** - hypnotised subjects can apparently perform behaviours that they would not normally be willing or able to do, such as controlling severe pain, experiencing hallucinations, retrieving forgotten memories, etc.

DEPTH OF HYPNOSIS

The Stanford Hypnotic Susceptibility Scale provides an indicator of how deeply hypnotised a person is by listing a set of suggestions of increasing difficulty, e.g.

- Arm lowering - being unable to resist the suggestion that one's arm is getting heavier.
- Taste hallucination - responding appropriately to a suggestion that a sweet or sour taste is being experienced.
- Age regression - following suggestions of going back in time to childhood where behaviour, speech, and even writing, should be age appropriate.
- Post hypnotic amnesia - forgetting information after hypnosis until cued.

About 15% of people are highly hypnotisable, another 15% are very resistant to it, and the rest are somewhere in between.

HOW IT IS DONE

Hypnosis is achieved by a mixture of relaxation and persuasive suggestion.

- Environmental conditions should be comfortable and free of distractions. The subject should sit comfortably.
- The hypnotist should adopt a quiet and calm, but authoritative tone of voice. Delivery of suggestions should be smooth and confident.
- Many methods employ fixed gaze techniques - getting the subject to focus their attention on something.
- Suggestions should be repeated to the subject that they are relaxed and sleepy and that their arms and legs feel heavy, warm and relaxed until their eyes close.
- Suggestions graded from easy to follow, to hard to follow, should gradually be presented to determine the degree of hypnosis. The Stanford Hypnotic Susceptibility Scale ranges from suggestions that an outstretched arm is getting heavier and heavier to hallucinations and post hypnotic amnesia.

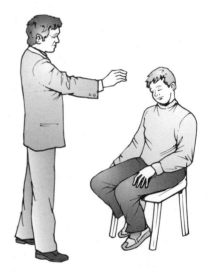

APPLICATIONS

MEMORY

Opinion is divided as to whether memory recall under hypnosis consistently provides more detailed and accurate data than other methods of retrieval.

Hypnosis and eyewitness testimony

For:

- The relaxed and focused state of hypnosis may lead to better recall as well as the use of more specific hypnotic techniques, such as context recreation (based on state dependent memory theory) or 'freeze-framing' scenes.

Against:

- The highly suggestible, compliant, and imaginative state of hypnosis may lead to a greater vulnerability to leading questions or confabulation in order to please the hypnotist.

Hypnosis and repressed memory

For:

- Research has indicated that hypnosis can retrieve previously inaccessible memories, but should not be relied upon without objective corroborative evidence.

Against:

- Hypnosis may lead to false memory syndrome, an especially sensitive issue when memories of child abuse are retrieved by the hypnotist in adulthood.

MEDICAL USE

- **Pain control** - Hypnosis has significantly reduced the perception of pain in a variety of situations from dentistry to child birth. James Esdaile amputated the gangrenous leg of an individual under hypnotic analgesia in the nineteenth century. Physiological measurement indicates that pain messages are received by the brain but attention does not seem to be paid to them. People have been taught to control pain without hypnosis, but as with hypnosis, there are large individual differences in the success of pain reduction.
- **Wart removal!** - Surman et al (1973) successfully caused wart reduction in 50% of those hypnotised.
- **Therapy** - Hypnotic role-play and regression can facilitate the cathartic effect of therapy and reduce inhibitions when recalling traumatic events. The same effects can be achieved without hypnosis, but the use of it can speed the therapeutic process up.
- **Addiction** - There are problems evaluating the success of hypnosis to overcome addictions, e.g. to smoking, Those who use hypnosis for such purposes may be more highly motivated, or may have personality traits more conducive to overcoming addiction.
- **Stress** - Hypnosis aids relaxation but one of the criteria for susceptibility to hypnosis is the ability to relax.

Theories of hypnosis

WHAT CAUSES IT?

ALTERED STATE

Some researchers support the state or special process approach to hypnosis, which proposes that

1 hypnosis represents an altered state of consciousness, distinct from both waking and sleep states. Hilgard proposes the neo-dissociation theory, which suggests that hypnosis divides consciousness into separate channels of awareness.
2 hypnosis is a special state, in that phenomena can be produced during it (such as immunity to pain) that cannot be shown under other conditions.

EVIDENCE
For proposition 1:

- *Hidden observer* - Hilgard and others have found that hypnotised subjects can show divided conscious experience. For example, when painful stimuli are applied under the hypnotic suggestion to feel no pain, although subjects will report no pain, another part of them (the hidden observer) will report agony. Similarly, instructions to the hidden observer to raise a finger will produce anxiety in the subject over this inexplicable movement. This supports the dissociation of consciousness theory.
- *Physiological evidence* - Brain scans have shown different areas of brain activity between low and highly susceptible subjects when hypnosis is attempted.

For proposition 2:

- *Task performance* - Orne et al (1968) found that hypnotised subjects responded to a suggestion to touch their forehead (when they heard the word 'experiment' mentioned throughout a 2 day period) more often, especially if highly susceptible to hypnosis, than simulators.
- *Hypnotic analgesia* - Many studies show that the experience of pain is reduced under hypnosis even if the physiological indicators of pain are present. Knox et al (1974) found that the average pain severity ratings reported by highly susceptible subjects exposed to 8 minutes of ischaemic pain (caused by restricting blood flow) was 1 out of ten when hypnotised to ignore it, but 9.9 when not hypnotised.
- *Trance logic* - Trance logic refers to the ability of hypnotised subjects to tolerate logical inconsistency. Orne showed that hypnotised subjects are able to hallucinate a person (which they often describe as transparent) sitting in a chair, even if that person was also seen standing next to them, without being perturbed by this inconsistency. Simulators asked to fake this hypnotic situation often described their 'hallucinated' person as opaque and report that the hallucination disappears when they turn to look at the real person next to them. Bowers (1976) states that people told to simulate (fake) hypnosis will bump into a chair if a hypnotist suggests they can not see it, whereas genuinely hypnotised people walk around it.

Colman (1987) argues that the fact that simulators can imitate many aspects of the hypnotic state, does not mean that the state does not exist. Simulators can convincingly fake drunkenness or sleep behaviour but we do not doubt that these are altered states.

Colman (1987) also notes that task motivated simulator subjects may unwittingly fall into a hypnotic trance due to their attempts to be a good simulator and imagine what hypnosis is like.

SOCIAL INFLUENCE

Other researchers support the non-state or social psychological approach to hypnosis which argues that:

1 Hypnosis is really only a form of social influence not an altered state, and that hypnotised people, deliberately or not, comply to the demands of the hypnotist and conform to the norms of the hypnotic situation (they behave as they think they are expected to act).
2 All phenomena produced under hypnosis can be produced without it (by people motivated to simulate hypnosis).

EVIDENCE
For proposition 1:

- *Lie detecting* - Coe and Yashinski (1985) found that people with post hypnotic amnesia increase their recall if led to believe that a lie detector test will find out if they are lying. Pattie (1937) showed that hypnotised subjects given the suggestion that they could not feel anything in one hand reported sensations administered to the fingers of both their hands if they were inter-linked (making it difficult to tell which was which). This suggests that the subjects were merely behaving as *if* they were hypnotised.
- *Physiological evidence* - Differences in brain activity levels between low and highly susceptible subjects when hypnosis is attempted may just reflect a state of relaxation rather than hypnotic trance.

For proposition 2.

- *Task performance* - The power of social influence to produce unexpected results in non-hypnotised subjects is underestimated. Task motivated control groups asked to behave as if they were hypnotised have performed many tasks in the same way as hypnotised subjects, e.g. eating onions under the pretence that they are apples, or following an instruction to throw 'acid' at another person. The human plank demonstration (where it is suggested that the body is so rigid it can be placed across two chairs and sat upon) can be performed by most fit, non-hypnotised people.
- *Hypnotic analgesia* - Relaxation and redirecting of attention in non-hypnotised subjects has yielded similar results in terms of pain reduction. Barber and Hahn showed that motivated subjects could reduce their experience of cold pressor pain (caused by immersing the hand in icy water) more than non-motivated and non-hypnotised control subjects, and to a similar degree to hypnotised subjects.
- *Trance logic* - Johnson et al claimed that simulators were just as able to show trance logic (e.g. reporting transparent hallucinations of a person that persisted when the real person was also present) as hypnotised subjects, although Hilgard accused the study of being flawed.
- *Task inability in hypnotised subjects* - Subjects under the hypnotic suggestion of deafness fail delayed auditory feedback tests that real deaf people pass.

Colman's argument that simulators can also fake drunkenness or sleep behaviour, ignores the many other physiological correlates of these states (such as the different EEG measurements involved in sleep) that justify the use of the term 'state'.

Motivated simulators often vigorously deny accidentally falling into a hypnotic trance.

Physiological theories of motivation

HOMEOSTATIC DRIVE THEORY OF MOTIVATION

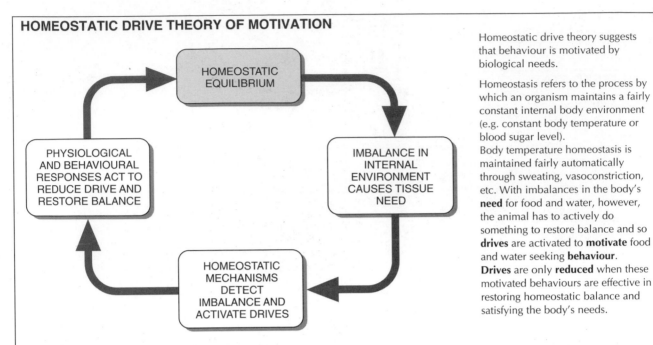

Homeostatic drive theory suggests that behaviour is motivated by biological needs.

Homeostasis refers to the process by which an organism maintains a fairly constant internal body environment (e.g. constant body temperature or blood sugar level).

Body temperature homeostasis is maintained fairly automatically through sweating, vasoconstriction, etc. With imbalances in the body's **need** for food and water, however, the animal has to actively do something to restore balance and so **drives** are activated to **motivate** food and water seeking **behaviour**. **Drives** are only **reduced** when these motivated behaviours are effective in restoring homeostatic balance and satisfying the body's needs.

EVALUATION
Behaviour is not always motivated by homeostatic needs and drives
Homeostatic drive theory ignores higher psychological and social needs (e.g. self-esteem and achievement). It only seems to explain a handful of motivated behaviours for basic physiological survival needs and, even with these, it does not provide a complete explanation. A number of social, developmental and psychological factors are involved in all the basic drives, from hunger and thirst to sleep and sex. In the case of the hunger drive, for example, the homeostatic level for food intake required to satisfy tissue needs may well be dictated by a biological set point (different people may naturally require different amounts of food). However, research has indicated that even this homeostatic set point may be influenced by early environmental factors, e.g. over or under feeding as a child. Furthermore, eating behaviour is not governed strictly by the hunger drive - we can refuse to eat when hungry or can over eat when already full.

Drive reduction is not always necessary to motivate behaviour
Studies have found that animals will still perform many behaviours when physiological drives have been reduced and will even actively seek stimulation rather than reduce arousal. Optimal arousal theory suggests that drive reduction only applies if the organism is over stimulated and that many behaviours indicate that a certain level of drive **arousal** is desired. This has been termed sensation seeking behaviour.

BRAIN PHYSIOLOGY AND MOTIVATION
Physiologists have identified many areas of the brain involved in motivating a variety of behaviours:

- **The medial forebrain bundle** - Olds and Miller found that electrical stimulation of this 'pleasure area' in rats massively reinforced behaviour. Male rats that could administer self stimulation by pressing a lever pressed it thousands of times a day, even in preference to food or sexually receptive female rats.
- **The hypothalamus** - a small area of the brain involved in homeostasis and the motivation of a vast variety of behaviours, from feeding and drinking to aggressive and sexual behaviour.
- **The reticular activating system** - controls general arousal and activity levels.
- **The cerebral cortex** - probably the location of the more rational, cognitive sources of motivation.

The hypothalamus   The cerebral cortex

The medial forebrain bundle   The reticular activating system

Evaluation
Even the most simple of motivated actions involve very complex interactions of many brain systems. Seeing brain centres as sources of motivation ignores the triggering influence of environmental stimuli. The most precise scientific studies have been conducted on rat brains due to the ethical objections of experimenting on human brains, raising the problem of generalising from animal studies to humans.

GENETICS, EVOLUTIONARY THEORY AND MOTIVATION
Evolutionary sociobiological theorists argue that ultimately all behaviour is motivated by evolutionary survival needs. Behaviours evolve to better adapt an organism to their environment to promote survival, therefore sexual behaviour is motivated by the genetic requirement to reproduce, aggression is motivated by the need to compete or defend against others; social behaviour is motivated by the survival benefits bestowed upon a socially integrated individual, etc.

Evaluation
Evolutionary theory is rather reductionist and often ignores contemporary social and cultural motives for behaviour.

Physiological mechanisms for the hunger drive

Much research has focused on the hunger drive as the best example of homeostasis affecting motivation. Many studies have sought to find both the short term mechanisms of feeding behaviour (the mouth, stomach, and duodenum) and the longer term mechanisms (the hypothalamus and blood glucose levels of the body).

THE HYPOTHALAMUS

Different areas of the hypothalamus are thought to be involved in different aspects of feeding behaviour:

The ventromedial nucleus of the hypothalamus (VMH) may act as a satiety centre - stopping eating once the animal has consumed the required intake.

The lateral nucleus of the hypothalamus (LH) may act as a feeding centre - initiating eating behaviour when intake is required.

Evidence

- Teitelbaum et al (1954) ablated the LH of rats which caused a loss of eating behaviour. Hess (1954) stimulated it with microelectrodes causing compulsive eating.

- Hetherington and Ranson (1942) damaged the VMH of rats, which caused dramatic over-eating (hyperphagia), whereas Olds (1958) found stimulation decreased eating.

Evaluation

Damage to the VMH may work not by just increasing appetite but by reducing the sensitivity to the internal cues of hunger and increasing sensitivity to external cues. The hyperphagic rats whose VMH had been removed became very fussy and sensitive about their food and would not eat it if quinine was added to give it a bitter taste. Schachter (1971) found that overweight people also seem to pay little attention to internal cues (hunger pangs) and base their eating habits more on external cues (the availability and taste of food). Overweight people respond less to the internal cues of stomach distension (Schachter et al, 1968) and are more likely to continue to eat food that is available but are less likely to search for it if it is not.

Although hypothalamic tumours have been associated with obesity in humans, it is more likely that the hypothalamus works differently in fat and thin eaters through the operation of a biological set point - a natural body weight determined by the balance between the VMH and LH. The set point may be affected by genetics, the number of fats cells in the body or damage to the LH or VMH to alter the balance between them.

BLOOD GLUCOSE LEVELS

Blood glucose levels are monitored by glucoreceptors in the hypothalamus, liver and blood system. When glucose levels drop, they may motivate eating behaviour to restore the loss.

Evidence

- Injections of glucose decrease appetite.
- Injections of insulin (which lowers glucose levels by converting it into fat) increases appetite.

Evaluation

Glucose levels remain very balanced and seem to be homeostatically controlled themselves, and so are unlikely to show the variation needed to respond to and activate eating behaviour.

THE MOUTH

Operations on rats, whereby the oesophagus was redirected out of the rat's body instead of connecting with the stomach, showed that the mouth and throat are only short term sensory receptors for hunger and satiety. The rats with the above operation stopped feeding after chewing and swallowing larger than normal meals, but soon began eating again.

THE STOMACH

Cannon believed that stomach contraction was the mechanism involved in monitoring and triggering the hunger drive.

Evidence

In an experiment by Cannon and Washburn (1912), Washburn swallowed a balloon so that stomach contractions could be measured and a correlation was found between contractions and self reports of hunger.

Evaluation

However, people whose stomachs have been surgically removed still get hungry, and hunger persists even if the neural pathways from the stomach to the brain are cut.

THE DUODENUM

A further short term mechanism of satiety is the release of cholecystokinin (CCK) by the duodenum in response to fatty acids in the intestine.

Evidence

Injections of this hormone into hungry rats or obese humans decreases their appetite.

Psychological theories of motivation 1

Some psychological approaches incorporate biological motivation in some way, e.g. Hull or Freud's drive theories, or Maslow's lowest hierarchical levels. Other approaches reject it.

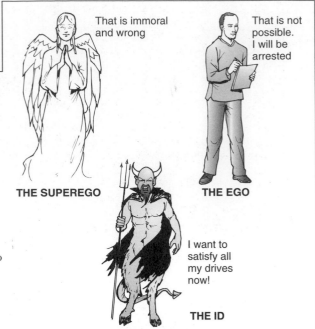

THE SUPEREGO — That is immoral and wrong

THE EGO — That is not possible. I will be arrested

THE ID — I want to satisfy all my drives now!

PSYCHOANALYTIC DRIVE THEORY OF MOTIVATION

Freud's ideas on motivation are based upon unconscious instinctual drives seeking expression in a society that imposes constraints upon them. Motivation stems from a dynamic struggle between the three aspects of the unconscious mind:

- **The id** - which seeks to release the two drives of sex (from Eros the life instinct) and aggression (from Thanatos the death instinct) regardless of time or place. The unconscious mind resembles a hydraulic closed energy system (like a steam engine) in that psychic energy from the drives builds up and, if not released, causes inner pressure or anxiety. Thus sex and aggression are the biological, instinctual motivating influences upon behaviour.
- **The ego** - which seeks to control the id in line with reality. The ego is motivated to defend the conscious mind and society against forbidden id impulses.
- **The superego** - which is motivated to control the id in line with moral principles.

Evaluation
Freud's ideas on motivation suffer from all the usual criticisms of drive theories, plus those of psychoanalytic theory in general, e.g. the lack of experimental evidence.

COGNITIVE THEORIES OF MOTIVATION

Cognitive theories emphasise the importance of psychological level motivational influences upon behaviour. Many of these influences go beyond biological needs and drives in that they
- may actually involve sensation-seeking behaviours - **increasing** arousal or drive levels rather than reducing them, and
- can combine with **social** motivational needs or desires to behave in socially appropriate ways - thus behaviour can be said to be **elicited** from without as well as motivated from within.

Examples of these cognitive and psychosocial motivational factors include:
- **Curiosity** - both animals and humans are motivated to explore and seek information, even when biological needs have been met.
- **Cognitive consistency** - humans are motivated to think and act in consistent ways to avoid unpleasant cognitive dissonance.
- **Need for control** - humans are motivated to assert control over their lives - perceived constraints upon freedom can produce resistance and a lack of control can lead to learned helplessness and depression.
- **Need for achievement** - the motive to achieve high standards of performance or success.

Evaluation
Many studies have supported cognitive motivational theories.
Harlow - found rhesus monkeys showed curiosity, since they would perform a task to be reinforced merely with **seeing something new**.
Festinger and Carlsmith - found humans would change their behaviour and opinions to make them consistent with their past actions.
McClelland - found evidence for the need for achievement with the Thematic Apperception Test (a rather subjective projective test).

HUMANISTIC THEORIES OF MOTIVATION

Maslow believes humans are motivated by needs beyond those of basic biological survival. Fundamental to human nature is the desire to grow and develop to achieve our full potential - referred to as 'self actualisation'.
Maslow proposed a hierarchy of needs ranging from lower level basic needs to higher level psychological and actualisation ones. Only when the bottom levels have been reasonably satisfied can the person move on to the higher ones.
Other researchers have proposed humanistic motivational influences upon behaviour - Rogers, for example, points out that individuals strive to achieve their ideal selves because they are motivated towards self-improvement.

Evaluation
Humanistic ideas on motivation gain strength from emphasising uniquely human motivational factors, rather than generalising from reductionist, biologically based theory and evidence gained from animal studies. Maslow's hierarchy integrates virtually all the other theoretical approaches to motivation. However humanistic concepts are difficult to test experimentally - how can self-actualisation be measured and how do we know when we have reached full potential?

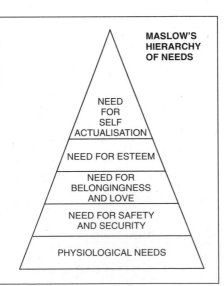

MASLOW'S HIERARCHY OF NEEDS

NEED FOR SELF ACTUALISATION

NEED FOR ESTEEM

NEED FOR BELONGINGNESS AND LOVE

NEED FOR SAFETY AND SECURITY

PHYSIOLOGICAL NEEDS

Psychological theories of motivation 2

HULL'S DRIVE REDUCTION THEORY

Clark Hull (1943) was a behaviourist who integrated the idea of homeostatic drives into an influential theory of learning to explain the motivation of all animal behaviour.

Hull believed that drives could be combined with other motivational factors, such as **incentive** and **habit** (past experience), in a **mathematical formula** that would be able to predict the likelihood of a behaviour being produced.

Hull argued that the organism's **level of drive** was important, since **drive reduction** was the basis of reinforcement. Hull proposed
- reinforcement is linked to **biological needs**, e.g. for food
- when needs are thwarted and the animal is **deprived**, physiological **drives** (states of tension) are **energised** to make the organism seek for ways to fulfil its needs
- by **trial and error**, some responses **satisfy the need** and, therefore, **reduce the drive** (drive reduction is experienced as pleasurable)
- the responses are thus **reinforced** and are more likely to occur again

Another important variable was the **incentive** of the **stimulus** or reward offered to the animal - given a certain level of drive, an animal may have a preference for certain behaviours that bring the greatest reward (have the greatest incentive).

All the variables in the motivational equation could be precisely **measured** or operationalised in **behavioural terms**, and could then be put to the test. Below is one of Hull's simple equations to show how, in addition to past experience (habit), drives and incentive may influence the motivation to show a behaviour.

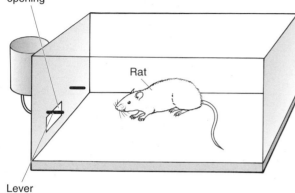

Food delivery opening

Rat

Lever

A Skinner Box
(pressing the lever releases a food pellet into the delivery opening)

sEr	=	sHr	×	D	×	K
Likelihood of response	=	**Strength of habit**	×	**Drive**	×	**Incentive**
e.g. The likelihood of a rat pressing the lever in a Skinner box	=	How much practise the rat has had at pressing levers	×	How hungry the rat is at that time	×	The desirability of the reinforcement for pressing

Objective measures:

Whether the rat presses the lever and how many times	=	Number of past reinforcements for lever pressing	×	Number of hours of food deprivation	×	The size, number or type of reward, e.g. food pellets

When will behaviour be most motivated?

Tendency to respond will be greatest, i.e. the rat will press the lever frequently	WHEN	Reinforcement has been frequent in the past, i.e. the rat has pressed levers before	×	Deprivation and drive is high, i.e. the rat is hungry	×	High desirability of reward, i.e. many food pellets are expected

EVALUATION

Hull's equations were precise and bold statements of behaviour, aiming to make psychology as predictable and testable as physics. Unfortunately for Hull, however, the tests on animal behaviour using his equations were not very successful and Hull found that more and more factors had to be taken into account. His final system (Hull, 1952) needed 32 separate postulates. Worse still for Hull's theory, the concept of drive reduction became increasingly criticised. Sheffield et al (1951) used female rats in the goal box of a maze as a sexual reinforcer for the male rats who had to learn to run it. The researchers found that the rats would still run the maze even if they were prevented from completing copulation with the females (certainly no drive reduction!).

Theories of emotion

Theories of emotion have mainly focused on the relationship between the physiological and psychological aspects of emotion.

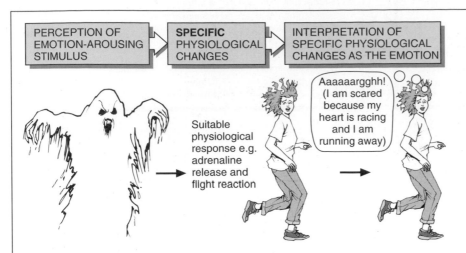

JAMES-LANGE THEORY

The James-Lange theory of emotion states that different emotion-arousing external stimuli will produce specific physiological responses that in turn directly cause specific emotional feelings.

Thus, the external stimuli of a dangerous object will cause the physiological response of adrenaline release/increased heart rate, which in turn is felt as the emotion of fear. Physiological **arousal** is **necessary** and **sufficient** for emotions to occur.

SUPPORT

Ax (1953) found different physiological changes associated with particular emotions, e.g. fear seemed associated with the physiological effects of adrenaline, anger with the effects of noradrenaline. Schwartz et al (1981) have also found distinct physiological reactions for anger, fear, happiness, and sadness. Laird (1974) found that facial feedback (e.g. making subjects adopt the muscular facial expression of a smile) affected mood (made them feel happier).

CRITICISMS

Specific physiological changes have not been found for every emotion, only the strongest and most basic ones.
Maranon (1924) found that physiological arousal is not sufficient to cause emotion, by injecting subjects with adrenaline. Over two thirds of them reported only physical symptoms - the rest merely reported 'as if' they were feeling an emotion.
Some researchers claim that physiological changes are not even necessary for emotion (see Cannon-Bard theory).

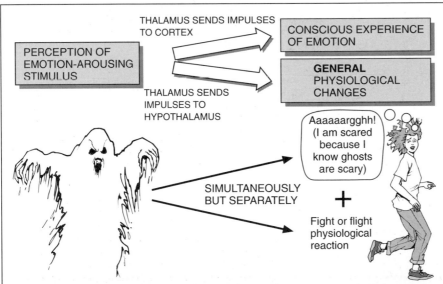

CANNON-BARD THEORY

The Cannon-Bard theory of emotion states that conscious feelings of emotion and physiological changes occur as separate but simultaneous reactions to external emotion-arousing stimuli.

Thus, the external stimuli of a dangerous object will cause the thalamus to send signals

- to the hypothalamus to trigger a general 'flight or fight' physiological response, and
- to the cortex to register the conscious emotion of fear.

Physiological **arousal** is, therefore, **neither necessary** nor **sufficient** for emotions to occur.

SUPPORT

Some studies have shown that physiological changes do not seem necessary for emotions to occur.
Sherrington (1900) severed the spinal cord of dogs and Cannon (1927) removed the nervous system of cats - finding in both cases that although no physiological feedback was possible, the animals showed normal emotional responses.
Dana (1921) conducted a case study on an individual with spinal cord damage who nevertheless still showed a range of emotions.
The theory importantly emphasised cognitive factors in emotion.

CRITICISMS

Cannon and Bard were wrong to assume that physiological factors have no influence on emotion - other studies have indicated that it plays some role.
The evidence presented for the theory is based on animal and case studies, which are of doubtful generalisability to human behaviour in general.
The Cannon-Bard theory over-estimated the role of the thalamus in emotion. Many other brain areas are involved in emotional reactions.

Schachter and Singer's cognitive labelling theory

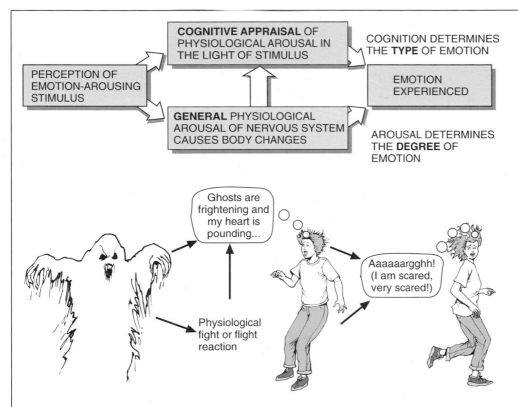

The cognitive labelling theory of emotion states that emotion-arousing external stimuli will cause a **general** physiological arousal response that will be **interpreted** by a cognitive appraisal of the stimuli as a **particular** emotional feeling. Thus, the external stimuli of a dangerous object will cause a general 'fight or flight' physiological response **and** a cognitive evaluation of this arousal in the light of, for example, past experiences involving this object (i.e. having learnt that ghosts are frightening) which leads to the appropriate emotion of fear. Physiological **arousal** is, therefore, **necessary** for most genuine emotions to occur but **not sufficient** (since cognitive appraisal can label it as a variety of emotions).

SUPPORT

Schachter and Singer (1962) told subjects that they were going to test the effects of a vitamin injection on their vision, but instead injected them with adrenaline. Subjects were then either:

A informed of the real effects (e.g. increased heart/respiration rate)
B misinformed of the effects - told false symptoms, e.g. itching
C given no information on the effects

A fourth group (**D**) were injected with a placebo of saline solution in place of adrenaline to provide a control group.

All subjects were then left in a waiting room with another subject (really a confederate of the experimenter) who began to act either

1 angrily, e.g. complaining about and then ripping up a questionnaire, or
2 Euphorically, e.g. laughing and throwing paper around.

The subjects were then rated by external observers who found groups **B** and **C** were more likely to follow the confederate's behaviour. The results showed some support for cognitive labelling theory in that

- those who did not have an accurate explanation for their physiological arousal (groups **B** and **C**) used the cues of the confederate's behaviour to identify and label their own emotion.
- those who already had an accurate explanation (group **A**) for the effects did not need other cues, so did not follow the confederate.
- those who changed their behaviour (groups **B** and **C**) did so according to cognitive appraisal of their emotions, rather than specific physiological arousal, indicating that only general arousal is required.

Dutton and Aron (1974) found further evidence for cognitive labelling of emotions. Male subjects approached by an attractive female experimenter on a high suspension bridge were shown to mislabel their fear as sexual attraction.

Hohmann's (1966) study appears to support the necessity of physiological arousal for genuine emotional feelings. He studied 25 males with spinal cord injury, and found the greater the damage to their nervous system feedback, the less intense were their emotional experiences. Subjects still reported emotions but when angry, for example, would describe it as 'a mental kind of anger'.

CRITICISMS

Schachter and Singer's (1962) experiment has been criticised in a number of ways:

- There was no assessment of the subjects' emotional state before the experiment began, or the emotional effect of receiving an injection.
- The emotional states produced by artificial injections under laboratory conditions are probably not typical of normal emotional reactions.
- Significant results were only found for the behavioural changes rated by the observers - no significant differences were found in the subjects' self report of their emotions.
- The results were not highly significant and other researchers such as Marshall and Zimbardo (1979) have not replicated Schachter and Singer's findings.

While the misattribution of emotions (the most typical experimental support for cognitive labelling theory) is perhaps an unusual occurrence in everyday life, it does indicate an important role for cognitive appraisal. Researchers such as Lazarus (1991) argue that cognitive processes can initiate both physiological arousal and emotion feelings, and that a cognitive appraisal of environmental stimuli at some level (conscious or unconscious) is a basic requirement for the elicitation of any emotion.

Although the majority of current theories on emotion involve cognitive appraisal, there is still some debate over its importance. Psychologists such as Zajonc (1984) still argue that cognition and emotion involve relatively separate systems, and that emotion can occur without any cognitive appraisal. Recent research indicates that emotional centres in the brain can receive information directly from the sensory areas.

'Cognitive, social, and physiological determinants of emotional state' Schachter and Singer (1962)

AIM

To describe an experiment that provides support for Schachter's (1959) theory of the interaction between physiology, cognition, and behaviour in emotional experience. Schachter believes that cognitive factors (thought processes) are very important in determining which emotion is felt. He argues that emotion-provoking stimuli, such as a gun being pointed at you, will automatically cause a general physiological level of arousal (the activation of the sympathetic nervous system), which is interpreted (cognitively) as fear (the emotion) in the light of our knowledge about the dangerous nature of guns. Schachter and Singer, therefore, propose the 3 following predictions from this theory:

A Given an **unexplained** state of general **physiological arousal**, the individual experiencing it will attempt to describe or **label it as a particular emotion** in terms of his **cognitive explanations** of its causes. Thus, the same state of arousal could be described or labelled as joy or fury, depending upon the situation he is in.

B Given a state of general **physiological arousal** for which an individual already has an **appropriate explanation** (e.g. I feel this way because I have been injected with adrenaline) there will be **no need** to use external situational cues **to label** his arousal as an emotion.

C Given **no** state of general **physiological arousal, despite situational cues** to label emotions with, an individual will experience **no** emotion.

METHOD

Subjects: 184 male college students, 90% of whom volunteered to get extra points on their exams.

Design: Laboratory experiment. Based on the above predictions, three independent variables were manipulated in an independent measures design to affect the dependent variable of experienced emotional state (measured by behavioural observation and self-report).

Independent variable	Conditions manipulated
1 Physiological arousal	a *Injection of epinephrine* (adrenaline) b *Injection of a placebo* (saline solution)
2 Explanation of arousal	a *Informed* (told correct symptoms) b *Misinformed* (told wrong symptoms) c *Ignorant* (told no symptoms)
3 Situational emotion cues	a *Euphoric stooge* b *Angry stooge*

Procedure: Subjects were told the experiment was a study of the effect of Suproxin - supposedly a vitamin supplement - upon vision. Subjects were tested individually and asked whether they would mind receiving a Suproxin injection (in fact either epinephrine or a placebo) and were assigned to one of the following conditions:

1 **Epinephrine informed** - given a Suproxin injection that was *really epinephrine* and told of its *real side effects* (general physiological arousal of the sympathetic nervous system causing accelerated heartbeat/breathing, palpitations etc.).
2 **Epinephrine misinformed** - given a Suproxin injection that was *really epinephrine* and told *false side effects* (e.g. itching, numbness, etc.)
3 **Epinephrine ignorant** - given a Suproxin injection that was *really epinephrine* and told there would be *no side effects* at all
4 **Control ignorant** - given a Suproxin injection that was *really a placebo* (a saline solution which has no direct effect on arousal of the sympathetic nervous system) and told there would be *no side effects* at all.

All subjects (with the exception of the epinephrine misinformed group, who were not exposed to the angry stooge) were then left alone with either
• **the euphoric stooge** (subjects saw a confederate behaving happily - throwing paper and playing with a hula hoop) or
• **the angry stooge** (subjects saw a confederate complain and behave in a outraged way, ripping up a questionnaire)
and then observed through a one-way mirror to rate their behaviour for how similar it was to the stooge's behaviour (implying that they were in the same emotional state). Self-report scales were also used to assess how good or angry they felt.

RESULTS

For subjects observing euphoric stooges:
• Self-reports of emotions and behaviour were mostly significantly happier in epinephrine ignorant and misinformed subjects (who did not have a relevant explanation for their arousal) than the epinephrine informed group (who did not need to use the external cues to explain their arousal). This supports predictions **A** and **B** above.
• There was no significant difference in mood between the epinephrine ignorant or misinformed subjects, and the placebo control subjects.
This indicates that prediction **C** above is not supported.

For subjects observing angry stooges:
Only behavioural observations were used, since subjects feared self-reports of anger at the experimenter would endanger their extra exam points.
• Epinephrine ignorant subjects behaved significantly more angrily than epinephrine informed or placebo subjects.
This supports predictions **A**, **B**, and **C**. However, placebo subjects still followed the angry behaviour more than the epinephrine informed subjects. The results support the predictions more strongly if adrenaline misinformed and ignorant subjects who attributed arousal to their injection and the placebo subjects who showed physiological arousal in response to just having an injection, are removed from the data.

EVALUATION

Methodological: *Artificiality* - Injection is an artificial way of generating physiological arousal and can cause (fear) arousal in itself. The laboratory lacks ecological validity and the situation of experiencing unexplained physiological arousal is rare.
Validity - Only male subjects and two-tailed tests were used and the results have not always been replicated.
Ethics - Deception over purpose of study and content of injection. Injection (although by permission) hurt.

Theoretical: Supports the importance of cognitive factors in emotional experience. Provides some support for Schachter's theory that physiological arousal and cognitive interpretation are **both necessary** but **not sufficient on their own** to cause emotions.

Links: Emotion.

The physiology of emotion

CEREBRAL CORTEX
Frontal cortex
The frontal cortex has been implicated in the mediation and expression of aggression. Bard removed the cortex of cats, causing attack behaviour that lacked appropriateness and co-ordination. Prefrontal lobotomies were used to pacify violent schizophrenics, although the precise reason for the effect is not known. Delgado stimulated the aggression centres of monkey brains but found that the aggression produced was usually directed towards weaker targets - indicating the modifying role of the frontal cortex. Unexplained arousal of the sympathetic nervous system can be labelled as a particular emotion by the more cognitive parts of the frontal cortex.

Hemispheric specialisation in emotion
Brain damage and brain scan research has indicated differences in emotional localisation between the hemispheres. The right hemisphere seems more involved in the perception and expression of emotional behaviour (particularly negative emotions) than the left hemisphere.

CROSS-SECTION OF THE BRAIN
(showing areas involved in emotion)

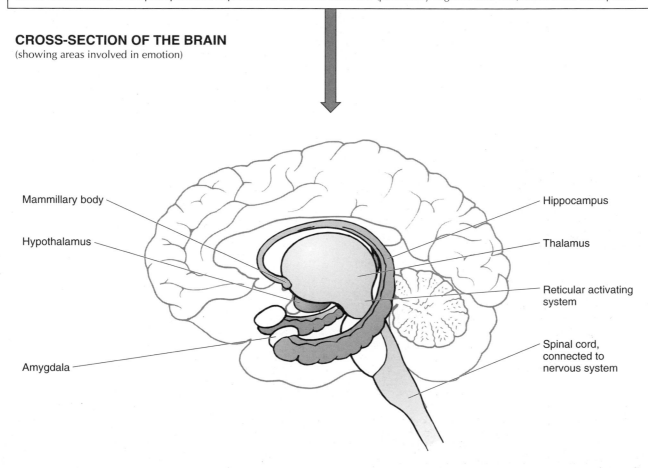

Mammillary body

Hypothalamus

Amygdala

Hippocampus

Thalamus

Reticular activating system

Spinal cord, connected to nervous system

LIMBIC SYSTEM
The limbic system is thought to play an important role in emotional experience and behaviour. It contains many brain structures, including the hypothalamus, septum, cingulate gyrus, hippocampus, and amygdala.
Papez (1937) proposed a model of how these structures were interlinked to regulate emotional behaviour, which became known as the Papez circuit. This model was modified by MacLean and is still regarded as an important contribution today, despite the acceptance that many other areas of the brain are involved in emotion.
One particular area of the limbic system that seems to be especially involved in strong emotions, such as aggression and fear, is the amygdala. Research has found that removing the amygdala from monkeys, rats, and humans has dramatically reduced aggressive behaviour, while stimulation has provoked it.

BRAIN STEM
The brain stem contains the reticular activating system and other structures responsible for releasing brain neurotransmitters, including:
- Norepinephrine - released by the locus coeruleus, it seems involved in pleasurable sensations while deficits are thought to be involved in depression.
- Dopamine - released by the substantia nigra and seems involved in the emotional disturbances of schizophrenia, as well as the positive feelings caused by drugs like cocaine.
- Endorphins - released by many neurones throughout the nervous system. They play a vital role in moderating the experience of pain, fear, and anxiety.

THE NERVOUS SYSTEM
The sympathetic branch of the autonomic nervous system, when activated, is responsible for the body's 'fight or flight' sensations.

HORMONES
Many hormones are involved in emotional behaviour.
Androgens released by the sex glands are implicated in feelings of aggression, for example.

The physiological effects of stress

Selye (1976) identified the **General Adaptation Syndrome** (GAS) - a **non-specific** physiological response that occurs to a **variety** of stressful stimuli. Much research has investigated the 3 phases of the GAS.

Definition of stress: 'A pattern of negative physiological states and psychological responses occurring in situations where people perceive threats to their well being which they may be unable to meet.' Lazarus and Folkman (1984).

PHASE 1
ALARM REACTION
The physiological response triggered by stressful stimuli.

Perception of stressful stimuli

HYPOTHALAMUS

Activates the sympathetic branch of the autonomic nervous system

Activates pituitary gland to release adrenocorticotrophic hormone (ACTH)

ADRENAL GLAND

Activates adrenal medulla to release adrenaline and noradrenaline

Activates adrenal cortex to release corticosteroids

Activates fight or flight reactions of increased heart and breathing rate, blood pressure, muscle tension, etc.

Activates immune system to repond, inhibits tissue inflammation, releases energy from the liver, etc.

PHASE 2
STAGE OF RESISTANCE
If the stressor persists or is not dealt with, the body seeks to maintain arousal at a constant if lower level.

Factors that could **mediate** in the resolving or continuation of stress arousal include:

- **Behavioural factors**

  Stress arousal will often not persist if fight or flight behaviours **deal with** the stressful stimuli. Optimal arousal theory states that up to a certain level stress can provide a beneficial motivating effect on behaviour (Selye called this type of stress 'eustress').

- **Personality factors**

  Friedman and Rosenman (1974) argued that some people have 'Type A' personalities that create and maintain high levels of stress in their life-styles. These people are often aggressive, competitive and highly driven perfectionists who will not delegate and are impatient towards others. Type B personalities, however, have a more relaxed attitude towards life that does not create, exaggerate or maintain high levels of stress.

  Kobasa (1979) proposes that people with 'hardy personalities' are less vulnerable to the effects of stress because, for example, they have a greater sense of control over, and a more positive attitude towards, stressful events and possess a stronger sense of purpose.

- **Cognitive factors**

  Rotter proposes that a sense of control over stressful events (i.e. an **internal** rather than external **locus of control**) appears to moderate the effects of stress.

  Weiss (1972) found that rats who could **predict** and **control** electric shocks were less likely to develop gastric ulceration than those who could do neither (who in turn were more healthy than those who could control but **not** predict when shocks would arrive, as in Brady et al's (1958) executive monkeys experiment).

PHASE 3
STAGE OF EXHAUSTION
Eventually continued high arousal levels exhaust bodily resources producing negative physiological & psychological effects.

- **Physiological effects:**

  a Reduced resistance to infection

  Stress has been associated with many illnesses, ranging from headaches (Gannon et al, 1987) and asthma (Miller and Strunk, 1979), to colds (Stone et al, 1987) and cancer (Jacobs and Charles, 1980). Studies on both animals and humans have shown that long term stress can have an adverse effect on the immune system - causing it to become over-reactive and attack healthy cells or suppressed in its activity.

  b Heart and circulatory disorders

  Rosenman et al (1975) found in a 9 year study involving over 3 thousand men that type A personalities were more prone to suffer heart disease than type B personalities. However, there is debate over whether the personality traits are a cause of stress or a result of it, and which traits are the most important, since some studies have not replicated Rosenman et al's results.

- **Psychological effects:**

  a Anger and frustration

  This can cause a vicious circle of stress production, as anger and frustration contribute to a more stressful environment. Hostility may be a key stress provoking factor in type A behaviour.

  b Depression and helplessness

  Seligman (1975) showed how continual and unavoidable stress could cause learned helplessness and depression which would be inappropriately generalised to different situations.

  c Anxiety

  Different types of stressful situation can produce different types of anxiety disorder, e.g. persistent, unresolvable stress could lead to generalised anxiety disorder, whereas 'one-off' traumatic events could cause post-traumatic stress disorder.

Coping with and reducing stress

IDENTIFYING STRESSORS

STRESSFUL LIFE EVENTS: Holmes and Rahe (1967) suggested that stress is caused by **change** and may lead to greater susceptibility to physical and mental health disorders. They compiled the 'Social Readjustment Rating Scale' (SRRS) - a list of 47 life events involving stressful change and rated them for their severity out of one hundred (e.g. death of a spouse = 100, marriage = 50, change in school = 20, etc.). Scores of over 300 life change units in a year would represent a high risk for stress related health problems.

HASSLES AND UPLIFTS: Lazarus et al (1981) proposed that **everyday problems** or pleasant occurrences were more likely to affect stress levels and health. They designed the 'Hassles and Uplifts Scale' to measure these incidents and their effects.

CATASTROPHIC STRESS: Single traumatic events such as natural disasters, warfare or violent assault can provoke long lasting stress and health problems. The classification systems for mental disorder term this post-traumatic stress disorder.

OCCUPATIONAL STRESS: Usually takes the form of continual levels of stress due to highly demanding work requiring consistently high levels of concentration, responsibility, frustration or exposure to suffering, e.g. air traffic controllers or nurses.

EVALUATION
The SRRS has been criticised for its over-generalised approach. There are many individual differences in what events people find most stressful and how they react to them. The evidence for the scale relating to health is mostly correlational, illness may have contributed towards the development of stressful life events such as losing employment, rather than vice versa. The 'Hassles and Uplifts Scale' has been found to be a better predictor of health. Continuous diary monitoring of everyday stresses has enabled a causal link to be made with later illness (Stone et al, 1987).

DEALING WITH THE EFFECTS

BIOLOGICAL APPROACHES

Anti-stress drugs
Beta-blockers - act on the autonomic nervous system to reduce physiological stress arousal.
Anxiolytic drugs - minor tranquillisers, e.g. valium, combat anxiety without causing sleepiness.
Anti-depressant drugs - less often used, but can be appropriate for dealing with severe anxiety.

Other drugs
Alcohol is an often sought remedy for stress, its sedative effects slow down neural and bodily functions and its effect on loosening inhibitions can lead to cathartic behaviour.

EVALUATION
Anti-anxiety drugs can cause
- psychological and physical dependence
- unpleasant side effects

Drugs are only short term stress remedies that reduce its effects rather than deal with its causes.

BEHAVIOURAL APPROACHES

Biofeedback
Feedback signals on body processes can help control the adverse physiological effects of stress, such as increased heart rate and blood pressure.

Appropriate behaviour
These range from dealing with the source of stress, e.g. time management planning, to behavioural reactions designed to combat its effects, e.g. exercise, cathartic expression (e.g. laughter, shouting), meditation, or rest and relaxation.

EVALUATION
Although there is debate over how it works, biofeedback can lower heart rate and blood pressure, but it only treats the symptoms not causes of stress.
Dealing directly with the source of the stress is most effective.

PSYCHOLOGICAL APPROACHES

Therapy - *Meichenbaum* and *Kobasa* have both developed cognitive behavioural techniques designed to increase the stress resistance or 'hardiness' of clients by getting them to
- learn to analyse sources and physical signs of stress
- learn coping strategies and techniques to combat stressful situations
- practice these skills in simulated and real situations, so a successful change is produced

Positive thinking - training oneself to think optimistically and possessing an internal locus of control helps stress control.

Social support - a sympathetic social network aids stress coping if not stress reduction.

EVALUATION
Cognitive behavioural therapies are effective, although the behavioural aspects (successfully dealing with a stressful situation) seem more important than the cognitive aspects (e.g. inner stress reducing statements). Social support is significantly correlated with lower mortality rates.

Abnormal psychology

Conceptions of abnormality

Psychopathologies

Therapeutic approaches

Medical model conception of abnormality

MEDICAL MODEL

ASSUMPTIONS

Also known as the somatic, biological, or physiological approach.

NOTION OF NORMALITY

- Properly functioning physiology and nervous system and no genetic pre-dispositions to inherit mental disorder.

NOTION OF ABNORMALITY

- Like physical illness, **mental illness** has an **underlying physical/bodily cause.**
- **Genetic, organic, or chemical disorders** cause mental illness, which gives rise to behavioural and psychological **symptoms.**
- These symptoms can be classified to **diagnose** the **psychopathology**, which can then be treated through **therapy** in psychiatric **hospitals** to **cure** the **patient.**
- Note the use of medical terminology which this approach has borrowed.

ETHICAL IMPLICATIONS

There are both positive and negative ethical implications of the medical model definition of abnormality:

1 Positively for the abnormal individual, the idea that they are mentally 'ill' means that the individual is **not** to be held **responsible** for their predicament - they are more likely to be seen as a **victim** of a disorder that is **beyond their control** and, therefore, they are **in need of care** and **treatment**. The medical model is, therefore, intended to be a more caring and humane approach to abnormality - especially given the blame, stigmatisation, and lack of care for abnormality that had been the norm before the approach.

2 Negatively, the medical model's assumptions have produced many unfavourable ethical consequences.

  a The assumption that abnormal people are mentally ill and, therefore, **not responsible** for their actions can lead to
  - the **loss of rights**, such as the right to **consent** to treatment or institutionalisation, and even the right to vote if sectioned under the Mental Health Act.
  - the **loss of an internal locus of control**, loss of self-care, and an abdication of responsibility to others.
  - the assumption that **directive therapy** is needed for the benefit of the mentally ill individual. The concept of directive therapy may be less debatable with acute schizophrenia, where insight may be totally lacking, but becomes more controversial when we consider the rights of depressed patients to withdraw from electro-convulsive therapy which may prevent their suicide.

  b The assumption that there is always a **biological underlying cause** for mental disorder may be incorrect and, therefore, lead to the **wrong** diagnosis and/or treatment being given.
  - There is not always a clearly identifiable underlying biological cause for disorders.
  - Many disorders have a large psychological contribution to their cause, such as the learning theory explanations of phobia acquisition.
  - Heather (1976) suggests that the basis of defining abnormality is often governed by social and moral considerations rather than biological - thus the inclusion of psychosexual disorders such as paedophilia.

  c The assumption that mentally ill people are **distinctly different** from mentally well people can lead to **labelling** and **prejudice** against those defined as abnormal under the medical model.

PRACTICAL IMPLICATIONS

The use of the medical model to define abnormality as mental illness can lead to:

1 **The use of sectioning** under the Mental Health Act (1983) - the compulsory detention and even treatment of those regarded as mentally ill, if they represent a danger to their own or others' safety. This is based on the medical model assumption that mental illness leads to a loss of self-control and responsibility; but note that a social worker is required to section somebody, in addition to a GP and a psychiatrist (implying that social as well as physical factors need to be taken into account).

Section 2 of the Act can be used to detain people for up to 28 days for observation and assessment of mental illness. Section 3 of the Act involves the enforced application of treatment and loss of rights.

Power is firmly in the hands of society, since

  a Section 5 of the act can prevent the right of even the nearest relative to withdraw the sectioned individual from care.

  b Section 136 gives the police the right to arrest in a public place anybody deemed to show mental illness to maintain security.

  c Section 139 removes all responsibility for mistaken diagnosis from those involved in sectioning, providing the diagnosis was made in good faith and the legal procedures were carried out correctly.

2 **Institutionalisation** - which can have both positive and negative implications:
  - **Positively,** institutionalisation allows the removal to a controlled environment of individuals who may represent a danger to themselves or others. The controlled environment allows the close monitoring, support, and treatment of those suffering from mental illness.
  - **Negatively,** institutionalisation may worsen the condition of the patient, providing them with an abnormal environment and causing the internalisation of the passive and dependent role of 'mental inmate'. Rosenhan's study 'On Being Sane in Insane Places' revealed the often negative treatment received in mental institutions.

3 **Biological treatments** - which include the administering of drug treatment, electro-convulsive therapy, or even psychosurgery, all of which have their dangers and side effects as well as the possibility of beneficial effects.

Alternative conceptions of abnormality

THE PSYCHOANALYTIC APPROACH

Notion of normality

Balance between id, ego, and superego. Sufficient ego control to allow the acceptable gratification of id impulses. No inconvenient fixations or repression of traumatic events.

Notion of abnormality

Emotional disturbance or neurosis is caused by thwarted id impulses, unresolved unconscious conflicts (e.g. Oedipus complex), or repressed traumatic events deriving from childhood. Psychological and physical symptoms are expressions of unconscious psychological causes. Conflict and neurosis is always present to some extent – the difference between the 'normal' and 'abnormal' is only quantitative.

ETHICAL IMPLICATIONS

- **Directive therapy** - due to the unconscious cause of psychological problems and the resistance patients put up to unconscious truths, the patient must trust the therapist's interpretation and instructions. However, psychoanalysis does occur under voluntary conditions.
- **Anxiety provoking** - psychoanalysis can reveal disturbing repressed experiences.
- **Humane** - psychoanalysts do not blame or judge the patient, who is not responsible for their problems.

PRACTICAL IMPLICATIONS

- **Expensive** - Freud argued you do not value what you do not pay for.
- **Long term** - several sessions a week for many months are usually required, although Mallan's Brief Focal Therapy is faster.
- **No institutionalisation** required.
- **Low success rates** - with many disorders, e.g. psychoses.

THE BEHAVIOURAL APPROACH
(Also known as the behaviourist or learning theory approach)

Notion of normality

A learning history that has provided an adequately large selection of adaptive responses.

Notion of abnormality

Maladaptive responses have been learnt or adaptive ones have not been learnt. Observable, behavioural disorder is all abnormality consists of. Abnormal behaviour is not a symptom of any underlying cause.

ETHICAL IMPLICATIONS

- **Directive therapy** - due to the environmental determinism of behavioural problems, patients need to be re-programmed with adaptive behaviour.
- **Stressful** - behaviour therapy can be painful and disturbing, e.g. flooding and aversion therapy.
- **Humane** - specific maladaptive behaviours are targeted, the whole person is not labelled.

PRACTICAL IMPLICATIONS

- **Relatively cheap** - due to the fairly quick nature of treatments.
- **High success rates** - with certain disorders.
- **Institutionalisation** - may be required to ensure environmental control with certain treatments, e.g. selective reinforcement for anorexia.

THE COGNITIVE APPROACH

Notion of normality

Properly functioning and rational cognitive thought processes that can be used to accurately perceive the world and control behaviour.

Notion of abnormality

Unrealistic, distorted, or irrational understanding and thoughts about the self, others, or the environment. Difficulty in controlling thought processes or using them to control actions.

ETHICAL IMPLICATIONS

- **Semi-directive therapy** - due to the client's problems controlling their thoughts, external aid has to be provided by the therapist, although this will vary in its directiveness depending on how forceful the persuasive techniques used by the therapist are.
- **Stressful** - rational emotive therapy can be disturbing although most cognitive therapy is humane.

PRACTICAL IMPLICATIONS

- **Relatively cheap** - depending on length of therapy.
- **Fairly high success rates** - with certain disorders and when combined with behavioural therapies.
- **No institutionalisation** is usually necessary.

THE HUMANISTIC APPROACH
(Also known as the phenomenological or existential approach)

Notion of normality

Positive self regard, ability to self actualise, healthy interpersonal relationships, and responsibility and control over life.

Notion of abnormality

It is wrong to talk of abnormality, since everyone is unique and experiences 'problems with living' occasionally. These problems stem from interpersonal relationships (which prevent healthy interpersonal relationships, and thwarting environmental circumstances (which prevent individuals being true to themselves) and thwarting environmental circumstances (which prevent self actualisation). The client should not be labelled or directed.

ETHICAL IMPLICATIONS

- **Non-directive therapy** - clients have free will and, therefore, the responsibility and capability to change their thoughts and behaviour (with insightful help).
- **Humane** - the happiness of the client is of most importance. The client is given unconditional positive regard.
- **Non-labelling** - humanist therapists believe labelling is counter-productive and irrelevant, since each person is a unique individual.

PRACTICAL IMPLICATIONS

- **Fairly expensive** - based on length of therapy required.
- **No institutionalisation** - is necessary, since treatment is completely voluntary.
- **Low success rates** - with many disorders, e.g. psychoses. Better success with 'problems with living' in interpersonal areas.

Diagnostic classification – aims and techniques

THE PURPOSE OF CLASSIFICATION

The classification of mental disorder involves the **identification of groups** or patterns of behavioural or mental **symptoms** that reliably occur together to form a **type** of disorder. This process of classification allows

- psychiatrists, doctors and psychologists to **identify** and talk more easily about **groups** of similar sufferers

- a **prognosis** (prediction about the future course of the disorder) to be made

- researchers to **investigate** these groups of people to determine what the **causes** (aetiology) of the disorder are

- a suitable **treatment** to be developed and administered to all those showing similar symptoms

Thus, classification fulfils important communicative and investigative functions, ultimately serving to benefit the individual who has been identified.

THE HISTORY OF MENTAL DISORDER CLASSIFICATION

Emil Kraepelin developed the first comprehensive classification system for mental disorders, believing that they could be diagnosed from observable symptoms, just like physical illness.

Two major western classifications systems exist today – the American Psychiatric Association's 'Diagnostic and Statistical Manual of Mental Disorder' (DSM IV), and the World Health Organisation's 'International Classification of Diseases' (ICD 10). These systems have undergone many revisions, e.g. from the first, very unreliable DSM in 1952, to the DSM II in 1968, DSM III in 1980, the revision of this (DSM III-R) in 1987, and currently the DSM IV in 1994.

TECHNIQUES OF ASSESSMENT

Behavioural observation, e.g. behaviour coding systems and rating scales.

- **Advantages** - provides direct and detailed information.

- **Weaknesses** - problems with inter-observer reliability and subject reactivity. Some symptoms cannot be observed.

Clinical interview, e.g. open-ended questions or the more standardised and reliable structured interview (such as 'The Schedule for Affective Disorders and Schizophrenia').

- **Advantages** - a detailed, flexible, and sensitive method.

- **Weaknesses** - lacks objectivity. Self report responses are interpreted by the therapist, and subjects may be unable or unwilling (due to embarrassment) to give accurate data.

Psychological tests, e.g. IQ tests or personality inventories (such as The Minnesota Multiphasic Personality Inventory).

- **Advantages** - objectively rated, quick, and standardised.

- **Weaknesses** - personality tests rely on self report and literacy.

Physiological tests, e.g. static brain scans (magnetic resonance imaging) or dynamic scans (positron emission tomography).

- **Advantages** - gives precise data on brain structure or activity

- **Weaknesses** - expensive and cannot be used to diagnose disorders alone.

THE DSM IV CLASSIFICATION SYSTEM

The 'Diagnostic and Statistical Manual of Mental Disorder' defines a mental disorder as a clinically significant syndrome associated with distress, a loss of functioning, an increased risk of death/pain, or an important loss of freedom.
The manual emphasises that the problem should stem from within the individual, but does not specify whether it is biological, behavioural, or psychological in nature.
The manual describes over 200 specific diagnostic categories for mental disorder and lists the **specific diagnostic criteria** that have to be met for a diagnosis to be given.
Assessment is usually made on five axes to provide a more complete picture of the individual.

AXIS 1 CLINICAL SYNDROMES

Axis 1 refers to the major diagnostic classification arrived at by the clinician, e.g. 'catatonic schizophrenia', 'major depressive disorder', 'generalised anxiety disorder', etc.

AXIS 2 DEVELOPMENTAL AND PERSONALITY DISORDERS

Additional diagnostic classifications that may contribute to an understanding of the Axis 1 syndrome.

AXIS 3 MEDICAL CONDITIONS

Physical problems relevant to the mental disorder.

AXIS 4 PSYCHOSOCIAL STRESSORS

All potentially stressful events (e.g. loss of job) or enduring circumstances (e.g. poverty) that might be relevant to the disorder are rated for severity on a scale ranging from 1 (none) to 6 (catastrophic) for the past year.

AXIS 5 GLOBAL ASSESSMENT OF FUNCTIONING

Rates the highest level of social, occupational, and psychological functioning on a scale of 1 (persistent danger) to 90 (good in all areas) currently and during the past year.

The practical and ethical implications of diagnostic classification 1

PRACTICAL IMPLICATIONS – CAN CLASSIFICATION BE EFFECTIVELY MADE?

RELIABILITY

For classification systems to be reliable, different diagnosticians using the same system should arrive at the same diagnosis for the same individual. The reliability of the early systems, e.g. the DSM II was very poor:

Beck et al (1962)

Found that agreement on diagnosis for 153 patients (where each patient was assessed by two psychiatrists from a group of four), was only 54%. This was often due to vague criteria for diagnosis and inconsistencies in the techniques used to gather data.

Cooper et al (1972)

Found New York psychiatrists were twice as likely to diagnose schizophrenia than London psychiatrists, who were twice as likely to diagnose mania or depression, when shown the same video-taped clinical interviews.

Rosenhan (1973)

Found that 8 'normal' people could get themselves admitted to mental hospitals as schizophrenics merely by claiming to hear voices saying single words like 'hollow' and 'thud'. Rosenhan also found that the staff of a teaching hospital, when told to expect pseudo-patients, suspected 41 out of 193 genuine patients of being fakers.

Classification systems have improved in reliability due to a multi-axial approach, more standardised assessment techniques (e.g. the Schedule of Affective Disorders and Schizophrenia), and more specific diagnostic criteria, but are still far from perfect.

Di Nardo et al (1993)

Studied the reliability of the DSM III-R for anxiety disorders. Two clinicians separately diagnosed each of 267 people seeking treatment for anxiety and stress disorders, and used the Kappa statistic to test how similar diagnosis was (the nearer 1 the value is, the closer the agreement). They found high reliability for obsessive-compulsive disorder but lower reliability for generalised anxiety disorder, due to problems with interpreting how 'excessive' a person's worries had to be (see table on the right). The DSM IV corrected this fault.

Diagnostic category	Kappa
Obsessive-compulsive disorder	.80
Generalised anxiety disorder	.57
Panic disorder with agoraphobia	.72
Social phobia	.79
Major depression	.65

VALIDITY

For a classification system to be valid it should meaningfully classify a real pattern of symptoms, which result from a real underlying cause, which can, therefore, lead to a suitable treatment and prognosis (predictive validity). Very few underlying causes are known, however, and there are a wide range of treatments for the same disorder. Some classifications such as 'undifferentiated schizophrenia' (for those whose symptoms do not fit into any of the other sub-types of schizophrenia), are rather meaningless as diagnostic categories. Valid diagnosis for mental disorder is more difficult than physical disorder, because of the lack of objective physical signs of disorder like temperature, blood pressure, etc.

BIAS

Since diagnostic classification is not 100% objective and reliable, bias may result from the expectations or prejudices of the diagnostician. Diagnosticians are likely to expect that people seeking psychiatric help are disturbed and are more likely to make what social psychologists call the fundamental attribution error - over-emphasising personality rather than situational/environmental causes of behaviour.

Temerline (1970)

Found that clinically trained psychiatrists and clinical psychologists could be influenced in their diagnosis by hearing the opinion of a respected authority. After watching a video-taped interview of (a completely psychologically 'healthy') individual, some subjects heard the respected authority state that, although the person seemed neurotic, he was actually quite psychotic. These diagnosticians were highly influenced by the statement in their own diagnosis of the individual.

ETHICAL IMPLICATIONS – SHOULD DIAGNOSIS BE MADE CONSIDERING THE DIFFICULTIES OF CLASSIFICATION?

Szasz questions both the validity and purpose of classification, arguing that in many cases diagnosis is made on a political and social basis, rather than a psychological or biological one, and suggests that the majority in power in a society attach stigmatising labels to those who show different or frightening behaviour and so justify their control and treatment.

Szasz in his book *The Manufacture of Madness* goes so far as to say that mental illness is actually created by society, and adds that where the biological causes of mental disorders are known, they should be defined as 'diseases of the mind', but if there is not a supportable underlying cause of disorder, then the term 'problem with living' should be used. Scheff (1966) proposes a similar criticism of the basis of classification, suggesting that labelling people as abnormal helps society overcome its anxiety and establish clear norms of reality and appropriate behaviour. The major ethical implication here is that the classification systems serve the purposes of the majority in society only, and that it is wrong to assume they are helpful.

Some would argue that society has merely tried to 'medicalise' disruptive behaviour - to find a cause 'within' the person for bad behaviour, rather than looking to the environment for causes. Thus, classifications such as anti-social personality disorder, or kleptomania, are really only medical terms for evil or bad people. Originally the medical model of mental illness was just a useful metaphor, but the underlying assumption has developed that there are underlying biological causes for mental disorder.

A counter argument to Szasz's proposal is the fact that medical and behavioural treatments have helped people to overcome their disorders, and that many people (such as those suffering from anxiety and depression) volunteer for treatment.

Classification aims to help those with mental disorders, and, therefore, fulfils a potentially very useful function - medical diagnosis had, and still has, problems with classification, yet we would not think of rejecting it today. The classification systems have led to the development of many effective therapies and treatments that have helped to either cure, alleviate, or control a wide variety of disorders. Perhaps diagnosis should be made more idiographic, and focus on particular problems rather than grouping people together in a category that may not be helpful, especially where biological causes are not known. However many categories have demonstrated themselves to be useful.

Diagnostic classification has improved as the classification systems have developed. Rosenhan's pseudo-patients would probably not succeed in gaining admission to mental hospitals today (or would have to lie a lot more!).

The practical and ethical implications of diagnostic classification 2

PRACTICAL IMPLICATIONS – WHAT ARE THE CONSEQUENCES OF CLASSIFICATION?

TREATMENT

Since there are problems with the validity of diagnostic classification, unsuitable treatment may be administered, sometimes on an involuntary basis. There are many practical and ethical problems involved in choosing and applying different treatments and therapies.

INSTITUTIONALISATION

Institutionalisation can lead to loss of responsibility. Rosenhan's study found that institutionalisation can lead to depersonalisation, dependency, and a loss of self care skills, thereby worsening the disorder. Goffman (in *Asylums*) speaks of the 'career' of the mental inmate, where the identity of the patient is gradually lost to the institution.

Patients may actually be taught abnormal behaviour from those around them in the institution, and conditions do not help normal functioning since they are not treated as normal people would be.

CARE IN THE COMMUNITY

Rosenhan talked of the 'stickiness' of diagnostic labels – when an individual returns to society, their record of mental illness goes with them (the pseudo-patients left with a diagnosis of 'schizophrenia in remission'). This can lead to stigmatisation, stereotyping, and discrimination against those who have been mentally disordered, making reintegration back into the community difficult.

LABELLING

Scheff (1966) points out that diagnostic classification 'labels' the individual, and this can have many adverse effects, such as

* **Self-fulfilling prophecy** - Patients may begin to act as they think they are expected to act - Goffman argues that they may internalise the role of 'mentally ill patient' and this could worsen their disorder rather than improve it. Doherty (1975) points out that those who reject the mental illness label tend to improve more quickly than those who accept it, although this is not always the case, since accepting the label of 'alcoholic' can help alcoholics recover.

* **Distortion of behaviour** - diagnosis of mental disorder tends to label the whole person - once the label of diagnosis is attached, then all the individual's actions become interpreted in the light of the label. Sometimes even normal behaviour is ignored or interpreted as a sign of the individual's mental disorder - in Rosenhan's study, the pseudo-patients' behaviours were regarded as symptoms of their psychopathology.

* **Oversimplification** - Labelling can lead to reification - making the classification a real, physical disorder, rather than just a descriptive term to help diagnosticians talk about patients or a hypothesis about what is troubling the person. Labelling may have a major effect not just on an individual's identity, but also on their self-esteem.

LEGAL IMPLICATIONS

Sectioning under the Mental Health Act (although rare) can lead to loss of rights and enforced treatment. Legally, the insane can be found not guilty due a lack of responsibility for their actions.

ETHICAL IMPLICATIONS – SHOULD DIAGNOSIS BE MADE CONSIDERING THE CONSEQUENCES OF CLASSIFICATION?

An ethical decision has to be made regarding the justification of classification, given the profound implications of being classified as mentally disordered.

* Do the benefits of classification (care, treatment, safety) outweigh the costs (possible misdiagnosis, mistreatment, loss of rights/self responsibility, and prejudice due to labelling)?

  Gove (1970, 1990) has found that the stigmatising effects of labelling are only short-lived, while Major and Crocker (1993) have found that the effect of labelling on a person's self-esteem is difficult to predict.

  Prejudice from society clearly does occur, however, and is even shown by mental health professionals. Langer and Abelson (1974) showed a videotape of a younger man telling an older man about his job experience. If the viewers were told that the man was a job applicant, he was judged to be attractive and conventional looking, whereas if they were told that he was a 'patient', he was described as tight, defensive, dependent, and frightened of his own aggressive impulses.

* Is society right to administer treatment when misclassification is quite likely and the underlying causes are not known?

  Some researchers have argued that, overall, there are too many criticisms of the basic assumptions of classification to justify its use and consequences.
  The assumption that mental disorder can be classified into types is ethically questionable. Classification ignores the fundamental uniqueness of human minds and goes against the right of every person to be treated as an individual.
  An idiographic, rather than a nomothetic, approach to mental disorder may be more appropriate, considering the huge individual variations in patients' symptom expression and individual circumstances. If nomothetic comparisons have to be made, then perhaps it is best to regard mental health and disorder as on a continuum, so that there is only a quantitative rather than qualitative difference between them. Classification only works if there are enough differences **and** similarities between patients.

* Should individuals lose their rights of consent and self-responsibility?

  Humanists would argue that the classification systems are over influenced by the medical model's assumptions about lack of control and freewill. In some cases these assumptions have been used as a method of political control.

* Why does society have double standards about responsibility and mental disorder?

  Legally, the insane can be found not guilty due to a lack of responsibility for their actions. However, 'insanity' is a decision made by the legal system and, due to society's need to blame people to make them account for their crimes, this verdict may not be given. Many criminals have been clearly mentally disordered, but have been found guilty of their crimes and sent to prison.

'On being sane in insane places' Rosenhan (1973)

AIM

To illustrate experimentally the problems involved in determining normality and abnormality, in particular
- the poor reliability of the diagnostic classification system for mental disorder at the time (as well as general doubts over its validity)
- the negative consequences of being diagnosed as abnormal and the effects of institutionalisation

METHOD

Subjects: Eight sane people (3 women and 5 men from a small variety of occupational backgrounds), using only fake names and occupations, sought admission to a range of twelve hospitals (varying in age, resources, staff-patient ratios, degree of research conducted, etc.).

Procedure: Each pseudo-patient arranged an appointment at the hospital and complained that he or she had been hearing voices. The voices were unclear, unfamiliar, of the same sex and said single words like 'empty', 'hollow', and 'thud'. Apart from the aforementioned falsifying of name and occupation and this single symptom, the pseudo-patients did not change any aspect of their behaviour, personal history or circumstances. On admission to the hospital ward, every pseudo-patient immediately stopped simulating any symptoms and responded normally to all instructions (except they did not swallow medication) and said they were fine and experiencing no more symptoms. Their tasks were then to
- seek release by convincing the staff that they were sane (all but one pseudo-patient were very motivated to do this)
- observe and record the experience of the institutionalised mentally disordered patient (done covertly at first, although this was unnecessary)

RESULTS

Admission: Pseudo-patients were admitted to every hospital, in all cases except one with a diagnosis of schizophrenia, and their sanity was never detected by staff - only by other patients (35 out of 118 of whom voiced their suspicions in the first three hospitalisations). To check the poor reliability of diagnosis, and to see if the insane could be distinguished from the sane, a later study was conducted where a teaching hospital (who had been informed of Rosenhan's study) was told to expect pseudo-patients over a three month period. During that time 193 patients were rated for how likely they were to be pseudo-patients - 41 patients were suspected of being fakes, 19 of which were suspected by both a psychiatrist and one other staff member, even though no pseudo-patients were sent during that time.

Release: Length of stay ranged from 7 to 52 days, with an average of 19 days. All except one were released with a diagnosis of 'schizophrenia in remission', supporting the view that they had never been detected as sane.

Observation results:
- **Lack of monitoring** - very little contact with doctors was experienced, and a strong sense of segregation between staff and patients was noted.
- **Distortion of behaviour** - all (normal) behaviour became interpreted in the light of the 'label' of 'schizophrenia', for example:
  a A normal case history - became distorted to emphasise the ambivalence and emotional instability thought to be shown by schizophrenics.
  b Note taking - pseudo-patients were never asked why they were taking notes, but it was recorded by nurses as 'patient engages in writing behaviour', implying that it was a symptom of their disorder.
  c Pacing the corridors out of boredom - was seen as nervousness, again implying that it was a symptom of their disorder.
  d Waiting outside the cafeteria before lunch time - was interpreted as showing the 'oral-acquisitive nature of the syndrome' by a psychiatrist.

- **Lack of normal interaction** - for example, pseudo-patients courteously asked a staff member 'Pardon me, Mr (or Dr or Mrs) X, could you tell me when I will be presented at the staff meeting?' or 'When am I likely to be discharged?'. They found mostly a brief, not always relevant, answer was given, on the move, without even a normal turn of the head or eye-contact (psychiatrists moved on with their head averted 71% of the time and only stopped and talked normally on 4% of occasions).
- **Powerlessness and depersonalisation** - was produced in the institution through the lack of rights, constructive activity, choice, and privacy, plus frequent verbal and even physical abuse from the attendants.

EVALUATION

Methodological:

Lack of control groups - Only the experimental condition was conducted.

Data analysis - Was mostly qualitative rather than quantitative.

Ethical problems - The study involved deception, but it might be argued that the hospitals had the power not to be deceived and were in fact being tested in their jobs. In addition, the study's ends (its valuable contribution) outweighed its slightly unethical means, and kept data confidentiality.

Theoretical: Despite the fact that 'schizophrenia in remission' is an unusual diagnosis according to Spitzer (1976), the study is widely held to have fulfilled its aim of showing the deficiencies of the classification system for mental disorder at the time (the DSM II) and the negative consequences of being labelled and institutionalised for mental disorder. Studies like these led to pressure to revise and improve the accuracy of the classification systems.

Links: Problems with the diagnosis and classification of mental disorders. Stereotyping.

Cultural and subcultural differences in the determination of abnormality

WHAT IS MEANT BY 'CULTURE' AND 'SUBCULTURE'?

CULTURE

Culture refers to all ways of thinking, feeling, and acting that people learn from others as members of society' (*New Grolier Encyclopaedia*, 1993). Culture involves shared beliefs, traditions, norms, and even physical man-made creations.

Different societies possessing different cultures may show cross-cultural variations in beliefs, traditions, norms, etc. and may, therefore, have different views on defining and classifying abnormality.

SUBCULTURE

A society can be divided into many different social groups, such as gender groups, age groups, social classes and 'racial' groups. Different groups within a society may possess different beliefs, norms, etc. to the dominant culture in that society, and may therefore represent a subculture.

Because of subcultures, there may be different views within a society over defining abnormality. The dominant culture within a society is likely to become the 'norm' and is more likely to regard other subcultures as abnormal.

CROSS-CULTURAL

SUBCULTURAL

Subgroups of the population, e.g.

* gender groups
* age groups
* social class groups
* ethnic/racial groups

POSSIBLE EXPLANATIONS FOR CROSS-CULTURAL AND SUBCULTURAL DIFFERENCES IN THE DETERMINATION OF ABNORMALITY

There is no doubt that there are many cultural and subcultural **differences** in the determination of abnormality - not just in terms of the **amount** of disorder but also in terms of the **types** of disorder found in different social groups and cultures. However, these differences could occur for many reasons, and each one needs to be examined to discover whether it is caused by (**a**) biological factors, (**b**) cultural/environmental leaning, or (**c**) cultural bias in diagnosis

BIOLOGICAL INNATE EXPLANATIONS	CULTURAL/ENVIRONMENTAL EXPLANATIONS	CULTURAL DIAGNOSTIC BIAS EXPLANATIONS
Differences in the amount and type of abnormality found in different social groups and cultures could reflect 'true' differences in underlying biological causes. If biological causes are found to explain differences, then the medical model of abnormality is supported.	Differences in the amount and type of abnormality found in different social groups and cultures could alternatively reflect different culturally created environmental conditions. Different social groups may conform to/learn different cultural behaviours or experience more stress from the environment, and so become more likely to develop disorder.	Differences in the amount and type of abnormality found in different social groups and cultures could also merely reflect diagnostic bias and **not** any true underlying differences between groups and cultures. Mistaken diagnosis could be made due to • the inability of the diagnoser to truly understand the 'patients' behaviour, or, • those in power being prejudiced and labelling out-groups for social control.

Research into subcultural differences in the determination of abnormality 1

GENDER DIFFERENCES IN DETERMINING ABNORMALITY:

Women in Britain are approximately **40%** more likely to be admitted to a mental hospital than men, and are around **twice** as likely as men to suffer from depression and neuroses. This is a trend common in the majority of industrialised countries.

BIOLOGICAL EXPLANATIONS

The **most popular**, but one of the **least supported**, explanations of greater female depression is that females are innately more susceptible due to sex-linked biological mechanisms, such as **hormonal** fluctuations caused by the menstrual cycle, childbirth, and the menopause.

Research, however, suggests that the impact of these factors accounts for only a small proportion of all cases (Weissman and Klerman, 1977). Cooper et al (1988) found that depression after birth increased to 8.7% (from 6% before birth) but also found that the rate of depression for a control group of non-pregnant women was 9.9%.

CULTURAL/ENVIRONMENTAL EXPLANATIONS

An alternative explanation of greater female mental disorder is that women live in cultural/environmental conditions that make them more likely to become depressed, anxious, etc. **Cochrane** proposes 3 environmental influences:

- The long-term effect of **child abuse** - Many studies show that physical and sexual child abuse is a major correlate of later depression. The rate of abuse for girls is between 1.5 to 4.5 times higher than for boys.
- The effects of **female gender role socialisation** - The traditional gender role expectations of the woman to be passive, nurturing, and yielding and, therefore, to get married, stay at home, and care for the children, are a significant cause of mental disorder. The inescapable **stresses, dependency,** and lack of reinforcement the female **house-bound** lifestyle provides, may lead to a state of **learnt helplessness,** while the inability to go out to work/attain goals can cause **low self-esteem**. The greatest difference in depression rates between men and women occurs between the **ages of 20-50,** when women are going through their marriage-childbearing-motherhood cycle. Gove (1972) discovered that there is **no difference** in mental disorder prevalence between **unmarried** men and women - married men are much healthier than single men, but this is not so with women!
- The effects of **female gender role coping strategies** - Cochrane (1983) suggests that men and women have different socially acceptable coping strategies available to them when faced with distressing problems. For **men,** heavy **drinking**/drug abuse is seen as more 'socially acceptable'; **women,** however, are 'allowed to cry' and 'have **less positive coping strategies** available to them.

DIAGNOSTIC BIAS EXPLANATIONS

Another explanation of greater female admissions to mental hospitals is that these higher rates do **not** reflect the **real prevalence** of depression in men and women.

This could be due to many factors, such as the greater willingness of women to **admit** to symptoms of depression, the lower threshold of women to **seek** psychiatric help, the unintentional **bias** to diagnose depression for women because of gender role stereotypes, or, worse still, the greater willingness of psychiatrists in a male dominated society to use the label of 'depression' on women to maintain their **social power** and the myth of female emotionality and dependence.

The evidence, however, does indicate **real increases** in depression in women in our society as measured by many different indicators, not just hospital admissions. The major effect of social/cultural bias is in the different environments that women occupy, rather than the diagnostic system.

SOCIAL CLASS DIFFERENCES IN DETERMINING ABNORMALITY

'The great majority of studies have shown that the highest rates of psychiatric disorder are in the lowest social groups' (Rutter and Madge, 1976). The **differences** between classes are most marked with psychoses such as **schizophrenia,** which is between twice to eight times more prevalent in the lower socio-economic groups of society than the higher, while **neuroses** and depression seem more frequent only in **working class women,** rather than working class men. Brown and Harris (1978) suggested that up to a third of working class women suffered some form of psychiatric disorder.

BIOLOGICAL EXPLANATIONS

Rutter and Madge (1976) suggest that the idea that abnormality could be the end-product of an inter-generational accumulation of genetically vulnerable individuals' in the lower social classes, has received **inconclusive support** - although genetic factors probably play a greater role in psychoses than neuroses.

CULTURAL/ENVIRONMENTAL EXPLANATIONS

A more likely explanation for social class differences is that the increased social **stresses** and **deprivation** of positive **rewards** experienced by the lower-socio-economic groups may directly cause disorders, such as depression, through learned helplessness, or may act as a **trigger** for a genetic predisposition to suffer from schizophrenia, for example.

DIAGNOSTIC BIAS OR ERROR EXPLANATIONS

Alternatively, increased rates of mental disorder may not reflect true causal differences, but rather the bias of predominantly middle to upper class psychiatrists to be more likely to **label** working class people 'mentally ill' than 'eccentric', or experiencing 'problems with living'. A more widely supported explanation, however, is the **social drift hypothesis** - that individuals who suffer mental disorder are more likely to lose their jobs, status, income, etc. and, therefore, drift down to lower socio-economic groups. Rather than social class causing abnormality, many 'research findings on parental social class and disorder show that the main mechanism is an illness determined downward social drift' Rutter and Madge (1976).

Research into subcultural differences in the determination of abnormality 2

AGE DIFFERENCES IN DETERMINING ABNORMALITY

The elderly - have always been proportionally more likely to be admitted to mental hospitals. In Britain the likelihood of admission increases by around 30% from the 55-64 to the 65-74 year old age bracket, and then virtually doubles again for those aged 75 and over.

The young - more recently there has been an alarming increase in psychiatric hospital admissions for young people, compared to a drop in admissions for adults. The rate of admission increased by around 65% for 10-14 year olds, and 21% for 15-19 year olds between 1985 and 1990, according to Department of Health figures, compared to a 20% drop in adult admissions.

BIOLOGICAL EXPLANATIONS

There is a good deal of evidence that biologically based psychoses, such as senile dementia, do significantly increase with age. However, the recent increase in child admissions to psychiatric care (which may lead to the use of forced biological treatments, such as drug therapy) is less easy to explain in terms of biological causes.

CULTURAL/ENVIRONMENTAL EXPLANATIONS

Social conditions can contribute towards the development of abnormality, both in the young and the old. The elderly are faced with increasing financial hardship and social stress, and the western cultural tendency not to care for the elderly in the family, but to institutionalise or give them home help, provides conditions of loneliness and lack of stimulation, productive activity, and social support. Children, it may be argued, are more prone to early family stresses in the form of increased divorce rates, for example, and some research has shown that parental privation or deprivation can have long term effects on mental health, such as depression or even affectionless psychopathy.

DIAGNOSTIC BIAS OR ERROR EXPLANATIONS

An alternative explanation of age differences suggests that the admission rates are not true reflections of the real prevalence of abnormality in the young and old. Stereotyping and expectations of the elderly as being prone to mental disorder, or the use of psychiatric care for the social control of deviant youngsters (the medicalisation of deviance) could be responsible.

ETHNIC DIFFERENCES IN DETERMINING ABNORMALITY

Subcultures can also be produced by immigrants of one country moving into and living in another country, and their different cultural beliefs, norms or religion have often been sufficient to somehow cause different levels of abnormality.

Higher rates of mental illness have been found in first generation immigrants in a number of countries including Hispanics in the USA, early Polish immigrants to Britain, and first generation 'French' Canadians (reported by Ballantyne, 1988). These increases can persist even into the second generation of immigrants - one study conducted in the late 1980s found that **children** of immigrants from the Caribbean living in Britain were 10 times more likely than white children to develop schizophrenia as adults. Although this second generation effect is not found in children from the Asian subcontinent, it still seems that black people in Britain are more likely to be diagnosed as suffering from disorder than white people, and may even receive higher doses of drug treatment.

Subcultural differences in the determination of abnormality are not just restricted to the northern hemisphere - for example, in New Zealand, Kramer (1980) found that involuntary admissions to mental hospitals were much more common amongst the Maori than the non-Maori population.

BIOLOGICAL EXPLANATIONS

Although differences in the type and prevalence of abnormality exist across different societies, it is difficult to separate out the possible cultural and biological reasons for them.

However, it seems less likely that biological causes could account for the increase in abnormality found when members of one society move to another and form a subculture - these immigrants show higher rates than both their adopted society and their originally native society. The only biological factors that have been suggested are the increased likelihood of stress during pregnancy or the exposure to viruses not found in the native country (viruses have been proposed as a possible causal factor in schizophrenia).

CULTURAL/ENVIRONMENTAL EXPLANATIONS

As usual, a major cause of ethnic differences in abnormality could lie in the environmental stresses that members of a subculture experience.

Dr Glynn Harrison, the psychiatrist who led the Nottingham University Hospital study on Schizophrenia in Caribbean immigrants (quoted in *The Guardian*, 31 October 1988) argues that 'Many young black men in Britain, faced with discrimination and limited opportunities, suffer from crises of identity, which could precipitate the illness in those already vulnerable', and suggested that more research should be conducted on the possible effects of living in decaying inner city areas.

DIAGNOSTIC BIAS OR ERROR EXPLANATIONS

A frequent explanation of subcultural differences in the determination of abnormality is that the increased rates of diagnosis are not truly reflective of the real rates, but are motivated by diagnostic bias.

This bias could involve unintentional mis-diagnosis due to not understanding the behaviour of the subculture, or could be due to deliberate prejudice on the part of psychiatrists in the society, who often represent the establishment - the dominant culture possessing the political power.

Subcultures are not always formed by immigrants in a society, any section of the population from the dominant culture different views and attitudes from the dominant culture could be regarded as subcultural. In Russia, the psychiatric system was used by the Communist Party in power as a means of social control - political dissidents were often defined as schizophrenic or suffering from delusions/paranoia so that they could be 'legitimately' removed from society, confined and 'treated'.

Szasz (1974), in his book *Ideology and Insanity*, argued that all diagnosis is a form of social control and that labels have always been attached to those who show different behaviours from the norm in a society because it 'justifies' their persecution and control.

Research into cross-cultural differences in the determination of abnormality

CROSS-CULTURAL DIFFERENCES IN ABNORMALITY

There are many cross-cultural differences in the determination of abnormality, both in prevalence and type of disorder. However, there are also many cross-cultural similarities. Gross (1995) argues that disorders show enough recognisable core symptoms in every culture to be regarded as **universal** (for example all schizophrenics world-wide show incoherent thought patterns and speech, delusions, etc.) but show cultural variations in

- the precise **form** that the **symptoms** take
- the **reasons** for the onset of disorder
- the **prognosis** for recovery

However, it has been proposed that some disorders are **culturally relative** - that is unique to a particular culture. Western psychiatrists are likely to say that if a syndrome is distorted beyond a certain point, then a **culture-bound syndrome** is identified. Researchers (e.g. Fernando, 1991) suggest that anorexia nervosa and pre-menstrual syndrome may be western **culture-bound syndromes**, while 'Amok' (which involves short-lived outbursts of aggressive behaviour in males involving attempts to kill or injure) may be a Southeast Asian culture-bound syndrome, since it is identified as a disorder in Malaysia, Thailand, and Indonesia. The ICD10 recognises that some disorders seem to be particularly frequent in some cultures, and includes, in subsection F48.8 called 'Other specified neurotic disorders':

- **Dhat syndrome** - anxiety involving 'undue concern about the debilitating effects of the passage of semen'.
- **Koro** - a disorder involving 'anxiety and fear that the penis will withdraw into the abdomen and cause death'.
- **Latah** - involving 'imitative and automatic response behaviour'.

BIOLOGICAL EXPLANATIONS

Biological effects can account for the widespread **similarities** in abnormality across cultures, but probably have a more limited role in determining cross-cultural differences. The idea that disorders are **absolute** - that is 'culture free' (found in all cultures in exactly the same form) has received very **little support**. Even with disorders with strong biological influences, it seems that cultural factors can affect the prevalence, types of symptoms, and prognosis for recovery.

CULTURAL/ENVIRONMENTAL EXPLANATIONS

The idea that disorders are **universal** - they occur in all cultures but are subject to cultural modification due to **learning influences** in their causes or expression, has received the most support. Many of the cross-cultural differences can be attributed to environmental factors, such as the different levels of stress, different social learning effects, different norms, etc. found in those societies. According to Gross (1995),

- different cultures will learn different ways of expressing their symptoms, for example schizophrenics complaining of thought invasion by mysterious forces in western societies have kept pace with technological developments. In the 1920s they thought that voices were being transmitted directly into their heads via radio, in the 1960s it was accomplished by space satellites, and in the 1970s and 80s it was done through microwave ovens. In Nigeria, where the culture believes that others can curse or direct evil spirits at you, schizophrenics show a higher prevalence of paranoia and persecution symptoms.
- many disorders are thought to be provoked by stressful environments. However, different cultures may differ in the amount of environmental stress their members experience and what they find socially distressful. Unless these culturally determined influences are understood, the causes of the disorder may remain a mystery.

Lin and Kleinman (1988) have found that schizophrenics are more likely to recover in a non-industrialised society than an industrialised society, despite more advanced medical resources in the latter. They argue that this is probably because non-industrialised cultures are less individualistic and competitive, providing more family and social support for the sufferer and more stable and predictable environments to aid recovery.

DIAGNOSTIC DIFFERENCE EXPLANATIONS

Different cultures vary in the way they perceive and identify abnormality, so the difference in disorders between cultures could be due to the **different notions** of normal and abnormal behaviour found in those cultures. Thus, it has been argued that in some cultures the symptoms of schizophrenia, such as strange visions, speech, and behaviour, might be regarded as special or sacred rather than abnormal and undesirable. However, research by Murphy (1976) on non western cultures (such as Inuit tribes) has indicated that linguistic distinctions are made between the 'shaman' and 'crazy people' in their society. Alternatively, other cultures may regard those defined as suffering from Anti-social Personality Disorder by western diagnostic systems as just plain evil or bad. Western societies have 'medicalised' disorder to a greater degree than non western societies in Africa and India for example, where mental well-being is far more tied up with religious and social well-being. Even in different western cultures, different diagnostic classification systems and expectations have been shown to influence the determination of abnormality, e.g. Cooper et al's (1972) study on New York and London psychiatrists.

'A case of multiple personality' Thigpen and Cleckley (1954)

AIM
To describe the case study of a 25 year old married woman referred to two psychiatrists for severe headaches and blackouts, but soon discovered to have a multiple personality. The article presents evidence for the existence of this previously rare condition in the subject, in a cautious but convinced manner.

SUMMARY OF THE CASE

The first few interviews with the woman, Eve White, only found her to have 'several important emotional difficulties' and a 'set of marital conflicts and personal frustrations'. The first indication of multiple personality was when the psychiatrists received a letter from Eve that she did not remember sending and which contained a note at the end written in a different and childish handwriting. On her next visit, after a period of unusual agitation, she reported that she occasionally had the impression that she heard a voice in her head - and then suddenly and spontaneously showed a dramatic change in her behaviour, revealing the character (and answering to the name) of Eve Black.

Over a period of 14 months and around 100 hours of interview time, the two psychiatrists investigated the two Eves, first using hypnosis, but later without the need for it. Eve White was found not to have access to the awareness and memories of Eve Black (experiencing blackouts when Eve Black took over control) although the reverse was true for Eve Black (who often used the ability to disrupt Eve White's life by taking over and getting her into trouble or by giving her headaches).

Later during the course of therapy, a third personality emerged called Jane - again suddenly and with a different set of characteristics. Jane had access to the consciousness of both Eves, but incomplete access to their memories before her emergence, and could only emerge through Eve White.

The authors admit the possibility of fakery, although they think it highly unlikely, and argue for more research to answer some fundamental questions concerning the multiple personality phenomena.

EVIDENCE FOR THE EXISTENCE OF MULTIPLE PERSONALITY

Personality distinctions gained through interview:
- Character - Eve White - self-controlled, serious, matter of fact, and meticulously truthful.
  Eve Black - childish, carefree, shallow, mischievous, and a fluent liar.
- Attitudes - Eve White - distressed about failing marriage, warm love for daughter.
  Eve Black - thought Eve White's distress and love was silly, seemed 'immune to major affective events in human relationships'.
- Behaviour - Eve White - responsible and reserved.
  Eve Black - irresponsible, pleasure and excitement seeking, seeks company of strangers to avoid discovery.
- Mannerisms - 'A thousand minute alterations in manner, gesture, expression, posture, of nuances in reflex... of glance' between the two Eves.

Personality distinctions gained through independent psychological testing:
- Psychometric tests - IQ of Eve White was 110, IQ of Eve Black was 104, differences between the two were found in memory function.
- Projective testing - Rorschach revealed
  a Eve Black to show regression and hysterical tendencies, but to be far healthier than Eve White.
  b Eve White to show repression, anxiety, obsessive-compulsive traits, and an inability to deal with her hostility.

The psychologist was of the opinion that the tests revealed one personality at two stages of life - that Eve Black represented a regression to a carefree state, as a way of dealing with her dislike of marriage and maternal pressures.

Personality distinctions gained through physiological EEG testing:
Eve White and Jane were found to show similar Electroencephalograph readings, with Eve Black definitely distinguishable from the other two.

Evidence for multiple personality as a distinct and valid disorder:
- Clearly distinguishable from other disorders, such as schizophrenia, but with some similarities to disorders like dissociative fugue.
- Eve's behaviour showed such remarkable consistency within characters that two psychiatrists were persuaded she was not deliberately faking.
- Shows similarities of symptoms with other multiple personality cases such as patterns of amnesia between personalities and similar causal circumstances that provoke a denial of parts of the self.

EVALUATION

Methodological:

Case study method - Lack of objectivity when involved with the patient, especially when trying to help through therapy, rather than attempting rigorous experiments to test the possibility of fakery.

Unreliability of testing - Those tests that were conducted were of doubtful validity, because they could have been affected by deliberate attempts to fake (except perhaps the EEG test, although what the differences found represented is open to interpretation) and projective tests are also of doubtful reliability due to the subjective nature of their interpretation.

Theoretical: Doubts about the validity of this study are caused by Chris Sizeman (the real name of Eve) later revealing that she had other personalities before (and after) 1954, yet these were not detected or mentioned at the time. Doubts about the validity of multiple personality disorder in general are caused by the fact that they are often investigated through hypnosis and are becoming increasingly common in America but not other countries. There are ethical and legal implications involved in accepting multiple personality as a valid disorder, e.g. culpability.

Links: Abnormality (particularly problems in diagnosing), personality, freewill debate. Case study of Freud.

Schizophrenia - symptoms and diagnosis

BACKGROUND
Some studies indicate that there is approximately a 1% life time risk of developing schizophrenia.
Kraepelin (1902) described the symptoms of 'dementia praecox' (senility of youth) as being delusions,
attention deficits, and bizarre motor activity, due to a form of mental deterioration that began in youth.
Bleuler (1911) observed that deterioration did not continue and often began after adolescence, and so
introduced the term 'schizophrenia' (split mind) to describe how psychological functions had lost their unity.

DIAGNOSIS

The DSM IV diagnostic criteria are:

1 **Two** or more of the following symptoms present for a significant amount of time in a one month period:
   - **Hallucinations** (if there are extensive auditory hallucinations of voices, then no other symptoms have to be present)
   - **Delusions** (if these are very bizarre, then no other symptoms have to be present)
   - **Disorganised speech**, e.g. incoherent
   - **Catatonic or disorganised behaviour**, e.g. repetitive movements or gestures
   - **Negative symptoms**, e.g. emotional blunting

2 Disturbance must last for 6 months (including 1 month of the above symptoms).

3 · The symptoms must have produced a marked deterioration in functioning at work, in social relations, and in self care (axis 5 of the DSM IV).

SYMPTOMS

EMOTIONAL
Emotions can be either
- flat, unresponsive and insensitive, or
- inappropriate to the situation and changeable

BEHAVIOURAL
Somatic disturbance, e.g.
- psychomotor agitation - fixed, repetitive gestures
- Catatonic stupor - keeping the same position for long periods of time

PERCEPTUAL
- Auditory hallucinations, usually voices commenting upon behaviour and thoughts in the third person, are heard.
- Visual hallucinations, such as size, space, and colour distortions occur

COGNITIVE
Disruption occurs to
- **thought processes** - schizophrenics show **cognitive distractibility** (they are unable to maintain a consistent train of thought); **attentional deficits** (focusing on irrelevant stimuli); and **thought passivity** (where they think that others block, insert or withdraw the thoughts in their head).
- **thought content** - includes delusions, e.g. of persecution, control, or grandeur.

SUBTYPES OF SCHIZOPHRENIA
The DSM IV lists five sub-categories of schizophrenia, because of the huge variety of symptoms shown.

DISORGANISED SCHIZOPHRENIA
Symptoms mostly involve
- **incoherent** thoughts and speech
- **bizarre** delusions and hallucinations
- **inappropriate** emotions and behaviour

UNDIFFERENTIATED SCHIZOPHRENIA
The classification for those whose symptoms are not classifiable under any of the other subtypes. This is the least useful of the diagnostic classifications.

CATATONIC SCHIZOPHRENIA
Involves alternating between
- catatonic **stupor** and **negativism**, and
- catatonic **excitement** - prolonged, frenzied, even violent behaviour

PARANOID SCHIZOPHRENIA
Involves organised and complex delusions (often of persecution), mostly auditory hallucinations, and relatively few other symptoms.

RESIDUAL SCHIZOPHRENIA
Involves the gradual development of many minor problems, e.g. unusual behaviour, social withdrawal, emotional blunting, and apathy.

ALTERNATIVE TYPOLOGIES
- **Type 1 schizophrenia** - is characterised by positive symptoms, e.g. hallucinations and delusions
- **Type 2 schizophrenia** - is characterised by negative symptoms, e.g. emotional blunting and avolition

Explanatory theories of schizophrenia

BIOLOGICAL THEORIES

**PSYCHOLOGICAL/
ENVIRONMENTAL THEORIES**

GENETIC CAUSES

Family studies - Children of two schizophrenic biological parents are around 46% likely to develop the disorder. These studies do not rule out environmental learning though.

Twin studies - Studies from many countries have produced different estimates, but Gottesman (1991) suggests that monozygotic identical twins (who have the same genes) have significantly higher concordance rates (48%) for schizophrenia than dizygotic non-identical twins (17%). Concordance rates refer to whether **both** twins develop the disorder.
However, identical twins also share more similar environments.

Adoption studies - When adopted subjects' environments are matched, the rates of schizophrenia are higher for adoptive children with schizophrenic biological parents compared to adoptive children with non-schizophrenic biological parents (Kety et al, 1975). Ideally, identical twins with schizophrenia, raised apart in different adoptive environments, would be the best evidence for genetic causes, but obviously these cases are extremely rare.

Genetic factors do not account 100% for schizophrenia, however. People probably inherit a genetic predisposition for schizophrenia, which **may** be triggered by environmental factors.

BIOCHEMICAL CAUSES

A very popular theory of schizophrenia was the dopamine hypothesis - that over-activity of the neurotransmitter dopamine in the synapses of the brain caused type 1 positive symptoms of schizophrenia. Evidence for the hypothesis included the findings that

- large doses of amphetamines (which increase dopamine activity) can create amphetamine psychosis, which closely resembles acute paranoid schizophrenia. Small doses can trigger symptoms in schizophrenics.
- anti-schizophrenic drugs like chlorpromazine work by blocking the post synaptic receptor sites of dopamine, thereby reducing its activity. If schizophrenics are given too much of these drugs, they develop symptoms similar to Parkinson's disease (caused by too little dopamine).
- post-mortems and Positron Emission Tomography scans have found higher amounts of dopamine and dopamine synaptic receptor sites.

However, the dopamine hypothesis is an over simplistic explanation, since new anti-schizophrenic drugs (e.g. clozapine) work by affecting other neurotransmitters, especially serotonin.

BRAIN STRUCTURAL CAUSES

Enlarged ventricles - research has found that these fluid filled cavities in the brain are larger in schizophrenics due to brain cell loss. Cell loss in the temporal lobes of the brain (responsible for cognitive and emotional functions) has been associated with negative symptoms. However, the evidence is correlational - enlarged ventricles may be a symptom not a cause, since non-schizophrenics can also show them.

Brain area activity - schizophrenics' brain scans do not show the usual prefrontal activation of the cortex when given problem solving tasks. Brain scanning can not yet predict the presence of schizophrenia.

PSYCHOLOGICAL CAUSES

A variety of theories have sought to explain schizophrenia at the psychological level, including:
Psychoanalytic theory - Freud suggested that regression to a state of 'narcissism' in the early oral stage could be responsible, where there is no developed ego to test reality. Psychotic thought resembles the id's primary process thinking, and is untreatable through psychoanalysis because the narcissistic person has given up any attachment to the outside world (preventing transference, for example).

Existential theory - Psychiatrists, such as Laing, have proposed that people withdraw from reality as a normal response to the pressures of a mad world. Schizophrenia is a social and interpersonal experience which can be regarded as a potentially beneficial journey of self discovery.

Labelling theory - Scheff (1966) has argued that schizophrenia may be largely a social role that, once assigned by diagnosis, is conformed to and becomes a self-fulfilling prophecy. The internalisation of the schizophrenic role is strengthened by the reactions of other people and hospitalisation. Szasz has taken these ideas further to argue that schizophrenia is a myth created by society to control those who are different.

Cognitive theory - Frith (1979) proposes that disruption to an attentional filter mechanism could result in the thought disturbance of schizophrenia, as the sufferer is overloaded with sensory information. Studies on continuous performance and eye-tracking tasks indicate that schizophrenics do show more attentional problems than non-schizophrenics. Perhaps reduced short term memory capacity could account for some schizophrenics' cognitive distractibility.

SOCIAL/ENVIRONMENTAL CAUSES

Social or environmental factors could act to trigger schizophrenia in those with a genetic predisposition.

Family stresses - Faulty interpersonal relationships in the families of schizophrenics have been found by Fromm Reichmann (who proposed the idea of the 'schizophrenogenic mother'); Bateson (who discovered ambivalent 'double bind' communication between schizophrenic children and their parents); and Lidz and Fleck (who described 'schism' and 'skew' in the families of schizophrenics).
However, the evidence is correlational - perhaps schizophrenics cause stress and disturbance in their families.

Environmental stresses - Some studies have found schizophrenia is 8 times more common in the lower socio-economic groups. However, this could be a cause (providing greater stress) or a result (of downward social drift) of schizophrenia.

Viruses - Many viruses, e.g. influenza have been proposed to trigger genetic causes of schizophrenia.

Mood disorders - symptoms and diagnosis

BACKGROUND
Mood disorders are one of the most frequently occurring psychopathologies, the risk of developing one is around 9%. The DSM IV distinguishes between two main categories of mood disorder: unipolar depression and bipolar (manic) depression. Major unipolar depression occurs at least 5 times more frequently than bipolar depression (it has been called 'the common cold of mental illness'), and mania can occur on its own (although this is very rare). It is important to remember that we all have our emotional 'ups and downs' but these mood disorders differ in degree from 'normal', natural reactions, both in their severity, frequency and duration, and may lead to suicide attempts.

UNIPOLAR DEPRESSION

Diagnosis - Unipolar depression can present four types of symptoms.
The DSM IV states that either depressed mood or loss of pleasure, plus at least another 4 symptoms (out of those listed opposite) must be shown during the same two week period for the diagnosis to be made.

Prevalence - There is at least a 5% lifetime risk of developing unipolar depression. It appears cross-culturally, but is diagnosed twice as often for women.

EMOTIONAL SYMPTOMS
Intense feelings of sadness or guilt, along with a lack of enjoyment or pleasure in previous activities or company.

MOTIVATIONAL SYMPTOMS
Passivity and great difficulty in initiating action and making decisions.

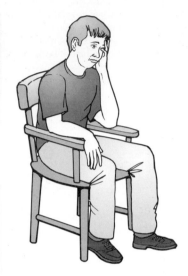

COGNITIVE SYMPTOMS
Frequent negative thoughts, faulty attribution of blame (blame themselves) low self esteem, and irrational hopelessness.

SOMATIC SYMPTOMS
Loss of energy or restlessness. Disturbance of appetite, weight, and sleep.

BIPOLAR DEPRESSION

Diagnosis - Bipolar depression involves the symptoms of depression, followed by mania or hypomania (shorter, less severe mania). Mania involves 4 types of symptoms.
The DSM IV states a manic episode must involve 'a distinct period of abnormally and persistently elevated, expansive or irritable mood, lasting at least a week', plus at least 3 additional symptoms (out of those opposite).

Prevalence - There is around a 1% lifetime risk of developing bipolar depression.

EMOTIONAL SYMPTOMS
Abnormally euphoric elevated or irritable mood, and increased pleasure in activities.

MOTIVATIONAL SYMPTOMS
Increase in goal-directed activity and increase in pleasurable activities that have a high risk of painful consequences.

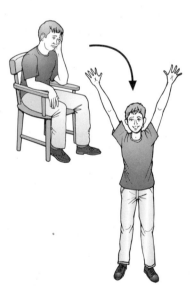

COGNITIVE SYMPTOMS
Inflated self-esteem or grandiosity, racing ideas and thoughts, distractibility of attention.

SOMATIC SYMPTOMS
Decreased need for sleep, psychomotor agitation, more talkative and rapid, pressured speech.

OTHER MOOD DISORDERS
The DSM IV and ICD 10 list many other varieties of mood disorder, including:
- **Dysthymia** - A classification given to those who suffer chronic mild depression over a period of not less than two years, where a depressed mood and other symptoms of mild depression are suffered **a** for most of the day, **b** on more days than not, and **c** without a break of more than two months in the two year period.
- **Cyclothymia** - The bipolar equivalent of dysthymia. It is a classification given to those who suffer from mild depression, interspersed with periods of hypomania, for more than two years.
- **Mania** - A classification given to those who suffer from full blown symptoms of mania without corresponding periods of depression. The symptoms must last for at least one week and must be sufficiently severe to interfere with social and/or occupational functioning.
- **Seasonal affective disorder** - A classification given to those who suffer a mood disorder that systematically varies with seasonal changes, often involving depression in winter months and sometimes also bipolar mania in the summer.

Explanatory theories of mood disorders

| BIOLOGICAL THEORIES | PSYCHOLOGICAL THEORIES | ENVIRONMENTAL THEORIES |

Genetics
There is moderate evidence for a genetic predisposition to suffer from unipolar depression, but much stronger evidence for the role of genes in bipolar depression. Monozygotic twin **concordance** studies and family studies have led Katz and McGuffin (1993) to suggest that genetic factors account for 52% of the variance in unipolar depression, but up to 80% of the variance in vulnerability in bipolar depression.

Learning theory
Looks at the role of **reinforcement** and **punishment**. Depressives may suffer from a lack of positive reinforcement that may lead to 'sad' behaviour which, when noticed, may itself be reinforced by the attention it draws. However, since depressed people tend to be avoided in the long run, this only leads to further lack of reinforcement and a vicious circle.
Seligman found that dogs repeatedly subjected to unavoidable punishment would no longer initiate any action to avoid electric shocks when it was made possible to do so. Seligman argued that the dogs had **learned helplessness** and showed behaviour similar to that showed by human depressives.

Life events
Depression occurs not only after major stressful life events (particularly the early loss of attachment figures), but is also reliably linked with continual levels of stress and 'hassles'.

Neurochemicals
One of the most popular theories is that a **lack** of the neurotransmitters **norepinephrine** (noradrenaline) and **serotonin** are responsible for depression. These biochemicals are involved in the areas of the brain involved in emotional behaviour, and evidence for their involvement in depression comes from studies into the action of anti-depressant drugs (which increase their activity) and the drug reserpine, which causes depression (because it decreases norepinephrine and serotonin levels).
The very successful effect of lithium carbonate in treating bipolar depression indicates a strong role for biological causes in this disorder.
Some studies have indicated that hormones, such as cortisol, have a role to play in unipolar depression.

Cognitive theory
Based on his experiments on **learned helplessness**, Seligman proposed a cognitive theory suggesting that people become depressed when they **believe** that nothing they do will improve their situation.
Learned helplessness makes the depressive see
- causes as internal (blaming themselves not the situation)
- situations as stable (showing extreme pessimism about the future)
- failure as global (not specific to one situation)
In other words the depressed person thinks 'its me, its going to last forever, and everything I do will go wrong'.

Aaron Beck came up with some similar ideas by proposing his **cognitive triad** of negative thoughts (about the self, present experience, and the future) and looked at the depressive's **errors in logic** (distortions of thought processes, such as false magnification or minimisation of events, over-generalisation, personalisation, etc.).
Cognitive psychologists emphasise faulty attributions.

Socio-economic background
Depression is proportionally more common in women, but especially in 'working class', house-bound women with three or more children. Clearly, stress and lack of environmental reinforcement is greater in these circumstances.

Seasonal variation
Seasonal affective disorder may be caused by the variations in daylight hours that occur as the seasons change. Less daylight in the winter months may account for the higher reports of depression at this time.

Psychoanalytic theory
Focuses on **unconscious** causes of depression. According to Freud, depressives turn their aggressive drive and anger that they feel towards other people or situations inwards and are, therefore, punishing themselves.

Evaluation
The role of the above neurotransmitters and hormones in depression is extremely complex, and anti-depressant drugs have effects on many other neurochemicals, apart from norepinephrine and serotonin, so we cannot guarantee that these are the only substances involved.

Evaluation
Learning theory does not take into account the idea that different people sharing a similar set of environmental experiences will not always become equally depressed. Seligman's finding on animals can not be legitimately generalised to humans. The psychoanalytic theory of depression lacks scientific support.

Evaluation
These factors should perhaps be regarded as **triggers** of depression for people who are already predisposed to suffer from it, since not all people will react in the same way to these environmental stresses - some cope, others do not.

INTERACTION EXPLANATIONS

Researchers, such as Checkley (1992), have pointed out that stress causes the release of adrenal steroid hormones, such as cortisol, and these hormones are thought to play a role in regulating the effect of genetic influences.

Other researchers such as Weiss and Simson (1985) have found that rats exhibiting the behavioural symptoms of learned helplessness induced by unavoidable shock, often showed large decreases in the production of the neurotransmitter norepinephrine.

Eating disorders - symptoms and diagnosis

BACKGROUND

Eating disorders like anorexia and bulimia are fairly recent arrivals to the classification manuals - appearing for the first time in the DSM III in 1980. There is debate over whether these disorders have always existed, but what is certain is that they have increased in prevalence in recent years. These disorders are ten times more common in women than men, and often occur together in the same individual.

Obesity, however, is not included in the diagnostic classification manuals, but can produce a range of serious physical as well as psychological consequences and may have a number of causes that do not always involve deliberate choice. Obesity occurs in men and women in roughly equal amounts.

ANOREXIA NERVOSA

Diagnosis - 'Anorexia' comes from the Greek term for 'loss of appetite' and involves problems maintaining a normal body weight. The DSM IV states that the four symptoms opposite must be shown for the classification to be made.

Prevalence - 0.5-1% of females in adolescence to early adulthood.

BEHAVIOURAL SYMPTOMS

A refusal to maintain a body weight normal for age and height (weight itself is less than 85% of that expected).

EMOTIONAL SYMPTOMS

An intense fear of gaining weight, even though obviously under-weight.

COGNITIVE SYMPTOMS

Distorted self-perception of body shape (over estimation of body size) and over emphasis of its importance for self-esteem. Denial of seriousness of weight loss.

SOMATIC SYMPTOMS

Loss of body weight and absence of menstruation for 3 consecutive months.

BULIMIA NERVOSA

Diagnosis - 'Bulimia' is derived from the Greek for 'ox appetite', and involves binge eating followed by compensatory behaviour to rid the body of what has just been consumed.

The DSM IV states that the symptoms opposite must be shown for the classification to be made.

Prevalence - Around 1-3% of females in adolescence to early adulthood.

BEHAVIOURAL SYMPTOMS

Recurring binge eating - excessive quantities consumed within a discrete period of time (e.g. 2 hours) without a sense of control over what or how much is consumed.

Recurring inappropriate compensatory behaviour to prevent weight gain - such as self-induced vomiting, misuse of laxatives, or fasting.

Binge eating and compensatory behaviours occur on average at least twice a week for three months.

COGNITIVE SYMPTOMS

Self image is overly influenced by body size and shape.

OBESITY

Diagnosis - Although not listed as a disorder in the DSM IV, obesity is defined as having a body weight in excess of 20% above the average for one's height.

Prevalence - Stewart and Brook (1983) estimated that 22% of Americans aged 14-61 were over-weight, 12% of these seriously so. More recent estimates in America have suggested that up to a quarter of the population is obese.

Consequences - Physically, obese people are more likely to suffer from a range of weight induced illnesses, including heart attacks and diabetes. Psychologically, there are many negative effects (for example on self-esteem) as a result of societal reaction and prejudice, especially for overweight children.

Explanatory theories of eating disorders

BIOLOGICAL THEORIES

Genetics
Family studies have shown that there is a higher risk of developing anorexia or bulimia if a first degree relative suffers from it, while monozygotic twin concordance studies have also suggested there may be a genetic link.
Adoption studies have indicated that obese adopted children are more likely to have obese biological than adoptive parents.

Physiology
Early research indicated that disruption to the ventromedial or lateral areas of the hypothalamus could severely affect eating behaviour - ablating the ventromedial hypothalamus in rats, for example, caused them to overeat until they became obese.
Although there is little conclusive evidence for their role in anorexia or bulimia, set point theory suggests these areas of the hypothalamus may have an imbalanced relationship which could lead to obesity. Obese people may have a higher physical set point for weight that the body constantly seeks to maintain (which explains why diets so often fail). Set point theory is supported by the fact that obese people have twice the number of fat cells of the average person, and the finding that dieting decreases the size of fat cells but not their number.
Hormonal disorders can cause obesity, although their comparative rarity can not explain all cases
Eating disorders have been linked to depression and some studies have found that anti-depressants are also effective in treating bulimia, although not necessarily by directly tackling any physical cause of it.

Evaluation
The biological cause and effect of eating disorders is difficult to determine, since the physical disorders found in anorexia and bulimia may be an effect of starvation and purging, rather than a cause. Environmental influences on obesity should not be ignored - a high set point may be the result of over-feeding at an early age, producing more fat cells rather than a genetic inheritance.

PSYCHOLOGICAL THEORIES

Psychoanalytic theory
Psychoanalytic theory has produced various explanations for eating disorders.
The anorexic's refusal to eat has been interpreted as an unconscious denial of the adult role and wish to remain a child (in figure at least) provoked by the development of sexual characteristics in puberty. This idea is supported by the timing of onset in anorexia. Another psychoanalytic interpretation is that anorexics are unconsciously rejecting their bodies as a reaction to sexual abuse in childhood.
Fixation at the oral stage has been suggested as a psychoanalytic explanation for obesity.

Cognitive theory
Cognitive psychologists have proposed that sufferers of anorexia and bulimia may be seeking to assert control over their lives to an excessively idealistic extent - Dura and Bornstein (1989) found this drive for perfection in hospitalised anorexics extended to academic achievements which were at a much higher level than their IQ scores would predict. Schachter has suggested that obese people may be more sensitive to external cues for eating (e.g. availability, appearance or taste) than internal cues (e.g. hunger).

Learning theory
Learning theory explains eating disorders in terms of reinforcement consequences for eating behaviour.
Weight loss or control may be rewarded by social praise or respect from a society that places a high value on slim female appearance. Alternatively, the attention and concern shown towards someone with an eating disorder may be rewarding.
A learning explanation for obesity is that food is a reinforcing stimulus that may become particularly rewarding for those who are bored or upset ('comfort eating').

Evaluation
Psychological level theories gain more strength when integrated with the social and cultural findings. However, although anorexics may develop their symptoms at puberty, and may have been sexually abused in some cases, the effects of these events are often more convincingly explained in non-Psychoanalytic terms.

ENVIRONMENTAL THEORIES

Social pressure
The idea that cultural pressures for individuals to conform to socially desirable conceptions of body shape are responsible for eating disorders has received much support. For example, anorexia and bulimia occur most in
- cultures where thinness is socially desirable, e.g. North America, Western Europe, and Japan. Indeed, evidence suggests that immigrants to these countries show higher levels of eating disorder than their native countries.
- western women - physical attractiveness is the best predictor of self-esteem in western girls, whereas physical competence is the best predictor for western boys.
- groups where thinness is particularly valued, e.g. ballet dancers, models, and gymnasts.
Social pressure for obesity appears to work primarily at the family level - children of obese parents conform to the family norms and patterns of eating.

Environmental stresses
Many researchers have found that the families of children with eating disorders show the following characteristics:
- Less emotional and nurturing - this may lead to eating disorders developing as an attention gaining tactic.
- Overly protective - restricting independence may force the child to assert its own control and autonomy through the eating disorder.
- Middle class, overachieving parents - whose high expectations of success may lead to overly idealistic notions of success in matters of weight control.

Evaluation
While social pressure is a powerful explanatory factor in eating disorders, not all people will react in the same way to these pressures and stresses - some undereat, others overeat.

Anxiety disorders - types of anxiety disorder

PHOBIAS

Diagnosis
The symptoms are unambiguous and diagnosis is easy:
- Persistent fear of a specific situation out of proportion to the reality of the danger.
- Compelling desire to avoid and escape the situation.
- Recognition that the fear is unreasonably excessive.
- Symptoms not due to another disorder, e.g. schizophrenia.

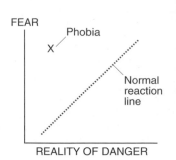

Although phobics perceive their disorder to be beyond their control and wish to be rid of it, with the exception of agoraphobics, the phobic's everyday functioning is unimpaired.

Symptoms of fear
There are various elements that make up the fear response:
- Cognitive elements - the expectation of impending harm.
- Somatic elements - the body's emergency reaction to danger and changes in appearance. The sympathetic nervous system is activated, releasing adrenaline.
- Emotional elements - the feelings of dread, terror, panic.
- Behaviour elements - usually fleeing or freezing.

Types of phobia
Most common phobias are found in the following 3 categories:
- **Agoraphobia** - involves fear of places of assembly, crowds and open spaces and is the most prevalent of all phobias. Occurring most often in women in early adulthood.
- **Social phobias** - involve fear of being observed doing something humiliating. Onset occurs most often in adolescence.
- **Specific phobias** - usually of three subtypes: **a** animals (e.g. spiders, snakes, rats), **b** inanimate objects (darkness, heights, enclosed spaces), **c** illness (injury, death, disease).

OBSESSIVE COMPULSIVE DISORDER

Diagnosis
According to the DSM IV, five criteria have to be met:
- Either obsession or compulsions must be experienced.
- The sufferer has to recognise that the obsessions or compulsions are excessive or unreasonable.
- The obsessions or compulsions are time consuming (taking over one hour a day), interfere with occupational or social functioning, and cause marked distress.
- The obsessions or compulsions are not confused with the preoccupations of other disorders, e.g. food with eating disorders, or drugs with substance abuse disorders.
- The obsessions or compulsions are not directly caused by medication or other known physical conditions.

Symptoms
- **Obsessions** - involve recurring and persistent thoughts, images or impulses that are experienced as inappropriate, intrusive and anxiety provoking, and are not just excessive worries about real life problems. The sufferer realises that these thoughts, etc. are the product of their own mind, and attempts to ignore or suppress them, often by thinking another thought or performing some action.
- **Compulsions** - involve repetitive and rule following behaviours (e.g. hand washing, checking) or mental acts (e.g. counting, praying) that the sufferer feels driven to perform (often in response to an obsession) to reduce distress or to avoid an imagined catastrophe. These acts are excessive and not realistically linked with what the sufferer is trying to avoid.

PANIC ATTACK

Diagnosis
According to the DSM IV a panic attack involves
- a discrete period of intense fear or discomfort, reaching a peak within 10 minutes.
- at least four (out of a list of 13) other symptoms occur very rapidly.

Symptoms
Somatic symptoms - such as sweating, trembling, palpitations, breathlessness, chest pain, nausea, dizziness, numbness, tingling or hot flushes.
Emotional symptoms - such as feelings of choking, smothering, derealization, depersonalisation, and fear of losing control, going mad or dying

GENERALISED ANXIETY DISORDER

Diagnosis
According to the DSM IV generalised anxiety disorder involves
- excessive, and difficult to control, worry and anxiety.
- significant distress and disruption to functioning.
- worry occurring more days than not for at least 6 months.
- worry not involving another disorder (e.g. depression).

Symptoms
Three additional symptoms must also be shown, e.g.
- restlessness and irritability,
- muscle tension, rapid physical fatigue, and sleep disturbance,
- concentration problems.

POST-TRAUMATIC STRESS DISORDER

Diagnosis
According to the DSM IV, post-traumatic stress disorder (PTSD) involves exposure to a traumatic event that was responded to with fear, helplessness or horror, plus the presence of the following symptoms for more than 1 month:
- The traumatic event is persistently re-experienced, e.g. as recurrent and intrusive recollections, flashbacks or dreams.
- Persistent avoidance of stimuli associated with the trauma and numbing of general responsiveness.
- Persistent symptoms of increased arousal, e.g. sleep difficulty, anger outbursts, exaggerated startle response, concentration difficulty.

Explanatory theories of anxiety disorders

BIOLOGICAL THEORIES

Genetics

The usual methods have been employed to assess the genetic causes of anxiety disorders:

- **Twin studies** - anxiety disorder concordance rates for monozygotic twins are fairly high, especially in comparison with dizygotic twin rates (Carey & Gottesman, 1981).
- **Relative studies** - some studies have shown that people with first degree relatives (e.g. mother, brother) who have experienced panic attacks are 10 times more likely than controls to also have them. Relatives of obsessive compulsives, however, are not more likely to develop obsessive compulsive disorder itself, but are more likely to suffer from some kind of anxiety disorder.

It appears that agoraphobia and panic disorder have the most **specific** genetic transmission, whereas other disorders seem to transmit a general tendency to inherit some kind of anxiety.

The genes for anxiety disorders have proven difficult to isolate however, and their method of action is unknown.

Evolutionary reasons for phobias

Seligman has talked of the 'biological preparedness' of phobias - that we are instinctively biased to acquire certain phobias because they have good evolutionary survival functions. Evidence for this comes from analysing the survival functions of the most common phobias (which usually involve dangerous stimuli, e.g. heights, snakes, the dark, etc.) and conditioning experiments, for example on monkeys which can be conditioned to fear snakes but not leaves or flowers. This also accounts for why modern dangerous objects, such as guns and cars, are rarely involved in human phobias - they have no evolutionary history.

Marks & Nesse argue that anxiety has evolved as 'a normal defence mechanism... People who are afraid of heights, for example, may "freeze" when confronted by a sudden drop, thereby reducing the chances of a fall'.

This does not explain why some people develop a particular phobic response compared to others.

Immediate biological causes

An excess of sodium lactate has been proposed as an explanation of panic attacks - infusions of this substance will provoke panic attacks in susceptible subjects significantly more than in controls. The same substance could be involved in phobias. Lactate may work by increasing blood carbon dioxide levels, thereby increasing respiration rates and provoking panic, or it may reduce serotonin, thereby reducing this neurotransmitter's calming effects. Evidence comes from the fact that anti-anxiety drugs block lactate effects.
PTSD may disrupt the locus coeruleus - the brain's alarm and arousal centre in the brain stem. This may be responsible for the PTSD symptoms of hyperalertness, difficulties in concentration and sleep, and exaggerated startle response.
Biological theories on their own can not provide a complete explanation - bodily effects still need to be cognitively interpreted, and an explanation of why certain people develop certain anxiety disorders needs to be provided.

PSYCHOLOGICAL THEORIES

Psychoanalytic theory

Freud proposed that phobias are caused by the displacement of unconscious anxiety onto harmless external objects. The anxiety stems from unconscious conflict, which has to be resolved before the phobia can be dealt with - even if one phobia goes, another will take its place until the underlying disorder is treated. The classic evidence that Freud provided was the case study of 'Little Hans' (1909), where Hans's unconscious fear of castration was displaced onto a fear of being bitten by white horses (which symbolised the father). Freud would have attributed PTSD to repressed traumatic events.
There are many criticisms of this approach and therapy.

Learning theory

Learning theorists propose that phobias come about as an originally neutral stimulus becomes associated with an unpleasant or traumatic experience and so becomes a fear-eliciting conditional stimulus. The classic example is the case of 'Little Albert' demonstrated by Watson & Raynor (1920).

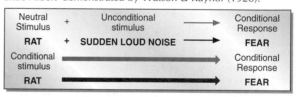

The persistence of phobias (i.e. why they do not extinguish easily) is explained by Mowrer's (1960) 'Two- factor' theory. It suggests that phobias are acquired through classical conditioning (as above) but are maintained through negative reinforcement - as the avoidance of unpleasant phobic situations is reinforced.
The degree of PTSD suffering is related to the severity of the trauma experienced, perhaps indicating a strong form of classical conditioning is involved.
Behaviourist views of phobia learning have to compromise with:
- biological preparedness (not all fears are equally easy to learn)
- vicarious learning of fear responses via social learning theory.

Cognitive theory

Clark (1986) proposes that faulty cognitive processes (thinking) are to blame for panic attacks. The sufferer tends to focus their attention internally, so are more aware of bodily sensations, and are more likely to misinterpret those sensations as catastrophic. This thinking can lead to a vicious circle as an increased heart rate is misinterpreted as a sign of impending harm - this leads to anxiety - which in turn leads to increased heart rate!
People suffering from generalised anxiety disorder show the attentional problem of over-vigilance - they are extremely sensitive to even minor danger cues.
Expectancies are important in determining whether traumatic events will cause PTSD. If people in the emergency services are not prepared for traumatic events, they are likely to suffer PTSD. Obsessive compulsives appear to use their obsessive thoughts and compulsive actions as a way of **suppressing** or controlling some underlying anxiety or worry. These thoughts and actions may be negatively reinforced by providing momentary escape from the underlying anxiety.

'Analysis of phobias in a five year old boy' Freud (1909)

AIM
To present the case study of Little Hans, a young boy who was seen as suffering from anxiety that led to a number of phobias. Freud uses this case study as strong support for his psychoanalytic ideas concerning:

- **Unconscious determinism** - Freud argues that people are not consciously aware of the causes of their behaviour. Little Hans was not consciously aware of the motivations for his behaviour, fantasies, and phobias.
- **Psychosexual development** - Psychoanalytic theory proposes that the sex drive seeks gratification through different erogenous zones at different ages, e.g. oral stage (0-1 years), anal (1-3 years), phallic stage (3-5 or 6 years). Little Hans was currently experiencing the phallic stage, according to Freud, gaining pleasure through masturbation and showing an interest in his own and other people's genitals.
- **The Oedipus complex** - Central to Freud's theory of personality, this occurs during the phallic stage as young boys direct their genital pleasure towards the mother and wish the father dead. However, young boys fear that their illicit desires will be found out by the father who will punish in the worse way possible - castration. Out of castration anxiety, the boy identifies with the father. Little Hans was regarded as a 'little Oedipus' wanting his father out of the way so he could be alone with his mother.
- **The cause of phobias** - Freud believed that phobias were the product of unconscious anxiety displaced onto harmless external objects. Little Hans's unconscious fear of castration by the father was symbolically displaced as a fear of being bitten by white horses.
- **Psychoanalytic therapy** - Aims to treat disturbed thoughts, feelings and behaviour by firstly identifying the unconscious causes of the disturbance, and secondly bringing them 'out into the open' to consciously discuss and resolve them. Thus Little Hans' behaviour was analysed, and its unconscious causes inferred and confronted.

SUMMARY OF THE CASE
Little Hans started showing a particularly lively interest in his 'widdler' and the presence or absence of this organ in others, and his tendency to masturbate brought threats from the mother to cut it off. When he was three and a half, he gained a baby sister, whom he resented, and consequently developed a fear of the bath. Later Hans developed a stronger fear of being bitten by white horses which seemed to be linked to two incidents - overhearing a father say to a child 'don't put your finger to the white horse or it will bite you' and seeing a horse that was pulling a carriage fall down and kick about with its legs. His fear went on to generalise to carts and buses. Little Hans, both before and after the beginning of the phobias, expressed anxiety that his mother would go away and was prone to frequent fantasies including imagining: **a** being the mother of his own children, whom he made to widdle, **b** that his mother had shown him her widdler, **c** that he had taken a smaller crumpled giraffe away from a taller one, **d** that a plumber had placed a borer into his stomach while in the bath on one occasion and had replaced his behind and widdler with larger versions on another occasion, and **e** that he was the father of his own children with his mother as their mother and his father as their grandfather. Having received 'help' from his father and Freud, his disorder and analysis came to an end after this last fantasy.

METHODS OF ANALYSIS
Little Hans was analysed and treated through his father (a firm believer of Freud's ideas) based on the latter's reports of Hans's behaviour and statements. Treatment was achieved by
- inferring the unconscious causes of Hans' behaviour through rich interpretation and decoding of psychoanalytic symbols
- confronting Hans with the unconscious causes by revealing to him his hidden motivations and consciously discussing them

RESULTS OF ANALYSIS

Event	Freudian Interpretation	Conclusion
Anxiety of mother's desertion	Sexual arousal of being taken into mother's bed for comfort	
Fear of bath	Death wish against sister due to jealousy over mother's attention	
Asking why mother did not powder his penis	Seduction attempt	Oedipus complex love for the mother
Taking smaller giraffe from the bigger one	Taking mother away from father	
Fear of heavily loaded carts and buses	Fear of another birth due to jealousy over mother's attention	
Fear of being bitten by white horses	Father (with spectacles and moustache) symbolic of white bus horse (with black blinkers and muzzle), bitten finger symbolic of castration	Fear of castration by father
Fantasy of plumber providing larger widdler	Wanting to be like (identifying with) his father	
Fantasy of being father with his mother	Fulfilment of growing up to have mother while making his father a grandfather instead of killing him	Resolution of Oedipus complex

EVALUATION
Methodological:
Case study method - Advantageous for therapeutic use but also many disadvantages, e.g. generalising results.
Lack of objectivity - Analysis was conducted second hand via the father and all data interpreted in the light of psychoanalytic theory. Freud was aware of objectivity problems and putting words in Little Hans' mouth, but argued 'a psychoanalysis is not an impartial scientific investigation but a therapeutic measure. Its essence is not to prove anything, but to alter something'.

Theoretical: There are many other explanations of Little Hans' behaviour that are more credible, e.g. those of Fromm (castration anxiety from the mother), Bowlby (attachment theory) and learning theory (classical conditioning of phobias).

Links: Freud's theory of socialisation, personality development and abnormality (its causes and treatment)
Links to case study of Thigpen and Cleckley in methodology.

Behavioural treatments

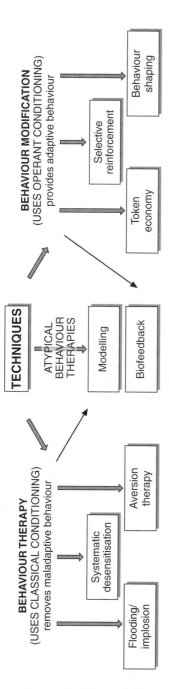

BEHAVIOUR MODIFICATION
(USES OPERANT CONDITIONING)
provides adaptive behaviour

→ Selective reinforcement → Behaviour shaping

→ Token economy

TECHNIQUES
ATYPICAL BEHAVIOUR THERAPIES
→ Modelling
→ Biofeedback

BEHAVIOUR THERAPY
(USES CLASSICAL CONDITIONING)
removes maladaptive behaviour

Systematic desensitisation → Aversion therapy

→ Flooding/implosion

AIM OF THERAPY

Aims to rectify specific maladaptive behaviours through relearning bad responses or learning good ones.

No underlying causes are considered, and the focus is on current observable behaviour only.

Has **high success rates** with a wide **variety** of behaviour disorders compared with psychotherapies. However it is argued that the approach **neglects underlying** mental or physical causes which could lead to symptom substitution, and cognitive and behavioural treatments **combined** show higher success rates than behavioural treatments alone.,

MODELLING

TECHNIQUE

Uses **social learning theory** as its basis, and is thus a more cognitive approach to learning therapy. Modelling aims to treat disorders, such as phobias, by showing a **model** interacting happily with the phobic object in the hope that the positive and relaxed feelings being demonstrated will be vicariously associated with it.

APPLICATION

Modelling has been applied to a range of anxiety and behavioural disorders (particularly for phobias) as well as in assertiveness and social skills training.

EFFECTIVENESS

Bandura has carried out modelling therapy on snake and dog phobics and claims a 90% success rate with children who watched models interacting with these creatures, particularly when they saw a live demonstration.

APPROPRIATENESS

However, the reasons for modelling's success rate are more debatable. Marks (1978) proposes that modelling might work by merely persuading the child to expose itself to the object of its fear; while Kazdin and Wilcoxin (1976) point to more cognitive explanations, namely that the phobic patient is made to **believe** and **expect** success.

BIOFEEDBACK

TECHNIQUE

Individuals are given information (i.e. feedback) about specific aspects of their biological functioning, such as heart rate, blood pressure, breathing rate, etc. and are then trained to **control** these **biological functions at will**, whereas they would normally be involuntary and beyond conscious control.

The feedback signal is thought to act as a reinforcer for the subject, and makes it more likely that the particular biological response that led to that reward will be repeated again. This is an example of operant conditioning, since the response comes before the stimulus reinforcer. However, it is unusual since the response made is usually a biologically **involuntary** rather than voluntary one.

APPLICATION

Miller and Dicara (1967) were the first to demonstrate biofeedback techniques with rats. Paralysed rats were rewarded by electrical stimulation to the hypothalamus whenever their breathing rate, or other autonomic functions changed in the desired direction. The rats then seemed to learn to manipulate their biological functions to gain the reward, implying that involuntary body processes could be voluntarily controlled.

Since this first crucial experiment, a number of other studies have claimed similar results using human subjects, who have been taught to control what were always regarded as involuntary phenomenon such as high blood pressure or the secretion of stomach acids. This type of learning has huge potential in medicine e.g. as a way of preventing heart attacks stomach ulcers or stress.

EFFECTIVENESS

Miller and Dicara's original study was never successfully replicated and those experiments claiming to have shown conscious control of involuntary processes in humans have either
a not been reliably replicated either, or
b been shown to be artificial and probably due to voluntary biological processes.

Le Francois (1983) argues that the application of biofeedback has huge but unproven potential in medicine. Johnston (1989) however claims biofeedback is less effective than drugs for controlling stress.

APPROPRIATENESS

In conclusion, it does seem that we may be able to influence involuntary biological processes to a small degree in the short term, but we probably do so using our existing voluntary nervous system and muscles. We probably cannot **directly** and consciously control autonomic functions, but anyone, for example, can speed up their heart rate indirectly by running a short distance!

Behavioural treatments - behaviour therapy (treatments using classical conditioning techniques)

SYSTEMATIC DESENSITISATION

TECHNIQUE
Aims to **extinguish** the fear response of a phobia, and **substitute** a relaxation response to the conditional stimulus **gradually**, step by step. This is done by

- forming a hierarchy of fear, a list of fearful situations, real or imagined, involving the CS that are ranked by the subject from least fearful to most fearful.
- giving training in deep muscle relaxation techniques.
- getting the subject to relax at each stage of the hierarchy, starting with the least fearful situation, and only progressing to the next stage when the subject feels sufficiently relaxed to do so.

APPLICATION
This therapy was developed mainly by Wolpe (1958). Mary Cover Jones applied systematic desensitisation to infants with phobias, such as the case of 'Little Peter'. Little Peter was a three year old child who had a strong phobia of rats and rabbits, and initially 'fell flat on his back in a paroxysm of fear when a white rat was dropped into his playpen', Walker (1984). Peter's treatment began by being presented with a rabbit in a cage at the same time as he ate his lunch, and ended 40 sessions later with him stroking the rabbit on his lap with one hand and eating his lunch with the other!

EFFECTIVENESS
This method of treatment has a very high success rate with specific phobias, e.g. of **particular** animals rather than agoraphobia (a **general** fear of being in open spaces), and is thought to work because it seems impossible for two opposite emotions (like fear and relaxation) to exist together at the same time.

APPROPRIATENESS
This conclusion is questioned by studies that claim to have found that neither relaxation or hierarchies are actually **necessary**, and that the essential factor is just **exposure** to the feared object or situation.
Systematic desensitisation is considered more ethical and less directive because the patient has more control over the treatment - progression only occurs when they feel suitably relaxed.

IMPLOSION/FLOODING

TECHNIQUE
Both methods of forced reality testing aim to produce the **extinction** of a phobic's fear by the **continual** and **dramatic** presentation of the phobic object or situation.
In implosion therapy, the phobic individual is, therefore, asked to continually **imagine** the worst possible situation involving their phobia, whereas in flooding therapy the worst possible situation is actually **physically** and continuously presented.

APPLICATION
Wolpe (1960) forced a girl with a fear of cars into the back of a car and drove her around for 4 hours until her hysterical fear completely disappeared, while Marks et al (1981) used flooding on agoraphobics. Prolonged exposure and compulsive response prevention is used for obsessive compulsives.

EFFECTIVENESS
Marks et al (1981) found continued improvement for up to nine years after the treatment. The key to the therapy is that the dramatic presentation is continuous and **cannot be escaped from or avoided**. Therefore, the patient's anxiety is maintained at such a high level that eventually some process of stimulus 'exhaustion' takes place (you can not scream forever!) and the conditioned fear response extinguishes.

APPROPRIATENESS
These methods are considered to be
- the most successful at treating phobias, especially flooding, which Marks et al, 1971, found to be consistently more successful than systematic desensitisation, suggesting that **in vivo exposure** is crucial.
- quick and cheap but involve ethical problems of suffering and withdrawal from therapy (which could worsen the phobia).

AVERSION THERAPY

TECHNIQUE
Aims to **remove undesirable responses** to certain stimuli **by associating** them with other **aversive** stimuli, in the hope that the undesirable responses will be avoided in the future. In essence, this therapy actually tries to condition some kind of 'phobia' of the undesirable behaviour, although it is important to note that fear is not always the conditioned response.

APPLICATION
Aversion therapy has been used to treat alcoholism.

More controversially, aversion therapy has been used to prevent a number of sexual behaviours, ranging from homosexuality to fetishism. Shocks have been paired with self damaging behaviours to stop them.

EFFECTIVENESS
Some studies have claimed limited success using aversion therapy to treat alcoholism - Meyer and Chesser (1970) found that about half their alcoholic patients abstained for at least one year following their treatment, although O'Leary and Wilson (1987) have reported mixed results. Marks et al (1970) claimed aversion therapy was effective on sexual behaviours for up to 2 years, although Marshall et al (1991) found no effectiveness.

APPROPRIATENESS
However, relapse rates are very high - the success of the therapy depends upon whether the patient can avoid the stimuli they have been conditioned against, to maintain the aversion. If the alcoholic continues to go to bars then the nausea response to alcohol may extinguish under repeated exposure.
There are ethical problems involved in deliberately conditioning aversions.

Behavioural treatments - behaviour modification (treatments using operant conditioning techniques)

BEHAVIOUR SHAPING

TECHNIQUE

This technique works by positively **reinforcing successive approximations to the desired behaviour** step by step.

Very complex behaviours can, therefore, be acquired from the more simple ones that make them up.

APPLICATION

Lovaas et al (1967) used behaviour shaping to improve the social interaction and speech of autistic children by

- associating food with verbal approval whenever the child made eye-contact with, or paid attention to, the therapist
- reinforcing any speech sound the child made with food and approval
- gradually withholding reinforcement until the child made the correct sounds, syllables, words then sentences.

EFFECTIVENESS

Lovaas et al (1976) reported long lasting gains in social and verbal behaviour that were maintained if the children were returned to a supportive home environment and parents who had also been trained in shaping techniques.

APPROPRIATENESS

Many serious psychoses, like schizophrenia, **cannot** fundamentally be 'cured' by learning treatments - when these treatments have been applied to them, they often show superficial short term effects unless continually reinforced.

SELECTIVE POSITIVE REINFORCEMENT

TECHNIQUE

This works by **reinforcing desirable behaviour** with a stimulus the individual finds rewarding, but **withholding** it if the desirable behaviour is not emitted.

The first task of the therapist is to find what is rewarding to the patient, so the therapist will look for a behaviour that the patient shows more frequently than others, presumably because they find it pleasant.

APPLICATION

Stunkard (1976) has successfully used selective positive reinforcement with anorexics to encourage them to eat normally. Once their rewarding behaviours have been identified, i.e. watching television or talking with other patients, then the therapist will **deprive** the patient of them until they first eat a required amount of food. If this is done, then the eating behaviour is positively reinforced with a certain amount of the rewarding behaviour (e.g. each mouthful of a whole meal might be rewarded with five minutes of television) making the eating behaviour more likely to occur again; if not, the reward is withheld.

EFFECTIVENESS

Selective positive reinforcement has been used very successfully for a long time on a number of different behaviours ranging from behaviour problems in educational situations to the eradication of self-mutilating behaviour.

APPROPRIATENESS

Reinforcement needs to be kept consistent and behaviour needs to be monitored closely for selective reinforcement to work efficiently.

Reinforcement for desirable behaviour appears to work better than aversion therapy for undesirable behaviour.

TOKEN ECONOMY PROGRAMMES

TECHNIQUE

Tokens act as **secondary reinforcers**, and many studies have shown that both animals and humans will emit behaviours for tokens that are exchangeable for primary reinforcers at a later time.

APPLICATION

Allyon and Azrin (1968) have used the principle of secondary reinforcement to reward the socially desirable behaviour of long term inmates in psychiatric institutions by giving **tokens** that can later be exchanged for certain primary reinforcers.

Each time an appropriate behaviour is demonstrated by the inmate, such as making their bed or brushing their teeth, then a token will be issued - and the more desirable the behaviour, the greater the number of tokens (e.g. 6 tokens for washing up for ten minutes). These tokens can then be used to **buy** desired rewards (e.g. 3 tokens for a favourite TV show).

EFFECTIVENESS

Token economies have produced improvements in self care and pro-social behaviour, even in chronic, institutionalised schizophrenics. Paul and Lentz (1977) found token economies more effective than other hospital management methods.

APPROPRIATENESS

Token economies can make the individuals involved dependent on the tokens. Some patients may become quite mercenary, **only** producing desirable behaviour if they are going to get a token for it, and there may be serious problems in transferring improved behaviour and skills to the outside world. In addition, the beneficial effects of token economy schemes may be, in part, a result of the improved attitude of the staff towards the patients - if the staff are more optimistic about improvements in patients' behaviour, then they may start treating them more positively, and this may become more reinforcing than the tokens.

Somatic/biomedical treatments 1

AIM OF THERAPIES

To cure the underlying physical causes of mental illness or to alleviate the symptoms of these causes.

Physically based treatments for mental disorder have a long and horrific history - ranging from bleeding, vomiting, and high speed rotation, to cold baths, and insulin coma therapy.

Biological treatments have been applied to a range of disorders and have the highest success rates with serious psychoses. However, they involve powerful techniques that can cause many side effects.

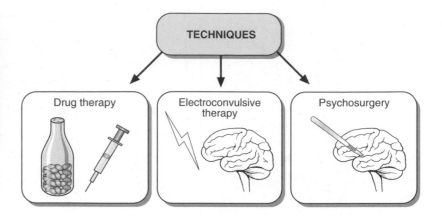

TECHNIQUES

Drug therapy

Electroconvulsive therapy

Psychosurgery

PSYCHOSURGERY

TECHNIQUE

Neolithic skulls with trepanned holes in were perhaps the first attempts at physically rectifying mental problems. When Moniz introduced psychosurgery in the form of prefrontal lobotomy in 1935, some might argue that the scientific justification and techniques were not much more advanced. Prefrontal lobotomy involved severing the connection between the frontal lobes of the brain and the deeper underlying structures (often by hammering a rod through the eye socket and rotating it around) in the hope of producing calm and rational behaviour. Today only very precise bundles of nerve fibres are destroyed, but it should still be noted that the effects are irreversible.

APPLICATION

Psychosurgery was originally performed on tens of thousands for a wide variety of mood, anxiety and personality disorders, but was especially employed for schizophrenia because of its dramatic symptoms and resistance to treatment (before drug therapy). Today it is usually used mainly as a last resort for severe depression or obsessive compulsive disorder, but virtually never for schizophrenia.

EFFECTIVENESS

Psychosurgery was initially hailed as a 'wonder cure' for psychoses, probably due to the need for a cheap, effective, and 'scientific' treatment to give the mental health profession respectability (Valenstein, 1986). However, long term follow up studies of prefrontal lobotomy patients found it to be ineffective at combating the precise symptoms of disorders. A National Commission review of psychosurgery in the USA in 1976, concluded that psychosurgery could be effective for certain disorders, such as severe depression.

APPROPRIATENESS

The indiscriminate use of psychosurgery between 1935 and 1955 led to it virtually becoming a method of social control. The development of drug therapy replaced it. Many undesirable psychological side effects were produced in most patients with prefrontal lobotomies, such as profound changes in personality, motivation, and cognitive abilities (Barahal, 1958). Patients also suffered seizures and a 1- 4% likelihood of death.

ELECTROCONVULSIVE THERAPY

TECHNIQUE

ECT involves applying an electric shock of approximately 100 volts to one side of the brain (unilateral ECT) or both sides (bilateral ECT) to induce a seizure. When the patient recovers, they remember nothing of the treatment, but report a relief of symptoms.

The treatment is usually repeated at least six times over a period of around 3 or 4 weeks. Unilateral shocks are usually administered to the non-dominant hemisphere and muscle relaxants and anaesthetic are given to reduce physical damage.

APPLICATION

ECT was originally applied to schizophrenics under the mistaken assumption that they did not suffer epilepsy (which involves disruptive electrical activity in the brain). Today ECT is rarely applied to schizophrenics but is used to treat severe cases of depression, usually if drug treatment has failed and the risk of suicide is high.

EFFECTIVENESS

ECT is considered a very effective treatment for depression, producing symptom relief in 60-80% of cases. However, its mode of action is unknown. Possible explanations are that the shock
- destroys neurones in brain areas responsible for emotion
- affects the balance of neurotransmitters involved in emotion
- acts as a form of punishment for depressive behaviour or negative reinforcement for recovery behaviour (feeling better to avoid shocks)
- produces memory loss that allows thoughts to be restructured

APPROPRIATENESS

ECT replaced insulin coma therapy, being a more controllable and less risky procedure. However, ECT has been over-used and abused in the opinion of many and does cause side effects such as memory loss and around a 3 in 10,000 mortality risk.

Ethical problems arise with using a treatment whose mode of action is unknown and also with consent (should ECT be forcibly applied to depressed patients with a high risk of suicide?). ECT can save lives.

Somatic/biomedical treatments 2

DRUG THERAPY

Many drugs are used to treat a wide variety of disorders. Neuroleptic drugs are thought to have their effect by controlling the activity of brain neurotransmitters at the synapse.

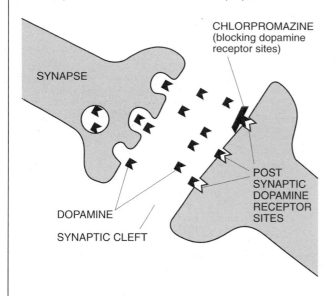

SYNAPSE

CHLORPROMAZINE (blocking dopamine receptor sites)

DOPAMINE

SYNAPTIC CLEFT

POST SYNAPTIC DOPAMINE RECEPTOR SITES

APPLICATIONS

Anti-psychotic drugs

Drugs such as the phenothiazine chlorpromazine are used to reduce the activity of the neurotransmitter dopamine by blocking its post synaptic receptor sites, while a more recent anti-psychotic drug, clozapine, blocks serotonin receptors.

Anti-depressant drugs

Each group of anti-depressant drugs work in a different way:
- Tricyclic anti-depressants, such as imipramine, work by blocking the re-uptake of neurotransmitters like norepinephrine, making more of it available.
- Monoamine oxidase (MAO) inhibitors, increase the amount of norepinephrine available by inhibiting the enzyme (monoamine oxidase) which breaks it down.
- Selective serotonin reuptake inhibitors (SSRIs), such as Prozac, specifically increase the amount of serotonin available in the synaptic cleft.
- Lithium carbonate effectively reduces both the effects of mania and depression in manic depressives.

Anti-anxiety drugs

Often termed minor tranquillisers, drugs like valium have been administered to reduce anxiety disorders and panic attacks.

EFFECTIVENESS OF DRUG TREATMENT

- Anti-psychotic drugs have massively reduced the need for institutionalisation, enabling many schizophrenics to be cared for in the community. However, around 25% of schizophrenics do not improve on traditional neuroleptics and a further 30-40% do not show full remission of symptoms. More recent anti-psychotic drugs, such as Clozapine have been found to improve both positive and negative symptoms in around 50% of those who resisted previous drugs, perhaps because they affect the neurotransmitter serotonin.
- The tricyclic anti-depressants have a delayed effect, providing relief in up to 75% of all cases after 2 to 3 weeks. Although all patients do not respond to them, they are generally more effective than MAO inhibitors. SSRIs, like Prozac, have been shown to be of equal effectiveness to prior anti-depressants, are easier to administer, and have less unpleasant side-effects. Lithium carbonate has proven very successful at countering bipolar depression - up to 80% show full or partial recovery, and its use can decrease the risk of relapse.
- Typically, anti-anxiety drugs, such as valium, have been shown to be beneficial for those suffering from generalised anxiety disorder, but not those suffering from panic attacks or obsessive compulsive disorder. Anti-depressant drugs are usually used in these latter cases, and some studies have shown them to be effective for obsessive compulsive disorder in up to 50% of cases.
- The effectiveness of drugs is best tested by using longitudinal studies with placebo (fake pill) control groups and double blind assessment techniques (where neither the patient nor the doctor assessing improvement knows who is receiving the real drug).

APPROPRIATENESS OF DRUG TREATMENT

Side effects:

- Phenothiazines can produce many unpleasant minor side-effects for schizophrenics, such as dryness of the mouth and throat, drowsiness, and weight gain or loss; and two major side-effects - symptoms similar to Parkinson's disease (body stiffness or body spasms), and tardive dyskinesia (involuntary movements of the tongue and mouth).
- Clozapine does not appear to produce the above side-effects in schizophrenics, but does produce a lethal blood condition in about 1% of patients. Weekly white blood cell monitoring is required.
- MAO inhibitors can be lethal if combined with certain foods such as cheese, and tricyclics can produce weight gain, drowsiness, and constipation. SSRIs are remarkably free of side-effects. Lithium carbonate requires close medical supervision.
- Anti-anxiety drugs can produce physiological and psychological dependence or addiction in approximately 40% of cases after 6 months.

Not a complete cure:

- Anti-schizophrenic drugs have been called pharmacological strait-jackets - they only alleviate or contain symptoms rather than providing a complete 'cure'. While they have enabled care in the community, hospital re-admission rates are very high - the relapse rate is around 70% in the first year after discharge if the patient discontinues medication (which is likely given the side effects). Anti-anxiety and depression drugs do not 'cure' either.
- No drug has provided a specific, 100% cure for any mental disorder, and the neurochemical reasons for their effectiveness are still a subject of much debate.
- The biological approach may neglect many important psychological or social factors that contribute to the development of the disorder or its treatment. Social skills training for schizophrenics and their families, for example, will help them readjust to living in society, while cognitive and behavioural therapy may be necessary to overcome anxiety disorders and depression completely.

Psychotherapy - psychodynamic therapies

AIMS OF THERAPIES
The notion of a cure, according to psychoanalysis developed by Freud, involves not merely eradicating symptoms, but identifying the deeper, underlying unconscious mental causes of disorder and dealing with them as best as possible. However, since Freud regarded all humans as neurotic to some extent, his notion of a cure was very modest, to 'turn neurotic misery into common unhappiness' by providing the client with more self-control: 'where id was, there shall ego be' (Freud, 1933).

TECHNIQUES
Traditional psychoanalytic therapy involves first identifying the unconscious source of disorder (such as the blockage of id impulses or the repression of traumatic experiences) and then trying to effect a cure by releasing the blockage or reliving the traumatic event in order to release the built up emotional energy associated with it.

1 Identifying the problem - Freud used three methods for unrooting the unconscious causes of disorder:
* **Free association** - which involved the uninhibited expression of thought associations from the client to the analyst. The content of the word list produced could contain useful information regarding the source of unconscious anxiety and pauses in, or drying up of, associations would mean that resistance to unconscious truths was being met.
* **Dream analysis** - which Freud regarded as the 'royal road to the unconscious'. By unravelling the disguised symbolism of the manifest content of the dream (what was remembered), the latent content (what the dream actually meant) could be revealed.
* **Behaviour interpretation** - Freud believed that both normal and abnormal behaviour were symptomatic of unconscious causes which could be carefully deduced from what people said and did - 'He that has eyes to see and ears to hear may convince himself that no mortal can keep a secret. If the lips are silent, he chatters with his fingertips; betrayal oozes out of him at every pore' (Freud 1901). Thus being late for, or refusing, therapy could indicate that progress was being made to uncover disturbing hidden truths.

2 Effecting a cure - this is achieved by
* **catharsis** - discharging the emotion (psychic energy) associated with repressed impulses or traumatic memories. However, this release can only occur if the unconscious conflict is brought out into the open for discussion. This is where transference is important.
* **transference** - the process whereby unconscious feelings of love and hate are projected onto the analyst. These feelings provide a basis for identifying, accepting, and discussing the analyst's interpretation of the problem.

Other psychoanalytically-orientated therapies include:
* **ego analysis** - which focuses more on conscious ego processes rather than unconscious id processes.
* **play therapy** - which interprets the symbolism underlying play (e.g. with dolls) to reveal unconscious conflict or repressed trauma.

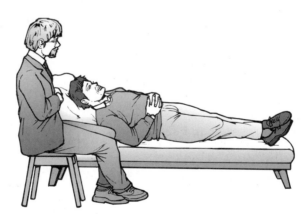

APPLICATION
Psychoanalysis was applied to treat a variety of neurotic anxiety disorders including:
* Hysteria - for example 'Anna O' a patient treated by Breuer who had hysterical symptoms, such as arm paralysis, relieved by remembering and discussing the repressed traumatic memories associated with them (she called this cathartic process 'chimney sweeping').
* Phobias - for example 'Little Hans' who had a phobia of white horses caused, according to Freud, by an unconscious fear of castration by the father.
* Obsessive compulsive disorder - for example the 'Rat Man' treated by Freud.

Freud argued psychotic patients could not be treated because they lacked insight and the ability to form transference attachments to the therapist. Play therapy has been applied to children.

EFFECTIVENESS
Eysenck (1952) found that psychoanalytic therapy had lower success rates (44%) than alternative therapies (64%) or spontaneous remission (70%).
This finding has been hotly disputed, because of its very high spontaneous remission rate (now estimated at around 30%) and criteria for success. A meta analysis of general success rates by Smith and Glass (1977) shows that psychoanalysis is more effective than no therapy for most people, but has slightly lower success rates than many other therapies.
Sloane et al (1975) found that psychoanalysis was most effective for clients with less severe problems.

APPROPRIATENESS
Psychoanalytic therapy can be distressing for the patient (it can actually be counter-productive for schizophrenics because of its emotional stress) and involves complete trust in the interpretations of the analyst.
The need for long term analysis makes this therapy very expensive, even though shorter versions have been developed, e.g. Malan's brief focal therapy. Psychoanalysis seems most appropriate for minor neuroses and anxiety disorders, not for patients with psychoses who lack insight into their condition.

Psychotherapy - humanistic therapies

AIM OF THERAPIES

To help the client achieve positive self-regard, acceptance of the self, and self-actualisation in order to overcome any problems with living. This is achieved through focusing on the client's unique conscious experience of the world as well as his or her aims and goals, and by providing them with insight into their lives so that they can make positive freewill choices to improve their condition.

TECHNIQUES

There are a variety of humanistic therapies that differ in technique and directiveness. All, however, regard the client's conscious experiences and aims in life as important, and are insight based.

Rogers' client-centred therapy

Rogers' therapy aims to provide the client with positive self regard and set them on the path to self actualisation in a non-directive way. Through providing unconditional positive regard (warmth), empathetic understanding, and accurate insight into the client's life, the therapist encourages the client to exert their free-will to make choices that will bring them closer to the person that they want to be. Rogers' therapy focuses on current behaviour and events rather than delving into the past like psychoanalytic therapy.

Fritz Perls' gestalt therapy

Fritz Perl's therapy aims to enable the client to recognise and accept all aspects of themselves to become a whole (gestalt) person. The therapist may be quite directive in forcing the client to avoid phoney or non-genuine behaviours and statements, and may employ the empty chair technique (where role play conversations with various aspects of the self or important others can be imagined) to make decisions or solve interpersonal problems.

Other humanistically orientated therapies include:

- **Existential analysis** - developed by therapists such as Rollo May to help clients find meaning in their lives.
- **Encounter groups** - developed by therapists like Rogers, the participants provide group therapy for each other by discussing members' problems aided by a therapist who acts as a facilitator.
- **Transactional analysis** - pioneered by Eric Berne, clients identify and explore the child, adult, and parent aspects of their character in role play situations.

APPLICATION

- Counselling for stressful life events or interpersonal problems, e.g. marriage, divorce, bereavement, etc.
- Advice for improving quality of life - some people go into therapy with no major problems, but to enrich or seek meaning in their lives.
- Milieu therapy - a humanistic based therapeutic community that acts as a 'half-way house' for chronic institutionalised patients where they can develop a sense of self-worth and control over their lives by participating in the running of the community.

EFFECTIVENESS

Smith et al's (1980) meta-analysis showed that humanistic therapies were the most successful for promoting self-esteem, but were the least successful for treating anxiety disorders when compared to other approaches.

Many researchers including Rogers have argued that the basic element for the success of any therapy is the supportive therapeutic relationship between therapist and client (involving genuiness, empathy, etc.), regardless of what is done in the therapy. While it is true that receiving any therapy is better than receiving none, some research indicates that genuineness and empathy are neither necessary nor sufficient for recovery - the expectations of improvement on the part of the client seem more important.

APPROPRIATENESS

Humanistic therapies cannot directly tackle the causes of serious disorders such as psychoses - where insight based therapy is not very effective.

As a supportive therapy, however, humanist based counselling has much to offer and is now extensively used in a wide variety of problems - including family therapy for the relations of schizophrenic patients.

Psychotherapy - cognitive therapies

AIMS OF THERAPIES

To cure or alleviate the underlying mental causes of disorder by restructuring the maladaptive thought processes that are causing it. Cognitive therapies aim to alter the way people think about themselves and their environment, to prevent illogical or irrational thoughts and to enable thought to control behaviour and emotion. Cognitive therapists concentrate on current thinking.

TECHNIQUES

There are a variety of cognitive behavioural therapies that differ in technique and directiveness. All, however, aim to alter thought processes (the cognitive part) and monitor the effectiveness of this on everyday behaviour or in role play situations (the behaviour part).

Beck's cognitive restructuring therapy

Beck's therapy (Beck et al, 1979) involves the identification and restructuring of faulty thinking as a collaborative process between the client and therapist. The therapist challenges the client's assumptions by gently pointing out errors in logic and contradictory evidence in their life and letting the client decide for themselves whether their thinking is accurate.

Ellis's rational emotive behaviour therapy

Ellis's therapy (Ellis, 1962) involves identifying generalised irrational and false beliefs (such as 'I must be successful at everything I do' or 'I must be liked by everyone') and forcibly persuading the client to change them, often through reality testing, to more rational beliefs.

Meichenbaum's self-instructional training

Meichenbaum (1975) assumes many problems are caused by negative, irrational and self-defeating inner dialogues - individuals may talk themselves into maladaptive behaviours with internal thoughts such as 'I can't do this' or 'something is going to go wrong'. The therapy identifies these maladaptive inner dialogues and gets the client to substitute them for better inner statements such as 'I can do this' by verbally repeating them until they become internalised, natural, and self guiding.

Kelly's personal construct therapy

Kelly's (1955) therapy is based upon his theory of personality. The client's personal constructs (ways of seeing the world) are identified through the use of the Repertory Grid technique and then altered or 'loosened' so they become more accurate or functional.

APPLICATION

Cognitive therapies have been applied to treat a variety of mental disorders including:

- **Depression** - Beck's therapy aims to correct the cognitive triad of negative thoughts about the self, the environment, and the future.
- **Anxiety disorders** - Beck's therapy and attribution training have been used to counter panic attacks and phobias.
- **Impulsive children** - Meichenbaum's self instructional training has been used to internalise dialogues of self-control.
- **Stress** - Meichenbaum has also applied his ideas to stress management in industry.
- **Schizophrenia** - Cognitive therapists, such as Beck, have even tried to help schizophrenics cope with, if not remove, their delusions and hallucinations.

EFFECTIVENESS

With depression, cognitive therapies have been shown to be just as effective as drug therapy - some studies have even reported higher success rates. Perhaps more importantly, lower relapse rates are gained if cognitive therapy is used in conjunction with medication.

Anxiety disorders also respond well to cognitive behavioural therapy although some research indicates that they are not superior to pure behavioural techniques, such as systematic desensitisation in some cases.

APPROPRIATENESS

Ellis's therapy is more forceful and directive than the others, but generally cognitive therapies aim to empower the patient with self-control strategies. Although cognitive behavioural therapies emphasise thought processes, they do tackle all aspects of a problem and are thus more complete in their approach. As Ellis's (1993) 'ABC' principle illustrates, many therapists assume that an activating event (A), such as being rejected for a job, directly causes an emotional consequence (C), low self-esteem. However, in reality it is often the intervening belief (B), such as 'I am suitable for all jobs', that is responsible for the emotional effect.

Difficulties assessing the appropriateness of intervention (should treatment be given, and if so which treatment?)

DIFFICULTIES ASSESSING EFFECTIVENESS

WHAT DO WE MEAN BY AN EFFECTIVE TREATMENT?

To consider how effective a treatment is, one must first define what its aim is. Some treatments aim to 'cure' the individual (e.g. flooding for phobias) while others seek only to alleviate or control the disorder (e.g. drugs for schizophrenia).

One major problem, however, is that different therapeutic approaches have different ideas about what constitutes a 'cure' - for behavioural therapists the removal of maladaptive responses may be sufficient, but for psychoanalysts an underlying unconscious solution must be found, regardless of current behaviour. Indeed, given Freud's quantitative views on abnormality, we may all be neurotic to some extent and so a cure may only involve 'reducing neurotic misery to common unhappiness'.

Relapse rates must also be considered when assessing effectiveness - how long should a cure last?

HOW DO WE KNOW WHEN WE HAVE CURED?

There are several difficulties involved in assessing when a treatment has been effective:

- Generalisability - an individual may appear cured in the controlled conditions of the clinician's place of work, but sometimes relapse will occur when the individual returns to the real world. For example, people exposed to token economy systems often do not generalise their improved behaviour, and alcoholics treated with aversion therapy often relapse when returned to public life.
- Monitoring effectiveness - who decides when a treatment has been effective - the therapist or the client? Both the therapist and the patient want to see success and may therefore make type one errors in assessment. The patient may show the 'hello-goodbye' effect, exaggerating their disorder at the beginning to ensure they are taken seriously, and exaggerating their recovery at the end of therapy out of gratitude. Psychometric tests used to monitor behaviour may be unreliable.

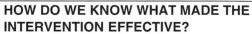

HOW DO WE KNOW WHAT MADE THE INTERVENTION EFFECTIVE?

There are many factors, other than those the therapy intends, that could affect recovery, such as

- spontaneous remission - many disorders disappear themselves, without any treatment and, in some cases, without reappearing again. Estimates of spontaneous recovery vary according to the disorder but overall it is generally thought to occur in around a third of all cases.
- mere attention - it has been suggested that just the increased attention and support from another can lead to improvement (the Hawthorne effect). In addition the expectation of recovery can cause self-fulfilling prophecy.

For the above reasons control groups are needed to test therapy effectiveness, e.g. using placebos in drug testing.

ETHICAL ISSUES OF INTERVENTION

TREATMENT VS. NO TREATMENT

The first ethical decision that has to be made, concerns whether treatment should be administered, given that

- there is a chance that spontaneous remission will deal with around a third of all cases anyway.
- there are potentially many costs involved in intervention, such as money, time, and side-effects.
- some therapies, such as psychoanalysis, have been accused of being less successful than spontaneous remission.

POWER AND CONSENT

One of the most difficult ethical problems involves the issue of power in the therapist-patient relationship.

- Treatment may be enforced if the patient is sectioned under the Mental Health Act (1983).
- The choice of goals in some therapies is determined by the therapist or the norms of society, not the patient. This is especially relevant in psychoanalytic therapy where the patient has to accept the therapist's interpretation.
- The therapist may deem it necessary to discourage the patient from exercising their right to withdraw - for example when close to the unconscious 'truth' in psychoanalytic therapy, during flooding, or when forcibly restructuring thoughts and perceptions in rational emotive therapy.

SUFFERING VS. SUCCESS

Many therapies involve making decisions between success and suffering. Drugs and electroconvulsive therapies can cause many unpleasant side-effects or even death. However, their use could be potentially very beneficial - preventing greater suffering from the disorder or suicide (especially in cases of depression).

TESTING ON HUMANS

Many therapies have to be tested on humans rather than animals for validity. However,

- should patients be given new treatments whose mode of action is unknown? Even in the case of ECT, which has been used for many years, its reason for effectiveness is unknown.
- should patients be allocated to control groups with no treatment? Should not every patient have the right to the best treatment available?

CONFIDENTIALITY

Should the patient's disorder be made publicly known, given the stigmatising effects of labelling in our society?

INDEX

Bold type indicates main entries.